FACING SOCIAL CLASS

FACING SOCIAL CLASS

How Societal Rank Influences Interaction

Susan T. Fiske
Hazel Rose Markus
Editors

Russell Sage Foundation
New York

Library of Congress Cataloging-in-Publication Data

Facing social class : how societal rank influences interaction / Susan T. Fiske and Hazel Rose Markus, editors.
     p. cm.
   Includes bibliographical references and index.
   ISBN 978-0-87154-479-7 (pbk. : alk. paper) – ISBN 978-1-61044-781-2 (ebook)   1. Social classes–United States.   2. Differentiation (Sociology)   3. Equality–United States.   4. Social interaction–United States.   I. Fiske, Susan T.   II. Markus, Hazel Rose.
   HN90.S6F33 2012
   305.50973—dc23   2011053386

Text design by Genna Patacsil.

RUSSELL SAGE FOUNDATION
112 East 64th Street, New York, New York 10065
10 9 8 7 6 5 4 3 2 1

CONTENTS

CONTRIBUTORS

SUSAN T. FISKE is Eugene Higgins Professor of Psychology at Princeton University.

HAZEL ROSE MARKUS is Davis-Brack Professor in the Behavioral Sciences in the Department of Psychology at Stanford University.

COURTNEY BEARNS is graduate student of psychology at Princeton University.

JESSICA MCCRORY CALARCO is graduate student of sociology at the University of Pennsylvania.

PAUL DIMAGGIO is A. Barton Hepburn Professor of Sociology and Public Affairs at Princeton University.

SUSAN R. FISK is doctoral student in sociology at Stanford University.

STEPHANIE A. FRYBERG is assistant professor of psychology and affiliate faculty in American Indian Studies at the University of Arizona.

JULIE A. GARCIA is associate professor of psychology at California Polytechnic State University.

CRYSTAL C. HALL is assistant professor of public affairs at the University of Washington.

MICHAEL W. KRAUS is social-personality psychologist and post-doctoral scholar at the University of California, San Francisco.

ADRIE KUSSEROW is professor of anthropology at St. Michael's College.

ANNETTE LAREAU is Stanley I. Sheerr Term Professor in the Social Sciences and professor of sociology at the University of Pennsylvania.

PEGGY J. MILLER is professor emerita of both communication and psychology at the University of Illinois, Urbana-Champaign.

MIGUEL MOYA is professor of psychology at the University of Granada, Spain.

PAUL K. PIFF is graduate student at the Institute of Personality and Social Research (IPSR) at the University of California, Berkeley.

MICHELLE L. RHEINSCHMIDT is graduate student of psychology at the University of California, Berkeley.

CECILIA L. RIDGEWAY is Lucie Stern Professor of Social Sciences in the sociology department at Stanford University.

ANN MARIE RUSSELL is graduate student of psychology at Princeton University.

DIANA T. SANCHEZ is associate professor of psychology at Rutgers University.

DOUGLAS E. SPERRY is doctoral candidate of psychology at the University of Illinois, Urbana-Champaign.

NICOLE M. STEPHENS is assistant professor of management and organizations at the Kellogg School of Management at Northwestern University.

JOAN C. WILLIAMS is Distinguished Professor of Law, Hastings Foundation Chair, and Founding Director of the Center for WorkLife Law at the Hastings College of the Law, University of California.

CHAPTER 1

INTRODUCTION: A WIDE-ANGLE LENS ON THE PSYCHOLOGY OF SOCIAL CLASS

Hazel Rose Markus and Susan T. Fiske

In the United States, people attach particular significance to the ideal of equality. Yet the empirical picture is clear. Social-class differences and the inequality they reflect now organize American society more than ever. Differences in resources and in the associated status and cultural capital influence whether we fight in a war, vote, or get divorced. They matter for the music we listen to, what we eat for dinner, how we talk, how much we weigh, and how long we live. Social class also shapes social interactions in every domain of life, and that is the focus of the current volume—*Facing Social Class*. The contributors—including social psychologists, sociologists, anthropologists, linguists, and legal scholars—illuminate this fact. They report, for example, that doctors, middle class by virtue of their occupation, prescribe simpler treatment regimes for their working-class than for their middle-class patients; that middle-class jurors tend to be more assertive than jurors from the working class; that working-class parents are more likely than their middle-class counterparts to defer to teachers' views of their children; that, relative to middle-class adults, working-class adults are more attuned to the emotions of others and relatively more concerned with helping and giving back to their communities; that working-class or first-generation college students can be disadvantaged by the university focus on self-expression and choice; and that middle- and working-class Americans together perpetuate a broad and deep stereotype of middle-class competence.

With the title *Facing Social Class*, we intend to signal that the comprehensive analyses of the everyday face-to-face social interactions that constitute social life have the potential to markedly extend our current social science understandings of social class. Until quite recently, social psychologists have concentrated their analyses on middle-class North American college students, leaving unexamined the social interactions and psychological tendencies of the working class and the more than 70 percent of

Americans without a college degree. Sociologists and other social scientists have addressed social class for years, as reflected, for example, in Annette Lareau and Dalton Conley's (2010) *Social Class: How Does It Work*? But on-the-ground interpersonal dynamics that create and maintain social-class differences remain to be understood.

The contributions in this volume show that social class, one of the most powerful ways in which societies rank their members, shapes selves (or identities) and the interactions of these selves. Together, the chapters generate a rich set of new empirical questions, yet they also afford a number of broad generalizations about societal rank and social interaction. Across the research reported here, it emerges that people are constantly and keenly aware of their ranking and that those at the top of the social ladder think, feel, and act differently from those on the lower rungs. This appears to be the case whether one's superior position is objectively anchored with resources and status, subjectively experienced, or manifest through the temporary assignment of power and influence. For example, in the North American settings described here, those with a higher rank have a sense of themselves as independent from others and as influencing and controlling social interactions. Those with a lower rank experience themselves as relatively interdependent with others and as adjusting and deferring to others in interaction. The self in a high-status position is likely to focus on expressing and promoting one's own interests, choices, and goals. The self in a lower-status position is more likely to be relatively socially responsive and to focus on avoiding threat or harm and tuning into others' goals, emotions, and needs. The research summarized here contributes to and creatively extends the analysis of how one's rank in a setting, community, or society is a major coordinate and determinant of behavior at every level.

The chapters here define social class in a variety of ways and analyze multiple forms of social hierarchy and inequality. Some researchers index social class with educational attainment, labeling those with a college degree as middle class and those without as working class. Others use occupation or income or a composite of several factors to categorize people into class groupings. Some focus on the objective indicators of social class using indices of educational attainment or occupational status, while others attend to subjective assessments such as perceived ranking within one's community or perceived financial security. Most of the comparisons discussed here involve people who are working and operating within the mainstream economic system. They do not focus on the nonworking poor. Nor do they consider the very wealthy or the owning class. All authors concur that defining social class is a significant and unmet challenge and that different indices of social class often correlate poorly and do not provide the same pattern of results. They acknowledge that a social-class designation is highly context dependent and that specifying social rank is a challenge; for example, who has a higher social rank, the highly paid woodworker with a high school diploma or the poorly paid substitute teacher with a master's degree? Yet the primary focus in this volume is the influence of one's rank in the social hierarchy, however determined or assessed, on the flow of everyday lived social experience. The emphasis is less on specifying the source of one's social rank than on understanding how social rank is communicated and translated into different types of relationships and into differences in thoughts, feelings, and actions.

The ethnographies, field studies, surveys, and laboratory experiments assembled in this volume demonstrate that social class is not a fixed set of inherent attributes. Neither is it simply a rank or position in the social hierarchy, a marker of prestige or status, or an index of access to or control over material resources. It is all of these, but it is also a form of doing that can pervade thought and action. It is manifest in shared understandings and perspectives and in everyday interaction—in practices of language, caretaking, schooling, money management, religion, health, politics, work, and the media. Social class is among the most significant of all sociocultural contexts, and as such it can have a broad and diverse influence on one's way of being a person (that is, an agent, a self, an identity) in the world.

Understanding the multifaceted psychological consequences of social class requires a view of people as ongoing participants in encompassing social, political, economic, and cultural systems. As indicated in the nested boxes depicted in figure 1.1, individuals—their brains, bodies, and psychological tendencies (box A)—are structured by their everyday social interactions (box B). These interactions are, in turn, organized and animated by larger societal institutions (box C) and historically derived pervasive ideas and values (box D).

The essays in this volume reveal that social class influences all aspects of psychological functioning: how people make decisions; how they perceive and are perceived by others; their sense of self, agency, and identity; their feelings of trust, certainty, belonging, or fit; their orientation to time; their perceptions of health, sickness, and well-being; their social responsiveness to others; their understandings of in-group and out-group and social hierarchy; their attitudes toward politics, religion, and life in general; their hopes and dreams and possible selves. To understand how these psychological tendencies are constituted and maintained, we focus a wide-angle lens on behavior: ideas, institutions, interactions, and individuals.

PERVASIVE CULTURAL IDEAS

Social-class distinctions in the United States are fueled, first, by a particular and historically derived constellation of powerful ideas, tacit assumptions, and cherished ideals. These include the primacy of the individual; a collective fear of the collective; the significance of independence, individual achievement, and hard work as the route to success, happiness, and well-being; and the still powerful although obviously flawed notions that social class is not important, that Americans are all middle class, that opportunity is equal, and that upward mobility reflects ability and effort and thus is fairly earned or merited. The American dream (which holds that anyone—not everyone—can make it to the top with hard work) and the foundational ideal of equality among individuals, coupled with the reality of major and growing inequality, results in a United States–specific set of tensions around the idea of status rankings and social hierarchies. These ideological tensions, and how people engage with them, are significant for understanding why and how social-class position influences behavior.

Social psychologists, both sociologists and psychologists, have grappled with why American social-class beliefs generally support existing inequality, for example, in

Figure 1.1   Influence of Social-Class Ideas, Institutions, and Interactions on Individual Psychological Functioning

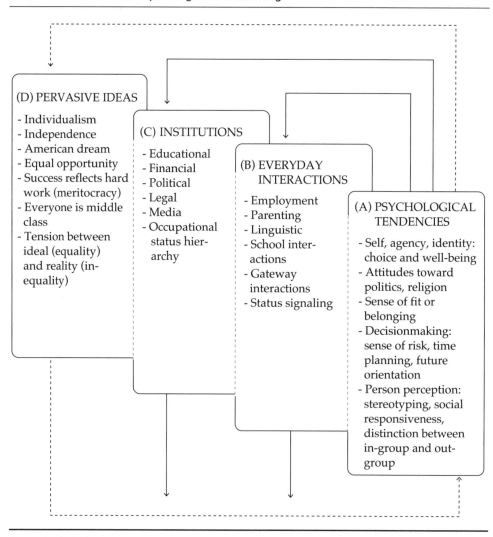

Source: Authors' figure.

this book chapters 5 (the poor economic situation of the working class being widely attributed to their lack of effort), 6 ("deeply held belief" in individual mobility and personal responsibility), and 12 (a cross-class stereotypic link between status position and competence). In sociology, the public ideology advocates working hard to get ahead: ideal Americans ought to, and do, prove their worth through effort (Rytina, Form, and Pease 1970). This belief justifies the current stratification system, and all strata agree in the abstract, although lower strata have more reservations about whether specific policies actually work. On a related note, James Kluegel and Eliot Smith (1986) show the shared belief system that, assuming equal opportunity, people get what they deserve, and therefore the system is fair. Even those who are massively disadvantaged by the status quo tend to justify the system (Jost and Kay 2010), though people do differ in how much they endorse existing group-dominance hierarchies as necessary and fair (Sidanius and Pratto 1999). All these ideologies reinforce current arrangements that advantage the middle and upper classes over the lower-income and working classes.

Part I of this volume starts with such widespread beliefs about class. Paul DiMaggio (chapter 2, "Sociological Perspectives on the Face-to-Face Enactment of Class Distinction") examines sociologists' work on social class and inequality for insights useful to psychologists who study face-to-face encounters, discussing the ambiguity of defining social class conceptually and operationally. Considering together the work of Basil Bernstein on class and language, Pierre Bourdieu on social and cultural reproduction, and Randall Collins on interaction ritual chains, the chapter yields an array of hypotheses focusing on the factors in play when cross-class encounters are more and less successful.

In another illustration of ideology's role, Joan Williams (chapter 3, "The Class Culture Gap") discusses the variety of ways that people in different social-class groups reinterpret foundational American ideas. These ideas, in turn, inform the behaviors and daily experiences of the working and middle classes. Using class-divided voting patterns as an example of class cultural phenomena, Williams also explores the different ways in which the social-class spectrum can be divided and discusses pros and cons of each.

INSTITUTIONAL PRACTICES AND POLICIES

Other chapters analyze how the ideals of equality and the reality of inequality are reflected in institutional practices and policies. Occupation, education, and income index social class, but they create and maintain social-class distinctions as well. The type of access people have to society's powerful institutions—political, legal, educational, financial, media, and more—and how these institutions function to provide or deny resources, privilege, and standing give rise to and maintain the various psychological tendencies that accompany social class. For example, the psychological tendencies often associated with working-class status are intimately bound up with the factors that reduce life chances in general: highly segregated living conditions that concentrate poverty, chronically low-wage jobs and economic subordination and insecurity, low-quality and inadequately funded schools, political underrepresentation, legal underrepresentation, discrimination, and inconsistent health care.

Part II addresses the influence of social class in American institutions. In chapter 4 ("Class, Cultural Capital, and Institutions: The Case of Families and Schools"), Annette Lareau and Jessica McCrory Calarco delve into class cultural change, showing how interactions between individuals in different social classes can transmit different class cultural capital (that is, the knowledge, beliefs, and behavior patterns used by particular class groups). They review class differences in institutional interactions, such as those between teachers and other school administrators. They show how such institutional interactions, although often disadvantaging the working class, also offer a means for the working class to learn and use the middle-class cultural habits that are generally valued more in institutional contexts.

Nicole Stephens, Stephanie Fryberg, and Hazel Rose Markus, in chapter 5 ("It's Your Choice: How the Middle-Class Model of Independence Disadvantages Working-Class Americans"), examine the way social class shapes agency or capacity to act in the world. They suggest that the middle-class experience allows people to see themselves as independent agents, free to choose their possible selves and to create their future worlds. For working-class Americans, independent agency is largely out of reach, yet this model is taken for granted as the natural, normal, or neutral way of being, built into the social machinery of everyday life. The chapter synthesizes various studies that show how the proliferation and instantiation of the independent model of the self can produce a hidden disadvantage for working-class Americans.

EVERYDAY INTERACTIONS

In part III, social class is shown to be reflected and maintained through everyday social interactions with teachers, bosses, neighbors, and friends in homes, schools, workplaces, and religious spaces. These are the informal and minute interactions that create and convey the consequences of one's class status and access to resources. It is in these local worlds that people learn either that the world is safe and welcoming, available for exploration and influence, or that the world is uncertain and threatening, requiring vigilance and toughness.

Peggy Miller and Douglas Sperry, in chapter 6 ("Déjà Vu: The Continuing Misrecognition of Low-Income Children's Verbal Abilities") explore class variations in linguistic style, drawing on ethnographic studies of families in different social classes. They show how class differences in parenting practices and daily language are turned into disadvantage or advantage in American educational systems. With vivid examples they demonstrate that schools value the highly individualized, psychologized, and abstracted expressions of experience characteristic of many middle-class contexts and simultaneously devalue the narrative, storytelling style common to many working-class contexts.

In chapter 7 ("Class Rules, Status Dynamics, and 'Gateway' Interactions"), Cecilia Ridgeway and Susan Fisk investigate class interactions at the interpersonal level and consider implications of these interactions for systematic group outcomes. Their focus is on "gateway" interactions—those involving people from different class backgrounds that are critical for class mobility. They reveal how these gateway interactions are molded by cultural capital and status assumptions, often leaving those from lower-class backgrounds in an imbalanced situation that is uncomfortable and disadvantageous.

Michael Kraus, Michelle Rheinschmidt, and Paul Piff's chapter 8 ("The Intersection of Resources and Rank: Signaling Social Class in Face-to-Face Encounters") explores current literature on the role of social class in face-to-face interactions, especially emphasizing the ways in which social class is signaled in subtle and previously unexplored ways. For instance, both conversational style and the amount that individuals talk in an interaction track social-class status. The same is true for nonverbal behavior. How close one stands to an interaction partner influences the balance of power in interactions and conveys social class. These social-status signals shape interactions in ways that advantage those from middle-class backgrounds. Furthermore, as these status differences are reflected back to a participant through interaction, they reinforce and influence that person's subjective feeling of status and power.

INDIVIDUAL PSYCHOLOGICAL TENDENCIES

As a consequence and a cause of the preceding levels—ideas, institutions, and interactions—people walk into cross-class encounters with expectations, habits, heuristics, and predispositions to respond. People acting in concert constitute the higher social levels and are constituted by them. This is the subject of part IV.

Crystal Hall, in chapter 9 ("Behavioral Decision Research, Social Class, and Implications for Public Policy") reviews the literature on behavioral decisionmaking and suggests new ways, beyond the prevalent models, to think about the role of social-class context in choice and decisionmaking. In particular, she explains how the material resources and the cultural capital associated with social class powerfully influence which psychological tendencies are enabled by different financial decisionmaking situations. She also connects this work to public policy: examining nutrition programs, she shows how the changing availability of healthy foods has a major impact on healthy food choices and decisions about diet among the poor.

From another perspective, Adrie Kusserow, in chapter 10 ("When Hard and Soft Clash: Class-Based Individualisms in Manhattan and Queens") explores intra-American cultural differences in individualism by investigating interactions among parents, children, and teachers. Social class, she argues, divides Americans into soft individualists, who emphasize emotional expression, creativity, and uniqueness, and hard individualists, who emphasize emotional control, self-reliance, and toughness. These behavioral patterns and value systems, in turn, shape different interactional and psychological outcomes. Kusserow shows with compelling examples that these different patterns have far-reaching consequences for the main engine of upward mobility—children's education.

In chapter 11 ("Putting Race in Context: Socioeconomic Status Predicts Racial Fluidity"), Diana Sanchez and Julie Garcia highlight the intersectionality of race and class. Across a variety of social contexts, they show how race and class influence one another and moderate relative advantages or disadvantages in social interaction. For example, whites often perceive working-class African Americans as more black than middle-class blacks. Furthermore, as one's social class changes, one's own racial identity also shifts, particularly for mixed-race individuals who may identify more as monoracial or multiracial, depending on their current social-class status.

Finally, Susan Fiske, Miguel Moya, Ann Marie Russell, and Courtney Bearns (chapter 12, "The Secret Handshake: Trust in Cross-Class Encounters") show that mistrust between those of different class backgrounds, fostered by institutional experiences and stereotyped beliefs, can foster inequality through everyday interactions.

Using the stereotype content model, they investigate affiliative and competence be-liefs toward different social-class groups and the role of these beliefs in producing feelings of misfit in cross-class interactions.

What is powerfully apparent throughout the chapters in this volume is that social-class positioning influences all aspects of everyday interaction—how to talk, if to talk and when, whom to trust, whether or not to plan or risk, what can or cannot be done, how to belong, and who to be. Of course, how people respond to these social interac-tions depends on how social class intersects with the meanings and practices associ-ated with other significant sociocultural categories (gender, race, ethnicity, age, cohort, religion, geography, sexual orientation) that also influence psychological tendencies. As the arrows in figure 1.1 indicate, people create the institutions, practices, and ideas to which they later adapt, and these, in turn, shape people's behavior in ways that perpetuate them. As people change their social-class positions through education, in-come, or job status, the nature of the social interactions and the social contingencies of their local worlds will change, and so will their psychological tendencies.

We have ordered the chapters according to their emphasis on one or another of the categories in figure 1.1. We begin with the chapters that focus on pervasive cultural ideas, move next to those chapters that emphasize the way social class is reflected and promoted in mainstream institutions, and then move to the chapters that illumi-nate everyday social interactions and practices, ending with chapters that concen-trate on the consequences of social class for individual psychological tendencies. The considerable literature referencing the biological level of analysis is not examined here (but see chapter 12). Some psychologists have already begun to scan the brain and examine the body for the physical implications of social class. What all of these chapters suggest is the importance of "scanning" social worlds, thus helping us un-derstand how social class conditions and structures people's worlds and their inter-actions within it. Social class will be revealed in the patterns of ideas and values, in-stitutional practices, social interactions, and psychological tendencies that people engage in and transmit to one another.

The time is right for a social psychological perspective on social class. We know from a great deal of research in sociology and public health that social class matters for all important life outcomes, but a social psychological perspective (one that takes particular account of the person in ongoing social interaction and the different forms these interactions can take) will help us understand why and how social-class dis-tinctions are made and maintained as well as how they can be undone. All of the chapters in this volume view the study of social class through the wide-angle lens advocated here.

FUTURE DIRECTIONS

Together, these chapters provide a substantial basis for further research and suggest a host of significant, unexamined questions. Illustrative issues include the following:

What are the interpersonal signals of social class? Although we have collec-tively made a start on determining this, how do people know at a glance, for example, who went to boarding school and who did not finish high school?

Cues include clothing, nonverbal behavior, speech, and appearance, all of which have some overlap with power and status indicators, about which we know a lot, but the social-class overlap is incomplete. For example, working-class dominance signals probably differ from upper-class dominance signals in certain ways. Some of these cues make potential employers and social partners decide that this person is not "like us."

What makes working-class students socially uncomfortable in selective colleges and universities, white-collar settings, and elite resorts? Although we have made a start on determining this, as this volume shows, we could know more about how this sense of displacement operates through self-concept and identity, as well as cultural differences and in-group–out-group behavior that create experiences of ostracism. Conversely, what makes an upper-middle-class person uncomfortable in a blue-collar setting, such as a factory floor, a construction site, a trailer park, or a working-class gym? One displacement matters more than the other because of who holds the resources, but both matter to the ways that people are divided from one another by status.

How do people who have been socialized in working-class contexts fare in the institutions that have been shaped by middle-class standards and rules? Are those without the middle-class experience—of being called on to develop one's own attitudes and ideas and to defend one's own versions of reality—at risk for being persuaded, bullied, or taken advantage of? Are they, for example, more likely to be victims of discriminatory workplace practices or to be induced into false confessions? How do people who cross over from working-class to middle-class contexts fare in the elite professions? What personal factors and social contexts determine success? What is the empirical evidence for Richard Sennett and Jonathan Cobb's *Hidden Injuries of Class* (1972)? When and how does social-class status become a source of stereotype threat? What are the costs and benefits of working-class tendencies toward constant vigilance to prevent unsustainable risks? What are the strengths and benefits of working-class culture? Should perpetuating professional middle-class cultural ideas and practices be the goal of mainstream institutions?

How do family ties both bolster and impede the upwardly mobile working class and poor? We know that working-class students in elite colleges and universities who maintain responsibilities and responsiveness to families endure much more difficult challenges than do their middle-class peers. The costs of caring for at-risk families are high, but the costs of deserting them would be higher. What are students' differential costs by social class of being alienated from family?

How well do "mixed" marriages work? What expectations do distinct social classes bring to close relationships? What gender, work, and parenting norms differ, and how do these play out when class cultures combine?

Who subscribes to what lay theories (attributions) about social class and therefore acts on them? We know that, in general, conservative interpretations endorse meritocracy and that liberal interpretations endorse circumstances. But how do these system-justifying and system-challenging beliefs play out across blue-collar, middle-class, and high-income conservatives and liberals? What are the ideas and social interactions that maintain the view that social class, status, and inequality are natural and inevitable and obscure the understanding that these are social distinctions of one's own making and thus malleable and changeable?

What is the route to quantitative understanding of Bourdieu's and Paul Fussell's astute observations of class aesthetics? How do we define and measure habits, sensibilities, and rituals? How can the insights of ethnography, surveys, systematic observation, and laboratory experiments be more effectively integrated to deepen our understanding of how social class works?

How are the super rich different from the rest of us, besides the fact that they have money? What is their gated habitat? How do they use their money and status to influence politics? How do they feel about rising inequality?

How do we define class psychologically, not just by socioeconomic variables? How can we distinguish between class and status and which might be prestige and which might be power or control over resources? What are the psychologically important social-class categories? The chapters here concentrate on comparisons between middle class and working class but use different defining criteria. Should the middle class be divided into two classes, separating the upper or professional middle class from the rest of the middle class? What distinctions should be made between working class and very low income or poor?

How should we refer to people participating in different social-class contexts? Labeling people in our studies as "middle class" or "working class" inevitably encourages the essentialist idea that people in different classes have different attributes or qualities that impel their behavior. These labels work against the most important insights of the volume. Social class (like gender, race, and ethnicity) is an ongoing system of social distinction that is created and maintained through implicit and explicit patterns of social interaction. Labels such as "people engaged in middle-class contexts," although less convenient, can highlight the importance of analyzing people as responsive to the normative ideas and practices of their contexts.

Our goal in this volume is to draw together new and heuristic research focused on the way social class shapes social behavior. Our hope is that the findings and insights of the chapters that follow stake a claim for the importance of facing social class.

REFERENCES

Jost, John T., and Aaron C. Kay. 2010. "Social Justice: History, Theory, and Research." In *Handbook of Social Psychology,* 5th ed., edited by Susan T. Fiske, Daniel T. Gilbert, and Gardner Lindzey. New York: Wiley.

Kluegel, James R., and Eliot R. Smith. 1986. *Beliefs About Inequality: Americans' Views of What Is and What Ought to Be.* Edison, N.J.: Aldine Transaction.

Lareau, Annette, and Dalton Conley. 2010. *Social Class: How Does It Work?* New York: Russell Sage Foundation.

Rytina, Joan Huber, William H. Form, and John Pease. 1970. "Income and Stratification Ideology: Beliefs About the American Opportunity Structure." *The American Journal of Sociology* 75(4, pt. 2): 703–16.

Sennett, Richard, and Jonathan Cobb. 1972. *The Hidden Injuries of Class.* New York: Vintage.

Sidanius, Jim, and Felicia Pratto. 1999. *Social Dominance: An Intergroup Theory of Social Hierarchy and Oppression.* New York: Cambridge University Press.

PART I

PERVASIVE IDEAS AND SOCIAL CLASS

CHAPTER 2

SOCIOLOGICAL PERSPECTIVES ON THE FACE-TO-FACE ENACTMENT OF CLASS DISTINCTION

Paul DiMaggio

Social scientists ordinarily define social class and related concepts in terms of such tangible measures as occupation, income, years of schooling, and home ownership. Humans experience inequality, however, in social interactions, which produce the orderings that our variables index. We learn where we stand by observing how others treat us: deferentially or dismissively; with interest in or indifference to our ideas or desires; with apprehension, reserve, or openness to intimate exchange. Although human status orders are never neatly transitive (Martin 2009), the enactment of status in face-to-face interaction gives us a good idea of our place in the world.

Work by sociologists on social class and inequality yields a rich harvest of insights and hypotheses for social psychologists interested in studying the enactment of class in face-to-face interaction; such work also complicates this enterprise by underscoring the analytic and practical ambiguity of "social class," such that one cannot study cross-class interactions by simply transposing methods that have been effective in studying interactions among people of different races or genders. This chapter focuses on the United States, with the understanding that class may operate differently in other parts of the world.

Research by ethnomethodologists (and social constructionists, more broadly) on categorical distinctions like gender or race (Garfinkel 1967; West and Zimmerman 1987) has demonstrated that social categories are actively produced and reproduced ("accomplished") by humans in the course of social interaction. Although I place more importance on structural sources of inequality than do most ethnomethodologists—institutions, after all, do much of society's dirty work in reproducing privilege and disadvantage—I share the view that class and social status have little meaning except insofar as they shape interaction and are reproduced face to face.

If we can grasp that something as apparently natural as gender is defined and instantiated in social interaction, recognizing that the same is true of social class should not be a stretch. Yet no comparably large sociological literature has focused on the production of class difference in social interaction (West and Fenstermaker 1993; Harris 2006). I begin by asking why this is the case and discuss some problems that sociologists encounter (and that psychologists may expect to encounter) when they study social class. With these cautions in place, I describe three theoretical traditions within sociology—those associated with the work of Basil Bernstein, Pierre Bourdieu, and Randall Collins—that may be useful to scholars contemplating empirical research on cross-class interactions, drawing distinct empirical predictions from each. I conclude with a discussion of issues social psychologists might expect to encounter in converting these traditions into research designs.

THE INVISIBILITY (AND INTRACTABILITY) OF SOCIAL CLASS

As students of American exceptionalism have recognized, class has been less salient in the United States, especially since the Great Depression, than in other advanced industrial countries (Karabel 1979). Moreover, social class is far less institutionalized in the United States than are gender and race. Our statistical agencies collect information about and build statistical tables comparing men with women and African Americans with whites. But though the Census Bureau may produce charts based on educational attainment or income level, it never categorizes persons by social class. Our legal system defines gender and race as salient for certain purposes (not least to regulate the tendency of organizations to treat the "suspect categories" of race and gender as salient). By contrast, social class is rarely if ever recognized in law or by the courts. (Poverty is a basis for administrative action, insofar as the poor are eligible for certain social programs; but poverty is depicted less as an identity than as an affliction from which low-income families are expected to recover.) Groups organize for political and social purposes along gender and racial lines. By contrast, working-class parties have never fared well in the United States, and political candidates shrink from even mild admonitions about economic justice lest they be accused of fomenting class warfare. As Charles Tilly (1998) pointed out, supposedly natural categories like gender and race are readily available social building blocks that other institutions (courts, political movements, labor markets) assemble into larger structures. The same is not true of class.

The absence of a large literature on the role of social class in face-to-face interaction results not only from the fact that social class is weakly institutionalized in the United States but also from the fact that there is little agreement about what social class is. (This lack of consensus is related to weak institutionalization because identities are more salient where institutions sort people into them.) Moreover, the notion of social class has traveled a great distance since the Industrial Revolution. Then, laborers were herded into huge factories, were housed near the factory door, worked long hours, and were paid starvation wages for their toil. It made sense to assume, as Karl Marx did, that under these conditions social class, defined as relationship to the means of production, would determine with whom people interacted, where they lived, and how they defined their interests—in short, that social class would be both a master identity and a focus of shared culture and community. Today it is difficult to find such occupation-based communities in the developed world. There are fewer big factories, many of those that survive are highly automated, and even where workers are numerous, they are ordinarily residentially dispersed. (Working-class concentration persisted longest in extractive industries like mining and forestry, but even these are less common and insular than they once were.) In the United States, class is probably most salient at the top and bottom of the hierarchy, among the wealthy and the urban poor. But the former rarely openly speak of class, and ethnoracial identities compete with class for many of the latter.

This is not to say that inequality is unimportant or that it fails to enter into face-to-face interaction. Inequality has risen dramatically in the United States over the past thirty years (Neckerman and Torche 2007). But the inequalities to which sociologists usually attend (those of income, education, and occupational status) are weak bases for class identities for two reasons. First, they are graduated rather than binary, indexed by dollars of income, years of education, or points on a scale of occupational status. Calling oneself a college graduate or a professional invokes a kind of status, to be sure, but not one that exhausts what we mean when we speak of class. Second, these dimensions are only imperfectly correlated: defining class on the basis of any one of them produces groups that are internally heterogeneous with respect to the rest (Blau 1977).

This poses a problem for experimental research: If one seeks to explore the dynamics of cross-gender or cross-race interactions in the contemporary United States, one ordinarily knows whom to place in which experimental condition and can be confident that the participants will share cultural knowledge of dominant gender and racial stereotypes. We cannot make such assumptions about class. Before studying cross-class interactions experimentally, we must either decide on an analytic basis on which to assign subjects to classes or first learn how people figure out what classes they and their interaction partners are in and what stereotypes they attach to those categories. Moreover, in the United States and increasingly in Western Europe, many cross-class interactions are cross-ethnoracial encounters as well. Therefore, although I refer to cross-class interactions throughout this chapter as a shorthand for encounters between people who differ in control over or access to resources, I do so simply to keep the lid on Pandora's box.

What Is Social Class?

Sociologists have debated the definition of class incessantly. Leading definitions are rooted in work, consumption, and identity. If we start from Marx's view of class as relationship to the means of production, we define class based on a person's job. Some approaches start with job titles, aggregating, for example, jobs whose occupants tend to be similar in social or occupational background or that cohere into such common-sense categories as blue collar, professional, or managerial. Approaches rooted in Marxian theory (of which Erik Wright's [1997] is best developed) define class on the basis of job characteristics rather than job titles. These ordinarily focus on such features of jobs as control over resources, control over persons, and autonomy with respect to both proximate goals and the means to achieve them. Such definitions perform well as predictors of many individual outcomes, as they reflect job characteristics that are related to economic interests and may shape broader orientations to social relations (Kohn et al. 1990), as well. They are limited, especially for experimental purposes, however, because respondents outside the labor force are difficult to classify and because they tend to generate complex typologies rather than a few simple strata.

A second set of approaches draws on the work of Max Weber, based on his view of the class situation as multidimensional (positions in markets for labor, land, credit, and commodities) or on his notion of style of life, or on both. Classic twentieth-century community studies combine indicators of education, occupation, and income with information about community members' residential status and group affiliations to assign families to strata defined by socioeconomic status (Lynd and Lynd 1929; Coleman and Neugarten 1971). This approach better reflects the range of attributes and experiences that shape class identity than occupational criteria. The trouble is that most of these indicators are only moderately correlated with one another. Thus neat typologies of socioeconomic status produce illusory groupness, and most scholars working in this tradition prefer instead to treat different dimensions of status independently, using multivariate statistics.

If we believe that class identification shapes how people approach social interactions, then we can ask people about their class identities directly: This is a third way to measure class, which makes sense if we believe that class operates primarily through attributions that participants in interactions make based on their own and their partners' class identities. It makes less sense if we think that class is an analytic category empirically associated with skills and orientations that influence interaction outcomes independent of labeling or subjective experience.

Do Americans Have Class Identities?

Measuring class by self-assignment raises the question of whether people have class identities at all, in the sense of stable elements of the self-schema. We know, of course, that when social surveys ask respondents what class they are in, almost everyone will emit an answer. But how salient are class identities in everyday life?

Social surveys suggest that class is not very salient. First, when Americans are invited to categorize themselves as lower, working, middle, or upper class, one finds many anomalies: Between 2000 and 2004, about one in four unskilled blue-collar workers who responded to the General Social Survey (GSS; and slightly more skilled blue-collar workers) identified themselves as middle class rather than working class. At the same time, one in five elite professionals, more than one in three managers, and more than two in five "lower professionals" like teachers or nurses labeled themselves as working class (Hout 2008, 33–34). Second, responses vary markedly depending on whether class-identification items are open ended or offer fixed choices. The most recent open-ended GSS (from the early 1990s) found a mere one in six Americans volunteering that they were working class (Hout 2008, 31), compared with 45 percent of respondents to the fixed-alternative items in the surveys taken between 1988 and 1996.[1]

Moreover, there is evidence from several English-speaking countries that people's self-identifications are not very stable over time. An Australian study found a .41 correlation between self-assessments made two years apart of respondents' positions on a seven-point scale ranking "groups that tend to be towards the top" and "groups that tend to be towards the bottom." This item, of course, does not ask about social class, and the respondent could define *group* in terms of lifestyle or ethnicity (Evans and Kelley 2004). A U.S. study using an item that referred to several indices of social status but not to class found a six-month test-retest correlation of .62 (Operario, Adler, and Williams 2004). A United Kingdom panel study that used class labels to track class identification over a five-year interval reported "a very high level of instability in class descriptions" compared with actual change in occupation or income (Lambert 2006). Thus surveys show that self-reported class identities diverge from common usage, are prone to strong question-wording effects, and are not very stable over time—all signs that class is not very salient.

Ethnographic studies tell us about the salience of class in ordinary social settings. Nina Eliasoph (1998, 92) reports that working- and lower-middle-class regulars at the Wisconsin country-western bars she studied "did not gather as members of a social class." On the contrary, "most did not know what the others did for a living or purposely forgot." An ethnography of a resort-town coffee shop reports that, although class differences among regulars shaped patterns of avoidance and interaction, the women never mentioned class, instead using such "euphemisms for class . . . as 'level,' 'elite,' or 'never had to work'" (Yodanis 2006, 347). In another study, working-class men defined themselves as working class on the job but middle class at home (Halle 1984). Other studies suggest that many Americans talk about class, when they are forced to, in moral rather than economic terms (West 1945; Lamont 1999).

Even when researchers ask respondents to discuss political issues related to social inequality, class references are rare: William Gamson (1992) reports that participants in only 19 percent of focus groups on deindustrialization spontaneously mentioned social class, and more than one third failed to mention class even after intense priming. When class was mentioned, people used inconsistent typologies, oscillating "among populist, consumption and work-based" frameworks. "Frequently a single person would begin using one term—say, *working people*—and would switch in the next sentence to the *little guy* or *poor people*. . . . The most common language of class discourse, however, was populist, illustrated by the symbols of `people with money' and `little people'" (1992, 91, emphasis in original).

That the language of class does not come easily to Americans, nor do they appear to have stable understandings of their class positions, does not mean that we cannot study the effects of socioeconomic status on interaction. There is a robust experimental literature on the effects of physical attractiveness (Mulford et al. 1998; Hosoda, Stone-Romero, and Coats 2003), which, like class, is best understood as continuous (and probably multidimensional). But it does mean that we cannot assume that people enter into interaction viewing themselves or others as representing stereotyped class categories. Rather, the nature and salience of concepts related to socioeconomic status, and the mechanism by which class differences influence interactions, should be primary foci of research.

THREE SOCIOLOGICAL APPROACHES TO CLASS IN FACE-TO-FACE INTERACTION

How then can we make progress in understanding the mechanisms through which class is instantiated in and influences the outcomes of face-to-face interaction? Three sociological approaches offer clues: Basil Bernstein's studies of the relationship between class and language, Pierre Bourdieu's work on social and cultural reproduction, and Randall Collins's theory of interaction ritual chains. Although none of these has generated a large body of empirical research on face-to-face encounters, each is full of implications for such research. And although they share common intellectual antecedents, they define class or status rather differently, emphasize different outcomes in social interaction, and hold different implications for research design.

First, the common theoretical ground. One source is Emile Durkheim (1954, 1997), whose work emphasized the importance of ritual and the collective effervescence (and sense of well-being and shared identity) that rituals generate, of social classification, and of the embodiment of social categories in persons. A second is Erving Goffman (1959, 1967), who translated Durkheim's ideas about large-scale public rituals (the sort that anthropologists studied in tribal societies) to the micro-rituals (greetings, conversations, face-saving behaviors) of everyday life in the modern world. A third is Max Weber (1968), whose ideas about how "status groups" produce solidarity called attention to the importance of shared culture in defining intergroup difference. A fourth is the anthropologist Mary Douglas (1966), who explored the role of ritual in producing categorical boundaries. Finally, from Karl Marx (1906) came the notion that social class (that is, relation to the means of production) is a particularly important social identity.[2] This element, it turns out, is the most fragile: Bernstein (1974) carefully confines his generalizations to working-class communities rather than working-class people; Bourdieu (Bourdieu and Passeron 1977), while using the language of class, focuses more intently on status differences rooted in schooling, especially among "fractions of the dominant class"; and Collins (2004) does not privilege social class at all.

Given these shared intellectual antecedents, Bernstein, Bourdieu, and Collins attend the same church, even if they sit in different pews. My intent is not to provide a full introduction to these scholars' relevant works, or even to respect the complexity of their ideas, so much as to plunder them for what they can offer empirical research on situated inequality. A schematic comparison of their ideas is presented in table 2.1.

Basil Bernstein: Three Forms of Interactional Disadvantage

Basil Bernstein was a British sociologist of education and sociolinguist best known for his three-volume work *Class, Codes, and Control* (1974), which combined theoretical writings, empirical studies, and observations about educational policy. Based on research conducted in the United Kingdom, Bernstein describes working-class speech as comprising a "restricted code," characterized by relatively simple grammatical constructions, concreteness, a paucity of counterfactual or conditional state-

Table 2.1 Microinteraction and Social Inequality

	Bernstein	Bourdieu	Collins
Key mechanisms	Linguistic competence (control of "elaborated code"; comfort and familiarity in unstructured places); comfort with individualistic modes of thought and relating)	Cultural capital (familiarity with high-status topics); linguistic capital (linguistic competence); bodily hexis	Energy maximization and domination in conversation; mutual orientation, entrainment in conversational rituals; shared topics of conversation; Erickson (1976): establishing comembership in first moments of interaction leads to conversational synchrony and positive outcomes
Antecedents	Durkheim: organization of mind mirrors organization of space and social relations; Douglas (1982): grid, group	Durkheim and Goffman: interaction as ritual; Bernstein: language; Weber: status groups and status cultures	Durkheim and Goffman: interaction as ritual; Weber: minimal groups; Garfinkel: ethnomethodology, fragility of interaction
Nature of class difference	Class, insofar as correlated with network closure and multiplexity of family networks; extent and type of schooling	Class, based on family socialization and educational attainment; associated with occupation	Class, instantiated only in interaction; class effects mediated by effectiveness of interaction ritual
Titles of key works	Class, Codes, and Control, esp. vols. 1 and 3	Reproduction; Distinction	Interaction Ritual Chains
Hypothesis: class effects on success of cross-class interactions are mediated by	Symmetry of code choice Comfort in setting, spatial match Assumptions about individualism and collectivism	Easy command of acceptable conversational contents Linguistic competence Habitus match Bodily hexis	Availability of common topics; establishing comembership (Erickson) Mutual entrainment Exchange-or-dominate "choice" of higher-status interactant

Source: Author's compilation.

ments, and situation in particular social contexts. By contrast, middle-class speakers not only possess the restricted code but also employ what he calls the "elaborated code"—a form of speech that is more abstract, is less tied to context, uses more subjunctives, and is syntactically more complex. When working-class speakers confront middle-class (or upper-class) speakers in situations that require them to speak about abstract or unfamiliar topics, they are placed at a disadvantage. Bernstein emphasizes the effects of this disadvantage on working-class children's school performance, but his argument applies as well to adult encounters in the workplace and other public settings. Erving Goffman (1967, 14) draws a similar connection between networks and what he calls "social skill," which he views as "well developed among those of high station . . . , for the more face an interactant has, the greater the number of events that may be inconsistent with it, and hence the greater the need for social skill to forestall or counteract these inconsistencies."

Although Bernstein is largely remembered as a sociolinguist, his work goes beyond language to explore classification and framing, the organization of space and time, as well. Here, the counterparts to restricted and elaborated codes are collection code and integrated code. Bernstein's argument is profoundly Durkheimian, exploring how the organization of space in working-class and upper-middle-class homes (especially homes of professionals and executives, as distinct from middle managers or small businesspeople) reflects the social organization of families. Bernstein argues that authority in working-class families inheres in formal roles ("Why? Because I'm your father!"), whereas in new middle-class families it resides in loosely structured, flexible persons. Differences in spatial organization, he argues, reflect differences in social organization, with working-class homes divided among strongly bounded rooms and middle-class homes characterized by more flexible, open spaces. These different orientations influence what happens in schools: working-class kids perform better, he suggests, in classrooms with well-defined and stable positions (desks in a row), clear boundaries, and tight schedules. Children of the new middle class, by contrast, excel in open classrooms, where space is flexible, schedules adapted to student needs, and roles less rigidly defined (for example, emphasizing teamwork). What outsiders might perceive as a working-class deficit is, in fact, a mismatch between cognitive orientation and school organization that helps children of professionals and hurts children of blue-collar workers and members of the traditional middle class. As with linguistic codes, the argument extends easily from school to workplace, positing that persons from working-class backgrounds will adapt less readily to open workspaces and flexible work organization than peers raised in professional households.

It follows from these arguments that different ways of organizing speech, time, and space are reflected in class differences in orientation to the self and to collectives, with working-class families placing less value on individualism and more on group identity and conformity than their new-middle-class counterparts. (This insight is consistent with experimental findings of Stephens, Markus, and Townsend [2007] that U.S. college students who grew up in working-class contexts resist individuating choices in comparison to middle-class peers.) It also follows that working-class persons may fare less well in interactions in settings that emphasize individualism and innovation as core values (for example, college classrooms where everyone is expected to have an opinion about everything) and that different orientations toward individuation may lead to asymmetric attributions in such interactions (for example, working-class participants coding middle-class actors as "pushy" and the latter dismissing the former as "dull").

Bernstein often uses the language of class in his work, but in fact his theory has much more to do with social networks and role systems than with occupation, except insofar as occupation shapes social milieus. Bernstein's working-class families are embedded in tightly knit residential communities, with strong kin relations and relatively weak connections to the outside world. Social networks in these communities are characterized by closure (one's friends and family tend to know one another) and multiplexity (one relies on the same people for many purposes, rather than compartmentalizing one's social relations into functionally distinct and isolated spheres). Restricted code flourishes in networks of this kind, for speakers can assume that listeners share both background information and a definition of social reality. By contrast, where networks are open, and functionally specialized and segregated, speakers must provide more information, make more connections (social and cognitive) explicit, and speak more abstractly. In other words, linguistic codes reflect the practical requirements of everyday communication in different social contexts. As Bernstein (1974, 177) puts it, "If you cannot manage the role, you can't produce the appropriate speech."

This last point is one of Bernstein's most important insights. But it is an inconvenient insight if one is interested in the impact of social class on social interaction, for it suggests that class, measured at the individual level, is an imperfect indicator of code. The theory works best for working families in isolated settings, such as company towns or communities built around an extractive industry. One can find restricted code in some elite contexts as well. (Transcripts of conversations among the Nixon White House inner circle contain excellent examples.) It provides less purchase in understanding a male blue-collar worker married to a female middle manager, living in a mixed-class suburban development, and maintaining contact with socially diverse family members and friends.

Nonetheless, if we bracket the definition of class, Bernstein's work yields potentially fruitful hypotheses. (All hypotheses presented in this chapter are governed by ceteris paribus assumptions.)

> Cross-class interactions will be less effective, and working-class speakers will be more disadvantaged, to the extent that conversational topics or context require or reward the use of elaborated code.

> Working-class speakers will be relatively disadvantaged in cross-class interactions that take place in unfamiliar or loosely bounded spaces, whereas middle-class speakers will be less disadvantaged by removal from accustomed bounded spatial contexts.

> Working-class speakers will be relatively disadvantaged in interactions that presume adherence to individualistic orientations and values, whereas middle-class speakers may be relatively disadvantaged in interactions oriented toward collective values and goals.

Pierre Bourdieu: Four Mechanisms of Domination in Face-to-Face Interaction

Pierre Bourdieu was a French philosopher, anthropologist, and sociologist known for his contributions to social theory and to the study of social inequality. Although he was not a microsociologist, he was a gifted ethnographer who was attentive to the ways in which class enters into social interaction. In his work on inequality, Bourdieu was primarily concerned with the reproduction of privilege and disadvantage across generations. His early research focused on schooling, which he contended was the main institution that reproduced and legitimated inequality in contemporary advanced societies.

To summarize indecently, Bourdieu argues that families in the dominant class (by which he refers to owners and executives of large businesses, top state officials, and highly educated professionals) use three primary forms of capital—economic, social, and cultural—to pass on their privilege to their children. Wealthy families invest in prestigious cultural forms, converting economic into cultural capital and equipping their kids with an easy familiarity with the arts, literature, and music that teachers mistake for intrinsic talent. Families who have lots of cultural capital (that is, lots of education and sophisticated tastes) but less wealth create especially enriching home environments to boost their kids' fortunes in school. Advantaged from the start, children from dominant-class families attend the most selective institutions of higher education, acquiring additional cultural capital (including "credentialed" cultural capital, that is, prestigious degrees) that is "reconverted" to economic capital (through privileged access to good jobs) and social capital (ties to high-status friends who can help one get ahead; Bourdieu 1985).

Four of Bourdieu's ideas are especially relevant here. The first is *cultural capital*, which refers to familiarity with and command of forms of knowledge that are prestigious within a given social field. The term has lost much of its specificity as it has been absorbed by U.S. sociologists, who often use it incorrectly to refer to any useful knowledge or values that families inculcate in children. By contrast, for Bourdieu, cultural capital bears the unmistakable influence of Max Weber's writings on status groups and status cultures, which emphasized the essentially arbitrary forms of knowledge from which groups derived honor (for example, calligraphy in fifteenth-century China, poetry in Victorian England). For Bourdieu, cultural capital is the status culture of a society's elite insofar as that group has embedded it in social institutions, so that it is widely and stably understood to be prestigious. For example, familiarity with art became a form of cultural capital with the rise of museums and the entry of art history into college curricula. Cultural capital plays a critical role in Bourdieu's theory because schools take it as a sign of native academic ability but do not themselves impart it, performing acts of "social alchemy" (1990, 120) that transform class privilege into individual merit. To generalize from the French case, Bourdieu's work points to the role of the content of talk in the processes of impression management in face-to-face interaction, as well as to standards for identifying the particular forms of knowledge (for example, familiarity with investing among upper-middle-class men or indie rock among suburban high school kids) that mark persons as worthy or unworthy in different social fields.

A second, related, concept is that of *linguistic capital*, which refers to how one speaks rather than the topics one addresses (Bourdieu 1991). Linguistic capital refers to syntax, vocabulary, fluidity of expression, and signs of comfort or discomfort (for example, hesitations, use of humor) in public interactions. (Bourdieu notes that members of the lower-middle classes betray their sense of cultural dispossession by using stilted, overly formal language at public events.) Linguistic capital is a broader and more pragmatically oriented concept than Bernstein's elaborated code (though related to it), similar to Dell Hymes's (1972) idea of "communicative competence." In face-to-face interaction, linguistic capital is a basis both of classification (deciding the class position of one's interlocutor) and of evaluation (attributing underlying abilities and orientations).

A third important Bourdieuian concept is the *habitus*, which includes habits of mind, dispositions to action, and evaluative orientations, operating largely outside consciousness, that both reflect one's life experience and incline one to reproduce the kinds of situations that generated those experiences. Central to Bourdieu's theory is the belief that early experience varies systematically by social class (and by "class fractions" within social classes) and that it is through the habitus (both a mental structure imposed by class and a generative basis for action) that class cultures are reproduced.[3] This concept suggests that, in observing cross-class social interactions, one should be attentive to the effects of what may be differing unrecognized assumptions about appropriate conduct.

A final concept we may take from Bourdieu is that of *bodily hexis*, by which Bourdieu refers to the inscription of class origins in persons' bodies, affecting posture, gait, and muscular control. Differences in bodily hexis are among the most subtle, yet, because of that subtlety, they are powerful cues to class standing, and they may shape cross-class interactions by influencing the way that conversation partners classify and make assumptions about one another. For example, consistent with this view, research in the United States suggests that people of high social status communicate their positions nonverbally, projecting insouciance that enables student observers to classify people by social class quickly and accurately (Kraus and Keltner 2009).

From this discussion we may generate four hypotheses to inform empirical research on face-to-face interaction across social-class lines:

> Cross-class interactions will be less successful insofar as lower-status conversation partners are unable to exhibit cultural capital, that is, easy familiarity with prestigious forms of knowledge.

> Interactions across class lines will be less successful to the extent that lower-status conversation partners possess less linguistic capital than their higher-status interlocutors.

> Interactions across lines will be undermined to the extent that conversational partners have fundamentally different habitus, expressed as incongruent dispositions to accept risk, moral orientations, or strategic aims.

> Cross-class interactions will be more successful to the extent that interaction partners share a similar bodily hexis, that is, to the extent that they physically orient themselves to the interaction and to one another in similar (or complementary) ways.

Randall Collins: Mechanisms Shaping the Success of Interaction Rituals

Randall Collins is a leading U.S. social theorist. His book *Interaction Ritual Chains* (2004) draws out the implications of Goffman's microsociology (and, to a lesser extent, of ethnomethodology) for social phenomena as diverse as sexual relationships and political revolutions. Unlike Bernstein and Bourdieu, Collins does not employ social class as a central analytic category. Yet his account of conversations as rituals has important implications for analyzing face-to-face interaction across class lines.

Collins draws on Durkheim to characterize rituals as forms of interaction that generate collective energy (what Durkheim called "collective effervescence") for the persons involved. Durkheim's analysis of ritual was based on anthropological studies of tribal societies, where, he believed, ritual life was grounded in shared experience and a collective conscience that included shared apprehensions of sacred objects around which rituals were organized. He notes (in *The Division of Labor in Society*, 1997) that as societies become larger and more differentiated, areas of common experience contract and sacredness is sucked out of the natural world into newly individuated persons. Thus selves become the most sacred objects of the modern world.

Durkheim views this development as reducing the importance of ritual for social solidarity, but Goffman (1959, 1967) contended that if individuals are sacred in modern societies then, like any sacred objects, they must be the focus of rituals. The social importance of interactions, Goffman argued, arises not only from their manifest purposes but also from their role as rituals affirming the value of sacred selves. His analyses of social interaction focused on the ways in which interaction partners accomplish successful rituals and the ingenuity with which they work around challenges to that end.

Collins draws on work in anthropology and psychology to characterize more pointedly the things that make conversations rituals and to recognize variability in the extent to which such rituals succeed in generating collective energy. Successful interaction rituals, Collins argues, enhance persons' well-being, buoyancy, and self-confidence. Participation in successful rituals renders people able to project themselves more effectively into future situations, more optimistic and more willing to take risks, and more attractive to potential interaction partners (high-energy persons being attracted to similar others) and therefore likely to have more rewarding interactions. Successful rituals cumulate into chains that generate ever more energy and, in some cases, collective action. Unsuccessful rituals, by contrast, drain interaction partners, rendering them less buoyant and optimistic and less attractive to high-energy partners in the future. This, Collins argues, is the major mechanism by which status orderings emerge in everyday life.

To understand the significance of Collins's approach for studying cross-class interactions, we must delve more deeply into his account of the mechanisms that produce successful interactions. Three are central. First, potential interaction partners assess one another's energy level and tend to choose partners whose emotional energy matches their own. Second, once an interaction begins, partners must find a common topic on which to focus. Among people from the same social milieu, gossip about mutual acquaintances is a popular choice, but partners may also talk about their personal histories, events taking place in their surroundings, shared aesthetic tastes (for example, music, art, or cuisine), or shared political or religious views. Third, successful interaction requires conversational synchrony, a physical and neural orientation of each partner to the other that results in what Collins (2004, 48) calls "mutual entrainment."

Collins notes that when higher- and lower-status persons interact, the former may dominate the latter (for example, by being inattentive or abrupt). If so, the interaction yields positive energy for the dominant partner and reduces the energy of the inferior. Although he notes that such interactions sustain hierarchy, Collins contends that returns to successful symmetric rituals are greater (even for the higher-status party) than are returns to domination. (Bourdieu [1977, 193] takes the opposite position, noting that cross-class interactions are often sites of "symbolic violence.")

Although it antedates Collins's work, Frederick Erickson's (Erickson 1976; Erickson and Shultz 1982) study of community-college counseling encounters provides an excellent empirical illustration of the theory applied to interactions between persons of unequal status (in his case, age and race, though the approach could be employed to study cross-class interactions). Erickson and his team videotaped conversations between white male counselors who were reputed to be competent and unprejudiced and African American and European American male students who were meeting the counselors for the first time. Painstakingly detailed analyses of both verbal and nonverbal aspects of the interaction were followed by interviews in which students and counselors were asked to comment on points in the videos at which investigators discerned signs of discomfort.

As expected, counselors offered more assistance to white students, but the more interesting finding is that this advantage was entirely mediated by characteristics of the interaction itself. The trajectory was set in the first moment or so, when students and counselors (as Collins's theory would predict) tried to find a shared identity (called "establishing co-membership"). Often they would begin by trying to discover a common friend or acquaintance. (White students had the edge here because many lived in the same neighborhoods as the counselors.) Failing that, they tried to identify a shared interest (often a sport or other leisure activity). Once a common identity was found, the discussion would shift to the matter at hand (the student's choice of courses and career plans). Conversations that went well exhibited both vocal and physical synchrony (trunk and arms moving in reciprocal rhythm, few conversational hesitations or interruptions, all indicating mutual entrainment). Successful discovery of a common focus in the interaction's first moments improved the chances of conversational synchrony, which predicted the likelihood that counselors would offer encouragement or special help (for example, assistance in gaining access to oversubscribed courses).

Collins's approach suggests that students of cross-class encounters should focus on conversation as ritual—on how what goes on inside the interaction shapes its outcomes—and indicates the following hypotheses.

Participants will find cross-class interactions more rewarding if they succeed in establishing a common focus early in the encounter.

Participants in cross-class interactions will be more strongly rewarded the greater the extent to which they find conversational topics in which both can sustain interest.

Participants will find cross-class encounters more rewarding the greater the extent to which they experience mutual entrainment (as indicated by conversational and physical synchrony).

Successful cross-class interactions will be more likely to the extent that previous interactions have been successful (interaction ritual chain theory).

Summary of Bernstein's, Bourdieu's, and Collins's Approaches

I have argued that one can find in the work of Bernstein, Bourdieu, and Collins substantial insight into the factors influencing cross-class encounters. I have assumed that interactions among people in different social classes vary in their outcomes and have articulated hypotheses predicting under what circumstances such encounters will be more or less successful. Alternatively, one could focus on all interactions—within class and across class—and posit that the mechanisms to which these hypotheses refer will account for any tendency observed for within-class encounters to turn out better than between-class interactions.

Several questions remain unresolved. In addition to the definitional problem addressed earlier, these theories raise questions about how to think about class in interaction as well as questions about the aspects of interaction that class difference might affect, how different interaction contexts might shape the role of class, and how systematic effects of class on interaction outcomes might influence broader social patterns.

SOME MORE QUESTIONS ABOUT CLASS

If, as Bourdieu and Bernstein suggest, class affects a person's personality structure, bearing, constitutive assumptions, and schemes of perception, then what is the better predictor: current social class or class as measured in childhood or adolescence? How does class interact with such other identities as race or gender? Is class a master identity that people bring into interactions? Or does class emerge out of the interaction itself?

When Does Class Leave Its Mark?

In Bourdieu's and Bernstein's views, class exerts much of its effect when people are very young. If that is the case, we must treat class as an analytic construct that shapes interactions through its early influence on actors' linguistic capital, habitus, bearing, social networks, and life experiences. It follows that subjects who have experienced social mobility should be categorized according to their class of origin. If, as Collins's perspective implies, class is also an emic concept, entering into interactions as a salient identity, a basis of attributions to the self or other, a basis for role expectations, or a conversational resource on which participants draw, then current class position is more relevant. In other words, different theoretical perspectives lead to different expectations about how large a shadow the past casts on the present.

How Does Class Interact with Other Identities?

People of every social class enter into encounters equipped with race, gender, and other characteristics that make it difficult to speak of pure class effects on interaction dynamics. To what extent should we expect the effects of such identities to be additive? To what extent do people with specific combinations of class, racial, and gender identities possess distinctive resources and perspectives and find themselves subject to distinctive attributions and expectations? Theories of intersectionality (Dill, McLaughlin, and Nieves 2007) hold the second view, which is consistent both with emic views of class and with Bourdieu's account of the formation of the habitus as a product of the totality of life experiences, not just those experiences related to class. In all likelihood, then, cross-class interactions that are also cross-race (or cross-gender) differ from those in which participants share a race and gender.

How Context Dependent Is the Middle-Class Advantage?

All of the theories reviewed either assert or imply that middle-class people are likely to be advantaged in social interaction.[4] And all are emphatic in viewing this advantage as built into social contexts rather than inherent in persons. Bernstein emphasizes the extent to which interactions in schools and workplaces are organized in ways consonant with professional households; Bourdieu describes the institutionalization of criteria of giftedness that fit the advantages of families from the dominant classes. It follows that institutions could be organized in ways that advantage working-class persons (for example, by arranging time and space according to collection code rather than integrated code or by legitimating and privileging skills and knowledge embedded in working-class life).

Yet there are hints in these theories that class differences are not purely symmetric. If, as Bernstein argues, middle-class people possess both elaborated and restricted code, they are better equipped to operate in situations with which they are unfamiliar. If, as Bourdieu argues, the habitus leads us to try (unwittingly) to reproduce prior experiences, low-income people may interact in ways that reproduce their status inferiority. If, as Collins argues, interactions go better when participants can find some cultural common ground, then people with the broad cultural repertoires that schooling provides may be able to do this more consistently. To be sure, any team—working class or middle class—can design a playing field on which it is likely to win. But if the playing field is level, it appears that the middle class may have an advantage. Experimental designs that simulate three conditions—conditions representing preferred environments of working-class and middle-class participants and conditions alien to both—would be helpful in discriminating between context-specific and transcontextual mechanisms.

Is Class A Priori or Situationally Emergent?

If we view class as an analytic concept that influences interaction by virtue of its behavioral and attitudinal concomitants, we need not worry about how interaction partners perceive it. But if we believe that interaction is guided by partners' representations of their own and their partners' social class (or something like it), then we need to understand how these representations emerge. If, as we have seen, class identities are not very stable, not very salient, and only weakly elaborated, then we must ask whether people bring them into interactions or, instead, whether they are situationally emergent. Is it possible that rather than affecting interactions, socioeconomic identities are actively negotiated and jointly constructed by partners as they interact? If so, three things follow. First, class and related identities may be as much outcomes of face-to-face encounters as inputs to them. Second, as we know from minimal-group and status-construction theories (Hogg 1992; Ridgeway 1991), any perceived difference may emerge as a basis for status ordering under the right conditions. Thus class effects on interaction may vary widely from encounter to encounter, depending on path-dependent details of local status ordering. Third, it may be difficult to distinguish effects caused by social-class differences (for example, effects of behavioral differences or social stereotypes) from generic effects of situationally emergent social power and subordination.

SOME QUESTIONS ABOUT INTERACTION CONTEXTS

People enter into interactions in different ways, with expectations that vary in the extent to which they are perceived as binding and with varying amounts of information about one another. Different mechanisms may operate under different conditions. Such complexity must be taken into account and, if possible, built into experimental designs if we are to understand how class operates in face-to-face encounters.

Situations vary with respect to at least two dimensions, institutional scriptedness and specific person information, as represented in table 2.2.

Some cross-class interactions are highly scripted if they occur in the course of the performance of well-defined occupational roles (for example, between a customer and a convenience-store clerk or a restaurant server). In many such cases, actors know little about one another as persons but understand status difference, expectations about task performance, and stereotyped scripts built into client-server interactions (see cell C in table 2.2). This makes life easier for the client, though not necessarily for the service provider, from whom demands for deference and cheerfulness may exact a heavy load, especially when expectations are gendered (Hochschild 1985). Such situations may be characterized by discomfort (when servers fail to accept their formal status inferiority) or by awkwardness owing to incongruity between formal roles and informal identities (for example, when the client is identifiably of lower social class than the server).

In other cases (see cell D), interactions are scripted and at least one partner has an

Table 2.2   Taxonomy of Interaction Contexts

	Personal Information Absent	Personal Information Available
Scripting absent	A. Negotiated	B. Experimental manipulation
Scripting present	C. Role governed	D. Stereotype governed

Source: Author's compilation.

identity that suffuses the person as well as the role, either positively (for example, royalty) or negatively (for example, a panhandler). In such situations, the labeled status of one actor may have decisive effects on the expectations, perceptions, and behavior of the unmarked partner. This is especially true for interactions with members of categorical groups with exceptionally low status, toward whom Lasana Harris and Susan Fiske (2006) have found tendencies toward dehumanization.

A third class of interactions includes those in which participants are out of role but have information about the class or status of the other (cell B). For example, a researcher may make one or both participants in an interaction aware of some fact (real or fictitious) about the social status of the other while limiting the amount of additional information to which subjects have access (for example, by employing a confederate, having participants interact online, or using a vignette design requiring subjects to make judgments about hypothetical cases). Thus class-relevant information may shape mutual behavior without the kinds of dense information that well-defined social roles, strongly stigmatized social identities, or well-established group identities provide, affording a clean canvas for discerning the impact of socioeconomic factors.

Finally, interactions may occur in which partners are guided neither by formal role nor by information about the other (cell A). In these circumstances, class identities must be divined before they can affect the interaction, providing an opportunity for the observer or experimenter to investigate the circumstances under which class identities become salient and the information on which assumptions about social class are based (Goffman 1951).

Lab experiments ordinarily fall into cell B: Participants have some information about each other as persons but do not operate in highly scripted roles. If I am correct that class is likely to enter into each type of situation in a different way, then understanding the role of class in face-to-face interaction will require methodological diversity and ingenuity.

What Makes a Cross-Class Encounter Successful?

The hypotheses presented earlier in this chapter suggest that certain conditions will make a cross-class encounter more or less rewarding or successful. The language of these hypotheses brackets the criteria for assessing an interaction's success. Defining "success" is a problem for both experimental design and social policy, as dependent variables often reflect the researcher's conception of the desirable. In choosing outcome measures, we must be aware that interactions that succeed in terms of one criterion may fail in terms of another.

Positive Feelings Toward Other   George Homans's (1961) classic dictum that interaction leads to liking has guided much research on intergroup interaction: if an interaction goes well, it should create positive affect between participants. We tend to be most interested in this outcome in intergroup contexts when there is reason to believe that the default state is antipathy, misunderstanding, or suspicion. It is not self-evident that this is the case for cross-class encounters.

Positive Feelings Toward Self   Given Western culture's preoccupation with the individual and his or her self-esteem (Markus and Kitayama 2010; Meyer and Jepperson 2000), it is natural to believe that a successful interaction will enhance the interactants' feelings of well-being and self-regard. Moreover, this follows from Collins's (2004) interaction-ritual theory, which emphasizes the interaction's function as a ritual of mutual ratification.

Individuation of the Other   Where status differences are large, a better normative goal for intergroup interactions than either increased liking or self-esteem (and perhaps a sine qua non for those) may be the individuation of the other (Fiske and Neuberg 1990). By *individuation,* I refer to the extent to which each partner experiences the other as more than the sum of representations and typifications associated with her or his social category, relying on cognitive processes that are more controlled and less automatic than when interaction is highly stereotyped. This criterion is reasonable when an interaction's emotional stakes are high or its instrumental stakes require complex mutual alignment. By contrast, individuation may detract from the success of routinized encounters (for example, commercial purchases of small items) that rely on efficiency.

Help, Assistance, or Cooperation   Erickson's (1976) criterion for a successful encounter was encouragement and special help from the dominant to the dependent partner in the exchange. Such concrete behavioral outcome measures are useful for two reasons. First (to continue with the college-counseling example), they constitute a higher standard of commitment, in that the superior actor actually provides something of value (help in accessing competitive rewards) and takes some risk (for example, that the student he helped gain access to a limited-enrollment class may perform poorly). Second, a significant reason to care about cross-class interactions is that they are venues in which opportunities are distributed, so their outcomes may tend to reproduce (or, potentially, ameliorate) social inequality. Where access to natural settings is limited, experimental games may help us understand the impact of class difference on trust and other-regarding behavior, as well as the mechanisms that produce that impact.

BEHAVIOR IN THE INTERACTION ITSELF   Some of the most interesting research on gender has focused on behaviors that take place during interactions and on how these vary between men and women (Ridgeway and Smith-Lovin 1999). Why, researchers have asked, do men and women differ (predictably) in the extent to which they defer to or interrupt one another, provide positive feedback to or disagree with one another, or hesitate as they speak? The answers to such questions tell us a lot both about power relations and about the mechanisms that may render interactions rewarding or unpleasant.

REFLECTIONS   Most of the outcome measures I have described entail a distinctly modern, Western understanding of personhood as a ritual status that requires and deserves affirmation. By contrast, observers from other historical eras or other places might view cross-class interactions as successful insofar as they reproduce and affirm the status order and troubling insofar as they fail to reinforce existing hierarchies.

A bias in favor of egalitarian transactions is nothing to be ashamed of, so long as it does not blind us to the possibility that some actors may find it gratifying in intergroup interactions to establish or confirm their superior status or to resist the status claims of others. When we ask what makes an interaction successful, we must also ask, "successful in whose terms?" And, if we regard successful interactions as ones that reward both partners, we must ask, "When do interaction partners try to make an interaction work in this way"? If higher-status participants seek validation by enacting the status order that privileges them, cross-class interactions may have a zero-sum quality. Goffman (1967, 26) suggested that legitimate selves, and therefore legitimate interactional practices and expectations, are differentiated by social class. High-status participants, he contended, are authorized to exhibit arrogance, whereas a lower-status actor "must demand only the amount of attention that is an appropriate expression of his relative worth." Collins (2004, chapter 7), by contrast, argues that class-based deference has all but disappeared. Especially in the United States, where high levels of inequality converge with a cultural commitment to universalism, tensions between status-based deference and acknowledgment of mutual personhood may be salient features of many cross-class encounters.

How Do Interactions Scale to Inequality?

How do interactions across class boundaries generate larger patterns of inequality, and to what extent? At this point questions are easier to generate than to answer (but see Fiske 2010, 966–68).

What, for example, is the cumulative effect on inequality of the extent to which lower-status actors can make claims on higher-status peers for access to information and assistance? How do social-class differences influence the probability that fortuitous social or business interactions will develop into enduring social ties? How do interactional dynamics influence access to information across social distance and inequality in stocks of social capital on which rich and poor can draw?

How do cross-class interactions shape the emotional tone of life in different social strata? If, following Collins, we believe that successful interactions generate positive affect, buoyancy, and optimism whereas failed interactions generate negative feeling and depression, then how do such factors influence the distribution of attitudes toward risk, conceptions of the possible, and willingness to define and achieve ambitious goals? How do interactional dynamics contribute to inequality in self-esteem and subjective well-being? To what extent do interactional effects spill over to within-class relations, for example affecting the quality of parent-child interactions or rates of marital dissolution (Sennett and Cobb 1972)? Do interactional dynamics generate class differences in collective mood that affect political attitudes or rates of political participation (Rahn, Kroeger, and Kite 1996)? Are lower-status people who interact the most with higher-status people better off or worse off than their peers who interact less?

CONCLUSIONS

This book marks the beginning of a concerted effort to understand the way that differences related to social class shape social interactions. Any conclusions, therefore, must be procedural, not substantive. A few of these follow.

First, class is not like gender or race. It is less categorical, less salient, and less stereotyped. Consistent with this, a meta-analysis of studies of status and dominance effects on nonverbal interaction emphasizes the difference in effects between vertical superiority and gender (Hall, Coats, and LeBeau 2005). Therefore we must be cautious in borrowing from research designs that have worked for studying cross-gender and interracial interactions in designing studies of class.

Second, the distinction between analytic and emic views of class has important methodological implications. If we think of class as an analytic category, we can focus on the mechanisms by which status differences influence interaction, and we can investigate, as an empirical matter, the types of status differences most strongly associated with those mechanisms. If we think of class as an identity that people use to understand themselves and one another and to guide their interactions, then a first priority is to understand social representations of class and the situations that make them salient.

Third, we must understand how contexts affect the role of class in social interaction. How do interclass encounters vary depending on the scriptedness of roles and the availability of personal information? Under what (if any) conditions do participants experience social categories as compelling social facts (that is, treat others in terms of social-class stereotypes, as members of a group)? Under what conditions do they use categorical differences electively as a resource in jockeying for position?

Fourth, to the extent that the latter is typical, we must learn more about motivation. Under what circumstances do interaction partners have an interest in enacting hierarchy or in ignoring it? What determines when persons of different status seek common ground and when they try to underscore difference?

Finally, we should combine naturalistic and experimental methods. The latter will be most useful for understanding the specific mechanisms that prime social class and drive the outcomes of interclass encounters. The former may be most helpful in understanding the circumstances under which class becomes salient in the wild and the way that socioeconomic difference is presented and negotiated face to face.

The author is grateful to Mitch Duneier for helpful conversation and to the editors and reviewers for insightful comments and suggestions on earlier versions.

NOTES

1. I calculated the latter figure from the 2009 release of the General Social Survey cumulative codebook.
2. Although Marx and Weber hold different views of class, those views are compatible. Weber views class as contingent on one's position in several markets, whereas Marx privileges labor markets. Weber views class position as a matter of objective position rather than social identity but develops a separate analytic category, the status group, to describe collectivities with fellow-feeling. Marx distinguishes between class-in-itself (Weber's labor-market class position) and class-for-itself (collective identity and mobilization; Andrew 1983), the latter essentially a Weberian status group whose identity is rooted in its members' common labor-market positions.
3. Bourdieu often implies that early childhood socialization is critical in accounting for adult variation in cultural capital and linguistic capital and in shaping the habitus and bodily hexis, to a degree that is probably inconsistent with current understandings of adult development.
4. I am grateful to a prepublication reviewer for an insightful question that induced this paragraph.

REFERENCES

Andrew, Edward. 1983. "Class in Itself and Class Against Capital: Karl Marx and His Classifiers." *The Canadian Journal of Political Science* 16(3): 577–84.

Bernstein, Basil. 1974. *Class, Codes, and Control: Theoretical Studies Towards a Sociology of Language.* 2nd ed. New York: Schocken.

Blau, Peter M. 1977. *Inequality and Heterogeneity: A Primitive Theory of Social Structure.* New York: Free Press.

Bourdieu, Pierre. 1977. *Outline of a Theory of Practice.* New York: Cambridge University Press.

———. 1985. "The Forms of Capital." In *Handbook of Theory and Research in the Sociology of Education,* edited by J. G. Richardson. New York: Greenwood Press.

———. 1990. *The Logic of Practice.* Translated by Richard Nice. Palo Alto, Calif.: Stanford University Press.

———. 1991. *Language and Symbolic Power.* Translated by Gino Raymond and Matthew Adamson. Cambridge, Mass.: Harvard University Press.

Bourdieu, Pierre, and Jean Claude Passeron. 1977. *Reproduction in Education, Society, and Culture.* Trans. Richard Nice. London: Sage Publications.

Coleman, Richard, and Bernice Neugarten. 1971. *Social Status in the City.* San Francisco, Calif.: Jossey-Bass.

Collins, Randall. 2004. *Interaction Ritual Chains.* Princeton, N.J.: Princeton University Press.

Dill, Bonnie Thornton, A. E. McLaughlin, and A. D. Nieves. 2007. "Future Directions of Feminist Research: Intersectionality." In *Handbook of Feminist Research: Theory and Praxis*, edited by S. N. Hesse-Biber. Thousand Oaks, Calif.: Sage Publications.

Douglas, Mary. 1966. *Purity and Danger: An Analysis of the Concepts of Pollution and Taboo*. London: Routledge and Kegan Paul.

———. 1982. "Cultural Bias." In *In the Active Voice*, by Mary Douglas. Boston, Mass.: Routledge.

Durkheim, Emile. 1954. *The Elementary Forms of Religious Life*. Translated by J. W. Swaine. London: Allen and Unwin.

———. 1997. *The Division of Labor in Society*. Translated by W. D. Halls. New York: Free Press.

Eliasoph, Nina. 1998. *Avoiding Politics: How Americans Produce Apathy in Everyday Life*. Cambridge: Cambridge University Press.

Erickson, Frederick. 1976. "Gatekeeping and the Melting Pot." *Harvard Educational Review* 45(1): 44–70.

Erickson, Frederick, and Jeffrey Shultz. 1982. *The Counselor as Gate-Keeper: Social Interaction in Interviews*. New York: Academic.

Evans, Mariah, and Jonathan Kelley. 2004. "Subjective Social Location: Data from 21 Nations." *The International Journal of Public Opinion Research* 16(1): 3–38.

Fiske, Susan T. 2010. "Interpersonal Stratification: Status, Power, and Subordination." In *Handbook of Social Psychology*, edited by S. T. Fiske, D. T. Gilbert, and Gardner Lindzey. New York: Wiley.

Fiske, Susan T., and S. L. Neuberg. 1990. "A Continuum of Impression Formation, from Category-Based to Individuating Processes: Influences of Information and Motivation on Attention and Interpretation." *Advances in Experimental Social Psychology* 23: 1–74.

Gamson, William. 1992. *Talking Politics*. New York: Cambridge University Press.

Garfinkel, Harold. 1967. "Passing and the Managed Achievement of Sex Status in an 'Intersexed' Person." In *Studies in Ethnomethodology*, by Harold Garfinkel. Englewood Cliffs, N.J.: Prentice Hall.

Goffman, Erving. 1951. "Symbols of Class Status." *The British Journal of Sociology* 2(4): 294–304.

———. 1959. *The Presentation of Self in Everyday Life*. New York: Doubleday Anchor.

———. 1967. *Interaction Ritual: Essays on Face-to-Face Behavior*. New York: Pantheon.

Hall, Judith, Erik Coats, and Lavania LeBeau. 2005. "Nonverbal Behavior and the Vertical Dimension of Social Relations: A Meta-Analysis." *The Psychological Bulletin* 131(6): 898–924.

Halle, David. 1984. *America's Working Men: Work, Home, and Politics Among Blue-Collar Property Owners*. Chicago: University of Chicago Press.

Harris, Lasana T., and Susan T. Fiske. 2006. "Dehumanizing the Lowest of the Low: Neuroimaging Responses to Extreme Out-Groups." *Psychological Science* 17(10): 847–53.

Harris, Scott R. 2006. "Social Constructionism and Social Inequality." *The Journal of Contemporary Ethnography* 35(3): 223–35.

Hochschild, Arlie. 1985. *The Managed Heart: Commercialization of Human Feeling*. Berkeley: University of California Press.

Hogg, M. A. 1992. *The Social Psychology of Group Cohesiveness*. New York: New York University Press.

Homans, George C. 1961. *Social Behavior: Its Elementary Forms*. New York: Harcourt.

Hosoda, Megumi, Eugene F. Stone-Romero, and Gwen Coats. 2003. "The Effects of Physical Attractiveness on Job-Related Outcomes: A Meta-Analysis of Experimental Studies." *The Journal of Personnel Psychology* 56(2): 431–62.

Hout, Michael. 2008. "How Class Works: Objective and Subjective Aspects of Class Since the 1970s." In *Social Class: How Does It Work?*, edited by Annette Lareau and Dalton Conley. New York: Russell Sage Foundation.

Hymes, Dell. 1972. "On Communicative Competence." In *Sociolinguistics*, edited by J. B. Pride and Janet Holmes. Harmondsworth, U.K.: Penguin.

Karabel, Jerome. 1979. "The Failure of American Socialism Reconsidered." *The Socialist Register* 18: 204–27.

Kohn, Melvin, Atushi Naoi, Carrie Schoenbach, Carmi Schooler, and Kazimierz Slomczynski. 1990. "Position in the Class Structure and Psychological Functioning in the United States, Japan, and Poland." *The American Journal of Sociology* 95(4): 964–1008.

Kraus, Michael, and Dacher Keltner. 2009. "Signs of Socioeconomic Status: A Thin-Slicing Approach." *The Psychological Review* 20(1): 99–106.

Lambert, Paul. 2006. "The British Household Panel Survey: Introduction to a Longitudinal Data Resource." University of Stirling, U.K. Available at: http://www.longitudinal.stir.ac.uk/wp/lda_2006_2.pdf (accessed April 11, 2010).

Lamont, Michèle. 1999. *Money, Morals, and Manners: The Culture of the French and American Upper Middle Class*. Chicago: University of Chicago Press.

Lynd, Robert, and Helen Lynd. 1929. *Middletown*. New York: Harcourt Brace.

Markus, Hazel R., and Shinobu Kitayama. 2010. "Cultures and Selves: A Cycle of Mutual Constitution." *Perspectives on Psychological Science* 5(4): 420–30.

Martin, John Levi. 2009. *Social Structures*. Princeton, N.J.: Princeton University Press.

Marx, Karl. 1906. *Capital: A Critique of Political Economy*. Translated by Samuel Moore and Edward Aveling. London: Charles H. Kerr.

Meyer, John W., and Ronald L. Jepperson. 2000. "The 'Actors' of Modern Society: The Cultural Construction of Social Agency." *Sociological Theory* 18(1): 100–20.

Mulford, Matthew, John Orbell, Catherine Shatto, and Jean Stockard. 1998. "Physical Attractiveness, Opportunity, and Success in Everyday Exchange." *The American Journal of Sociology* 103(6): 1565–92.

Neckerman, Kathryn M., and Florencia Torche. 2007. "Inequality: Causes and Consequences." *The Annual Review of Sociology* 33: 335–57.

Operario, Don, Nancy Adler, and David R. Williams. 2004. "Subjective Social Status: Reliability and Predictive Utility for Global Health." *Psychology and Health* 19(2): 237–46.

Rahn, Wendy, Brian Kroeger, and Cynthia Kite. 1996. "A Framework for the Study of Public Mood." *Political Psychology* 17(1): 29–58.

Ridgeway, Cecilia. 1991. "The Social Construction of Status Value: Gender and Other Nominal Characteristics." *Social Forces* 70(2): 367–86.

Ridgeway, Cecilia, and Lynn Smith-Lovin. 1999. "The Gender System and Interaction." *The Annual Review of Sociology* 25: 191–216.

Sennett, Richard, and Jonathan Cobb. 1972. *The Hidden Injuries of Class*. New York: Knopf.

Stephens, Nicole, Hazel Rose Markus, and Sarah S. M. Townsend. 2007. "Choice as an Act of Meaning: The Case of Social Class." *Journal of Personality and Social Psychology* 93(5): 814–30.

Tilly, Charles. 1998. *Durable Inequality*. Berkeley: University of California Press.

Weber, Max. 1968. *Economy and Society*. Edited by Guenther Roth and Claus Wittich. New York: Bedminster.

West, Candace, and Sarah Fenstermaker. 1993. "Power, Inequality, and the Accomplishment of Gender: An Ethnomethodological View." In *Theory on Gender / Feminism on Theory*, edited by Paula England. New York: Aldine de Gruyter.

West, Candace, and Don Zimmerman. 1987. "Doing Gender." *Gender and Society* 1:125–51.

West, James. 1945. *Plainville, USA*. New York: Columbia University Press.

Wright, Erik Olin. 1997. *Class Counts*. New York: Cambridge University Press.

Yodanis, Carrie. 2006. "A Place in Town: Doing Class in a Coffee Shop." *The Journal of Contemporary Ethnography* 35(3): 341–66.

CHAPTER 3

THE CLASS CULTURE GAP

Joan C. Williams

> The right tool is half the job.
> —*Blue-collar saying*

Presumably on the theory that no tree falls if no ear hears it, Americans display a convenient tone deafness when it comes to class. One way we make class disappear is to describe virtually everyone as middle class: both the lawyer earning $175,000 a year and the truck driver earning $60,000 a year are likely to think of themselves as middle class. In fact, the lawyer would likely refer to himself as upper middle class. This usage has real consequences, as when Harvard decided to offer financial aid to "middle and upper-middle income families" earning up to $180,000 a year (Roger Lehecka and Andrew Delbanco, "Ivy-League Letdown," *The New York Times*, January 22, 2008, A21). The confusion is easy to clear up. The top-earning 13 percent of American families are professional-managerial households with earnings in the top 20 percent of the income distribution and at least one adult with a professional degree. The median income of this top 13 percent is $147,742. In the middle are the 50 percent of American families that are neither rich nor poor, with a median income of $64,465 (Williams and Boushey 2010).

Is this the only way to cut the apple? Of course not. My class taxonomy is a tool designed for a specific job: to help explain why American politics have veered so sharply to the right since 1970. Drawing on ethnographies that document that class is expressed through the cultural differences that shape everyday life—child rearing, food preparation and consumption, entertaining, social networks, and more—I sketch (à la Bourdieu) the contours of a class culture gap between the professional-managerial elite and the white working class (Bourdieu 1998). Then I show how this class culture gap fuels class resentments that have driven American politics in a sharply conservative direction in the last forty years.

THE CLASS CULTURE GAP

Class is expressed through cultural differences. Pierre Bourdieu explains why by pointing out that our instincts and the assumptions we take for granted—what he calls our "dispositions"—are profoundly influenced by class location. He urges us to examine workers' "culture repertoires," the taken-for-granted categories "they use for interpreting and organizing" their lives (Bourdieu 1990, 4). A central organizing principle for the white working class is what Michèle Lamont (2000, 22) calls the "disciplined self," which paves a path toward a solid middle-class life.

Before elaborating the key values animating white working-class life, we need to address some terminological issues. The people who call themselves the upper middle class I call the professional-managerial elite. Working-class people see them as an elite—and, in fact, they are, as illustrated by the demographic data given earlier (Williams and Boushey 2010). I also need to clarify what I mean by *working class*. Many commentators use this term to refer to the lowest-income Americans (for example, Bartels 2006). I do not. Following the practice in the ethnographies on which I rely, I use the term *working class* to refer to Americans who are neither rich nor poor (for example, Lamont 2000). This group typically calls itself middle class, not working class. The important point, rarely noted, is that even the terminology one uses to talk about class reflects localized class traditions.

Finally, an initial note on sources. I have read every ethnography of the white working class written since 1976 that I could locate. I also use essays and memoirs by a group I call class migrants: people born into the working class who have entered professional-managerial jobs. Because class migrants have "double consciousness," their comments often pin down the class culture gap with startling precision (DuBois 1994, 2). This material is viewed through the ethnography of my own life, given that I married into a working-class family (from a distinctly silver-spoon one) thirty-five years ago.

The Class Culture Gap

The class culture gap reflects both differences in everyday social interactions and differences in worldview. Because the two are inextricably intertwined, my description melds them (Bloch 1961).

Hard Versus Settled Living

American working-class families feel themselves on a tightrope where one misstep could lead to a fall into poverty and disorder. "My father made a religion of responsibility," notes a reporter whose father was a bricklayer with "a well-developed work ethic, the kind that gets you up early and keeps you locked in until the job is done, regardless of how odious or personally distasteful the task" (Lubrano 2004, 16–17). Workers are acutely aware that their ability to survive and thrive depends on "hanging in there." As Michèle Lamont (2000, 26–27) explains, "Their labor is often painful and time-consuming, yet underpaid, physically demanding, or psychologically challenging because repetitive. Being able to stick to it demands emotional energy and moral fortitude."

Thus "work signals a form of moral purity" (Lamont 2000, 24). A study of white working-class families in rural California found that strong work ethics were the crucial form of social capital and determined not only social acceptability and community support in times of need but also access to ever-scarcer jobs (Sherman 2009).

Blue-collar men paint themselves in heroic terms by stressing that theirs is heavy, manly work. "You have to keep going. . . . It's heavy work, the managers couldn't do it. . . . There's not many strong enough to keep lifting that metal," noted one (Willis 1990, 186). This focus on strength "is vastly out of proportion to the number of people actually involved in heavy work," Paul Willis (1990, 186) noted in the 1970s, an insight ever truer with the withering of the manufacturing section in the United States. Workers stress both strength and perseverance. A firefighter told Lamont (2000, 18) that he did things that "99% of other people in this world can't or won't do." For this reason, he viewed himself as part of an elite.

Workers see themselves as doing the real work and white-collar men as pencil pushers. One class migrant recalled "with what scorn my parents and their friends used to talk about pencil pushers, who included anybody in a white-collar job. . . . We disrespected pencil pushers, considered them lesser people who nonetheless had all the power" (Christopher 1995, 141). The daughter of a carpenter noted that her work as a professor "doesn't feel like work because it isn't hard, it isn't unpleasant, it isn't boring or frustrating" (Christopher 1995, 141).

The crucial importance of the disciplined self is best understood in conjunction with the specter of "hard living." The distinction between hard and settled living, introduced forty years ago by Joseph T. Howell (1972), is more important than has been recognized. It remains important today, as illustrated by Julie Bettie's (2003) study of working-class high school girls in California's Central Valley. Bettie found that settled families typically had at least one stable job, with health care benefits. They lived lives that were, in Howell's (1972, 258) words, "very routine," and they were conscientious about house upkeep and neighborhood respectability (Bettie 2003). They maintained strict control over their children and expected them to graduate from high school and perhaps attend a local college. Much the same picture emerges from Maria Kefalas's study of working-class families in Chicago. She explains why these families are so house proud and starch happy: "I came to see the Beltway [the neighborhood studied] from the viewpoint of its full-time inhabitants. I took note of the elaborate lawn decorations, manicured grass, color-coordinated kitchens, fastidiously cared-for American-made cars, and the graffiti-free alleys and streets. . . . The people of Beltway willingly dedicate themselves to the care of the neighborhood landscape with an unquestioned, nearly spiritual devotion" (Kefalas 2003, 12).

More is at stake than dust bunnies. These families are enacting the importance of a world in moral order, which Lamont (2000) identifies as the central organizing principle of working-class life. Settled families stress routine and "keeping your nose clean" to protect their families from falling from middle-class status. And it works, to a significant extent. Bettie found that kids from settled Mexican American families generally completed high school and hoped to attend technical school or a community college, while their white counterparts typically were looking to community college and planned to transfer to a four-year state university. Children of hard-living families saw no future. "My life is shit," one noted laconically (Bettie 2003, 134). Sherman's study of rural families in California found a hard line drawn between settled and hard-living families, such that the children of the latter found it difficult to get a job that might break the cycle of marginalization from social and economic life (Sherman 2009).

Understanding the settled working class is impossible without an appreciation of the specter of hard living. That specter anchors working-class culture to stability rather than novelty, to self-discipline rather than self-actualization. Whereas self-development of individual thoughts and talents holds the economic key for upper-middle-class kids, a similar focus among working-class kids would be counterproductive. "Working class kids who had really absorbed the rubric of self-development," notes Willis (1981, 177), would face a "terrifying battle" as they reported day after day to deadening jobs. "I just figure I get paid from the shoulders down," joked a construction worker (Paap 2006, 155). In many working-class jobs, thinking for yourself can get you fired. Said one class migrant, "In the working class, people perform jobs in which they are closely supervised and are required to follow orders and instructions. [So they bring their children] . . . up in a home in which conformity, obedience, and intolerance for back talk are the norm—the same characteristics that make for a good factory worker" (Lubrano 2004, 10).

The central value placed on the settled life helps explain why workers place such a high value on religion, traditional morality, and the military. All are bulwarks against hard living. "When hard-living people talk of changing their ways and of getting their lives straightened out," noted a pastor who works with them, "the image of what they considered the good life looked a great deal like" what Howell defines as settled living (Sample 2006, 47). Elites head for a therapist when the going gets tough, paying thousands of dollars for someone to work with them one on one to develop a customized interpretation of their past and an individualized plan to move toward ever-more-perfect self-actualization. This approach is unaffordable for workers, who turn instead to tried-and-true institutions for staying on, or regaining, the straight and narrow.

Settled families' insistence on self-regulation may seem heavy handed to the upper middle class. But these families have no safety net. Upper-middle-class children are encouraged to experiment, secure in the knowledge that if they get into scrapes, parents usually can get them out. Because money can buy second chances, those who have it have a different attitude toward novelty and risk.

Morality and religion also offer a social resource for people who lack economic clout. A letter carrier compared himself favorably with his brother, who was a congressman: "I'm successful now because I know Jesus Christ. . . . I don't put success on a monetary level." Another blue-collar man "feels that being very religious gives him authority. . . . 'There's a certain authority when I walk in. They really listen to what I say, you know. I like that'" (Lamont 2000, 40). Religion offers a resource by which some can "put themselves a notch above the others" in contexts where their jobs do not (Lamont 2000, 44). As Jennifer Sherman (2009, 6) points out, as blue-collar jobs disappear, "morality is one of the few remaining axes upon which to base" a sense of personal dignity and self-worth. The moral discourses that emerge "do not form a single, coherent ideology but rather [are] a conglomeration of ideas drawn from social, cultural, religious, and psychological sources" (Sherman 2009, 7). Morality "figures not as formal norms or teachings based on religion or on ethical theories tenuously linked to sentiments, but as grounded in the social psychology of emotional responses as evaluative," notes the British sociologist Andrew Sayer (2005, 117).

Developing and Displaying Human Capital

To attain, and to keep, a professional-managerial job requires class-specific human capital. Developing and displaying that capital is a central preoccupation of upper-middle-class life.

Consider dinner. In such families, children learn to engage in discussions of their ideas and their days and imbibe class norms: "At dinner, we would discuss current events. . . . During each holiday season, the discussion included an article about the New York Times Neediest Cases Fund" (Kari Haskell, "A Sense of Duty Takes Shape During Dinner Conversations," *The New York Times*, January 6, 2008, 20). Dinner table conversations train children for jobs that are "open-ended, with wide-ranging responsibilities that involve ambiguity, problem solving," and networking—all typical of professional and managerial jobs (Peckham 1995, 269–70).

At a more basic level, dinner table behavior inculcates the message about the importance of talk. Among professionals, the norms of when and how to speak are governed by speech norms in professional jobs. Children are taught how to use talk to display intelligence, engage with the outside world, forge relationships by searching out shared interests, and learn the limits of challenging authority. A class migrant noticed that professional-managerial parents teach different rules about rules: that it is okay to "question them and reshape them to make them fit ever-changing situations" (Peckham 1995, 269). While working-class parents tend to use directives, professional-managerial ones use "reasoning as their chief method of control," again teaching the norms expected in professional jobs (Lareau 2003, 130).

At the dinner table and elsewhere, children are expected to have opinions and supply reasons for them. Annette Lareau notes the "steady stream of speech" in professional and managerial families, including extensive negotiation and verbal jousting and play (Lareau 2003, 130). Parents seek to develop curiosity and knowledge; social bonding comes second. One class migrant summed this up by noting that class affects "what we tell our children at the dinner table (conversations about the Middle East, for example, versus the continuing sagas of the broken vacuum cleaner or the half-wit neighbors)" (Lubrano 2004, 20).

Having the television on during dinner is a dead give-away of a working-class family. "Since informality is the order of the day, there is no reason not to keep an eye on the television," notes Bourdieu (1990, 195). Family time is associated with an escape from the rigorous time-discipline of closely supervised jobs. "Informality is the rule of the game, amongst guests as well as the family itself. The common root of all these 'liberties' is no doubt the sense that at least here there will not be self-imposed controls, constraints, and restrictions—especially not in eating, a primary need and a compensation—and especially not in the heart of domestic life, the one realm of freedom" (Bourdieu 1990, 197).

Dinner table conversation is just one way upper-middle-class life develops and displays human capital. Annette Lareau documents how child-rearing cultures vary by class. Professional and managerial families engage in an ever-more-frantic sprint to ensure that "every child is above average," to quote Garrison Keillor, the prophet of National Public Radio (itself a pure expression of upper-middle-class culture). Children's tailored leisure is designed to develop the drive, resumé, and social skills for high-status jobs: to "set priorities, manage an itinerary, shake hands with strangers, and work on a team," to develop time-management skills, "gain poise and learn how to 'negotiate institutions,'" work smoothly with acquaintances and adults unrelated to them, and handle both victory and defeat with grace (Lareau 2003, 39, 62). Annette Lareau documents a frantic round of enrichment activities: "They rush home, rifle through the mail, prepare snacks, change out of their work clothes, make sure the children are appropriately dressed and have proper equipment for the upcoming activity, find their car keys, put the dog outside, load the children and equipment into the car, lock the door, and drive off. This pattern repeats itself, with slight variations, day after day" (Lareau 2003, 43).

Lareau found that children of white professionals participated in an average of 4.6 organized activities a week; black professionals' children participated in even more (5.2). In sharp contrast, working-class kids had far fewer activities: 2.8 a week for blacks and 2.3 a week for whites, at least one church related. Lareau tried hard, but failed, to find a single child from a professional-managerial family who did not participate in any organized activities (Lareau 2003). Again, we see the ethic of self-development that dominates upper-middle-class life. Lareau calls it, as applied to children, the ideology of concerted cultivation. Parents "actively fostered and assessed their children's talents, opinions, and skills. They scheduled their children for activities. They reasoned with them. They hovered over them and outside the home they did not hesitate to intervene on the children's behalf. They made a deliberate and sustained effort to stimulate children's development and to cultivate their cognitive and social skills" (Lareau 2003, 238).

Nonprofessional families look at the frantic schedules of upper-middle-class kids with wonder and disapproval. One class migrant who described herself as being from a "hillbilly" family, who had babysat for an upper-middle-class family, said, "I just kept thinking these kids don't know how to play. When I went to [their] . . . rooms, it didn't seem like [they] had a whole lot of toys . . . it just seems like there were mostly books, and more educational things" (Blumberg 2001). When Lareau recited the schedule of an upper-middle-class child to her less affluent informants, they were distinctly dubious: "I think his parents are too strict. I think he's not a child [*laughter*]." Another acknowledged that the activities might well "pay off 'job-wise'" but felt, "I think he must be a sad kid." "He must be dead-dog tired," said another (Lareau 2003, 251).

Children in nonprofessional families, to Lareau, seemed more relaxed. They had few restrictions on television and video games, in sharp contrast to the limits placed on more affluent kids. Less affluent children spent far more time on informal games they organized themselves and relied far less on adults to organize their lives and to entertain them. These kids tended to hang out more, thereby informally and independently learning how to construct and maintain friendships, how to entertain themselves, and how to organize and negotiate with their peers. In short, their childhoods were not lived under the shadow of a frantic felt need to "realize their full potential" and make sure that potential was above average (Lareau 2003).

Food is another aspect of life in the households of the professional-managerial class that revolves around the felt need to develop and display human capital. Because food is a class code, we see the quest for stability anchoring the food culture of the working class, while the development and display of human capital provides the central logic of food culture among professional-managerial elites. Notes the sociologist Marjorie DeVault (1991, 214), "The contrast is between a taken-for-granted expectation that good will be good because [it is] familiar, and an elaborated standard based on an expanded (and constantly expanding) field of knowledge about food that links pleasure with novelty and entertainment."

Working-class women typically have a standard repertoire of recipes. "I cook all my meats the same, you know. . . . And as long as he doesn't complain, why should I change it? He likes it, so there's no reason for me to change it" (DeVault 1991, 214). Again, we find the focus on stability, the tried-and-true, "nothing fancy." The working class tends to meals that are "plentiful and good," not "interesting and exotic" (DeVault 1991, 210–12). Maria Kefalas (2003, 13) recalls working-class celebrations in Chicago where the food was served "'family style,' which means massive platters are passed around so the guests may have a choice of three or four entrées that are 'popular staples.'" The restaurant of choice among the working-class families who voted for Hillary Clinton in 2008 was Red Lobster, with its generous portions of standard dishes (Kim Severson, "What's for Dinner? The Pollster Wants to Know," *The New York Times*, April 16, 2008, D1). In short, working-class food culture celebrates bounty and stability. So does entertaining: the classic event is the backyard barbeque. "What is your idea of entertaining?" asked the upper-middle-class spouse in a cross-class marriage. "Having people over for a barbeque on Labor and Memorial Days, and an open house at Christmas," replied her class-migrant husband, whose father was a factory worker (Williams 2010). "These gatherings are comfortable precisely because they are familiar," notes DeVault (1991, 208). Such events typically involve only family and people whom the hosts have known for decades.

In sharp contrast, the children of the upper middle class learn that food should be varied and interesting. One mother commented, "I get a lot of feedback for experimenting. Even my little one will say, 'Mom, this is fantastic.' And he's very diplomatic, you know he came up to me and he said, 'I know you tried your hardest, but this doesn't have any zing to it'" (DeVault 1991, 213). Unlike working-class women, who tend to follow recipes passed down from their mothers, upper-middle-class cooks are expected to turn food into a research project. They search out and experiment with new recipes for family but especially for guests. "It's almost an unspoken law, you know," one woman told DeVault. "You have to think up a really acceptable menu, with a fancy dessert. It has to be beautiful, and it has to be platters, and it has to be served a certain way" (DeVault 1991, 209). Even if the hostess dislikes fancy cookery, she feels social pressure to prepare such meals: "I used to subscribe to *Gourmet* magazine when I was married, and I use to—if I had people over for dinner— really try to go all out. My friends were into it, too, so—but I hated it. . . . I don't know why I did it. I guess I felt like people wouldn't like me, you know, there was part of that, too, that I had to show how good, how talented I was" (DeVault 1991, 210).

Note the conflation of being "good" and being "talented." All the recipes, all the focus on novelty and sophistication—all show how upper-middle-class food culture revolves around showing that one has world knowledge and book learning, that one is ever increasing one's book learning, and that one knows how to enact elite status. For both workers and the elite, food is a class act, a way of enacting the key values of one's class.

Attitudes Toward Work and Family

Different opportunities and values also create different attitudes about work and family. Though the identities of both working-class and professional-managerial men are closely intertwined with the provider role, attitudes toward work nonetheless differ substantially. For working-class men, work proves their manliness both because it is dirty and heavy and because it takes manly resolve to stick with work that is often boring and repetitive.

Although working-class men highly value "keeping your nose to the grindstone," ambition is approached with ambivalence. A bank salesman criticized overly ambitious people who "have blinders on. You miss all of life. . . . A person that is totally ambitious and driven never sees anything except the spot they're aiming at" (Lamont 2000, 110). While upper-middle-class men "often view ambition, dynamism, a strong work ethic, and competitiveness as doubly sacred because they signal both moral and socioeconomic worth, one-third of white workers view it with suspicion" (Lamont 2000, 115–16). An electronics technician distanced himself from people who are "so self-assured, so self-intense that they don't really care about anyone else. . . . It's me, me, me, me, me. I'm not that sort of person at all, and that's probably why I don't like it" (Lamont 2000, 110).

Thus working-class men may dismiss as narcissism the work devotion expected of professional men. The norm of work devotion requires high-level professionals "to demonstrate commitment by making work the central focus of their lives" and to "manifest singular 'devotion to work,' unencumbered with family responsibilities" (Blair-Loy and Wharton 2004, 151, 153). This approach violates another central blue-collar tenet: that family comes first. Observes Lamont (2000, 30), "Blue-collar men put family above work, and find greater satisfaction in family than do upper-middle class men. Family is the realm of life in which these workers can be in charge and gain status for doing so. It is also a realm of life that gives them intrinsic satisfaction and validation—which is crucial when work is not rewarding and offers limited opportunities."

Consider Thomas Fell, who sold auto parts in a car dealership. Fell's thirteen-year-old son called him shortly before his shift ended. The boy was frightened because his coach and teammates had left earlier, leaving him alone in a school building into which shots had been fired the week before. So Fell left work fifteen minutes early to pick up his son. Fell called that evening to explain why; his manager said he had done the right thing, saying that family came first (Tom Rice Buick 2001). (Fell was fired the next day, presumably because he had been active in union organizing.)

When it comes to work and family, workers often see professionals as having their priorities seriously misplaced. "Writing is what makes me happy," one class migrant told his father, who corrected him by articulating "a key blue-collar rule": "No, you're happy with your family" (Lubrano 2004, 108). Workers express disapproval of people who live to work rather than work to live. "How much money can you spend?" one asked rhetorically. What mattered to him is that "I'm cared for by a lot of people." "Family is very important in my life," said another. "You need to work to support your family. . . . I mean, I don't care what I have to do, I'll go out and do it to support my family" (Lamont 2000, 112).

For professional-managerial men, "work is the means by which they develop, express, and evaluate themselves" (Lamont 2000, 33). "Work is the place I feel most empowered [and] . . . competent," said an engineer. "It's just a place where I've been recognized as a star. . . . and that means a lot to me" (Sharone 2004, 206). Workers feel differently. "My father's job was a means to an end. . . . a way to put food on [the] table," noted a class migrant. Working-class men "measure the success of their lives by having good productive children and grandchildren. . . . Jobs are just the means that allow you to provide the best you can for your children" (Tokarczyk and Fay 1993, 65).

"Many [working-class men] equate a high quality of family life with 'being able to keep the wife at home,'" notes Lamont. Said a foreman at a tin factory, "My wife was always there for [the kids], which I thought was right. . . . I'm old-fashioned that way, where I feel my mother was home, my wife's mother was home and I feel that a mother should be home to raise her child in most circumstances" (Lamont 2000, 31, 29).

White workers, more than blacks, hold themselves to this now-unattainable ideal. "The husband should take care of the family but, realistically, it's hard. Hard to support a wife," a white firefighter said wistfully (Lamont 2000, 26).

Workers' focus on the family is both a cause and an effect of their different social networks. Recall the barbeque, peopled by a stable group of family and friends. "In the world of the working class, the world of reciprocal invitations, spontaneous or organized, is restricted to the family and the world of familiars who can be treated as 'one of the family,'" to quote Bourdieu (1998, 197). DeVault and Lareau both observe that working-class families tend to socialize with kin. Class migrants report the same thing: that their parents expect "regular and close association with nuclear and extended family members in the same geographical area" (Lang 1995, 165). Lamont notes that workers "are often immersed in tight networks of sociability, in part because their extended family often resides within a few miles" (Lamont 2000, 11). Children play with their cousins, and adults often speak daily with their siblings and their parents (Lareau 2003, 57). Class migrants who attempt to follow what the professional-managerial elite considers a natural career path are greeted with disbelief: "Ohio?" wept the mother of a cub reporter. "Where the hell is Ohio?" (Lubrano 2004, 107).

Network scholars see working-class networks as impoverished—although they could equally easily see the networks of the professional-managerial class as superficial. Working-class networks trend small and dense (that is, relationships are more intense), while professional-managerial networks trend larger (often nationwide or even global) and more diffuse. "The strength of weak ties" reflects the importance, for the latter group, of diffuse networks that provide access to a greater number and variety of jobs over a broad geographical range (Granovetter 1973). Nationwide job markets for professionals clash, in the lives of class migrants, with the "cultural obligation to remain near the clan" (Lubrano 2004, 131).

Resent the Educated, Admire the Rich

Progressives are often mystified that white workers are resentful toward middle-class people like themselves but admire the rich. Workers typically admire the rich but resent the educated because their goal is not to lose their way of life but to continue it, with more money. I "can't knock anyone for succeeding," a laborer told Lamont (2000, 103). A receiving clerk joked, "You can't associate money with happiness. But I'd sure like to give it a try" (Lamont 2000, 104). The dream of many working-class families is to work for themselves. "The main thing is to be independent and give your own orders and not have to take them from anyone else," said a machine operator (Vanneman and Cannon 1987, 86–87). Owning your own business, to many workers, is the American dream.

Workers feel very differently about managers and professionals. They often see managers as college kids "who don't know shit bout how to do anything, but are full of ideas about how I have to do my job," reported one class migrant (Howell 1972, 314). Barbara Ehrenreich's working-class father "could not say the word *doctor* without the virtual prefix *quack*. Lawyers were *shysters*, as in *shyster-lawyers*; and professors were without exception *phonies*" (Ehrenreich 1990, 137, emphasis in original). Resentments stem in part from unsatisfying or even humiliating encounters with professionals with whom workers lack the social capital to communicate effectively or who downright disrespect them. "Doctors will screw you every time," noted one worker (Howell 1972, 315). Lareau writes of tremendous resentment against professionals and intimates that it may be justified: a college student whose learning disabilities never get diagnosed; another whose dreams to be a nurse end when no one advises her to drop a course she is failing; a seriously ill woman who refuses to see a doctor because she feels she will be treated like "white trash" (Lareau 2003, 39, 239). In contrast, most workers never encounter the truly wealthy and so carry no sense of class affront.

Workers disapprove of professionals for other reasons as well, stemming from the requirements of professional and managerial jobs. There, career success depends in significant part on tact, friendliness, conflict avoidance, and teamwork; the successful manager makes others feel comfortable, knows how to "fit in," and knows how to engage in savvy self-promotion (Williams 2010). Workers find this distasteful. The archetypical blue-collar job requires technical skills, not people skills. Workers take pride in their ability to "be their own men" and to "call a spade a spade" (Howell 1972, 310). Indeed, workers' adoption of long hair may well signal that while the white-collar kids who originated that style had eventually to bow to the demands of convention in order to support their families, workers do not: they can be their own men and dress however they choose. (Think Clint Eastwood.)

The politicking and networking inherent in professional and managerial jobs also alienate workers. A firefighter who left a messenger job on Wall Street explained why: "In big business, there's a lot of false stuff going on. A lot of people are, 'How are you doing?' And then you turn your back and they are like, 'He's a jerk'" (Lareau 2003, 99). A car mechanic agreed: "You know what I hate? Two-face. I can't stand that. . . . Well, if you have to become snobby for them to want to be around you, well, then screw this person" (Lamont 2000, 108). A policeman expressed disdain for "Barbie and Ken people . . . with facades or snotty people. I just like regular people. I don't hang around with lawyers or doctors" (Lamont 2000, 109). Networking feels inauthentic. "Too much politicking," opined a pipefitter, criticizing "shirt and tie types . . . jockeying for jobs and worrying about whether they are making the right moves and stuff" (Lamont 2000, 108). Julie Bettie's (2003, 84) working-class California girls agreed, expressing distaste for the "preps" who used friendships to further social ambition, a move less affluent girls saw as fake, phony, and insincere.

In conclusion, a culture gap yawns between the professional-managerial elite and the white working class. Before beginning to discuss how the class culture gap has influenced American politics, I take time out for a methodological interlude, to discuss why class analysis needs to be embedded within an analysis of other patterns of social inequality.

EMBEDDING CLASS ANALYSIS WITHIN THE CONTEXT OF SOCIAL INEQUALITY

For too long, commentators who focus exclusively on a single axis of social subordination have dominated the analysis of social inequality. One group studies gender, another race, and still a third studies class. A serious drawback of this approach is that it does not allow theorists to recognize the patterned interactions between different axes of social inequality.

Two interlinked phenomena emerge. One is that people tend to try to offset their axes of privilege against their axes of subordination. David R. Roediger (1999) documents the way white working-class men have sought to offset their subordinated class status by insisting, sometimes violently, on their privileged place in the racial hierarchy. Karen Pyke (1996) notes that class-subordinated men sometimes seek to compensate for their class status by insisting on perceived male prerogatives, enforced by domestic violence. And hypermasculinized street culture among inner-city blacks puts masculine privilege front and center, complete with gangsta rap references to women as "bitches" and "hos" (Rhym, n.d.). In all these contexts, men quest for masculine dignity in social contexts where human dignity of any stripe is hard to find.

Men are not the only ones to play off their axis of privilege against their axis of subordination. The first-wave feminists Elizabeth Cady Stanton and Lucretia Mott argued for the vote for women by protesting that "[man] has withheld from [women] rights which are given to the most ignorant and degraded men—both natives and foreigners" (Bartlett and Rhode 2010, 16). In other words, they used class privilege to demand gender equality. In a later document, Stanton protested that "you place the negro, so unjustly degraded by you, in a superior position to your own wives and mothers; for colored males, if possessed of a certain amount of property and certain other qualifications, can vote" (Bartlett and Rhode 2010, 20). Thus early feminists called on not only class but also racial privilege to offset their gender disadvantage. This consistent pattern is rarely noted.

When one embeds a class analysis within an analysis of social disadvantage a second pattern emerges: people tend to problematize their axes of social disadvantage while treating their axes of privilege as unproblematic. Thus white professional women problematize gender but not race and class privilege. This was the central message of the anti-essentialist movement in feminism, in which women of color pointed out, in no uncertain terms, that white feminists accepted white racial privilege as uncontroversial even as they treated gender privilege as unethical. (Here I am thinking of Ruth Frankenberg's *White Women, Race Matters* [1993] and the flood of similar works.) A similar pattern, rarely noted, is evident when white men problematize class but treat gender and race privilege as unproblematic, as in earlier class analysis that asserts that gender and race problems will be solved automatically once class privilege is eliminated.

One cannot gain a robust appreciation of class without understanding the patterned interactions of gender, race, and class. One reason gender has proved so unbending is that class and racial aspirations often reinforce gender traditionalism. After all, the breadwinner-homemaker family has symbolized middle-class status since its invention in the late eighteenth century (Cott 1977). The breadwinner-homemaker dyad is a central feature of the ideology that men and women have separate spheres, which was invented as part of the shift to the Industrial Revolution after 1780. The housewife allowed men's work to shift outside the home, from farms and artisans' shops to factories and offices. Middle-class husbands went to work freed from child care responsibilities, in the process (for the first time) coding child rearing as entirely feminine. The woman's role shifted away from the traditional duty to serve her husband to the "moral mother" (Welter 1966), dedicated to her children, in particular, to developing the human capital of middle-class boys, who were freed from family duties so they could concentrate of their education. The housewife was part of the practical infrastructure of enacting middle-class status and, at a symbolic level, became a symbol of arrival into the middle class. In many communities, the breadwinner-homemaker family remains an important symbol of middle-class status to the present day (Williams 2000). In these ways, class aspirations constantly reinvigorate the hold of traditional gender roles.

Racial aspirations, too, cement traditional gender roles because of the role of traditional gender performances in expressing class aspirations. In African American families, class aspirations intertwine with the history of racial exclusion. After Reconstruction in the American South, some states passed laws prohibiting freed slave families from keeping wives at home to care for their families (Jones 1985). Far more effective, in the long term, was the strategy of denying decent jobs to black men, thereby making them unable to support a wife at home full time. Thus many American blacks still aspire to be (or to support) stay-at-home mothers, claiming title to a cultural ideal from which blacks traditionally have been excluded, at first by law and now by lack of means (Barnes 2008; Williams 2000). Black professional women sometimes defend their choice to stay home full time as critical to creating stable middle-class families, as do organizations such as Mocha Moms (Barnes 2008; Mocha Moms website: http://www.mochamoms.org/).

This analysis is just the tip of the iceberg. But this discussion, I hope, will begin to focus scholars' attention on the ways different axes of social disadvantage interact.

HOW THE CLASS CULTURE GAP INFLUENCES AMERICAN POLITICS

The class culture gap has a profound influence on American politics. Space constraints prohibit more than a brief sketch of how class resentments have fueled America's shift toward conservatism between roughly 1970 and today.

Culture Wars as Class Conflict

As noted earlier, working-class people see religion and morality as anchors to the settled life. Intellectualism and irony are less highly valued than sincerity and "telling it straight." "High school graduates generally uphold more rigid moral norms than college graduates: they are less supportive of freedom of choice and self-expression, especially in the area[s] of sexual morality, divorce, abortion," notes Lamont (2000, 43). A trainman described his goal as teaching his daughters to "believe in God, and you know, all the rights and wrongs, no grays. I don't believe in gray. Truth, honesty and responsibility, that's what I believe in. . . . Believe in God and believe in parents. Must have two parents in the family" (Lamont 2000, 38–39). The irony so fashionable in the professional-managerial elite is distinctly out of sync with workers' worldview. They neither read Nietzsche nor watch *The Daily Show*.

Progressives' focus on self-expression is equally alienating. "Without religion or some sort of background, we would have anarchy, total breakdown," continued the trainman (Lamont 2000, 39). Note the felt threat posed by postmodern sexualities to the disciplined self. Abortion rights rhetoric, in particular, runs into important shoals. Abortion rights advocates can easily be seen as ignoring the important "fact" that family comes first and proposing to sacrifice family values on the altar of ambition. (This is not how I see abortion rights; my point is to understand how others might see the issue.)

Today religion plays a major role in American politics, with traditionalists pitted against modernists, to use the accepted (upper-middle-class-inflected) terminology (Williams 2010). Although modernists see themselves as tolerant, in fact they are just as cocksure as the traditionalists, just in a different direction. The most current example concerns gay marriage. I fully support gay marriage, yet I can see why working-class opponents feel dissed. Gay marriage advocates are as uninterested in compromise as are their opponents, because both sides have defined legalization of gay marriage as a moral issue on which any compromise is unthinkable.

The question is whether progressives truly want a coalition that includes white workers. African Americans, although they tend to agree with white workers about many issues (including gay marriage), have not left the Democratic Party. White workers have left in droves: the percentage of working-class whites who identify as Democrats fell from 60 percent in the mid-1970s to 40 percent in the mid-1990s, and it has not risen substantially since (Kenworthy et al. 2007). Reassembling the New Deal coalition between workers and progressives—and attracting Latinos, who hold conservative views on religion and family values—will require progressives to bridge the class culture gap.

Government Spending on Means-Tested Programs

Back when most workers voted Democratic, Democrats focused on universal social programs such as Social Security, unemployment insurance, Veterans Administration and Federal Housing Authority mortgages, educational benefits for veterans, and good public schools and universities. Gradually after 1960, Democrats' focus shifted to means-based social programs targeted to the poor, such as welfare, housing subsidies, Head Start, and Medicaid. The new focus on means-tested programs means that "the have-a-littles fight the have-nots," to quote a Brooklyn lawyer in the 1970s. A working-class housewife agreed: "The taxes go to the poor, not to us. . . . The middle-income people are carrying the cost of liberal social programs on their backs" (Rieder 1985, 199).

Means-tested programs give benefits to the poor, whom workers conflate with the hard living, while excluding workers, who see themselves as leading disciplined lives and struggling against social disadvantage to build a decent life. Meanwhile, means-tested programs, by targeting the poor, exclude working-class people who are only a little richer. Republicans have very effectively leveraged white working-class anger against means-tested social programs into a generalized disdain for, and lack of faith in, government.

Tax Cuts

Democrats remain mystified that Republicans gain such traction by advocating tax cuts. One reason is that Republicans have deftly used means-tested programs to discredit government in a sweeping way, and Democrats have never posed an effective response. Democrats remain particularly bewildered by public support for tax cuts for the rich, most recently Republicans' insistence on leaving in place Bush-era tax cuts for people earning more than $250,000 a year. Again, workers admire the rich. Democrats' failure to understand this, which led to their use of outdated anti-big-business rhetoric, made it impossible for them to tap populist anger at the banks during the recession of 2008 to 2011.

The Role of Class

The most famous person to make an argument similar to mine is Thomas Frank (2004), in *What's the Matter with Kansas?* Frank argues that Republicans have used wedge issues such as guns and abortion to lure working-class Americans to vote against their own self-interest. The result is "a working-class movement that has done incalculable, historic harm to working-class people," Frank (2004, 109) concludes. "All they have to show for their Republican loyalty," he says, "are lower wages, more dangerous jobs, dirtier air, a new overlord class that comports itself like King Farouk—and, of course, a crap culture whose moral freefall continues, without significance from the grandstanding Christers whom they send triumphantly back to Washington every couple of years" (Frank 2004, 136).

Frank and I observe the same phenomenon but have different attitudes toward it. Frank argues that working-class voters have been duped and that they should wake up and smell the coffee. My message is that progressives (including Frank) regularly express disrespect for the working class while Republicans have gone out of their way to signal respect for the values that are central to working-class dignity. My message is that Democrats should change.

Some political scientists have documented a shift to the right among working-class whites. As noted earlier, the percentage of working-class whites that identified as Democrats fell sharply, from 60 percent to 40 percent, in the twenty years following the mid-1990s (Kenworthy et al. 2007). Another study found that the percentage of white working-class voters that voted for Democratic presidential candidates fell precipitously between 1960 and 1996 (Teixeira and Rogers 2000).

Other political scientists contest the claim that working-class voters have shifted right. Most prominent among these is Jeffrey M. Stonecash (2000, 13), who argues in *Class and Party in American Politics* that "Democrats have not suffered losses, as many scholars have assumed, among the less-affluent population outside the South. Quite the contrary, the less affluent outside the South have become *more supportive* of Democrats in recent decades" (emphasis added). More recently, Larry M. Bartels, in "What's the Matter with *What's the Matter with Kansas?*," also argues that less affluent Americans have not shifted toward the GOP (Bartels 2006).

Bartels (2006) begins by confirming prior studies' findings of declining support for Democrats among whites without college degrees. Yet he goes on to argue that class has declining significance in American voting, showing that whereas in the past whites with college degrees trended strongly Republican while whites without college degrees trended strongly Democratic, this divergence has diminished in recent decades.

His findings are mathematically accurate but methodologically flawed. The net effects Bartels documents reveal three separate class-linked voting patterns. The first is that upper-income voters (who tend to have college degrees) have shifted toward the Democrats (Gelman, Kenworthy, and Su 2010). The second is that working-class voters (most of whom lack college degrees) have shifted toward the Republicans (Kenworthy et al. 2007; Teixeira and Rogers 2000). The third is that the poor, who trend Democratic and presumably always have, have become increasingly detached from politics and are playing a progressively weaker role in determining the voting complexion of whites without college degrees (Baldassarri and Gelman 2008; Bartels 2006). While the net effect of class on voting may look smaller than when the rich voted Republican and the less affluent voted Democratic, this does not prove that class no longer plays a central role in American politics. It is just playing a different role—one veiled by Bartels's focus on net effects.

Bartels builds on earlier work by Stonecash. Stonecash's analysis is also flawed. He compares Americans in the bottom third of family income with those in the top third, reflecting his use (like Bartels's) of the term *working class* to refer to the poor (Stonecash 2000, 100; Bartels 2006, 207n3). Stonecash makes Americans who are neither rich nor poor disappear by quite literally leaving them out of his analysis and out of the picture. This is a particularly dramatic illustration of a common and troubling pattern: progressives focus on the poor and the professionals and leave out the "missing middle" (as Theda Skocpol, 2000, 3, calls working-class Americans in her critique of this peculiar habit). Ethnographers have documented at length that Americans in the middle are culturally and politically different from both the professional-managerial class and the poor. Political scientists need to read these descriptions and reshape their mathematical analyses so that they stop erasing working-class voters.

CONCLUSION

Class has too often been theorized from forty thousand feet. The important premise of this volume is that we need to "come down, now" and theorize class as it structures interactions in daily life (The Postal Service 2003). My proposal is to take that approach toward the study of different class cultures as the first step to understanding why white workers, much to the consternation of progressives, have persistently trended Republican since 1970, even in a context in which Republican economic policies have hurt nonaffluent Americans (Bartels 2004). The short answer, I suggest, is that while Republicans have consistently defended the interests of the rich in a manner best described by vulgar Marxism, Republicans simultaneously have bent over backward to signal respect for working-class culture and the values it enshrines in everyday life. Until progressives follow suit, I am sad to say I see little prospect for progressive politics.

REFERENCES

Baldassarri, Delia, and Andrew Gelman. 2008. "Partisans Without Constraint: Political Polarization and Trends in American Public Opinion." *The American Journal of Sociology* 114(2): 408–46.

Barnes, Riché Jeneen Daniel. 2008. "Black Women Have Always Worked: Is There a Work-Family Conflict Among the Black Middle Class?" In *The Changing Landscape of Work and Family in the American Middle Class: Reports from the Field,* edited by Elizabeth Rudd and Lara Descartes. Lanham, Md.: Lexington.

Bartels, Larry M. 2004. "Partisan Politics and the U.S. Income Distribution." Working paper, Princeton University. Available at: www.princeton.edu/~bartels/income.pdf (accessed August 28, 2011).

———. 2006. "What's the Matter with *What's the Matter with Kansas?*" *The Quarterly Journal of Political Science* 1(1): 201–26.

Bartlett, Katharine T., and Deborah L. Rhode. 2010. *Gender and Law: Theory, Doctrine, Commentary.* Austin, Tex.: Aspen.

Bettie, Julie. 2003. *Women Without Class: Girls, Race, and Identity.* Berkeley: University of California Press.

Blair-Loy, Mary, and Amy S. Wharton. 2004. "Mothers in Finance: Surviving and Thriving." *The Annals of the American Academy of Political and Social Science* 596(1): 151–71.

Bloch, Marc. 1961. *Feudal Society,* vol. 1. Translated by L. A. Manion. Chicago: University of Chicago Press.

Blumberg, Alex. 2001. "Return to Childhood." In Ira Glass, *This American Life,* episode 180. WBEZ, March 23.

Bourdieu, Pierre. 1990. *The Logic of Practice.* Translated by Richard Nice. Palo Alto, Calif.: Stanford University Press.

———. 1998. *Distinction: A Social Critique of the Judgment of Taste.* Translated by Richard Nice. Cambridge, Mass.: Harvard University Press.

Christopher, Rennie. 1995. "A Carpenter's Daughter." In *This Fine Place So Far from Home: Voices of Academics from the Working Class,* edited by C. L. Barney Dews and Carolyn Law. Philadelphia, Pa.: Temple University Press.

Cott, Nancy F. 1977. *The Bonds of Womanhood: "Woman's Sphere" in New England, 1780–1835.* New Haven, Conn.: Yale University Press.

DeVault, Marjorie L. 1991. *Feeding the Family: The Social Organization of Caring as Gendered Work.* Chicago: University of Chicago Press.

DuBois, W. E. B. 1994. "Of Our Spiritual Strivings." In *The Souls of Black Folk.* Chicago: Dover. First published in 1903.

Ehrenreich, Barbara. 1990. *Fear of Falling: The Inner Life of the Middle Class.* New York: Perennial.

Frank, Thomas. 2004. *What's the Matter with Kansas? How Conservatives Won the Heart of America.* New York: Henry Holt.

Frankenberg, Ruth. 1993. *White Women, Race Matters: The Social Construction of Race.* Minneapolis: University of Minnesota Press.

Gelman, Andrew, Lane Kenworthy, and Yu-Sung Su. 2010. "Income Inequality and Partisan Voting in the United States." *The Social Science Quarterly* 91(5): 1203–19.

Granovetter, Mark S. 1973. "The Strength of Weak Ties." *The American Journal of Sociology* 78(6): 1360–80.

Howell, Joseph T. 1972. *Hard Living on Clay Street: Portraits of Blue-Collar Families.* New York: Doubleday.

Jones, Jacqueline. 1985. *Labor of Love, Labor of Sorrow: Black Women, Work, and the Family from Slavery to the Present.* New York: Basic Books.

Kefalas, Maria. 2003. *Protecting Home, Community, and Nation in a Chicago Neighborhood.* Berkeley: University of California Press.

Kenworthy, Lane, Sondra Barringer, Daniel Duerr, and Garrett Andrew Schneider. 2007. "The Democrats and Working-Class Whites." Working paper. University of Arizona, Department of Sociology. Available at: www.u.arizona.edu/~lkenwor/thedemocratsandworkingclass whites.pdf (accessed January 4, 2010).

Lamont, Michèle. 2000. *The Dignity of Working Men: Morality and the Boundaries of Race, Class, and Immigration*. New York: Russell Sage Foundation.

Lang, Dwight. 1995. "The Social Construction of a Working-Class Academic." In *This Fine Place So Far from Home: Voices of Academics from the Working Class*, edited by C. L. Barney Dews and Carolyn Law. Philadelphia, Pa.: Temple University Press.

Lareau, Annette. 2003. *Unequal Childhoods: Class, Race, and Family Life*. Berkeley: University of California Press.

Lubrano, Alfred. 2004. *Limbo: Blue Collar Roots, White Collar Dreams*. Hoboken, N.J.: Wiley.

Paap, Kris. 2006. *Working Construction: Why White Working-Class Men Put Themselves—and the Labor Movement—in Harm's Way*. Ithaca, N.Y.: Cornell University Press.

Peckham, Irving. 1995. "Complicity in Class Codes: The Exclusionary Function of Education." In *This Fine Place So Far from Home: Voices of Academics from the Working Class*, edited by C. L. Barney Dews and Carolyn Law. Philadelphia, Pa.: Temple University Press.

Postal Service, The. 2003. "Such Great Heights." Sub Pop Records.

Pyke, Karen. 1996. "Class-Based Masculinities: The Interdependence of Gender, Class, and Interpersonal Power." *Gender and Society* 10(5): 525–49.

Rhym, Darren. n.d. "'Here's for the Bitches': An Analysis of Gangsta Rap and Misogyny." *Womanist Theory and Research*. Available at: http://www.uga.edu/womanist/rhym2.1.htm (accessed January 4, 2010).

Rieder, Jonathan. 1985. *Canarsie: The Jews and Italians of Brooklyn Against Liberalism*. Cambridge, Mass.: Harvard University Press.

Roediger, David. 1999. *The Wages of Whiteness: Race and the Making of the American Working Class*. New York: Verso.

Sample, Tex. 2006. *Blue-Collar Resistance and the Politics of Jesus: Doing Ministry with Working Class Whites*. Nashville, Tenn.: Abingdon.

Sayer, Andrew. 2005. *The Moral Significance of Class*. Cambridge: Cambridge University Press.

Sharone, Ofer. 2004. "Engineering Overwork: Bell-Curve Management in a High-Tech Firm." In *Fighting for Time: Shifting Boundaries of Work and Social Life*, edited by Cynthia Fuchs Epstein and Arne L. Kalleberg. New York: Russell Sage Foundation.

Sherman, Jennifer. 2009. *Those Who Work, Those Who Don't: Poverty, Morality, and Family in Rural America*. Minneapolis: University of Minnesota Press.

Skocpol, Theda. 2000. *The Missing Middle: Working Families and the Future of American Social Policy*. New York: W.W. Norton.

Stonecash, Jeffrey M. 2000. *Class and Party in American Politics*. Boulder, Colo.: Westview Press.

Teixeira, Ruy, and Joel Rogers. 2000. *Why the White Working Class Still Matters*. New York: Basic Books.

Tokarczyk, Michelle M., and Elizabeth A. Fay. 1993. *Working-Class Women in the Academy: Laborers in the Knowledge Factory*. Amherst: University of Massachusetts Press.

Tom Rice Buick. 2001. *Labor Relations Reference Manual* 67: 1342–47.

Vanneman, Reeve, and Lynn Weber Cannon. 1987. *The American Perception of Class*. Philadelphia, Pa.: Temple University Press.

Welter, Barbara. 1966. "The Cult of True Womanhood: 1820–1860." *American Quarterly* 18(2): 151–74.

Williams, Joan C. 2000. *Unbending Gender: Why Family and Work Conflict and What to Do About It*. New York: Oxford University Press.

————. 2010. *Reshaping the Work-Family Debate: Why Men and Class Matter*. Cambridge, Mass.: Harvard University Press.

Williams, Joan C., and Heather Boushey. 2010. *The Three Faces of Work-Family Conflict: The Poor, the Professionals, and the Missing Middle*. Washington, D.C.: Center for American Progress.

Willis, Paul. 1981. *Learning to Labor: How Working Class Kids Get Working Class Jobs*. New York: Columbia University Press.

————. 1990. "Masculinity and Factory Labor." In *Culture and Society: Contemporary Debates*, edited by Jeffrey C. Alexander and Steven Seidman. New York: Cambridge University Press.

PART II

INSTITUTIONS AND SOCIAL CLASS

CHAPTER 4

CLASS, CULTURAL CAPITAL, AND INSTITUTIONS: THE CASE OF FAMILIES AND SCHOOLS

Annette Lareau and Jessica McCrory Calarco

Americans are persuaded by the power of individualism and thus believe that individuals shape their own life chances by the choices they make (Warner, Meeker, and Eels 2006). As a result, Americans generally do not accept that the social class of parents shapes the life chances of their children. Social scientists are much more likely to recognize the power of social class in shaping life chances. Nevertheless, when social scientists have studied social class, they often have viewed it as an individual trait: a marker of relative status (Adler et al. 1994; Karabel and Astin 1975; Kohn 1963; Rosenberg and Pearlin 1978; Tajfel 1982) or a measure of an individual's material resources (Macleod et al. 2005; Teachman 1987), using it to predict individual outcomes like educational performance or attainment (Jencks et al. 1972; Marjoribanks 1979; Teachman 1987). These findings are important, but there are also signs that social class matters not only for its relationship to status or material resources but also for the cultural resources (for example, knowledge, skills, and competences) it provides (Lareau and Weininger 2003). Considering these cultural resources, some scholars have examined social class as a key component of interpersonal interaction (chapters 7 and 8, this volume). Less is known, however, about how these class-based cultural resources facilitate interactions with institutions and how they offer individuals different advantages for complying with expectations in these settings.[1]

   This chapter addresses these questions by examining the ways in which parents' class backgrounds provide them with different repertoires of cultural resources for use in interacting with their children's schools and thus different advantages for meeting the schools' expectations for these interactions. We begin by discussing the concept of cultural capital and its usefulness in understanding how social class shapes interactions. We then present data from two different ethnographic studies of middle-class and working-class white families and their elementary-school-aged children. With the first study, we examine social-class differences in parents' interactions with their children's schools. With the second, we suggest that while there are stable class-based cultural repertoires, in some instances it may be possible for individuals to transform and supplement their cultural resources. We then take up the implications of these findings for our conceptual models of cultural capital.

CULTURAL CAPITAL AND PARENT INVOLVEMENT IN SCHOOLING

Class matters for social interaction in that it provides access to different cultural repertoires. As Ann Swidler's (1986) "tool kit" model suggests, cultures provide individuals with sets of knowledge, skills, and strategies that they can use to navigate the experiences of daily life. Pierre Bourdieu (1984) adopts a similar, resource-based view of culture but takes it somewhat further. Bourdieu uses the concept of cultural capital to explore not only how class-based cultures provide individuals with different interactional resources but also how these resources can be invested to yield different social profits.

Cultural capital first entered English-speaking social science research in the early 1980s (DiMaggio 1982). A number of empirical studies followed, often using large-scale data sets that usually (but not always) found measures of cultural capital to be associated with educational outcomes (DiMaggio and Mohr 1985; De Graaf, De Graaf, and Kraaykamp 2000; Farkas et al. 1990; Roscigno and Ainsworth-Darnell 1999). Other scholars, however, question the extent to which these studies accurately capture Bourdieu's original concept. For example, Annette Lareau and Elliot Weininger (2003) argue that cultural capital research has been unduly focused on high-status cultural signals such as museum attendance, art lessons, and other forms of cultural consumption. They suggest that a close look at Bourdieu's writings reveals that the elements of high-status cultural signals are not crucial to his original formulation of the concept; his view is much broader. Lareau and Weininger (2003, 569) also stress the importance of assessing cultural practices in light of "institutional standards of evaluation." Hence their view of cultural capital (which we adopt here) "emphasizes micro-interactional processes whereby individuals' strategic use of knowledge, skills, and competence comes into contact with institutionalized standards of evaluation. These specialized skills are transmissible across generations, are subject to monopoly, and may yield advantages or 'profits'" (Lareau and Weininger 2003, 569).

A few works do explore how different forms of cultural capital have different values within a given setting. Rubén Gaztambide-Fernández (2009) and Dirk Wittenborn and colleagues (2003) show that class backgrounds provide individuals with microinteractional resources for use in particular situations. They demonstrate that young people raised in upper-middle-class families show levels of ease and comfort in certain social settings, including parties, while working-class youth who are upwardly mobile report feeling out of place in their clothing or in interactions with middle-class peers in those same situations. Similarly, Jenny Stuber (2005) finds that upwardly mobile white adults often view their working-class backgrounds as a liability in workplace settings and that this dissonance between the cultural standards of the workplace and the cultural practices of the worker creates stress for these employees (see also Lubrano 2004).

These studies, though they highlight the cultural significance of social classes and the repertoire of resources class provides, are also limited. While the social interactions they describe are important in terms of cultural familiarity, they are arguably less important than institutional interactions in which parents seek to secure key resources for their children. In these interactions, parents likely draw on their class-based cultural resources and use them to transmit advantages. Research shows that institutions such as schools and workplaces play a critical role in shaping life chances. School attendance is legally compulsory, and education credentials determine access to high-quality jobs and opportunities (Davis 1963; Kalleberg, Reskin, and Hudson 2000; Kingston et al. 2003). There has been little research, however, on the cultural resources that parents possess as a result of their own class backgrounds and the ways they use these resources in interactions with institutions to secure advantages for their children.

Numerous studies have identified important class differences in parenting behaviors, such as aspirations for children, willingness to discuss school matters, or literacy practices (Deutsch 1967; Gerris, Deković, and Janssens 1997; Heath 1983; Kohn 1959, 1963; Levine 1974). These studies, however, do not adopt Bourdieu's (1984) and Lareau and Weininger's (2003) notion of institutionally situated cultural dominance and thus do not look critically at school standards (see Bourdieu and Passeron 1990). They assume that "good" parents read to their children, attend school conferences, and volunteer at school; thus they view middle-class parenting as inherently better than that of the working class. As a result, these studies fail to see that the cultural standards promoted and privileged by the school may align with particular class-based styles of parental involvement in schooling. Nor do they examine how class-based cultural repertoires unequally equip parents with resources to comply with schools' standards.

Other research has shown, however, that schools have a historically specific set of standards governing the curriculum that children are taught, the way children should behave, and the way parents can best support children's schooling (Tyack and Tobin 1994; Tye 2002). Because schools are essentially middle-class institutions, they tend to privilege and reward the cultural styles of the middle class over those of the working class (Bourdieu 1984). As a result, families from middle-class backgrounds are better able to comply with some school standards, particularly those regarding parental involvement, for example, by attending parent-teacher conferences, volunteering at school, and assisting with schoolwork at home (Useem 1992; Brantlinger 1987; Lareau 2000; Baker and Stevenson 1986). In a study of social class and parental involvement, Lareau and Erin Horvat (1999, 43) found that teachers prefer parents who "expressed sympathy with the difficulty of teachers' work, and had detailed information about their children's school experiences." By activating their cultural resources (for example, knowledge of teachers' expectations, skills for fostering interactions with teachers), middle-class parents were better equipped to embody this ideal parent model.

Among those who have focused on class-based cultural capital and its role in family-school relationships (Reay 1998; Reay, Crozier, and James 2011; Weiss 2008; Lareau 2011), a different problem arises. As Jay MacLeod (1995) suggests, existing views of cultural capital are overly deterministic, viewing social class and class-based cultural repertoires as relatively fixed attributes of individuals. Cultural capital is often defined as a stable set of practices linked to family of origin. Although research has not fully explored the process through which individuals adopt these practices, most studies suggest that it is in the routine, dispositions, and habits of family life (what Bourdieu, 1977, 18, calls "habitus") that individuals absorb taken-for-granted cultural repertoires. While they do not study this explicitly, Bourdieu and others assume that although individuals might learn new practices later in life, in the same way that individuals learn a second language, they will always lack the ease and fluency of native "inhabitants" of a given social class and the native "users" of its associated culture.

Although some scholars recognize that individuals may alter their class-based styles and orientations, they offer no evidence of the processes by which such cultural learning occurs. The lack of discussion of cross-class learning may reflect the fact that most individuals have limited contact with others outside their social class group (Erbe 1975; Farley 1977; Holme 2002; Iceland and Wilkes 2006; White 1987). Furthermore, because class and occupational status are closely aligned, when cross-class interaction does occur "it tends to be on a narrow, role-specific rather than a personal basis" (Archibald 1976, 820), as when a working-class person visits a middle-class doctor or a middle-class person purchases something from a working-class store clerk.

While few scholars have considered cross-class interactions and their consequences for participants in those interactions, this does not mean that such exchanges never occur. Many families live in communities and send their children to schools that are relatively segregated by social class (Farley 1977; Rumberger and Palardy 2008), but segregation is not absolute. Some communities and social settings (schools, doctor's offices, and so on) are more socioeconomically integrated and thus might provide opportunities for cross-class interactions, which could then facilitate cross-class exchange of cultural styles, strategies, and orientations. Similarly, the types of gateway interactions—opportunities for class mobility provided, for example, by transitions to college or a new job—that Cecilia Ridgeway and Susan Fisk discuss in chapter 7 of this volume may also provide individuals with access to new cultural knowledge, skills, and competences. Despite these possibilities, however, prior research has largely failed to examine opportunities for cross-class learning.

In this chapter, then, we address two lingering questions. First, how do class-based cultural repertoires provide individuals with different resources (knowledge, skills, and competences) for use in securing social profits in institutional settings? Second, can these cultural resources be acquired outside of the home? We answer these questions using data from two ethnographic studies of middle-class and working-class white families and their elementary-school-aged children. We focus specifically on white families both for comparability between the two studies and to avoid conflating issues of race and class.[2] Drawing on prior research by Lareau (2011), we begin by examining how parents' class-based cultural repertories equip them with different resources for use in deriving advantages from their interactions with teachers and other school officials. The working-class parents studied were often frustrated in their encounters in institutions. They felt that their efforts to make claims were rebuffed, but because of their limited knowledge of the inner workings of the school, they generally deferred to the expertise of educators and did not press on with their concerns. Middle-class parents did not always have smooth interactions with educators, but they often made much more progress than working-class parents. These parents felt empowered to intervene at school and possessed the socioemotional strategies necessary to do so. As a result, middle-class parents were often able to activate their cultural resources to gain advantages for their children, securing school services on their behalf. Using data from Jessica Calarco's study, we show that while there are stable patterns of cultural knowledge, in some instances it may be possible to transform and supplement cultural repertoires. More specifically, we describe how middle-class "cultural mentors" can help working-class parents acquire a limited set of middle-class cultural resources (for example, knowledge, skills, and competences) for deriving advantages from their interactions with the school.

METHODS

Briefly, the Lareau study compares the middle-class families of children attending a middle-class elementary school (Swan—all names are pseudonyms) with the poor and working-class families of children attending two different working-class elementary schools (Lower Richmond and Lawrenceville; for detailed descriptions of the research sites and methods, see Lareau 2011).[3] Lareau identified children's social-class backgrounds by their parents' occupation and educational attainment. Middle-class families are those in which at least one adult is employed in a position that either entails substantial managerial authority or draws on highly complex, educationally certifiable skills. Working-class families are those in which no adult is employed in a middle-class position but for at least one adult is employed in a position with little or no managerial authority that does not draw on highly complex, educationally certifiable skills. This category includes lower-level white-collar workers. Poor households are those in which parents receive public assistance and do not participate in the labor force on a regular, continuous basis.

From 1993 to 1994, Lareau, along with a team of graduate students, conducted participant observations at the three schools, repeatedly visiting two classes of third-grade students in each school and, at Swan and Lower Richmond, following them from third to fourth grade. In addition to making classroom observations, the researchers attended a wide variety of family-school events, allowing them to observe both children and their parents and guardians. At Swan and Lower Richmond, the researchers also observed and tape-recorded parent-teacher conferences; afterward, they asked parents and teachers to reflect on these conferences. Additionally, Lareau and her assistants conducted formal interviews (two hours in length) with the students' classroom teachers, asking about child and parent involvement in schooling.[4]

At each of the schools, Lareau also selected smaller samples of focal families to participate in interviews and home-based observations.[5] Lareau, along with a team of graduate students, conducted formal interviews with children's parents (usually both) and also had many informal conversations with students, parents, and teachers. The research team also conducted home-based observations of a sample of twelve families between 1993 and 1995, visiting each family about twenty times, usually over one month's time, and following family members through various activities at home, at school, and in the community. While the presence of the researchers in the participants' homes did affect the family dynamics that they observed, there was also evidence that this influence waned over time (for further details, see Lareau 2011).

Briefly, the Calarco study compares the middle-class and working-class white families of children who attend the same suburban, public elementary school, Maplewood.[6] Calarco identified students' social-class backgrounds by their parents' occupation and educational attainment. Middle-class families had at least one parent with a four-year college degree and at least one parent employed full time in a professional or managerial occupation. Working-class parents generally had only a high school diploma (some were high school dropouts; some had completed some college) and worked in blue-collar or service jobs.

From 2008 to 2010, Calarco observed about twice weekly at Maplewood, following a cohort of four classes of students from third to fifth grade. Calarco also conducted audio-recorded, in-depth interviews with the children's third-, fourth-, and fifth-grade teachers and, after fifth grade, with a smaller sample of middle-class and working-class students and their parents (usually mothers).[7] The project also included countless informal conversations with teachers, parents, and students. Calarco conducted two parent surveys (in 2008 and 2010) with questions about students' home lives and activities. Finally, at the end of the students' fifth-grade year, Calarco collected data from students' school files, including grades, test scores, and teacher comments as well as records of contact between parents and school personnel (for example, notes, emails, memos, and descriptions of conversations. For detailed descriptions of the research site and methods, see Calarco 2011).

There are important differences between these two studies. For one thing, they took place nearly fifteen years apart and in different school settings. Despite these differences, however, we found many of the same patterns. Similarly, while these studies define social class in somewhat different ways, the experience of families within these social class groups was largely consistent across the two studies. While Lareau identified three different social-class groups (compared with two in the Calarco study), she found few differences between poor and working-class families (at least in terms of their interactions with the school) and thus discusses them together as one group, which is very similar to the working-class group discussed in the Calarco study. Despite their differences, the two studies use similar methodologies—observing students in school, conducting in-depth interviews with teachers and parents, and collecting records of parent-teacher interaction. This methodological approach is labor intensive and is thus hampered by small, nonrandom samples as well as enduring questions about the role of the researcher in shaping the results. Nonetheless, the method also has the potential to illuminate the meaning of events to individuals as well as the ways in which parents enact them in daily life.

CLASS, CULTURAL CAPITAL, AND FAMILY-SCHOOL RELATIONSHIPS

In both data sets we found class differences in the ways that parents interacted with schools. Working-class parents were deeply concerned about their children's progress in school, but they intervened rarely. They did, however, report having open displays of anger in some of their (infrequent) family-school interactions. By contrast, middle-class parents approached educators much more frequently with questions and requests. These family-school interactions were often more informal and cordial, and some included joking. Middle-class parents also tended to probe for detailed information from teachers about their children, and some sought alternative educational options.

Working-Class and Poor Parents: Choosing When and How to Intervene

The working-class and poor parents in the Lareau study watched their children carefully, made assiduous efforts to get them ready for school, and worried about their well-being. Yet like similar parents in other studies (Brantlinger 1987; Useem 1992), they also had relatively limited information about their children's schooling, and what information they had tended to be vague and blurry. This restricted knowledge reflected parents' cultural styles (their deference to the school) and provided them with limited resources for use in securing advantages from their interactions with educators. As a result, these parents (as discussed elsewhere—see Baker and Stevenson 1986; Brantlinger 1987; Lareau 2000, 2011; Useem 1992) rarely tried to intervene to alter their children's educational environments or experiences.

Working-class and poor parents were generally reluctant to approach teachers with questions or concerns. At Back-to-School Night at Lower Richmond, for example, parents did not talk with one another:

> None of the parents chattered with one another as they were waiting for things to start or popped over to talk to one another after the speech ended. People didn't smile at one another or appear to engage in banter. Everything seemed stiff and awkward and difficult as if it made the parents really uncomfortable. While the parents were waiting for the teacher to begin, it was overwhelmingly quiet.

As shown elsewhere, working-class parents tended not to socialize with other parents at their children's schools, whereas middle-class parents did (Horvat, Weininger and Lareau 2003). Interviews also suggested that working-class and poor parents had a clear expectation that educators (rather than parents) had primary responsibility for children's education and that education takes place at school.

These parents' cultural styles and orientations seemed to limit their access to the kinds of detailed information that they might have needed to feel comfortable intervening at school. Because of their infrequent, awkward interactions with educators and other parents, working-class and poor parents tended to have vague knowledge of children's schooling. Many parents could not remember teachers' names and had limited knowledge of their children's current educational standing. For example, Ms. King, an African American high school dropout, gave the following response in an interview when discussing the reading level of her adopted daughter, Tina:

> I don't know what reading level Tina is at. I know that this year when she comes in she'll sit at the table and do her homework. The other day she came in and said

I have to read. She told me that she did her homework in school and I said, "Tina, read my lips. If you have homework it says *home* work and that means you do it at home. It doesn't say school work. You're supposed to bring it home and do it." I said, "What you do at school you call school work." I said, "The next time you come in here and you don't have that homework to do you'd better take your pants down so I can tear up your behind." And that's what I'm gonna do.

Although working-class parents were concerned for their children's education, they also sometimes misunderstood school practices, as in this instance in which Tina's teacher encouraged students to finish homework during their spare time in class so that they would not have to take it home.

Similarly, some mothers were alarmed by their children's lack of educational progress but had limited knowledge of the details of their children's struggles and of ways to improve their performance. Ms. Grover, a high school graduate who cleaned house for a living (off the books), had older children and reported in an interview that she "knew" something was wrong with the educational progress of her youngest son, Gary, though her description of it was vague:

> Since he was in kindergarten, even when he was a baby, I was like, he doesn't learn like the other kids do, you know, he's just not as up-to-date as they were. I was like, you know, something's different about him, and I don't know, I'm not exactly sure what it is, so when I took him to kindergarten he was doing bad, and they were like, uh, he didn't complete this. I was like, "Don't you realize that something might be wrong?" [They said,] "No, he's just a kid."

Parents like Ms. Grover expected educators to handle such matters. Thus even when working-class and poor parents had thoughts about modifications that would benefit their children, they rarely requested accommodations. Mr. McNaulty, for example, was a high school dropout, widower, and retired roofer who was raising his ten-year-old son John with the help of his daughter, Maureen (thirty-one years old). Maureen, a high school graduate who worked as a secretary, had a clear sense of the kind of teacher John needed: "I think that if he would have a male teacher I think he would be a lot better than [with] a female. I think he takes advantage of that by not listening and not paying attention. . . . I know there's one in fifth grade and I'm just hoping that maybe he'll get him next year." But when asked if they would request this teacher for next year, Maureen and her father both indicated that they would not:

> Maureen: I think they know what they are doing. No, I won't request. I feel all the teachers are qualified to teach.
>
> Mr. McNaulty: They're doing the best they can. They have a lot of pressure.

The McNaulty family appeared to see initiating a request for a teacher as a violation of teachers' professional expertise ("I think they know what they are doing"). Because they turned over responsibility for schooling to education professionals, they did not feel entitled to intervene.

"I Raised Hell": Strategies for Intervention   The working-class and poor parents in this study rarely interceded to alter their children's educational experiences. This does not mean that working-class and poor parents were never frustrated with their children's schooling. Some working-class and poor parents complained to researchers about their children's teachers (saying things like, "They don't push him enough") or said they disagreed with the teachers about the best ways to manage their children's learning. Rather than intervene to assert their own preferences, however, these parents tended to defer to the expertise of the educators, trusting them to make key educational decisions on their children's behalf.

Despite their hesitancy to intervene, working-class and poor parents sometimes felt that they had to express their concerns. In doing so, however, these parents often found that their socioemotional strategies for managing frustrations (such as anger and direct confrontation) were largely incompatible with the complex and often unarticulated standards of the school. Educators expect parents to be deferent, respectful, and appreciative in their interactions with the school but rarely voice these expectations (Lareau and Horvat 1999). Thus, when working-class and poor parents did (on rare occasions) try to intercede at school, they often did so angrily and confrontationally. This aligns with prior research, which has found some evidence that working-class individuals are more likely than middle-class individuals to use verbal and physical aggression in dealing with the frustrations they encounter (Day, Gough, and McFadden 2003; Fox 2004; Lamont 1994; Willis 1981). For example, Ms. Grover, a house cleaner and high school graduate, was livid that "the school" wanted her son, Gary, to repeat first grade. As she reported in her interview,

> I had a fight with school first. I was like, "He failed, he failed first grade." And they were like, "Oh, well, he failed." And I was like, "No, no, no, no, he didn't fail, you failed." I said, "My son didn't fail, you failed. You're a teacher; it's your job to notice that this child is not doing what he's supposed to be doing in school."

Ms. Grover attempted to insist that her son be tested for special education and even "wrote a registered letter to the school district." The school, however, denied her requests, telling her that they would not test her son and suggesting that she have her son's eyes examined. Ms. Grover had Gary fitted for glasses but was aggravated that the school did not honor her demand for services. As we see in this example, working-class and poor parents like Ms. Grover sometimes tried to intervene at school. However, they found that their strategies for intervention did not always comply with educators' definitions of helpful parent involvement.

In some instances, working-class parents' efforts to intervene exploded into direct, angry behaviors that educators considered unacceptable. One working-class man, Mr. Mallone, was raising his third-grade grandson, Brandon (whose mother had a drug problem and did not have regular contact with her son). As Mr. Mallone explained in his interview, he and his wife were upset when the school enrolled Brandon in the school's special education program:

> They gave him some test at school which, to me, is absolutely, totally ridiculous. . . .
> I guess it was an IQ test. I really don't know what it is. I don't know the technical

thing but he came out below average or average. I just laughed, you know. How in the name of God can somebody teach at school if they don't know what you have. . . . And my wife said, "They're totally wrong." I know what he is. I mean I went out and bought him a piano for Christmas and within a week he was doing things that just blew my socks off.

Mr. and Ms. Mallone were convinced that their grandson did not belong in special education: "So we went down to school and I raised hell. I got downright belligerent and nasty and cops, the whole thing. To say that they had to put him in special classes because he has a learning disability and they gave him one of those stupid tests too, that said he was below, whatever. I forget the name of the test." Mr. Mallone had limited knowledge of Brandon's educational situation (for example, the name of the test, Brandon's score, and the nature of the learning disability). He also did not know that he could ask to have Brandon retested or that a learning disability would entitle Brandon to special services. Yet while Mr. Mallone's knowledge about Brandon's educational situation was blurry, the anger and frustration that he felt were clear. His effort to deal with this frustration, however, rapidly escalated to aggressive confrontation—the educators called "the cops" to assist. The school might have been willing to reconsider placing this student in special education had the boy's grandfather framed his request in an "appropriate" way (see also Lareau and Horvat 1999).

Other working-class and poor parents responded in similar ways. In an African American family on public assistance, Nikkia had been raised from birth by her aunt, Ms. Cook, who was a high school dropout. Nikkia told her aunt that her male teacher had been pulling her hair; this information prompted Ms. Cook to write a note to the teacher:

I told him, "You put your damn hands on my daughter's head one more fuckin' time and I'll be there to fuck you up, period. Keep your hands off her. You don't have to pull her hair because she's not doing anything that bad and I know Nikkia. Nikkia don't do nothin'—she said somebody was messin' with her. You keep [your] hands off her."

Nikkia's aunt considered this intervention effective, saying, "so I had no more problems out of him for the whole year." Although we did not interview this particular teacher, educators did not consider threats from parents to be an appropriate form of parent involvement. Because the working-class parents we studied did not use strategies compatible with educators' expectations, they often were unable to achieve the accommodations they desired.

Working-class and poor parents had to rely on their knowledge, skills, and strategies to guide their interactions with the school. Yet because schools are predominantly middle-class institutions (Lareau 2000; Bourdieu 1984), working-class parents' resources were often incompatible with those expected by the school. Because of this incompatibility, schools tended to dismiss working-class and poor parents (and their concerns) as irrational and even dangerous.

"JUST LET IT GO": THE PROCESS OF INTERVENTION   Even when working-class and poor parents did try to intervene at school, they were often unable to secure the services or modifications that they wanted for their children. In the face of such disappointment, however (and often despite their continued frustrations), these parents rarely continued to pester the teacher with their demands. This was the case for one working-class mother, Ms. Martin, who was disappointed with her child's teacher:

> He went to first grade and he got the teacher Miss Robinson and she had a baby during the summer and they had to ask her at the school, "Are you sure that you're ready to come back?" And at first she would come in full, regular, [but it] got to the point where she was coming in maybe once out of the five. Then she stopped coming altogether. She wouldn't quit so they could get a full-time teacher in there. So they kept going through substitutes. And so in first grade my son learned to color and that's about it. Because no one was there; the work wasn't consistent. Almost the whole class failed. They like only just passed. Well, since then he's been like just passing every year. He's got Cs and Ds.

Ms. Martin's complaints fell on deaf ears: "I complained. I wanted his room changed but, you know, they couldn't. Everybody, they said if they would have put him in the other first grade they would have had to put everybody in the other first grade." This working-class mother was deeply disturbed by the events of her son's first-grade year. She tried to intervene, but the school dismissed her request. Rather than continue to hound the teacher with her demands, however, Ms. Martin gave up, feeling frustrated but powerless to alter the outcome.

When working-class and poor parents did contact the school, their efforts to intervene were limited. These parents trusted teachers to make key educational decisions on their children's behalf. Thus even when educators did not fully satisfy their concerns, these parents did not push back. Ms. Walters, for example, was concerned when her daughter, Courtney, came home complaining that she had "failed" after receiving "an 80" on a test. While Ms. Walters was not upset about the grade, she was worried about her daughter, who was "very emotional." She called "the school" for reassurance. While the teacher agreed with Ms. Walters that "it's a B; it's not a failing grade," she also noted that Courtney had been "defiant" at school. After this conversation, Courtney was still very upset, and Ms. Walters was even more concerned, worrying about both her daughter's behavior at home and her defiance at school. In attempting to deal with these issues, Ms. Walters turned to her own mother for advice: "I had to call my mom and . . . and I said, 'I don't know what to do.' And she said, 'Just let it go.' And tell [Courtney], let her know that when she gets to school you would appreciate her apologizing [to the teacher]." The advice that Courtney's mother received was not to press on or adopt a different strategy but rather to "just let it go." Ms. Walters's mother also did not urge Courtney to challenge the grade or ask for extra help for future tests, instead suggesting that she should apologize to the teacher for being defiant. Other working-class and poor parents who tried to intervene in their children's schooling reported similar experiences of having the school deny or dismiss their efforts.

In sum, most of the working-class and poor parents in this study were reluctant to intervene to manage their children's school experiences and opportunities. Like working-class and poor parents in other studies (Lareau 2000), they saw teachers and schools as educational experts and trusted them to make key educational decisions on their children's behalf. These parents also lacked the kind of detailed knowledge of the school and their children's educational experiences that would allow them to request specific accommodations on their children's behalf. Thus when these parents did try to intervene, their efforts were often rebuffed, leading to angry confrontations or disappointed withdrawal and rarely to satisfactory outcomes.

Middle-Class Parents: Choosing When and How to Intervene

The middle-class parents were, like those in other studies (Ball 2003; Baker and Stevenson 1986; Brantlinger 2003; Useem 1992), very involved in their children's schooling and had ample, detailed information about their children's school environments and experiences. As a result, these middle-class parents were also aware of a wide variety of opportunities for intervention in their children's schooling. They knew that they could request testing or accommodations and that children could be placed with particular teachers or peers. The middle-class McNamara family, for example, opted to delay their son Drew's entrance into kindergarten. Mr. and Ms. McNamara, both former public school teachers, were well versed in contemporary theories of child development. When Drew, a tall, popular, gregarious boy, was in preschool, his parents concluded that he was not ready for kindergarten at the legally designated date. In making their decision, Drew's parents went to a university library and read articles in education journals regarding age of enrollment and school success and psychological functioning. They also drew on their informal social networks and spoke with the preschool teacher and friends about the matter. School district officials were not even consulted: "We didn't get advice from anyone in the public school. . . . I didn't think it was any of their business. Next year when we went in and had him tested they just all thought it was wonderful." Other middle-class parents also had extensive knowledge of their children's educational development relative to school standards. As a result, they felt comfortable asserting their own preferences, even if it meant overriding the school's recommendations.

While working-class parents trusted teachers to manage their children's educations, middle-class parents followed their children's schoolwork very closely, gathering detailed information about their children's schooling and using this information to advocate on their children's behalf. Many middle-class parents, for example, came to conferences armed with substantial knowledge of their children's academic performance and their standing in the class, information that working-class and poor parents tended to treat as the exclusive province of professionals. Unlike their working-class counterparts, middle-class parents also felt comfortable using this knowledge to try to secure advantages (such as services or accommodations) on their children's behalf.

"SAVE YOUR AMMUNITION": STRATEGIES FOR INTERVENTION   The middle-class parents in our study often tried to intervene in their children's schooling, seeking services and accommodations to better meet their children's individual needs (also see Baker and Stevenson 1986; Ball 2003; Brantlinger 2003; McGrath and Kuriloff 1999; Useem 1992). In these exchanges, middle-class parents also drew on different cultural strategies from those of their working-class peers. While working-class parents tended to approach the school (when they did so) with anger and accusations, middle-class parents took a much less confrontational approach: During parent-teacher conferences, for example, many middle-class parents asked probing questions about the quality of the education that their children were receiving. While teachers often tried to dismiss such concerns, these parents would then, in a light, friendly, and conversational tone (rather than in an angry or demanding one), disagree with the teacher. This was the case for Ms. Hopewell, a middle-class mother who used a parent-teacher conference to probe her daughter's standing in the class by asking detailed questions:

> Teacher: I would say that she falls sort of right in the middle. I don't see her as being an extreme case of always forgetting and lagging behind. But she's not maybe the top end.
>
> Mother: No. I wouldn't say. Now, how do you feel, do you feel that Therese is doing work to the best of her ability?
>
> Teacher: When she's working I do.
>
> Mother: See, I always feel like she's not.

Working-class parents either suppressed their frustrations or expressed them by angrily challenging educators. Middle-class parents instead took an assertive but cooperative approach, asking questions and establishing themselves as partners with the teachers. Ms. Hopewell was assertive with the teacher but also spoke in a light and airy fashion; she smiled frequently, leaned forward to signal that she was listening carefully to what the teacher said, and went out of her way to offer a critical assessment of her daughter before disagreeing with the teacher about whether her daughter was working to the best of her ability.

By adopting such socioemotional strategies, middle-class parents gained an advantage in complying with the schools' elaborate and unarticulated expectations. They understood that schools preferred to deal with parents who were respectful, appreciative, and cooperative (Lareau and Horvat 1999), and they tailored their styles and strategies to align with these expectations. Mothers at Swan, for example, were aware that the educators did not like requests from parents to place children with a particular teacher. While one middle-class mother, a former school teacher, recognized the potential benefits to be gained from placing her children with particular teachers, she knew that it was important to be highly selective in making these types of requests: "I requested for Drew last year. . . . I try not to request very often. Because if you do that it's like you get ignored. It's better to save your ammunition for 'when you really need it' kind of thing." Middle-class parents like this one used their detailed knowledge of teacher expectations and their socioemotional strategies to navigate the school's complicated and unarticulated preferences and successfully assert their own and their children's interests. Unlike working-class and poor parents, middle-class parents often had close friends who were teachers, and some were even teachers themselves. Thus while working-class parents were often awkward in their interactions with teachers, middle-class parents were generally comfortable in these exchanges, calling teachers by their first names and approaching them with a variety of requests.

Not all middle-class parents were so casual in their interactions with teachers. Compared with their working-class counterparts, however, middle-class parents had more frequent and friendlier exchanges with teachers. As a result, these parents were better able to comply with teachers' expectations for "appropriate" parental involvement. Teachers, in turn, tended to respond favorably to the strategies that middle-class parents used in their interventions and were thus often willing to grant them the services and accommodations they desired.

"AGAINST EVERYONE'S ADVICE": THE PROCESS OF INTERVENTION   Middle-class parents' initial efforts at intervention did not always produce the intended results. In these situations, however, and unlike their working-class counterparts, middle-class parents were rarely willing to "just let it go." Instead, they approached interactions with the school as an ongoing negotiation. This was the case for Ms. Hall, who refused to accept the teacher's recommendation that her son, Tommy, repeat kindergarten. At the end of Tommy's kindergarten year, Tommy's teacher was adamant that he should not go to first grade. Ms. Hall, however, did not want him to be held back. As she told us in her interview, this mother argued with the teacher for another alternative, suggesting a wide variety of educational options:

> Well, the whole year we just argued about it. I said, "Give me some options." I said, "I don't care if he [doesn't] go to first grade, but how about if he repeated a kindergarten that's only half day, could he have extra reading? Could he have extra math? Could I come in and work with him or do something? This kid wants more and I don't know what to give him." And she's like, "No, I have nothing to offer you." So I said, "Well, could we have him tested?" Someone had told me that they have facilities for testing. "Could we have him tested for first-grade readiness?"

In the end, Ms. Hall refused to have her son held back, as did four or five other mothers in similar situations: "I just could not see him repeating kindergarten. I couldn't do it. And they have never questioned Tommy's placement after kindergarten. And I wasn't the only mom either. It wasn't like all these kids were flourishing and Tom was standing out." Ms. Hall did not go against the teacher's advice easily, noting that "it was the hardest decision for me, putting him in first grade against everyone's advice." In the end, though, Ms. Hall stood her ground, refusing to accept that the teacher had "nothing to offer" her son.

Like other middle-class mothers, she approached the situation as a negotiation, pushing until she was satisfied that she had received the solution she desired. While working-class parents usually conceded to educators' recommendations, middle-class parents instead persisted in their demands. As a result, their efforts to intercede were generally multistage processes that involved repeated interactions with multiple school officials and sometimes outside parties, such as doctors or lawyers.

Despite middle-class parents' persistence, not all issues were resolved to their satisfaction. Yet even when schools denied middle-class parents' requests, they still tended to take these parents and their concerns seriously. They did so, in part, by granting these parents repeated and lengthy audiences with school and district officials who listened intently to their concerns.

In sum, there were class differences in the stance that parents took toward the school and in their interactions with teachers and other school officials. One indicator of this pattern is that it was common for working-class and poor parents to use the term *the school* when discussing the children's elementary school (that is, "I called the school" or "I got a letter from the school"). The term suggests a faceless, bureaucratic institution. By contrast, middle-class parents tended to discuss principals or teachers by name, often even using their first names (for example, Noelle) or nicknames (for example, Mr. I.). These terms suggest differences in the familiarity and quality of the relationships that parents had with their children's schools.

ACQUISITIONS OF CULTURAL CAPITAL

Broadly, the results of the Calarco study echoed those of the Lareau study. Like the middle-class parents at Swan, those at Maplewood were highly involved in their children's schooling, often volunteering at school and interacting both formally and informally with parents and teachers. Middle-class parents at Maplewood also had ample, detailed information about their children's school environments and experiences. As a result, they were both aware of and well-equipped to take advantage of a wide array of opportunities for intervening in their children's schooling. Middle-class parents at Maplewood, like those at Swan, also approached these interventions strategically, carefully choosing their battles, presenting their requests in a calm and pleasant manner, and often doggedly pursuing their demands through multi-stage negotiations. These parents often (though not always) experienced considerable success.

Compared with their middle-class peers, working-class parents at Maplewood had limited knowledge of when and how to intervene at school. Like their counterparts at Lower Richmond, working-class parents at Maplewood were also largely unaware of the school's expectations for parental involvement. As a result, when these parents were frustrated with something at school, they tended to either hide their frustrations from the school or express them in ways that the school deemed inappropriate (for example, by yelling). Furthermore, these working-class parents' efforts at involvement and intervention also tended to be much more limited (briefer and involving fewer contacts) than those of their middle-class peers.

Despite these similarities, however, we found important differences between the working-class parents in Calarco's study and those in the Lareau study. Unlike working-class parents at Lower Richmond, those at Maplewood lived in a socioeconomically diverse community and thus had more opportunities to interact with others from middle-class backgrounds (some had children who participated on sports teams with middle-class peers, and others had jobs—for example, day care provider—that put them in frequent contact with middle-class parents). While not all working-class parents took equal advantage of these opportunities, such cross-class interactions sometimes created opportunities for cross-class learning.

For example, middle-class parents sometimes acted as cultural mentors, providing strategic advice and guidance to their working-class peers. Ms. Carson, for example, was a high school graduate and mother of three who worked as a waitress at a local (upscale) restaurant. In her interview, Ms. Carson relayed a story about a conversation that she had at her son's Little League game. It was the spring of Jared's third-grade year, and Ms. Carson was sitting with a group of middle-class mothers of boys in Jared's grade. These other women had heard bad things about Ms. Nelson, one of the fourth-grade teachers at Maplewood:

> It was at a [Little League] baseball game! Sitting in the stands. And the conversation came up and they go, "How do you feel about Ms. Nelson?" And, "How's your year going?" They asked me, 'cuz they knew my older son Trevor had Ms. Nelson. And I said, "Well, I think it's okay. I don't think he comes home with enough homework. . . . I feel like he's doing okay, but I don't know. I look at his work and [*makes a skeptical face*]."

The other mothers then asked Ms. Carson if she had considered the possibility that Jared might also get Ms. Nelson in fourth grade and have the same problems that Trevor had. As Ms. Carson went on to note in her interview (the emphasis reflects the inflection of the speaker):

> And [one of the other mothers was] like [*in a warning voice*], "Well, you know, next year, who do you want Jared to have next year?" And I'm like, "How do I know?" She goes, "Oh yeah! You can *help place* a little bit, especially 'cuz you don't want him to have Ms. Nelson." And I'm like, "Really?". . . . And, it's funny that was brought to my attention, 'cuz I would never *say* anything.

The other mothers (one of whom was a teacher herself) then advised Ms. Carson on the specific strategies she should use in requesting that her son not be placed in Ms. Nelson's class. They knew that the school did not like dealing with confrontational and demanding parents, and they shared this insight with Ms. Carson. She explained all of this in her interview, dropping her voice to a whisper, as if sharing a secret: "And [the other parents] said: 'You know what, if you feel this way [about Ms. Nelson], you should do this, and write a letter. Because you can't *tell* them, but you can *ask* them, that you would like your child placed with [a different teacher].' And they kind of explained to me how to do it."

The other mothers also gave her the language to use in making this request, encouraging her not to "demand" that Jared be placed with a specific teacher but rather to explain that because of her son's personality he "needed" a particular type of teacher. Ms. Carson continued,

> I didn't say anything negative. I said, "I really feel my son needs. . . . " I was told to write, "He has a strong personality, and he needs a teacher that can dada-dada. . . . " And [the school] chose a teacher for him that was like that. I let them do it. I didn't tell them who I thought that he should have. *They* had me do it like that. The other parents, *they* had me do it the right way.

In light of his mother's letter, Jared was not placed in Ms. Nelson's fourth-grade class. Like the parents in this example, middle-class cultural mentors advised working-class parents to use particular (and "middle-class") socioemotional strategies in their interactions with the school. In doing so, they helped these parents tailor their requests to align with the school's complex and unarticulated expectations.

Other working-class parents also recounted incidents in which middle-class parents had encouraged them to approach the school with requests. Ms. Marrone, for example, a home day-care provider and mother of five, said in her interview that when her second daughter, Cindy (now twenty-six), was struggling in school, she received some advice on how to deal with the situation while talking with a middle-class mother who lived nearby:

> Cindy also had [a learning disability], and [the school] didn't know about it. . . . I would say something, and they would say, "Oh, she just doesn't test well. She's just not good in tests, and blah blah blah." And then, when Cindy was, like, in fifth grade, I kept saying to myself, "I don't know, there's just something about her." But I didn't know, I mean, Cindy was my second kid, and [my older daughter] didn't have those problems. And then, I was talking to [a middle-class mother], and she said, "Well, has [Cindy] ever been tested?" And I'm like, "No! The school's never tested her!" And they're like, "Well, why don't you request it?" And I'm like, "Oh! You can do that?" I mean, you don't *know* these things.

The other mother then explained to Ms. Marrone that she should write a letter to the principal requesting that her daughter be tested for a learning disability and even offered suggestions about the language to use in the letter. Following the advice and guidance she received from this middle-class cultural mentor, Ms. Marrone wrote the letter. The school granted Ms. Marrone's request, and Cindy was eventually enrolled in a learning support program.

Ms. Marrone's experience with Cindy had a lasting effect on her interactions with the school. When her son Shawn (now eleven) also showed signs of learning disabilities, the school wanted to hold him back. Ms. Marrone, however, drew on the lessons she had learned from her cultural mentor to insist that Shawn not repeat a grade:

> So when it came to Shawn, and I could see Shawn was like a little slower and stuff, same thing they debated on [keeping him back]. [They said,] "Boys! You know, that's what it is, boys need the extra time [in a grade]." And I just turned around and said, "No. You need to test him. And if you test him and he doesn't have a problem, then I will keep him back, 'cuz he needs to grow up. But if he has a problem, he's not staying back." . . . And here it was, they tested him, and he had the learning disability, so they never had him stay back. So you learn. It took me five kids, but you learn [*laughs*]. But now, you see me, and if I talk to somebody, I tell everybody. I tell 'em, "Write the note. You have an ounce of a question, write the note. And if you're not sure, just do it."

With each of her children, Ms. Marrone grew increasingly more assertive in her interactions with the school. She moved from simply asking to have her child tested for learning disabilities to politely refusing to allow the school to hold her son back a grade. She also moved from writing a single letter (as she did with her older daughter, Cindy) to engaging in multiple, in-person exchanges with teachers and other school officials.

Through interactions with cultural mentors, working-class parents learned when and how to intervene in their children's schooling. As a result of the advice, guidance, and encouragement that they received from their cultural mentors, these working-class parents then felt comfortable interceding at school on their children's behalf. Even when the school denied their requests, these parents politely persisted in their demands, engaging in multistage negotiations to secure the services and accommodations that they wanted for their children.

THE LIMITS OF CROSS-CLASS LEARNING

While cultural mentors clearly provided working-class parents with important resources for use in navigating and negotiating their interactions with teachers and other school officials, these cross-class exchanges were also limited in a number of important ways. Not all of the working-class parents at Maplewood received cultural mentoring; on the contrary, only a few parents benefited from such exchanges. Furthermore, even for those who did, cultural mentoring did not completely transform their parenting styles. While these working-class parents did gain new knowledge, skills, and strategies for interacting with the school, they also maintained many other aspects of their working-class culture. For example, Calarco observed all these parents using directives in speaking with their children, an interactional style that is common among working-class families (Lareau 2011). Similarly, while these working-class beneficiaries of cultural mentoring seemed to be somewhat more comfortable than other working-class parents in their interactions with the school, they still exhibited a stronger sense of distance and deference in these interactions than did their middle-class peers. What this means, then, is that while the instruction they received from their "cultural mentors" prompted working-class parents like Ms. Marrone and Ms. Carson to alter some aspects of their class-based cultural repertoires (particularly the skills, styles, and strategies used in negotiating with school officials), it did not lead them to adopt a fully middle-class style of parenting and parental involvement.

DISCUSSION

Like those in chapters 3, 5, 7, and 9 of this volume, our findings suggest that social class matters for interactions primarily through its relationship to class-based cultural repertoires. In this view, class backgrounds shape individuals' habits and dispositions (Bourdieu's "habitus") and also provide access to different cultural resources. We argue that the primary importance of these class-based cultural repertoires lies not in the clusters of tastes and preferences that they represent (DiMaggio 1982) but rather in the microinteractional resources (knowledge, skills, and strategies) that they provide to individuals who possess them. As Bourdieu (1984) and others have suggested, the value associated with class-based resources can vary across settings (what Bourdieu calls "fields"). This means, in turn, that institutional processes are not class neutral. On the contrary, the possession of particular cultural skills and strategies gives some individuals an advantage in complying with the standards of a given setting.

There are real and meaningful social-class differences in the microinteractional resources that parents possess for navigating the complex and often unarticulated expectations of schools. Broadly speaking, we find that parents' class-based cultural resources can facilitate or hinder their interactions with school officials and their willingness and ability to intervene at school on their children's behalf. Compared with the knowledge, skills, and strategies of working-class parents, those of middle-class parents are much more synchronized with the (ever-changing) standards of schools. Middle-class parents tend to have more knowledge of when and how they can intervene in their children's schooling and can thus tailor the strategies they use to align with the expectations of teachers and other school officials. Because of this alignment between middle-class repertoires and school expectations, schools tend to respond more favorably to the interventions of middle-class parents than to those of their working-class peers. While dealing with schools is not easy for middle-class parents, when they confront problems, they have more cultural resources on which to draw. As a result, they are able to persist in spite of the challenges they face, approaching interventions as an ongoing process of negotiation. Working-class parents also want their children to succeed in school and experience considerable anxiety when their children struggle. Yet because they have less knowledge of when and how to intervene at school, and because their cultural styles and strategies are not closely aligned with those privileged by educators, it can be quite difficult for them to negotiate educators' expectations. Parents' cultural resources, then, seem to give them different tools for interacting with schools and navigating school standards and thus differential options for managing their children's educational experiences and opportunities.

Such findings have important theoretical implications for our understanding of the role of social class in stratifying both the nature and outcomes of social interactions. These results suggest that particular (and usually middle-class) class-based cultural repertoires provide key advantages for individuals in complying with institutional expectations. We also believe, however, that this advantage is tied more to the knowledge, skills, and strategies that individuals possess than to the status group to which they belong. Through interactions with middle-class cultural mentors, some working-class parents in the Calarco study acquired a small but meaningful set of middle-class knowledge, skills, and strategies for navigating the complex and unarticulated standards of the school. These working-class parents were also able to activate these newfound resources to achieve real social profits for themselves and their children.

These findings add more nuance to our understanding of social class, culture, and interaction. They suggest that cultural mentoring can allow individuals to transform or supplement certain aspects of their class-based cultural repertoires and that these changes can have meaningful consequences for individuals' interactions with institutions. Similarly, other research has found some success in programs designed to increase poor and working-class parents' involvement in schooling and improve relations between these families and their children's schools (Epstein and Dauber 1991; Horvat and Davis 2010; Olds, Sadler, and Kitzman 2007). Yet while these results could be taken to suggest that class-based cultural repertoires are far less fixed than most scholars assume, we emphasize here that there are also real and meaningful limits to the types of knowledge, skills, and strategies that can be learned. Other studies have shown, for example, that programs have had little success in changing parenting behaviors (Goodson et al. 2000) and that even intensive, home-based parent mentoring generally has, at best, a short-term impact on children's educational outcomes (Campbell and Ramey 1995; Sweet and Appelbaum 2004).

Furthermore, while cultural mentoring may help some working-class parents to better navigate specific types of interactions with teachers (for example, writing a letter to request testing for learning disabilities), most family-school interactions are much more complex. In parent-teacher conferences, for example, parents need a deep understanding of school practices to know what questions to ask and also the confidence to interrupt the teacher and to doggedly follow up if the teacher does not fully respond to their requests (Horvat, Weininger, and Lareau 2003). Thus while cultural mentoring may give working-class parents some additional knowledge, skills, and strategies for use in navigating these complex interactions, we suspect, following Bourdieu, that these parents will not demonstrate the same ease and fluency that their middle-class counterparts exhibit in using these resources (Lamont and Lareau 1988). Hence in evaluating the success of programs like the Harlem Children's Zone's "Baby College," future research should also consider whether native fluency with dominant cultural repertoires continues to give middle-class families an advantage over their less privileged peers.

Scholars should also consider whether programmatic interventions are as effective as organic cross-class interactions in promoting the exchange of cultural resources. As Thomas DiPrete and colleagues (2011) suggest, the social networks of Americans are becoming more homogenous. This means that opportunities for meaningful cross-class interaction (and the cross-class learning that they facilitate) will likely become increasingly rare.

Overall, this chapter highlights the need for further qualitative research (some of which can be found in this volume) on the ways in which social class shapes social interactions, particularly through its relationship to class-based repertoires of micro-interactional resources. While these resources are critical to family-school relationships, we are impressed by how difficult it can be to capture them in social science research. We found, for example, that parents were not particularly aware of the class-based nature of their knowledge, skills, and strategies. In the Calarco study, it was striking that the working-class mothers felt that they were being let in on a secret; the middle-class mothers saw the information as common knowledge. It was only in cross-class interactions that the parents became aware of other strategies. Given this limited awareness, it would be hard for parents to describe the distinctiveness of these interactions in a survey. Hence in their interviews, middle-class mothers did not report that they asked pointed questions while maintaining a light and airy tone, nor did working-class parents report that after trying several times to influence the process they exploded in demands and anger. Socioemotional dynamics are critical to interaction; they are worthy of study. But they are hard to capture in large, representative studies.

As researchers try to study this topic, however, they also confront the problem that parents' support of their children's education is infused with standards of social desirability. Getting a good education is a universally accepted value. It is also widely accepted that "good parents" should be involved in their children's schooling. Hence survey questions on these topics are inflected with these broader cultural standards. We are not optimistic that these results could be easily confirmed by including additional questions about cultural resources or interactions in survey research; qualitative research, however, necessarily leads to small, nonrandom samples. But the fact that these patterns are not easily captured by fixed-response categories does not mean that they should be excluded from studies. Indeed, highlighting class differences in the rituals of daily life, and the ways that these differences in social rituals transmit important advantages for children, remains an important topic for researchers and policymakers in the future.

We are grateful to Susan Fiske, Hazel Markus, and the anonymous reviewers for their helpful comments and also to the Spencer Foundation for their generous support of this research. The opinions expressed are our own, and we are responsible for any errors. Versions of this chapter were presented at The Secret Handshake: Social Class Divides in Face-to-Face Encounters, a conference held by the Russell Sage Foundation in June 2010.

NOTES

1. While scholars have shown that class-based cultural resources matter for outcomes in institutional settings (DiMaggio 1982; Dumais 2002; Roscigno and Ainsworth-Darnell 1999), they rarely explore how these cultural resources actually operate in interactions.
2. Although qualitative research typically suggests that class matters more than race in shaping parent involvement in schooling (Lareau 2011), other quantitative studies have found race effects on parenting behaviors (Cheadle and Amato 2010; Cheadle 2009).
3. Swan is an elementary school located in a middle-class suburban district. Lower Richmond is a predominantly working-class elementary school in a large urban district. Swan and Lower Richmond are located in the same metropolitan area, outside of a large eastern city. The third school, Lawrenceville, is located in a university community about two hours from a major midwestern city. As the only school in the area, Lawrenceville serves both the white middle-class children of professors and the poor African American children who live in historically black neighborhoods in the community. While there is no significant free lunch program at Swan, 64 percent of students at Lower Richmond and 40 percent of those at Lawrenceville receive free lunches.
4. Some of the interviews in Lawrenceville were drawn from students in another nearby school district that served relatively similar student populations. The classrooms in Lower Richmond and Swan did not generate enough poor white families and middle-class black

children for the study, so additional families in these categories were recruited. The whites were recruited through flyers posted at social service agencies and on telephone poles; the African American families were recruited through a snowball sample started through informal social networks.

5. The interview sample involved eighty-eight white children and their families. Of these, thirty-six were from middle-class families, twenty-six from working-class families, and twenty-six from poor families. The home-based observations sample involved twelve white children and their families—four families from each of the three class groups. Both samples included approximately equal numbers of African American families. In this chapter, however, we focus only on the white families in this study, which composed half of each sample. Further details about the study samples and race-class comparisons can be found in Lareau (2011).

6. Maplewood is a K–5 school located approximately one hour outside a large eastern city. The school is not a charter or magnet school but draws students from both working-class and middle-class neighborhoods. Approximately 18 percent of Maplewood's students are from minority backgrounds (primarily Asian American and Hispanic-Latino), and 15 percent qualify for the school's free or reduced-price lunch program.

7. The observation sample comprises fifty-six white students: forty-two middle class and fourteen working class. The interview sample involved twenty-one families: twelve middle class and nine working class. For the purpose of this analysis we exclude students who moved away during the course of the study and students who were from minority backgrounds.

REFERENCES

Adler, Nancy E., Thomas Boyce, Margaret A. Chesney, Sheldon Cohen, Susan Folkman, Robert L. Kahn, and Symes Leonard. 1994. "Socioeconomic Status and Health: The Challenge of the Gradient." *The American Psychologist* 49(1): 15–24.

Archibald, W. Peter. 1976. "Face-to-Face: The Alienating Effects of Class, Status, and Power Divisions." *The American Sociological Review* 41(5): 819–37.

Baker, David P., and David L. Stevenson. 1986. "Mothers' Strategies for Children's School Achievement: Managing the Transition." *The Sociology of Education* 59(3): 156–66.

Ball, Stephen J. 2003. *Class Strategies and the Education Market: The Middle Classes and Social Advantage.* New York: Routledge Falmer.

Bourdieu, Pierre. 1977. *Outline of a Theory of Practice.* Cambridge: Cambridge University Press.

———. 1984. *Distinction: A Social Critique of the Judgment of Taste.* Cambridge, Mass.: Harvard University Press.

Bourdieu, Pierre, and Jean-Claude Passeron. 1990. *Reproduction in Education, Culture, and Society.* 2nd ed. Thousand Oaks, Calif.: Sage.

Brantlinger, Ellen A. 1987. "Making Decisions About Special Education: Do Low-Income Parents Have the Information They Need?" *The Journal of Learning Disabilities* 20(2): 94–101.

———. 2003. *Dividing Classes: How the Middle Class Negotiates and Rationalizes School Advantage.* New York: Routledge.

Calarco, Jessica M. 2011. "'I Need Help!': Social Class and Children's Help-Seeking in Elementary School." *American Sociological Review* 76(6): 862–82.

Campbell, Frances A., and Craig T. Ramey. 1995. "Cognitive and School Outcomes for High-Risk African-American Students at Middle Adolescence: Positive Effects of Early Intervention." *The American Educational Research Journal* 32(4): 743–72.

Cheadle, Jacob E. 2009. "Parent Educational Investment and Children's General Knowledge Development." *Social Science Research* 38(2): 477–91.

Cheadle, Jacob E., and Paul R. Amato. 2010. "A Quantitative Assessment of Lareau's Qualitative Conclusions About Class, Race, and Parenting." *Journal of Family Issues* 20(10): 1–28.

Davis, James A. 1963. "Higher Education: Selection and Opportunity." *The School Review* 71(3): 249–265.

Day, Katy, Brendan Gough, and Majella McFadden. 2003. "Women Who Drink and Fight: A Discourse Analysis of Working-Class Women's Talk." *Feminism and Psychology* 13(2): 141–58.

De Graaf, Nan Dirk, Paul M. De Graaf, and Gerbert Kraaykamp. 2000. "Parental Cultural Capital and Educational Attainment in The Netherlands: A Refinement of the Cultural Capital Perspective." *The Sociology of Education* 73(2): 92–111.

Deutsch, Martin. 1967. "The Disadvantaged Child and the Learning Process." In *The Disadvantaged Child*, edited by M. Deutsch. New York: Basic Books.

DiMaggio, Paul. 1982. "Cultural Capital and School Success: The Impact of Status Culture Participation on the Grades of U.S. High School Students." *The American Sociological Review* 47(2): 189–201.

DiMaggio, Paul, and John Mohr. 1985. "Cultural Capital, Educational Attainment, and Marital Selection." *The American Journal of Sociology* 90(6): 1231–61.

DiPrete, Thomas, Andrew Gelman, Julien Teitler, Tian Zheng, and Tyler McCormick. 2011. "Segregation and Social Networks Based on Acquaintanceship and Trust." *The American Journal of Sociology* 116(4): 1234–38.

Dumais, Susan A. 2002. "Cultural Capital, Gender, and School Success: The Role of Habitus." *Sociology of Education* 75(1): 44–68.

Epstein, Joyce L., and Susan L. Dauber. 1991. "School Programs and Teacher Practices of Parent Involvement in Inner-City Elementary and Middle-Schools." *The Elementary School Journal* 91(3): 289–305.

Erbe, Brigitte Mach. 1975. "Race and Socioeconomic Segregation." *The American Sociological Review* 40(6): 801–12.

Farkas, George, Robert P. Grobe, Daniel Sheehan, and Yuan Shuan. 1990. "Cultural Resources and School Success: Gender, Ethnicity, and Poverty Groups Within an Urban District." *The American Sociological Review* 55(1): 127–42.

Farley, Reynolds. 1977. "Residential Segregation in Urbanized Areas of the United States in 1970: An Analysis of Social Class and Racial Differences." *Demography* 14(4): 497–518.

Fox, Aaron A. 2004. *Real Country: Music and Language in Working-Class Culture*. Durham, N.C.: Duke University Press.

Gaztambide-Fernández, Rubén A. 2009. *The Best of the Best: Becoming Elite at an American Boarding School*. Cambridge, Mass.: Harvard University Press.

Gerris, Jan R. M., Maja Deković, and Jan M. A. M. Janssens. 1997. "The Relationship Between Social Class and Childrearing Behaviors: Parents' Perspective Taking and Value Orientations." *The Journal of Marriage and Family* 59(4): 834–47.

Goodson, Barbara D., Jean I. Layzer, Robert G. St. Pierre, Lawrence S. Bernstein, and Michael Lopez. 2000. "Effectiveness of Comprehensive, Five-Year Family Support Program for Low-

Income Children and Their Families: Findings from Comprehensive Child Development Program." *The Early Childhood Research Quarterly* 15(1): 5–39.

Heath, Shirley Brice. 1983. *Ways with Words: Language, Life, and Work in Communities and Classrooms*. Cambridge: Cambridge University Press.

Holme, Jennifer Jellison. 2002. "Buying Homes, Buying Schools: School Choice and the Social Construction of School Quality." *The Harvard Educational Review* 72(2): 177–207.

Horvat, Erin McNamara, and James Earl Davis. 2010. "Schools as Sites for Transformation: Exploring the Contribution of Habitus." *Youth and Society* 43(1): 142–70.

Horvat, Erin M., Elliot B. Weininger, and Annette Lareau. 2003. "From Social Ties to Social Capital: Class Differences in the Relations Between Schools and Parent Networks." *The American Educational Research Journal* 40(1): 319–51.

Iceland, John, and Rima Wilkes. 2006. "Does Socioeconomic Status Matter? Race, Class, and Residential Segregation." *Social Problems* 53(2): 248–73.

Jencks, Christopher, Marshall Smith, Henry Acland, Mary Jo Bane, David Cohen, Herbert Gintis, Barbara Heyns, and Stephan Michelson. 1972. *Inequality: A Reassessment of the Effect of Family and Schooling in America*. New York: Basic Books.

Kalleberg, Arne, Barbara F. Reskin, and Ken Hudson. 2000. "Bad Jobs in America: Standard and Nonstandard Employment Relations and Job Quality in the United States." *The American Sociological Review* 65(2): 256–78.

Karabel, Jerome, and Alexander W. Astin. 1975. "Social Class, Academic Ability, and College 'Quality.'" *Social Forces* 53(3): 381–98.

Kingston, Paul W., Ryan Hubbard, Brent Lapp, Paul Schroeder, and Julia Wilson. 2003. "Why Education Matters." *The Sociology of Education* 76(1): 53–70.

Kohn, Melvin L. 1959. "Social Class and Parental Values." *The American Journal of Sociology* 64(4): 337–51.

———. 1963. "Social Class and Parent-Child Relationships: An Interpretation." *The American Journal of Sociology* 68(4): 471–80.

Lamont, Michèle. 1994. *Money, Morals, and Manners: The Culture of the French and American Upper-Middle Class*. Chicago: University of Chicago Press.

Lamont, Michèle, and Annette Lareau. 1988. "Cultural Capital: Allusions, Gaps, and Glissandos in Recent Theoretical Developments." *Sociological Theory* 6(2): 153–68.

Lareau, Annette. 2000. *Home Advantage: Social Class and Parental Intervention in Elementary Education*. London: Falmer.

———. 2011. *Unequal Childhoods: Class, Race, and Family Life*. 2nd ed. Berkeley: University of California Press.

Lareau, Annette, and Erin McNamara Horvat. 1999. "Moments of Social Inclusion and Exclusion: Race, Class, and Cultural Capital in Family-School Relationships." *The Sociology of Education* 72(1): 37–53.

Lareau, Annette, and Elliot B. Weininger. 2003. "Cultural Capital in Educational Research: A Critical Assessment." *Theory and Society* 32(5–6): 567–606.

Levine, Robert A. 1974. "Parental Goals: A Cross-Cultural View." *The Teachers College Record* 76(2): 226–39.

Lubrano, Alfred A. 2004. *Limbo: Blue Collar Roots, White Collar Dreams*. New York: Wiley.

MacLeod, Jay. 1995. *Ain't No Makin' It*. Boulder, Colo.: Westview.

Macleod, John, George Davey Smith, Chris Metcalfe, and Carole Hart. 2005. "Is Subjective Social Status a More Important Determinant of Health than Objective Social Status? Evidence from a Prospective Observational Study of Scottish Men." *Social Science and Medicine* 61(9): 1916–29.

Marjoribanks, Kevin. 1979. *Family and Their Learning Environments: An Empirical Analysis*. London: Routledge and Kegan Paul.

McGrath, Daniel J., and Peter J. Kuriloff. 1999. "'They're Going to Tear the Doors Off This Place': Upper-Middle-Class Parent School Involvement and the Educational Opportunities of Other People's Children." *Educational Policy* 13(5): 603–29.

Olds, David L., Lois Sadler, and Harriet Kitzman. 2007. "Programs for Parents of Infants and Toddlers: Recent Evidence from Randomized Trials." *Journal of Child Psychology and Psychiatry* 48(3–4): 355–91.

Reay, Diane. 1998. *Class Work: Mothers' Involvement in Children's Schooling*. London: University College London Press.

Reay, Diane, Gill Crozier, and David James. 2011. *White Middle Class Identities and Urban Schooling*. London: Palgrave Macmillan.

Roscigno, Vincent J., and James W. Ainsworth-Darnell. 1999. "Race, Cultural Capital, and Educational Resources: Persistent Inequalities and Achievement Returns." *The Sociology of Education* 72(3): 158–78.

Rosenberg, Morris, and Leonard I. Pearlin. 1978. "Social Class and Self-Esteem Among Children and Adults." *The American Journal of Sociology* 84(1): 53–77.

Rumberger, Russell W., and Gregory J. Palardy. 2008. "Does Segregation Still Matter? The Impact of Student Composition on Academic Achievement in High School." *The Teachers College Record* 107(9): 1999–2045.

Stuber, Jenny M. 2005. "Asset and Liability? The Importance of Context in the Occupational Experiences of Upwardly Mobile White Adults." *The Sociological Forum* 20(1): 139–66.

Sweet, Monica A., and Mark I. Appelbaum. 2004. "Is Home Visiting an Effective Strategy? A Meta-Analytic Review of Home Visiting Programs for Families with Young Children." *Child Development* 75(5): 1435–56.

Swidler, Ann. 1986. "Culture in Action: Symbols and Strategies." *American Sociological Review* 51(2): 273–86.

Tajfel, Henri. 1982. "Social Psychology of Intergroup Relations." *The Annual Review of Psychology* 33:1–39.

Teachman, Jay D. 1987. "Family Background, Educational Resources, and Educational Attainment." *The American Sociological Review* 52(4): 548–57.

Tyack, David, and William Tobin. 1994. "The 'Grammar' of Schooling: Why Has it Been So Hard to Change?" *The American Educational Research Journal* 31(3): 453–79.

Tye, Barbara Benham. 2002. *Hard Truths: Uncovering the Deep Structure of Schooling*. New York: Teachers College Press.

Useem, Elizabeth. 1992. "Middle Schools and Math Groups: Parents' Involvement in Children's Placement." *The Sociology of Education* 65(4): 263–79.

Warner, W. Lloyd, Marchia Meeker, and Kenneth Eels. 2006. "What Social Class Is in America." In *Social Class and Stratification: Classic Statements and Theoretical Debates*, edited by Rhonda F. Levine. Lanham, Md.: Rowman and Littlefield.

Weiss, Lois, ed. 2008. *The Way Class Works: Readings on School, Family, and the Economy*. New York: Routledge.

White, Michael J. 1987. *American Neighborhoods and Residential Differentiation*. New York: Russell Sage Foundation.

Willis, Paul. 1981. *Learning to Labor: How Working-Class Children Get Working Class Jobs*. New York: Columbia University Press.

Wittenborn, Dirk, Jamie Johnson, Sheila Nevins, and Bingo Gubelmann [producers]. 2003. *Born Rich*. Film. Los Angeles, Calif.: Shout Factory.

CHAPTER 5

IT'S YOUR CHOICE: HOW THE MIDDLE-CLASS MODEL OF INDEPENDENCE DISADVANTAGES WORKING-CLASS AMERICANS

Nicole M. Stephens, Stephanie A. Fryberg, and Hazel Rose Markus

Middle-class standing confers considerable, yet invisible, advantage in American society. Beyond greater material resources, the hidden advantage of middle-class standing is psychological: a sense of ownership, influence, entitlement, and control over oneself and the world. The middle-class experience, defined here by the attainment of a four-year college degree, encourages people to see themselves as independent actors, free to choose their possible selves and to create their future paths. For many working-class Americans, who have less than a four-year college degree, this independent sense of self is largely out of reach. Working-class standing typically denies people the material resources, the authority or status, and the cultural knowledge or information needed to influence the world according to personal preference and to experience the self as an independent, freely choosing actor.

The middle-class standard of the independent self has increasingly become the default American standard for how to think, feel, and act in the world (Twenge 2006; Twenge and Campbell 2009). In mainstream American contexts, this standard is promoted as the cultural ideal and is widely perceived as the "right" way to be a person. This middle-class self is not just a matter of individual attitudes or beliefs; it is an understanding of what it means to be a person that is built into and promoted by the social machinery—law, politics, education, employment, media, and health care—of mainstream American society. For example, the middle-class independent self is reflected in the idea of the "reasonable man" of the law, the "authentic self" of clinical and counseling psychology, and the "rational actor" of economics (Markus and Schwartz 2010). Although the independent self is widely accepted as the cultural standard, it is not the natural, normal, neutral, or even the most effective way of being a person (Markus and Hamedani 2007; Markus and Kitayama 2010). Instead, it is a privileged and culture-specific understanding of what it means to be a person that flows seamlessly from the resources, opportunities, and experiences linked with middle-class American standing in society (Snibbe and Markus 2005; chapter 8, this volume).

In mainstream America, one important consequence of the proliferation of the cultural standard of the independent self, and the central theme of this chapter, is that working-class Americans are often unfairly measured against these cultural norms, despite their limited opportunities to act accordingly. Specifically, this chapter first highlights the way in which the pervasive ideas, practices, and institutions of mainstream America are structured according to the middle-class understanding of behavior as independent. Then it reveals how the exclusive reliance on these middle-class understandings can inadvertently disadvantage working-class Americans, who often are equipped with a different style of agency that is defined not by independence and separation from others but by interdependence and connection with others (see DiMaggio, chapter 2 of this volume, for discussion of the role of cross-class interactions in generating inequality).

We refer to the independent understandings of behavior common in middle-class American contexts as the *independent model of agency*. This model assumes that normatively appropriate actions are independent from others and the social context; freely chosen, personally controllable, and contingent on one's preferences, intentions, and goals; and directed toward influencing and standing out from others (Markus and Kitayama 2003). Alternatively, we refer to the interdependent understandings of behavior that are prevalent in working-class contexts as the *interdependent model of agency*. This model assumes that normatively appropriate actions are interdependent with others; responsive to and contingent on expectations of others, social roles, situations, and the larger social context; and directed toward adjusting to and fitting in with others.

Throughout this chapter, we focus on variation in models of agency based on experiences in different social-class contexts. We use the term *middle class* to refer to individuals who have earned a four-year degree and *working class* to refer to individuals who have not.[1] The chapter contains four sections. The first describes the growing, yet largely unrecognized, social-class divide in America. The second explains how this divide systematically influences people's conceptions of the "good" or "right" way to act as a person in the world. The third describes mainstream America as a middle-class world that is built according to middle-class understandings of agency as independent. Finally, the fourth section summarizes research that illustrates how the proliferation of the independent model as the default standard of behavior produces a hidden disadvantage for working-class Americans.

THE SOCIAL-CLASS DIVIDE

In the past fifty years, the social-class divide between the working class and the middle class has continued to grow (Burkhauser et al. 2009; Picketty and Saez 2003). In terms of the resource divide in the United States, income inequality is at an all-time high and has increased dramatically since the 1970s (Saez 2010). For example, in the 1970s the top 1 percent of Americans earned 9 percent of the total income, and the top

10 percent earned 33 percent of total income. By 2008 the top 1 percent of Americans earned 21 percent of the total income and the top 10 percent earned 48 percent of the total income (Saez 2010). In other words, the top tenth of Americans currently earn nearly half of the total income in America—nearly a two-fold increase from three decades earlier. The same pattern is reflected in the income earned by the chief executive officers of the largest U.S. corporations relative to the average American. In 1980 chief executive officers earned forty-two times as much money as the average American, whereas in 2001 they earned 531 times as much as the average American (Frank, Levine, and Dijk 2010).

One consequence of these growing material divides is that many people in working-class contexts are increasingly disconnected from the resources and skills needed to take full advantage of the opportunities that American society has to offer. Working-class contexts offer limited access to the material resources and cultural capital that enable the middle class to act as autonomous agents, to freely choose and control their fates, and to pull themselves up by their proverbial bootstraps. For example, working-class Americans more often live in neighborhoods that have limited or no access to stores with healthy food, high-quality schools, parks or facilities in which to exercise, and health care for their children (Kozol 1991; Morland et al. 2002). As for cultural capital, they are also less likely to know how to successfully negotiate the types of social interactions that foster upward mobility (chapter 7, this volume).

Given these differences in material resources and cultural capital, social-class standing powerfully predicts both the barriers to opportunities that people encounter and their chances of realizing the American dream—the belief that with hard work and effort Americans can improve their social standing and achieve their dreams. Adults with lower social-class standing, for example, are at higher risk for various chronic diseases (for example, heart disease and diabetes) and die younger than adults with higher social-class standing (Adler et al. 1994; Adler et al. 1993; Chen, Martin, and Matthews 2006; Marmot, Shipley, and Rose 1984). Lower class standing for adults also carries over to their children's educational prospects. Alexander Astin and Leticia Oseguera (2004) report that students who have two parents without college degrees have only a 9 percent chance of attending highly selective universities, whereas students who have two parents with college degrees have a 62 percent chance. As a result of this growing divide, the American dream is largely inaccessible to working-class Americans, regardless of sustained hard work and effort.

SOCIAL-CLASS CONTEXTS SHAPE WAYS OF BEING A PERSON

The material and social conditions of working- and middle-class contexts foster and promote different cultural models of agency, or sets of ideas and practices about how to be a culturally appropriate person (Markus and Kitayama 2003).[2] These models guide individual behavior and provide a blueprint for interpreting one's own and others' behavior. Understanding how social class shapes models of agency requires attention both to the material resources—such as income, accumulated wealth, and access to transportation—and to the social resources—such as relationships with family and friends—that are available in different social-class contexts. It also requires consideration of how the availability of these material and social resources shapes the way people are able to act (for example, whether the context provides the opportunity to influence the situation). How people act over time, in turn, influences which types of behavior will be understood as normal, appropriate, and valued (Bourdieu 1977; Correll 2004).

How, then, do the material and social resources prevalent in diverse social-class contexts shape patterns of behavior and psychological functioning? Consider how the resources of middle-class American contexts—those characterized by the attainment of a four-year college degree—encourage the development of independent agency (Markus and Kitayama 2003). These middle-class contexts provide greater access to economic resources (Day and Newburger 2002; Pascarella and Terenzini 1991) and to opportunities for choice, control, and influence than do working-class contexts (Kohn 1969). People in middle-class contexts also tend to have more predictable environments, to encounter fewer environmental risks, and to have better physical health (Adler and Snibbe 2003; Chen 2004). The plentiful economic resources provide different pathways to adulthood. Compared with the working class, middle-class individuals are more likely to be encouraged to leave home, to go away to a four-year college or university, and to find their own way in life. As a result, they are more likely to move to multiple geographic locations throughout their lives (Argyle 1994), to have extended social networks (Bowman, Kitayama, and Nisbett 2009), and to spend more time in relationships that are freely chosen and based on personal interests or preferences (Reay et al. 2001; Rossi 2001).

The material and social conditions prevalent in middle-class contexts foster particular socialization patterns that also play an important role in fostering norms of independence. Through the experience of attaining four-year college degrees, middle-class individuals learn that their opinions and ideas are respected and that promoting oneself, being confident, and standing out are valued and rewarded activities. When these individuals become parents, they foster and promote these culture-specific values and norms through their interactions with their children. For example, middle-class parents engage in concerted cultivation, or efforts to elaborate children's personal preferences and interests (chapter 4, this volume). They also give their children a variety of opportunities for self-expression through choices such as what to eat, whom to play with, what activities to participate in, and what books to read (chapter 10, this volume; Miller, Cho, and Bracey 2005). Through these interactions, parents convey to children that their thoughts and feelings are important and that they are on equal footing with everyone else (Wiley et al. 1998). The convergence of material and social conditions prevalent in middle-class contexts, coupled with the socialization processes these conditions foster, allows children to experience themselves as independent agents, to develop the sense that they are in charge and the world is their own, and to grow into adults who reflect and further promote the middle-class model of agency.

In contrast, the conditions of working-class American contexts—characterized by having less than a four-year college degree—encourage the development of interdependent agency. These contexts offer less economic capital, more environmental constraints, greater risks and uncertainty, and less choice, control, and influence than middle-class American contexts (Kraus, Piff, and Keltner 2009; Lachman and Weaver 1998; Patillo-McCoy 1999). Given limited economic resources and parents who have not attained a four-year degree, working-class students are more likely to attend a local community college or to go straight from high school to work. There is little opportunity for trying on a variety of potential future identities and for reflecting on how to define the self. Moreover, people who do not leave home to attend college are more likely to live in the same town for most of their lives, to have frequent contact with family, to be embedded in densely structured social networks, and to maintain lifelong friendships (Argyle 1994; Lamont 2000; Markus et al. 2004).

The material and social conditions prevalent in working-class contexts foster particular socialization patterns that also play an important role in fostering norms of interdependence. By spending their lives in a more unpredictable and uncertain environment, in which there is often no economic safety net to fall back on, parents quickly learn the dangers of stepping out of line and learn the value of following the rules, working together, and helping one another in times of need. Consequently, their children are more likely to learn that "life is not just about them," that the world is "not their own," and that they need to fit in, play by the rules, and make the best of the situation (Kohn 1969; Lareau 2003; Miller, Cho, and Bracey 2005). The convergence of the material and social conditions prevalent in working-class contexts, coupled with the patterns of socialization these conditions foster, encourages people to recognize the importance of interdependence: of fitting in and being responsive to others' needs, interests, and preferences.

THE INFLUENCE OF INDEPENDENT AGENCY ON THE STRUCTURE OF MAINSTREAM AMERICAN CONTEXTS

Models of agency not only reside in individual minds; they are also reflected in and promoted by the ideas, practices, and institutions that structure people's everyday experiences (Markus and Kitayama 2003). In mainstream America, institutions are largely organized and framed according to the independent model of agency. This model of agency is so thoroughly ingrained in the cultural and social machinery that American institutions—in education, health care, politics, and the media—promote middle-class expectations for how to act as the default standard (Adams et al. 2008). But there are other viable models for how to think, feel, and act as a person in the world.[3]

American colleges and universities reflect and promote the independent model of agency as the cultural standard. Although most universities seek to create a diverse student body, these efforts do not always translate into diverse expectations of students. In fact, most American universities convey the message that being an independent agent is the right or best way to be a student (Fryberg and Markus 2007; Kim 2002; Li 2003). Students are asked to make their own choices, to be individually motivated, to develop their own interests, and to pave their own innovative pathways. Invitation letters, student guidebooks, and mission statements communicate these expectations. Even before students arrive on campus, they are told how to be a student. For example, the Stanford University student guidebook informs students, "It is not the task, first and foremost, of an advisor to tell you what to do. . . . Your advisor should be seen as a compass, not as a roadmap" (Stanford University 2004). In other words, students are instructed not to rely on others for guidance but instead to know what they want and to find a way to achieve it on their own. These messages are by no means unique to Stanford. Washington University in Saint Louis encourages students to "create your own path" (Washington University 2009) and Harvard University tells students that the purpose of education is to "liberate students to explore, to create, to challenge, and to lead" (Harvard University 2009). Across university and college campuses nationwide, students are expected to enact these middle-class norms of independent agency.

In the health care domain, people are similarly expected to navigate the system as independent agents (Iyengar 2010). Throughout all stages of the process, patients are expected to research and choose doctors who fit with their personal preferences and values. An ad for the University of Chicago Medical Center features a middle-aged woman in front of a laptop and states, "Getting sick wasn't her choice. How she gets better is." The ad provides potential patients with the following script describing the expected movement through the health care system: "You're up all hours crawling the web to find every option, advanced treatment and nugget of hope you can. You want two or three—even four—opinions from the brightest medical minds in the world. And when it comes to making decisions about your health care, you're in charge. You're at the forefront of medicine." Patients are expected to seek out and explore multiple treatment options ("two or three—even four"!), to be fully in charge, and to make their own decisions—that is, to act with independent agency.

Patients are also expected to make their own choices because Americans presume that individual choice is necessary to maximize positive health outcomes. For example, describing what he viewed as the essential role of choice in prescription drug plans for senior citizens, President George W. Bush said, "The more choices you have, the more likely it is you'll be able to find a program that suits your specific needs" (Thaler and Sunstein 2008, 159). Choice is so central to the idea of health care in America that health policy debates center around the importance of keeping choice in the hands of the individual consumer. For instance, in opposition to recent efforts to pass universal health care legislation, a Cato Institute advertisement claimed, "When it comes to healthcare, what really matters is who decides. Under reform proposals before Congress, government would take over more and more of your health care decisions" (a 2009 Cato Institute healthcare advdertisement). The message conveyed is that patients should reject government intervention and protect their individual right to decide what types of health care best fit their individual needs.

In mainstream American media, across a wide variety of advertising campaigns, the language of individual choice is used to appeal to and promote the independent model of agency. Burger King, for example, declares, "We give your kids more than toys. We give them choices." American Family Insurance uses the same language: "Insurance is a matter of choice." Beyond consumer products, advertisements encourage people to adopt healthy eating and exercise habits ("Exercise, it's your choice") and to support policies, such as school vouchers ("School choice means better educational opportunity"), that are designed to increase the number of choices available to individuals. These advertising campaigns promote the idea that individual choice maximizes freedom and produces positive outcomes (Iyengar 2010; Iyengar and Lepper 2000; Markus and Schwartz 2010; Schwartz 2004).

Across education, health care, and the media, people are expected not only to choose but to choose in a way that affirms and reinforces their experience of independent agency. That is, they are expected to use choice to display their individuality, uniqueness, independence, and separation from others. In fact, in some advertisements the link between choice and individuality is made explicit. Camel cigarettes, for example, encourages people to "choose anything but ordinary." The Harvard Business School advises students to "break free. Start thinking and acting differently." These messages about independent agency are not unique to American education, health care, or media. They are pervasive in mainstream American culture.

RELIANCE ON INDEPENDENT AGENCY DISADVANTAGES WORKING-CLASS AMERICANS: THREE AREAS OF RESEARCH

Given the working-class emphasis on interdependent models of agency—on the importance of being in relationships with others, of fitting in, and of being responsive to others—the reliance on the independent model of agency as the cultural standard creates the experience of a cultural divide that serves to systematically disadvantage working-class Americans. To illuminate this claim, we review research studies from three areas of focus: everyday choice, the transition to a four-year college, and responses to natural disasters.

Everyday Choice

Choice is a central component of the independent model of agency. By making choices, people in middle-class American contexts are able to enact independent agency: they exert control over their environments, express their individual selves, individuate the self from others, and influence the world according to personal preference (Savani, Stephens, and Markus 2011). Given the centrality of choice to independent agency, individuals participating in mainstream American institutions, such as education, health care, and law, are often required to make choices with little support or guidance from others. This choice requirement might have very different consequences for hypothetical parents from different social-class contexts who seek to choose the best school for their children.

The first parent, Lauren, is a practicing lawyer and the mother of a ten-year-old boy. On receiving the book that explains the defining characteristics of the thirty different public elementary school options in the area, she sits down to review the materials and to make a decision about where to enroll her son. Among other issues, Lauren considers teacher quality, teaching pedagogies, class schedules, cost effectiveness, commuting times, and student diversity. She supplements the information with her own Internet research—perusing blogs, forums, and other sites that provide firsthand accounts from parents with children at the different schools. She ponders the options for a few days and debates with her husband and colleagues the pluses and minuses of different options. She ranks the options and decides on three schools in the area that she wants to visit and into which she might want to enroll her son.

The second parent, Sharon, is a waitress at a local diner and the mother of an eleven-year-old girl. Like Lauren, Sharon receives the book that explains the key features of the same thirty school options. Although she wants the best for her daughter, Sharon often works two shifts at the diner and has little control over her schedule. Given the limited resources of her working-class context and her limited prior experience with choice, she finds the number of schools and the process of considering the different dimensions of those schools to be overwhelming. She tries to reach out to the school district for advice about the best school for her daughter, but she is told that it is her job to determine which school is most likely to meet her daughter's particular needs, interests, preferences, and goals. School employees have been trained not to interfere but instead to ensure that parents independently choose which school is best for their children. They assume that parents are best equipped to choose for their children, and they do not want to be held responsible for biasing parents in the decisionmaking process. In the end, given Sharon's work schedule and the fact that she does not have a car to take her daughter to an academically rigorous school in the neighboring city, she picks the school that is close to home and most conveniently located.

The stories of Lauren and Sharon illuminate two very different experiences with the act of choosing. While both may find selecting a school stressful, the process and expectations of independent choice lead to quite different outcomes. Lauren finds the process time consuming, but given her own extensive educational experiences, she has the necessary time, resources, and cultural capital needed to identify a set of criteria that reflect her son's preferences, to measure the schools against these preferences, and, in the end, to choose the school that is the best fit for her son's needs and that will give him a solid foundation for future academic success. Sharon, in contrast, lacks the time, resources, and middle-class cultural capital needed to choose the school best equipped to meet the needs of her daughter. As a result, she ultimately picks the school that is closest to home rather than a school that will provide her daughter with the best chance of success in a middle-class world.

This requirement to choose is pervasive in American culture, in large part because individual choice is considered a fundamental right, an indicator of freedom, and the route to individual self-expression and agency. In other words, it is assumed that the provision of choice bestows freedom and that not providing choice is equivalent to taking away people's freedom. Empirically testing this assumption, Alana Snibbe and Hazel Markus (2005) conducted a series of studies that asked whether choice is central to people's conception of agency and freedom in working-class contexts. In one study, shoppers were approached and asked to evaluate one of five pens. In a free-choice condition, participants chose a pen, wrote with it, and then evaluated it. In a usurped-choice condition, just as participants chose a pen, the experimenter said, "I'm sorry, you can't have that one, it is my last," and then gave the participant another pen to write with and evaluate. Middle-class participants reported being upset when their choice was denied; as a result, those in the usurped-choice condition were less happy with the pen than those in the free-choice condition. Working-class participants, in contrast, liked the pens in both conditions equally well. In other words, choice was less central to agency for the working-class participants than for the middle-class participants.

In another set of studies, we explored whether the interests of others take precedence over individual choice in working-class contexts (Stephens, Fryberg, and Markus 2011). In one study, an experimenter offered participants a pen as a thank-you gift for their participation. Participants were told that if they wanted a different pen, the experimenter could offer them a choice of other pens. Working-class participants were more likely than the middle-class participants to accept the gift from the experimenter rather than ask to choose for themselves. These studies suggest that for working-class Americans focusing on and attending to others (interdependent agency) is normative and often takes precedence over choosing for oneself (independent agency).

Next, we examined whether a second assumption of independent agency—that choice is an act of independence—fits with the experiences of working-class Americans (Stephens, Markus, and Townsend 2007). We hypothesized that working-class participants would use choice not to distinguish themselves from others but to be similar to and to connect with others. In one study, we approached college students and asked them to choose a pen for an alleged marketing study. After participants made their own pen choice, they were exposed to one of two different conditions. In the similar condition, a confederate approached and said, "I would like a pen just like hers"; in the different condition, the confederate approached and asked for a pen that was different from the pen that the earlier participant had selected. While middle-class participants liked their pen more when the other person's choice made them appear unique and different, working-class participants liked their pens more when the other person's choice revealed similarity in preferences.

In a related study, firefighters and students with master's degrees in business were asked to imagine a scenario in which they bought a new car and then the next day their friend purchased the exact same car. As in the pen study, the middle-class students said that they would feel irritated that their friend had taken away the uniqueness of their choice. In contrast, the working-class firefighters said that they would feel flattered or happy about their friend's choice. One working-class participant exclaimed, "If I bought the car that I wanted and then my friend bought it too, I would say, 'Great, let's start a car club.'"

The assumption that choice equals agency and independence reflects the model of agency that is prevalent in middle-class contexts but diverges from the understandings of choice that are common among working-class Americans. Our studies reveal that working-class Americans understand acts of independence and individual choice as less important than acts of interdependence and connection to others. If highly consequential, mainstream American contexts are built according to the middle-class standard that people must choose independently and without others' influence, what then are the implications for working-class Americans, who often choose among undesirable alternatives, have limited resources to select the best option, and understand choice differently?

The reliance on an independent model of agency is likely to put working-class Americans at a significant disadvantage. In the case of school choice, as illustrated earlier with the example of Sharon, parents are often required to choose a school for their children without guidance from the school staff who are most knowledgeable about which schools are the most effective in meeting peoples' needs (Thaler and Sunstein 2008). One problem with this approach is that working-class parents are much less likely than middle-class parents to have the time and resources to research school options and to choose the school that will best educate their children (chapter 4, this volume). Thus a lack of advice or guidance is perhaps especially harmful to these working-class parents. Similarly, the health care system assumes that the consumer is independent and has the time and resources to make the right choice. Making a choice among treatment plans may be difficult even for those who have practice making choices and who have middle-class cultural capital at their disposal to identify the best option. For those who have less experience in making choices and little knowledge about how the health care system works, navigating the system may prove daunting, especially without sufficient guidance from someone who is knowledgeable about the potential benefits of various options.

Transition to College

Higher education ostensibly seeks to provide equal opportunities to all students from different circumstances and backgrounds (Bowen et al. 2005). The reality, however, is that American university settings are not neutral institutions but instead reflect and promote particular cultural norms and expectations of students. These understandings derive largely from the independent model of agency that is normative in middle-class contexts (Fryberg and Markus 2007; Greenfield 1994; Li 2003). The independent model matches the expectations of students from middle-class backgrounds, in this case, continuing-generation students whose parents have four-year college degrees. However, the independent model does not match the expectations of students from working-class backgrounds, in this case, first-generation students whose parents do not have four-year college degrees.

Imagine, for example, two students—one continuing-generation college student and one first-generation college student—who arrive on campus for the first time. Julie, the continuing-generation student, is excited to set up her dorm room and to discuss potential classes and activities with her academic adviser. For years her parents have talked about all the amazing experiences they had in college, and she has always envisioned what it would be like. Given what she has learned from her parents, Julie feels well prepared academically and personally, and she knows what to expect. When she meets with her academic adviser, her enthusiasm and confidence is reinforced. Her adviser asks about her interests and goals and tells her about the many exciting opportunities on campus that can help her achieve those goals. Julie cannot wait to explore all her interests, map out her academic plans, and take charge of her future. For the first time, she feels like an adult who is free to choose her own path.

Jen, in contrast, is the first person in her family to attend college—a first-generation college student. She has worked her whole life for the opportunity to go to college, but she has no idea what to expect when she gets there, and she is not sure if she has what it takes to succeed. When she arrives on campus, she is surprised by the confidence of the other students. She wonders whether they are as prepared and as confident as they seem and whether her own uncertainty is a sign that she is not ready. These concerns are amplified by her first meeting with her academic adviser. He is welcoming but is not very interested in getting to know her. His agenda involves identifying her long-term goals and plans, but Jen is unsure about his motives. For example, he offers Jen many choices of potential courses, activities, and majors, but when she seems confused, he is unwilling to advise her about which options might be best for her. She wonders whether he really cares or just wants to get her out of the office as quickly as possible. Jen leaves feeling intimidated, overwhelmed, and even more uncertain about whether the college environment is the place for her.

This example reveals how two students from different social-class backgrounds can experience and respond differently to the same college culture of independence. For Julie, the independent model was familiar and served as a sign that she belonged in the college environment. In the terms of our research, she experienced a cultural match between her own cultural models and the cultural models that were institutionalized in the university setting. For Jen, however, the focus on independent agency signaled that she was out of her element and led her to question whether she should be there. She experienced a cultural mismatch between her own cultural models and those that were institutionalized in the university setting.

Building on theories of social identity threat (Davies et al. 2002; Murphy, Steele, and Gross 2007; Steele and Aronson 1995; Steele 2010), we sought to capture the experience of cultural mismatch for first-generation students (Stephens et al., forthcoming) and to examine its consequences. Identifying the hypothesized mismatch required an analysis of both universities' and students' expectations. First, to assess the university culture, we surveyed a diverse sample of high-level university administrators from the top fifty national universities and the top twenty-five liberal arts colleges in the United States (*U.S. News and World Report* 2010). Specifically, high-level university administrators, who are experts in both creating and maintaining institutional norms, were asked to indicate their institutions' expectations for college students. They were presented with six pairs of institutional expectations, each divided into one statement reflecting independence and another interdependence, and asked to choose the one most often emphasized at their university (for example, "developing personal opinions" versus "appreciating opinions of others"). As expected, we found that more than two-thirds of administrators (72 percent) characterized the university culture as more independent than interdependent.

To assess students' motives for attending college, we surveyed a sample of incoming students at a large private university and asked them about the reasons why they chose to attend college. They were presented with twelve options that reflected either independent or interdependent motives for attending college and were asked to mark each motive that applied to them. We found that continuing-generation students' motives for attending college focused on independence, self-exploration, and self-development and therefore matched the university culture's focus on independence. In contrast, first-generation college students' motives diverged from the university culture's focus on independence: they were less likely than continuing-generation students to say that they were motivated to attend college for reasons relating to independence (for example, to explore their personal interests) but much more likely to say that they were motivated by interdependent reasons (for example, to give back to their communities or to help their families).

Finally, we examined the performance consequences of a cultural match or mismatch for first-generation students. Specifically, a series of experiments—one at a public and one at a private university—created the experience of a cultural match or mismatch and then assessed students' performance on a common measure of verbal ability (anagrams) and a common measure of spatial ability (tangrams). Participants were randomly assigned to read one of two welcome messages, ostensibly from their universities, composed by us to reflect either the independent or the interdependent model of agency. Adapted from actual university materials, the letter reflecting independent agency framed the university culture and college experience as one in which students are guided to pave their own pathways, to explore personal interests, and to learn to work independently. In contrast, the message reflecting interdependence framed the university culture and college experience in the context of being part of a community, working collaboratively, and connecting with fellow students and faculty. After reading a message, the participants completed one of the performance tasks. As expected, when the college culture was framed as independent (a cultural mismatch with first-generation students' motives), first-generation students experienced the tasks as more difficult and performed less well than continuing-generation students. Yet when the college culture was framed as interdependent (a cultural match with first-generation students' motives), this performance gap was eliminated (Stephens et al., forthcoming).

These studies suggest that American universities' focus on independence represents the perspectives of middle-class students and thereby places them at a distinct advantage. The same norms of independence can disadvantage first-generation students from working-class backgrounds, whose interdependent motives do not match the dominant norms of the college culture. As a result, first-generation college students often feel uncomfortable in college settings, construe academic tasks as difficult, and fail to perform up to their potential. If universities want to provide truly equal opportunities for all students, they might begin by recognizing that there is more than one way to succeed as a student and by expanding the university cultural repertoire to include more ideas and practices of interdependence. For example, universities' guidebooks and admissions letters could be adapted to include more messages about the importance of connection to others and working together. Teachers might think creatively about how to expand teaching practices to recognize and harness first-generation students' relatively interdependent motives, for example, by building trusting relationships in the classroom or by encouraging students to study with their peers and interact more in groups.

Response to Natural Disasters

The assumption that people freely choose their actions is widely used to explain negative life outcomes such as obesity, disease, poverty, academic underperformance, and unexpected tragedy (Hanson and Hanson 2006; Savani, Stephens, and Markus 2011). These assumptions about choice can disadvantage working-class Americans, whose contexts often place constraints on behavior and provide fewer opportunities to "freely choose" their actions. For example, after Hurricane Katrina destroyed the city of New Orleans, many outside observers assumed that the survivors had had a choice about whether to stay or evacuate before the storm. In response to the rising death toll in New Orleans, Federal Emergency Management Agency director Michael

Brown said, "That's going to be attributable a lot to people who . . . chose not to evacuate." Similarly, Secretary of Homeland Security Michael Chertoff explained, "Officials called for a mandatory evacuation. Some people chose not to obey that order. That was a mistake on their part" (CNN Transcripts 2005, 60–72). This assumption of choice differentially reflected the realities of residents in different social-class contexts. Here we present interview excerpts from the personal narratives of two survivors who had divergent experiences with the hurricane.

This assumption of free choice coincided with and reflected the reality of a male middle-class survivor, who describes the decisionmaking process leading to his evacuation before the hurricane hit:

> Initially my wife and I didn't know what to do. Whether we were gonna stay, whether we were gonna leave, it was all up in the air. She was very nervous about it. Uh, we were slightly panicked. At first I decided that I would stick around during the storm so that I could check on our house and my wife would evacuate. But when we saw the news reports on Saturday my wife said, "You're not gonna stay. You are coming—you and I are leaving and we're gonna get out of town." I said, "Where are we gonna stay?" and she said, "There's no place in the area. Jackson's full, Baton Rouge is full, Houston is filling up," and she couldn't even find a hotel in Memphis so I suggest[ed] we stay in west Memphis, and we tried to get a reservation online at the Red Roof and that didn't work and so I called them in person and made a reservation and they accepted it. So, I stayed up all night watching the weather reports to see what was gonna happen. My friend left at 2:33 in the morning and I passed out on the couch for maybe an hour. I got up at five, we loaded up the car figuring we'd only be gone for a few days at most, and packed our dogs, and me and my wife headed out of town. It took us twelve hours to get to Memphis. . . . So the evacuation went fairly well, I thought, and, the day the hurricane hit, we woke up—we were at the hotel in Memphis and we were watching the news.

Consider, in contrast, the experience of a female working-class survivor who did not have the resources to evacuate:

> I started watching the news and that Sunday, it was twenty-four hours before the storm was supposed to hit, and that's when the mayor got on the TV and he said just get out, just go or what have you. How are we supposed to go anywhere? You understand, for the ones that did leave, they was able to go. They had money. They had this, they had that, you see what I'm saying? My daughter had a little raggedy car that barely moved. So how are we going to leave or what have you, 'cause we had nowhere to go and no way to get there. . . . But they knew what Katrina was gonna do before Katrina got to New Orleans. You know what I'm sayin? So I feel as though, maybe even the president knew about it. All the way down, I'm speakin' the chain of command. They knew. They coulda got us out of there, out of that place, when they knew about three major storms, and they knew one of 'em was gonna come in, was gonna hit New Orleans. I feel as though they shoulda got all of the people that's skilled and can do for theirself and just help people, you un-

derstand, like me for instance. Get us out of there. Get everybody out of New Orleans. And it wouldn't a been so many deaths. People wouldn't a been choppin' through their roof, sittin' on their roof. Superdome wouldn't a been like it was. The Convention Center wouldn't a been like it was. If they would have planned ahead of time, and you can't tell me they didn't know. 'Cause they knew. Our government knew. Everybody. But we just didn't know, you see.

In our research we sought to illuminate the disconnect between the dominant representation of survivors' experiences as freely chosen and the experience of the survivors themselves. We asked observers of the Hurricane Katrina disaster to describe the residents who stayed for the hurricane and those who evacuated beforehand. We found that relief workers (for example, from the Red Cross) who had direct contact with survivors, as well as lay observers who watched the disaster from afar, interpreted survivors' actions based on an independent model of agency. Specifically, they assumed that survivors' actions were unconstrained by the context and that all people could have influenced the situation, overcome situational constraints, and found a way to evacuate before the hurricane hit. As a result, observers thought that the behavior of residents who stayed behind during the hurricane did not make sense; they viewed them as lazy, passive, irresponsible, and lacking agency.

Next, we examined the models of agency that the survivors used to make sense of their own experiences with the hurricane. In interviews with survivors from diverse social-class contexts, we asked them to tell their stories of what happened to them before, during, and after the hurricane. Our analysis of the themes common in survivors' narratives revealed that the middle-class and European American survivors, most of whom evacuated, understood their actions primarily in terms of choice, independence, and control. These themes clearly reflected an independent model of agency. Like the survivor whose story is told earlier in this chapter, many of the middle-class survivors had the necessary resources (time, money, a place to go) to make a plan for how to evacuate. If the situation did not go according to their evacuation plan, they then had the resources at their disposal (Internet, phone, money) to proactively influence the situation and to create another alternative that could meet their needs.

In contrast, like the survivor who explained that she did not have anywhere to stay or the necessary transportation to evacuate, the working-class and African American survivors were much less likely to have the resources necessary to influence the situation and evacuate before the storm. In contrast to the dominant rhetoric of choice employed by the media ("Why did they choose to stay?"), most of the survivors who stayed did not experience their actions as choices. One survivor said, "I didn't have a choice. Me and my three girls, my children, we didn't have a choice but to stay 'cause even the family members that came over to the house with the transportation they all had family with them, so we couldn't—we couldn't all fit in the cars." Instead of focusing on independence, influence, and choice, the working-class and African American survivors recognized the need to adjust to the constraints of their contexts and relied on a model of agency that involved connecting to and helping others, being strong and resilient, and maintaining faith in God (Stephens et al. 2009). These themes reflect some of the key elements of interdependent agency.

This study illustrates how the dominance of the notion of independent agency, specifically the assumption that actions are freely chosen, can lead to a misunder-standing of behavior across the social-class divide. Observers' reliance on an in-dependent model to understand survivors' actions was consistent with how the middle-class and European American survivors understood their experiences but di-verged from the understandings common among the working-class and African American survivors. In this case, the exclusive use of an independent model of agency concealed the relationship between people's actions and the resource structure of the environment and, in doing so, fostered a lack of empathy for the survivors who stayed and who bore the brunt of the hurricane. Unlike explicit racism or classism, criticism of people on the basis of adherence to cultural norms may not be identified as prejudice but may instead seem like a logical inference from the facts of the sit-uation. However, because independent agency is often possible only for people in middle-class worlds who have access to the types of resources and experiences that foster an independent sense of self, devaluing other forms of agency may be a power-ful form of discrimination against people who lack the resources to adhere to middle-class standards for behavior. These types of cultural norms and assumptions about behavior can serve as a potent form of system justification (see, for example, Jost, Kay, and Thorisdottir 2009; Jost and Major 2001). That is, they may serve to justify, maintain, and reproduce the very conditions in society that serve to limit and con-strain the types of opportunities that are available to working-class Americans.

DISCUSSION AND IMPLICATIONS

As the power of social class in shaping the economic and social realities of Americans has increased (Saez 2010), so too has the assumption that people are equally autono-mous and free to choose their actions (Hanson and Hanson 2006; Twenge 2006). As a consequence, working-class Americans are often susceptible to a double jeopardy: they have less access to the resources that are needed to freely choose their own fates and to create their own futures, yet their fates and futures are erroneously believed to be the sole product of their individual effort or lack thereof. In other words, working-class Americans not only have fewer opportunities to attain the independent self of the middle class but also, because of the prevalence of the ideology of independent agency in mainstream America, are likely to be held accountable or even penalized for the often negative results of their limited opportunities (Savani, Stephens, and Markus 2011; see also Stephens and Levine 2011).

The experience of double jeopardy is, in part, a product of the social machinery of mainstream America. It is built into and promoted by America's workplaces, schools, and media outlets. Across these highly influential contexts, the widely held and often taken-for-granted message is that people can and should make their own decisions and act accordingly and, in doing so, display their individuality and independence from others. This assumption that all behavior is a product of individual choice and that choice is a natural or universal unit of behavior is the cornerstone of the middle-class standard. The middle-class standard, however, obscures the fact that the ability to freely choose and to proactively influence the world according to personal prefer-ence is not equally available to all people.

This inequality hinges on one rarely recognized, yet critical, insight: that experi-encing oneself as independent requires a particular set of contextual conditions that are most readily available in middle-class worlds. For example, freely choosing according to personal preference—the signature of independent agency—cannot occur without the presence of important structural supports. The act of freely choosing requires that people have a number of positive alternatives from which to choose and also requires resources such as financial assets, time, and information to be able to select the most effective option. In many working-class contexts, however, people often do not experience the advantage of freely choosing their actions but are left to choose between a rock and hard place. In other words, when it comes to making choices that satisfy individual preferences, interests, and goals, working-class individuals have fewer desirable or effective alternatives among which to choose, and the resources at their disposal to make a good choice are also quite limited.

Despite the best efforts of social scientists across a variety of disciplines, the understanding that agency is not separate from the sociocultural world remains poorly integrated into popular understandings of behavior. Instead, as this chapter has shown, the popular assumption in mainstream America is that all people, irrespective of place or circumstance, are independent from their contexts and can freely choose their actions. This assumption represents a fundamental misunderstanding of behavior. Although the middle-class standard of the independent self is often taken for granted as the "right" or "best" way to be a person, the reality is that actions are not caused solely by either individual psychological qualities or social contextual influences. All people, even those who experience their actions as separate from the context and unaffected by others, are necessarily shaped by the prevalent cultural norms that structure the contexts in which they operate.

This misunderstanding of behavior has important implications. It serves to disadvantage people in working-class contexts, for whom the middle-class standard of the independent self is often out of reach. It can also inhibit the development of effective programs and policies that seek to remedy the effects of growing social-class inequality. Many such initiatives focus on how to provide more choices for people in schools and in health care. For example, parents with limited resources and information are expected to choose, with limited guidance from the experts, which schools their children will attend. The research presented here suggests that such policies and programs can undermine working-class Americans because they are informed by middle-class standards of acceptable behavior. Creating more effective programs and policies to bridge the social-class divide will require taking into account the divergent forms of agency that pervade different social contexts. Specifically, it will be important to recognize that working-class contexts are often characterized by social responsiveness and interdependence rather than individual choice and independence.

We would like to thank Sarah S. M. Townsend for her helpful feedback on earlier drafts.

NOTES

1. Educational attainment is among the best indicators of social class for two key reasons. First, attaining a bachelor's degree predicts job stability and is often a prerequisite to finding a high-status professional job. It also confers substantial advantages in lifetime earn-

ings. Specifically, college-educated people make twice as much money over the course of their lives as those who are high school educated (Day and Newburger 2002; Pascarella and Terenzini 1991). Second, among the three commonly used indicators of social-class status (education, income, and occupation), education is the indicator that is most closely associated with the lifestyle, behavior, beliefs, and psychological tendencies related to agency (Kohn and Schoenbach 1983; Matthews et al. 1989; Newcomb 1943).

2. We use the term *cultural model of agency* rather than *cultural model of self* because our research refers broadly to how people understand the sources, goals, and consequences of action.

3. While independence is the cultural standard in America, in most of the world interdependence is the cultural standard (Markus and Hamedani 2007).

REFERENCES

Adams, Glenn, Monica Biernat, Nyla R. Branscombe, Christian S. Crandall, and Lawrence S. Wrightsman. 2008. "Beyond Prejudice: Toward a Sociocultural Psychology of Racism and Oppression." In *On the Nature of Prejudice: Fifty Years After Allport*, edited by John F. Dovidio, Peter Glick, and Laurie A. Rudman. Malden, Mass.: Blackwell.

Adler, Nancy E., W. Thomas Boyce, Margaret A. Chesney, Sheldon Cohen, Susan Folkman, Robert L. Kahn, and Syme S. Leonard. 1994. "Socioeconomic Status and Health: The Challenge of the Gradient." *The American Psychologist* 49(1): 15–24.

Adler, Nancy E., Thomas Boyce, Margaret A. Chesney, Susan Folkman, and Leonard Syme. 1993. "Socioeconomic Inequalities in Health: No Easy Solution." *The Journal of the American Medical Association* 269(24): 3140–45.

Adler, Nancy E., and Alana C. Snibbe. 2003. "The Role of Psychosocial Processes in Explaining the Gradient Between Socioeconomic Status and Health." *Current Directions in Psychological Science* 12(4): 119–23.

Argyle, Michael. 1994. *The Psychology of Social Class*. New York: Routledge.

Astin, Alexander W., and Leticia Oseguera. 2004. "The Declining 'Equity' of American Higher Education." *The Review of Higher Education* 27(3): 321–41.

Bourdieu, Pierre. 1977. "Cultural Reproduction and Social Reproduction." In *Power and Ideology in Education*, edited by Jerome Karabel and A. H. Halsey. New York: Oxford University Press.

Bowen, William G., Martin A. Kurzweil, Eugene M. Tobin, and Susanne C. Pichler. 2005. *Equity and Excellence in American Higher Education*. Charlottesville: University of Virginia Press.

Bowman, Nicholas A., Shinobu Kitayama, and Richard E. Nisbett. 2009. "Social Class Differences in Self, Attribution, and Attention: Socially Expansive Individualism of Middle-Class Americans." *The Personality and Social Psychology Bulletin* 35(7): 880–93.

Burkhauser, Richard V., Shuaizhang Feng, Stephen P. Jenkins, and Jeff Larrimore. 2009. "Recent Trends in Top Income Shares in the USA: Reconciling Estimates from March CPS and IRS Tax Return Data." Working Paper 15320. Cambridge, Mass.: National Bureau of Economic Research.

Chen, Edith. 2004. "Why Socioeconomic Status Affects the Health of Children: A Psychosocial Perspective." *Current Directions in Psychological Science* 13(3): 112–15.

Chen, Edith, Andrew D. Martin, and Karen A. Matthews. 2006. "Understanding Health Disparities: The Role of Race and Socioeconomic Status in Children's Health." *The American Journal of Public Health* 96(4): 702–08.

CNN Transcripts. 2005. "Interview with Homeland Security Secretary Michael Chertoff." Available at: http://transcripts.cnn.com/TRANSCRIPTS/0509/01/ltm.03.html (accessed April 30, 2009).

Correll, Shelley J. 2004. "Constraints into Preferences: Gender, Status, and Emerging Career Aspirations." *The American Sociological Review* 69(1): 93–113.

Davies, Paul G., Steven J. Spencer, Diane M. Quinn, and Rebecca Gerhardstein. 2002. "Consuming Images: How Television Commercials that Elicit Stereotype Threat Can Restrain Women Academically and Professionally." *The Journal of Personality and Social Psychology* 28(12): 1615–28.

Day, Jennifer C., and Eric C. Newburger. 2002. "The Big Payoff: Educational Attainment and Synthetic Estimates of Work-Life Earnings." *The Current Population Report* P23-210 (July). Washington: U.S. Census Bureau.

Frank, Robert H., Adam S. Levine, and Oege Dijk. 2010. "Expenditure Cascades." Social Science Research Network. Available at: http://ssrn.com/abstract=1690612 (accessed November 18, 2010).

Fryberg, Stephanie A., and Hazel R. Markus. 2007. "Cultural Models of Education in American Indian, Asian American, and European American Contexts." *The Social Psychology of Education* 10: 213–46.

Greenfield, Patricia M. 1994. "Independence and Interdependence as Developmental Scripts: Implications for Theory, Research, and Practice." In *Cross-Cultural Roots of Minority Children Development,* edited by Patricia M. Greenfield and Robert R. Cocking. Hillsdale, N.J.: Erlbaum.

Hanson, Jon, and Kathleen Hanson. 2006. "The Blame Frame: Justifying Racial Injustice in America." *The Harvard Civil Rights–Civil Liberties Law Review* 41(2): 413–80.

Harvard University. 2009. "Harvard University Viewbook" [brochure]. Cambridge, Mass.: Harvard University.

Iyengar, Sheena S. 2010. *The Art of Choosing.* New York: Twelve.

Iyengar, Sheena S., and Mark R. Lepper. 2000. "When Choice Is Demotivating: Can One Desire Too Much of a Good Thing?" *The Journal of Personality and Social Psychology* 79(6): 995–1006.

Jost, John T., Aaron C. Kay, and Hulda Thorisdottir, eds. 2009. *Social and Psychological Bases of Ideology and System Justification.* New York: Oxford University Press.

Jost, John T., and Brenda Major, eds. 2001. *The Psychology of Legitimacy: Emerging Perspectives on Ideology, Justice, and Intergroup Relations.* New York: Cambridge University Press.

Kim, Heejung S. 2002. "We Talk, Therefore We Think? A Cultural Analysis of the Effect of Talking on Thinking." *The Journal of Personality and Social Psychology* 83(4): 828–42.

Kohn, Melvin L. 1969. *Class and Conformity: A Study in Value.* Homewood, Ill.: Dorsey.

Kohn, Melvin L., and Carrie Schoenbach. 1983. "Class, Stratification, and Psychological Functioning." In *Work and Personality: An Inquiry into the Impact of Social Stratification,* edited by Melvin L. Kohn and Carmi Schooler. Norwood, N.J.: Ablex.

Kozol, Jonathan. 1991. *Savage Inequalities: Children in America's Schools.* New York: Crown.

Kraus, Michael W., Paul K. Piff, and Dacher Keltner. 2009. "Social Class, Sense of Control, and Social Explanation." *The Journal of Personality and Social Psychology* 97(6): 992–1004.

Lachman, Margie E., and Suzanne L. Weaver. 1998. "The Sense of Control as a Moderator of Social Class Differences in Health and Well-Being." *The Journal of Personality and Social Psychology* 74(3): 763–73.

Lamont, Michèle. 2000. *The Dignity of Working Men.* New York: Russell Sage Foundation.

Lareau, Annette. 2003. *Unequal Childhoods: Class, Race, and Family Life.* Berkeley: University of California Press.

Li, Jin. 2003. "U.S. and Chinese Cultural Beliefs About Learning." *The Journal of Educational Psychology* 95(2): 409–28.

Markus, Hazel R., and MarYam G. Hamedani. 2007. "Sociocultural Psychology: The Dynamic Interdependence Among Self-Systems and Social Systems." In *Handbook of Cultural Psychology*, edited by Shinobu Kitayama and Dov Cohen. New York: Guilford.

Markus, Hazel R., and Shinobu Kitayama. 2003. "Models of Agency: Sociocultural Diversity in the Construction of Action." In *Nebraska Symposium on Motivation*, vol. 49, *Cross-Cultural Differences in Perspectives on the Self*, edited by Virginia Murphy-Berman and John J. Berman. Lincoln: University of Nebraska Press.

———. 2010. "Cultures and Selves: A Cycle of Mutual Constitution." *Perspectives on Psychological Science* 5(4): 420–30.

Markus, Hazel R., Carol D. Ryff, Katherine B. Curhan, and Karen A. Palmersheim. 2004. "In Their Own Words: Well-Being at Midlife Among High-School Educated and College-Educated Adults." In *How Healthy Are We? A National Study of Well-Being at Midlife*, edited by Orville G. Brim, Carol D. Ryff, and Ronald C. Kessler. Chicago: University of Chicago Press.

Markus, Hazel R., and Barry Schwartz. 2010. "Does Choice Mean Freedom and Well-Being?" *The Journal of Consumer Research* 37(2): 344–55.

Marmot, M. G., M. J. Shipley, and Geoffrey Rose. 1984. "Inequalities in Death: Specific Explanations of a General Pattern?" *Lancet* 323(8384): 1003–06.

Matthews, Karen A., Sheryl F. Kelsey, Elaine N. Meilahn, Lewis H. Muller, and Rena R. Wing. 1989. "Educational Attainment and Behavioral and Biological Risk Factors for Coronary Heart Disease in Middle-Aged Women." *The American Journal of Epidemiology* 129: 1132–44.

Miller, Peggy J., Grace E. Cho, and Jeana R. Bracey. 2005. "Working-Class Children's Experience Through the Prism of Personal Storytelling." *Human Development* 48: 115–35.

Morland, Kimberly, Steve Wing, Ana Diez Roux, and Charles Poole. 2002. "Neighborhood Characteristics Associated with the Location of Food Stores and Food Service Places." *The American Journal of Preventive Medicine* 22(1): 23–29.

Murphy, Mary C., Claude M. Steele, and James J. Gross. 2007. "Signaling Threat: How Situational Cues Affect Women in Math, Science, and Engineering Settings." *Psychological Science* 18(10): 879–85.

Newcomb, Theodore M. 1943. *Personality and Social Change: Attitude Formation in a Student Community.* New York: Dryden.

Pascarella, Ernest T., and Patrick T. Terenzini. 1991. *How College Affects Students: Findings and Insights from Twenty Years of Research.* San Francisco, Calif.: Jossey-Bass.

Patillo-McCoy, Mary. 1999. *Black Picket Fences: Privilege and Peril Among the Black Middle Class.* Chicago: University of Chicago Press.

Picketty, Thomas, and Emmanuel Saez. 2003. "Income Inequality in the United States, 1913–1998." *The Quarterly Journal of Economics* 118(1): 1–39.

Reay, Diane, Jacqueline Davies, Miriam David, and Stephen J. Ball. 2001. "Choices of Degree or Degrees of Choice? Class, 'Race,' and the Higher Education Choice Process." *Sociology* 35(4): 855–74.

Rossi, Alice S. 2001. "Domains and Dimensions of Social Responsibility: A Sociodemographic Profile." In *Caring and Doing for Others: Social Responsibility in the Domains of Family, Work, and Community*, edited by Alice S. Rossi. Chicago: University of Chicago Press.

Saez, Emmanuel. 2010. "Striking It Richer: The Evolution of Top Incomes in the United States (Updated with 2008 Estimates)." Unpublished paper. Department of Economics, University of California, Berkeley.

Savani, Krishna, Nicole M. Stephens, and Hazel R. Markus. 2011. "The Unanticipated Interpersonal and Societal Consequences of Choice: Victim-Blaming and Reduced Support for the Public Good." *Psychological Science* 22: 795–802.

Schwartz, Barry. 2004. *The Paradox of Choice: Why More Is Less*. New York: HarperCollins.

Snibbe, Alana C., and Hazel R. Markus. 2005. "You Can't Always Get What You Want: Educational Attainment, Agency, and Choice." *The Journal of Personality and Social Psychology* 88(4): 703–20.

Stanford University. 2004. "Stanford University Viewbook" [brochure]. Palo Alto, Calif.: Stanford University.

Steele, Claude. 2010. *Whistling Vivaldi: And Other Clues to How Stereotypes Affect Us*. New York: Norton.

Steele, Claude M., and Joshua Aronson. 1995. "Stereotype Threat and the Intellectual Test Performance of African Americans." *The Journal of Personality and Social Psychology* 69(5): 797–811.

Stephens, Nicole M., Stephanie A. Fryberg, and Hazel R. Markus. 2011. "When Choice Does Not Equal Freedom: A Sociocultural Analysis of Agency in Working-Class Contexts." *Social and Personality Psychology Science* 2(1): 33–41.

Stephens, Nicole M., Stephanie A. Fryberg, Hazel R. Markus, Camille Johnson, and Rebecca Covarrubias. Forthcoming. "Unseen Disadvantage: How American Universities' Focus on Independence Undermines the Academic Performance of First-Generation College Students." *Journal of Personality and Social Psychology*.

Stephens, Nicole M., MarYam G. Hamedani, Hazel R. Markus, Hilary B. Bergsieker, and Liyam Eloul. 2009. "Why Did They 'Choose' to Stay? Perspectives of Hurricane Katrina Observers and Survivors." *Psychological Science* 20:878–86.

Stephens, Nicole M., and Cynthia S. Levine. 2011. "Opting Out or Denying Discrimination? How the Framework of Free Choice in American Society Influences Perceptions of Gender Inequality." *Psychological Science* 22(10): 1231–36.

Stephens, Nicole M., Hazel Rose Markus, and Sarah S. M. Townsend. 2007. "Choice as an Act of Meaning: The Case of Social Class." *The Journal of Personality and Social Psychology* 93:814–30.

Thaler, Richard H., and Cass R. Sunstein. 2008. *Nudge: Improving Decisions About Health, Wealth, and Happiness*. New Haven, Conn.: Yale University Press.

Twenge, Jean M. 2006. *Generation Me: Why Today's Young Americans Are More Confident, Assertive, Entitled—and More Miserable Than Ever Before*. New York: Free Press.

Twenge, Jean M., and W. Keith Campbell. 2009. *The Narcissism Epidemic: Living in the Age of Entitlement*. New York: Free Press.

U.S. News and World Report. 2010. "Best Colleges." Available at: http://colleges.usnews.rankingsandreviews.com/best-colleges (accessed November 18, 2011).

Washington University. 2009. "Washington University Viewbook" [brochure]. St. Louis, Mo.: Washington University.

Wiley, Angela R., Amanda J. Rose, Lisa K. Burger, and Peggy J. Miller. 1998. "Constructing Autonomous Selves Through Narrative Practices: A Comparative Study of Working-Class and Middle-Class Families." *Child Development* 69(3): 833–47.

PART III

INTERACTIONS AND SOCIAL CLASS

CHAPTER 6

DÉJÀ VU: THE CONTINUING MISRECOGNITION OF LOW-INCOME CHILDREN'S VERBAL ABILITIES

Peggy J. Miller and Douglas E. Sperry

There is an old debate in education and developmental psychology about whether the language of young children from low-income and minority backgrounds is defi-cient or simply different from the mainstream standard. According to the language deprivation position, such children underachieve because they enter school with a language deficit that originates in the linguistic deprivation of their preschool home environments. This view was ascendant in the 1960s, generating a great deal of classroom-based research comparing poor (mainly African American) and middle-class (mainly white) children and leading to educational interventions designed to teach poor children to talk (for example, Bereiter and Engelmann 1966; Deutsch 1963; Hess and Shipman 1965). The language deprivation position was vigorously chal-lenged by other social scientists (for example, Baldwin and Baldwin 1973; Baratz 1973; Bernstein 1972; Cole and Bruner 1971; Leacock 1971). The most famous critique is the sociolinguist William Labov's "The Logic of Nonstandard English" (1972a), which appeared in *Language in the Inner City*, his classic collection of studies of black English vernacular. Labov demonstrates that black English is a distinct dialect with its own grammatical rules, that it is just as congenial as standard English to logical thought, and that African American children in inner-city neighborhoods participate in a highly verbal culture that affords a great deal of verbal stimulation.

It may seem odd to begin with such an old controversy; indeed, we suspect that most readers with an interest in social inequality will assume that this debate has long since been settled in Labov's favor. Scholars steeped in contemporary theories of language in social life—such as Dell Hymes, Elinor Ochs, Basil Bernstein, and Pierre Bourdieu—likely start from the premise that children from less privileged back-grounds are not linguistically deficient but acquire linguistic practices that differ from those of their more privileged counterparts, differences that stigmatize them in the linguistic marketplace.

A TIME WARP

There is growing recognition, however, that the notion of language deprivation has not disappeared, prompting a new wave of contestation (Dudley-Marling and Lucas 2009; Michaels 2011; Sperry and Sperry 2011). One focus of these critiques has been Betty Hart and Todd Risley's (1995) study of the preschool verbal environments of children from across the socioeconomic spectrum, including six welfare children (all African American) and thirteen children of professional parents (all but one European American). The most famous claim from this oft-cited study is that there is a thirty million word gap between the number of words spoken to children in the highest- and lowest- class families. Hart and Risley (2003, 110) call this disparity "the early catastrophe." Although they do not use the term *language deprivation* to describe this disadvantage, they nevertheless assert that it cannot be remedied: "By the time children are four years old, intervention programs come too late and can provide too little experience to make up for the past" (Hart and Risley 1995, 2). Even more intractable than vocabulary, they say, is the attendant disadvantage in confidence and motivation that poor children incur as a result of failing to receive "years of practice and encouragement in manipulating a vocabulary of symbols and using them to solve problems" (Hart and Risley 1995, 194). As Sarah Michaels (2011) points out, however, Hart and Risley did not assess children's confidence, motivation, or problem-solving skill.

Labov (1972a) not only takes issue with portrayals of low-income children's verbal environments but also challenges depictions of their verbal performance once they entered school. Invoking the fundamental sociolinguistic principle that social context is the most powerful determinant of verbal behavior, Labov argues that when children's abilities are measured at school on standardized tests of verbal ability in evaluative contexts that are inherently asymmetrical, assessments will necessarily be distorted. He also raises a related concern that contemporary scholars would see as a matter of language ideology (Kroskrity 2000; Schieffelin, Woolard, and Kroskrity 1998), namely, the systematic linking of the idea of language deficiency to certain categories of persons (in this case, poor African Americans). According to Susan Gal (1998, 319), the notion of language ideology encompasses both "verbalized, thematized discussion and . . . implicit understandings and unspoken assumptions embedded and reproduced in the structure of institutions and their everyday practices." Labov warns that the dissemination of the idea of language deficiency (verbalized language ideology, in Gal's terms) is likely to shadow teacher-pupil interactions (language ideology as unspoken assumptions). If teachers assume that poor children are linguistically deficient, their perceptions of individual children will be filtered through this stigmatizing lens. Repeated face-to-face interactions will reify negative stereotypes, undermine motivation, and create self-fulfilling prophecies.

Echoes of Labov's voice can be heard in Celia Genishi and Anne Haas Dyson's recent book *Children, Language, and Literacy: Diverse Learners in Diverse Times* (2009).

"Typically students in schools in need of funding do not pass the mandated tests and live in under-resourced neighborhoods where families have low incomes. Their children are labeled 'at risk' and are often cast as deficient problems-to-be-fixed, especially in the areas of language and literacy" (2009, 3). Genishi and Dyson reject this discourse, noting that contemporary conceptions of language from across the theoretical spectrum—whether envisioning language as a species-wide instinct (Steven Pinker), a social tool (Lev Vygotsky), or a congeries of ideological positions (Mikhail Bakhtin)—do not align with the idea that wide swaths of young children lack verbal ability.

This prompts them to ask, If almost all young children learn language with ease and display remarkable sociolinguistic flexibility when conditions permit, why not create diverse curricula that would allow diverse children to build on what they already know about language? Genishi and Dyson (2009) argue that exactly the opposite is happening in urban classrooms: language and literacy curricula are becoming more standardized and regimented, not more variegated and spacious. They argue further that the ideas about language that undergird this trend derive from long-outdated behaviorist theories. (These are the same theories, we might add, that supported the educational interventions intended to ameliorate language deficits in the 1960s.) They conclude, "In the early 21st century, we seem stuck in a time warp" (Genishi and Dyson 2009, 10).

In sum, the discourse of language deficiency remains very much alive. We argue, however, that its premises are now largely unspoken and implicit in institutional practices or cast in different terms (low-income children are "at risk" or "disadvantaged" rather than "deficient"), reflecting the chameleon-like fluidity of deficit thinking (Valencia 1997). While there may no longer be any advocates for the language deprivation position as such, the most influential scholarship and policy continue to focus overwhelmingly on the verbal limitations of low-income children and their families.

In this chapter we draw on ideas from the study of language socialization and language ideology to address the question of how misperceptions of young children's language as deficient continue to be created and sustained. Because language "deficits" supposedly originate in poor and working-class children's early experience, we turn first to studies of preschoolers in their homes and communities, studies that yield very different findings from those of Hart and Risley. A key finding of these studies is that poor and working-class children develop advanced narrative skills at an early age. Next we turn to studies of the systematic misrecognition that occurs when poor and working-class children carry their narratives into kindergarten and first-grade classrooms.

We argue in the final section of the chapter that this process of misrecognition parallels practices in the policy arena, where greater attention is given to studies that report poor children's verbal limitations than to studies that report their strengths. Because both of these processes of misperception operate to distort or occlude the verbal abilities of low-income children in institutions defined by middle-class norms and values, a critical part of our argument rests on the contrast between how the language of children from low-income backgrounds appears when they interact with familiar others on their home turf and how it appears when they interact with middle-class speakers under conditions of implicit inequality. Our guiding principle is that the establishment of secure vantage points within working-class worlds is a necessary though often-neglected aspect of the study of children's language development and achievement; without such vantage points, it is difficult to see anything except how poor children fall short of middle-class standards (Miller, Cho, and Bracey 2005; chapter 5, this volume).

LANGUAGE SOCIALIZATION IN LOW-INCOME COMMUNITIES

From its inception in the 1980s, the field of language socialization has investigated the cultural organization of child rearing and language learning (Ochs and Schieffelin 1984; Schieffelin and Ochs 1986a, 1986b). Drawing from anthropology, linguistics, developmental psychology, and sociology and recognizing that knowledge of language and knowledge of the social world are fully entwined, researchers have sought to understand language as a tool and outcome of socialization. A major goal has been to discover the variety of ways in which language is used by and with novice learners within and across cultures, treating the practices of middle-class, European-descent communities not as the standard but as one cultural variant among many (Ochs and Schieffelin 1984).[1]

In keeping with the goal of understanding the meaning of socializing practices from the perspectives of the participants themselves, the methodological hallmark of this field is a type of ethnography that combines sustained fieldwork in the local scene with micro-level analysis of talk. Applied to the study of children from low-income communities, this approach has yielded three key insights: children and adolescents of lower socioeconomic status participate routinely with their families, peers, and other community members in complex verbal practices that form systematic socializing pathways; these practices and pathways vary greatly within and across low-income communities, depending on gender, ethnicity, and culture; and oral narrative, of various stripes, involving precocious participation by young children is a vital feature of social life in many communities (see, for example, Haight 2002; Heath 1983; Miller 1982; Miller, Cho, and Bracey 2005; Miller and Sperry 1988; Philips 1983; Schieffelin and Ochs 1986b; Scollon and Scollon 1981; Shuman 1986; Sperry and Sperry 1996, 2000).

Thus when children are followed in the contexts of their everyday lives—in homes, neighborhoods, and churches—they emerge as able language learners, navigating a myriad of local practices and acquiring specific discursive skills, especially narrative. It is worth dwelling for a moment on the latter. Narrative is widely recognized to be a complex form of mental representation, a rich venue for identity construction, and the quintessential tool of meaning making. Oral stories told by working-class adults form the basis for William Labov and Joshua Waletzky's (1967) enormously influential structural-functional analysis of stories of personal experience (see Bamberg 1997) as well as Richard Bauman's (1986) classic analysis of oral narrative as intricately patterned, highly performed verbal art. In short, many working-class communities seem to have a knack for cultivating narrative talent. In the next two sections we take a closer look at the conditions that nurture narrative early in life in three working-class communities.

Personal Storytelling in South Baltimore and Daly Park

When Peggy Miller went to South Baltimore many years ago to study child language, she did not set out to study stories. It soon became obvious, however, that this working-class neighborhood, inhabited by descendants of Irish, Italian, Polish, and German immigrants and migrants from Appalachia, was alive with oral narrative. Personal storytelling was highly valued and avidly practiced, and virtually every adult was highly skilled; some could have held their own against the virtuoso narrators in Harlem (Labov 1972b), west Texas (Bauman 1986, 2004), the Piedmont Carolinas (Heath 1983), and Salt Lake City (Hudley, Haight, and Miller 2003).

The following example is typical of the stories she heard while making observations in the homes of young children. In this story Marlene, a young mother, recalls an experience that occurred the week before when she and her friends worked late and had to walk home "in the pitch black dark" (Miller and Moore 1989, 430).

> So the next night we had to work over again 'til six. And I said to Molly, "Well, Molly, it looks like it's just you and me again." Hazel said, "Well, I'm walkin' too. My husband can't come and get me so we're all gonna go together." She said, "I'll tell you what, Mar," she said, "being's I'm an old lady, I'll stand there and fight 'em off and all you young ones can scream." [*Laughs*] "I got news for you, Hazel, I'll scream and I'm gonna be runnin' at the same time. You can just take care of yourself." [*Laughs. Narrator's mother and ethnographer laugh*]

This story was the final episode in a chain of stories illustrating the dangers of city streets, a highly tellable topic in this community, and the good-humored pluckiness of the narrator and her friends. Marlene addressed her stories to her mother and the ethnographer in the presence of her two-year-old daughter. Although her audience supported her telling by their attention and appreciative laughter, Marlene assumed sole responsibility for telling the story. She crafted a linear, coherent account around a quoted conversational exchange. The story is set off from surrounding discourse by its internal structure, by an introductory comment that links the story to those that preceded it ("So the next night we had to work over again 'til six"), and by shared laughter at the end of the story.

In four families studied longitudinally in South Baltimore, mothers, fathers, grandparents, aunts, uncles, siblings, and cousins maintained a steady stream of such stories. Stories enacted in this configuration, in which the young child was a bystander and listener, occurred at an average rate of 8.5 an hour in forty hours of recorded observations (Miller 1994). Although story content encompassed enormous variety, pregnancy and childbirth were favorite topics among women (Miller, Cho, and Bracey 2005). At baby showers—intergenerational, all-female events—every mother regaled the others with her personal repertoire of childbirth stories, each rendered in gory detail. Stories about raising children were also common. In the following story, Sharon relates an incident in which she lost sight of her young daughter when they were swimming.

> So the lifeguard comes over, and he gets ahold of my arms and he's looking at me, and . . . I say, "My little girl's not here, she's in the water! She's in the water!" and he says, "Check the bathroom. We'll go in the water, you go check the bathroom." So I'm running. The whole time I'm running, I'm thinking, "Please God! Please let her be in the bathroom. I'm not going to be able to handle this if she's in the water." And I get up there and what do I see? These two little feet swinging by the toilet [*uses her index finger to enact the swinging movement*]. . . . Well, I busted in the door . . . here she is, she's on the toilet! I whip her up, I'm like, "Oh my God!" and I'm hugging her, "Don't you ever come to the bathroom without telling me!" I'm crying my eyes out. . . . She sees I'm so upset and then she looks at me and says, "Mom, I'm not finished pooping yet. Put me down."

Narrating the story from her perspective as the terrified mother, Sharon crafts a suspenseful story. In the opening scene she depicts herself seeking help from the lifeguard, rendering her frantic conversation in direct quotation. She then heightens the suspense by quoting her desperate mental prayer, using the progressive tense to slow down the action. When the self-protagonist finally arrives in the bathroom, she evokes in words and gesture the climactic visual image of "two little feet swinging by the toilet." She then signals her relief by dramatizing her emotional outburst. The story closes on a note of comic relief—a punch line that deftly inserts the perspective of the little girl, very much alive. Sharon told this story at a reunion with the researcher hosted by Sharon's mother on her back porch. On this occasion, unlike that of Marlene's storytelling, the family was primed to tell stories: they had known the researcher for fifteen years but had not seen her in some time, and two female radio producers who wanted to meet a family of skilled storytellers were also present. Under these circumstances, stories occurred at the astounding rate of forty stories an hour in a four-hour sample.

These two examples not only convey a sense of the narrative genre that flourished in South Baltimore but also offer a glimpse into the narrative life in which young children participated. These youngsters inhabited home environments that were saturated with stories: adults and older children cast young children as bystanders and listeners to stories of their own and others' experiences. They also encouraged very young children to tell stories about their own past experiences, collaborating with them to produce narrations in which the child was both story protagonist and conarrator. During the second and third years of life, the children narrated their own past experiences with considerable skill, providing temporal ordering and using evaluative devices to convey the point of the story (Miller 1994; Miller and Sperry 1988).

Findings from another European American working-class community, the Daly Park neighborhood of Chicago, resembled those from South Baltimore: adults participated prolifically, avidly, and artfully in personal storytelling in the family context and brought children into this valued activity from an early age (Burger and Miller 1999). Moreover, the children from Daly Park produced two to three times as many conarrated stories as their middle-class counterparts from Longwood, a middle-class neighborhood in Chicago. At three years of age, the average rates were 6.3 an hour in Daly Park compared with 2.3 an hour in Longwood. To our knowledge, this is the only study that has actually compared the frequency of narratives produced by working-class and middle-class youngsters in their home environments. A similar disparity was found in interviews conducted with mothers in the two neighborhoods. The working-class mothers produced three times as many stories as the middle-class mothers, with no overlap in the two distributions (Cho and Miller 2004). The Daly Park mothers also produced longer stories and more complex sequences of stories. In effect, they converted the interview into a forum for personal storytelling.

When the stories from Daly Park and South Baltimore were examined side by side, further similarities emerged in how the genre was practiced in these geographically dispersed working-class communities (Miller, Cho, and Bracey 2005). First, the stories privileged dramatic language and negative story content. This is best illustrated by the children from South Baltimore, who narrated many events of physical harm, casting them in a dramatic language that favored verbs of aggression and pejorative names (Miller and Sperry 1987, 1988). This inclination to dramatize negative experience mirrored stories that the children heard and jibed with their mothers' socializing goal of toughening children for the harshness of life in a poor community (Miller and Sperry 1987). The Daly Park children's stories were also skewed negatively, reflecting their mothers' belief in being open and honest with children about the realities of life (Burger and Miller 1999; Cho and Miller 2004). Although the negative slant was less pronounced in the more economically secure Daly Park families than in the South Baltimore families, both working-class groups differed from the middle-class Longwood families, where children's stories were skewed positively and favored a psychological language of emotion-state words. This narrative differentiation between working-class families on the one hand and between working-class and middle-class families on the other helps to constitute what Adrie Kusserow (2004 and chapter 10, this volume) has called "hard" and "soft" forms of individualism.

The second feature of the working-class children's narratives is also relevant to these different versions of individualism. In South Baltimore and Daly Park young children's stories were hybridized (Bakhtin 1986) with genres of dispute, challenge, and self-defense, a pattern discernible in stories by older working-class children and adolescents (Corsaro, Molinari, and Rosier 2002; Goodwin 1990; Shuman 1986). For example, Daly Park mothers tended to contradict the children in a matter-of-fact manner; they did not soften their stance or give in quickly, impelling children to defend their claims in the face of resolute opposition (Wiley et al. 1998). Thus these working-class children had to earn and defend the right to express their views, a lesson in "hard" individualism. In contrast, the middle-class Longwood children were granted a great deal of latitude to express their views, even when those views were factually inaccurate (Wiley et al. 1998). They were learning that the right to express one's views could be taken for granted, a lesson in "soft" individualism.

Oral Narrative in the
Black Belt of Alabama

Linda Sperry and Douglas Sperry's (1996, 2000) work with twelve African American families in the Black Belt of Alabama provides another example of a vibrant yet different oral narrative tradition.[2] Early hypotheses in this four-year ethnographic study were oriented to the possibility that narrative-like talk would emerge only gradually in the conversations of the two- and three-year-old participants. However, the children were engaging in such discourse from our earliest observations at twenty-four months.

The families living in this rural African American community varied considerably in economic means but were similar in the separation of their everyday lives from the minority European American population in their midst. Participants in this investigation included five welfare families, six working-class families, and one middle-class family. All members of the community expressed concern about their children's success within the educational system. In fact, early entry into the community was achieved through the ethnographers' volunteer participation in a local community education center: teaching children piano, helping them with homework, and providing instruction to adults on child development. Furthermore, independent observations made of the children in their homes often featured catalogs, magazines, school books, crayons, and other writing tools belonging to caregivers or older siblings.

Within this context, caregivers demonstrated extreme pride in their young children's often prodigious ability to recite the alphabet, the counting numbers, nursery songs, and prayers. Unlike those in South Baltimore, caregivers in our Alabama group did not usually choose to tell stories about the community or about their individual, adult experiences; rather, they let their children take center stage, encouraging them to entertain the ethnographer with their accomplishments. When Alicia was thirty-two months old, she, her mother, and her nine-year-old brother Robert were entertaining the investigator (Linda) with stories about past and future festivities surrounding the upcoming Christmas holiday. Alicia had already participated in the community parade, getting to ride on the float sponsored by her mother's employer. Soon after Alicia told about this event, her mother asked,

Mother: Did you sing, did you tell her [*Linda*] what you gonna do Wednesday?

Alicia: I sing . . . [*pausing expectantly, jumps off the chair on which she is sitting and glances directly at the camera as if to anticipate her upcoming performance*]

Robert: Yeah, sing, sing, sing, sing, sing, "Old Santa Claus is going to, to town." [*also gazes at the camera*]

Mother: Tell her what you gonna sing.

Alicia: [*singing*] "Santa Claus." [*spoken*] Sing, "Santa Claus is coming to town." [*still gazing at the camera, gets up and lays across the chair with her head on the chair's arm begins chanting, rhythmically*] "Santa Claus is coming to town."

Alicia: "Santa Claus"—[*interrupted by brother*]

Robert: Nuh uh. No. Lookit. No. No, look at the camera and s-sing it.

Alicia: [*turns toward camera and places her foot on brother's back; begins chanting rhythmically*] "Santa Claus is coming to town."

Robert: [*joins in Alicia's singing, midsentence*] "—Claus is coming to—" [*interrupted by mother*]

Mother: Nuh uh, let her sing it.

Alicia: [*gazes directly at camera*] "He make a list. He check it twice. Gon' find out who naughty or nice. Santa Claus is coming to town." [*at this point, Alicia stands on the chair and turns her back to the camera*] "He make a list. He gonna find out who naughty or nice." [*in the middle of this last utterance, both mother and brother exhort Alicia to face the camera*]

Mother: Turn around.

Robert: No. Nuh uh. [*pulls Alicia around on the chair*] See, look at the camera. "Bad or good. Good or bad." [*encouraging Alicia to continue*]

Alicia: "Santa Claus is coming to town."

In this episode, Alicia is encouraged to talk about a future event, the song she will sing at the preschool program later in the week. Both her mother and brother (of whom she was particularly fond) are simultaneously supportive and solicitous of her performance, guaranteeing its success. Alicia's mother appears relatively certain that her daughter will be able to offer a polished performance; whereas in many other episodes she encourages her son to participate in Alicia's conversation, here she dissuades him from continuing. Robert quickly adjusts his approach to the scenario, picking up on his mother's cues that the show belongs to his sister. He turns his attention to making sure that Alicia is presenting herself to her best advantage, repeatedly admonishing her to face the camera. This episode provides an excellent glimpse into the worlds of parents and children within this community, worlds that are focused on the family, the education of children, and the roles of both within a larger social context. At the same time, the unique way in which Alicia and her family situate their talk about a future event within a performance signals a customary approach to conversational storytelling for these caregivers.

Overall, narrative episodes were frequent and substantial in the children's conversations, encompassing more than 25 percent of their sampled talk from the ages of twenty-four to forty-two months. Episodes occurred across a relatively large repertoire of distinct genres, including talk about actual events that occurred in the past or would occur in the future. Children were also encouraged by their caregivers to participate frequently in fictional episodes, where the characters or actions did not exist outside of the imaginations of the participants. Many of the fictional episodes emerged as transformations of situations in the here and now, refracted through a prism of make-believe. For example, thirty-two-month-old Lamont, his mother, and his sister engaged in the theme-and-variations word game "Old Lady Witch Fell in a Ditch" while sitting on their front porch with the investigator. In this example, the word play holds much in common with remembered nursery rhymes and songs, such as those that the children encounter in day care, yet the focus on the performance aspects of the narrative serves purposes other than the demonstration of past learning and accomplishment.

Lamont: "Old lady witch fell in a ditch." [*stares absentmindedly out in-to the yard*]

Sister: [*joining in the game*] "Old lady witch."

Lamont: [*presumably encouraged by his sister's participation*] "Old lady witch fell in a ditch."

Mother: Old lady witch fell in a ditch? [*questioning but prompting further storytelling*]

Lamont: Yeah. [*turns head back toward his mother*]

Sister: Yeah.

Mother: How y'all know? Y'all seen her?

Sister: Yeah.

Mother: Nuh uh. [*denial, in a teasing manner*]

Lamont: Uh huh. [*affirmation*]

Mother: Y'all didn't see her. [*still teasing*]

Lamont: I saw her to the store. I see her to the store.

Mother: Y'all seen her to the store? How, how she look?

Lamont: Ugly.

Mother: [*laughs*]

Lamont: [*begins stomping across the porch, chanting*] "Old lady witch fell in a ditch."

Mother: You'll be like old lady witch. You'll fall in that ditch.

Lamont: Nuh uh, fell in ditch. [*Lamont kicks up his feet behind him, to demonstrate his control over his actions to his mother; the verbal game continues for a few conversational turns, then Lamont suddenly runs to the edge of the porch and bends over the edge in an exaggerated, precarious manner*] "Old lady witch fell in the ditch." [*glances at mother*]

This brief example suggests that for the children of rural Alabama, verbal games are not just play but are also a bridge to the child's narrated life. Lamont's mother quickly seizes on an opportunity to animate a word game within his mental world, changing the game into an experienced activity by asking her children if they had seen the witch (Sperry and Sperry 2000). In this manner, she not only gives voice to knowledge and opinions about worldviews (witches are ugly, and therefore bad) but also provides an opportunity for her children to situate this knowledge within their previous experiences, contributing to their static and dynamic concepts of self (Sperry and Sperry 1995).

The two different ways of telling illustrated in these examples privilege open-ended contributions by children. These opportunities for personal demonstration of skill (Alicia) and open-ended story spinning (Lamont) may serve to socialize a type of soft individualism, one where the child's contributions to conversation (and by extension, society) are valued on an individual basis, in contrast to the hard individualism encouraged in storytelling among the children of South Baltimore. However, there were also many times within the narratives we observed where truth was important, a value that more often than not led to narratives co-constructed between mother and child. Although the children of Alabama were more likely to tell fantasy narratives (4.5 episodes an hour), past narratives also occurred frequently (3.0 episodes an hour). Furthermore, caregiver preferences in narrative style for boys and girls diverged. Although both boys and girls were encouraged to tell stories of past, personal experience in addition to fantasies, boys in particular were encouraged to tell fantasies, while girls were encouraged to talk about the past. In the following episode, the investigator Linda asks thirty-six-month-old Daphne whether she has been fishing with her family recently.

Mother: Tell her what you did the last time you went out. Tell her.

Daphne: [*gazes at Linda*] Fishes. . . . My daddy catch a fish. . . . My daddy catch a fish.

Mother: How big was it, Daphne?

Daphne: One was this too big. [*verbally stressing "this too big," holding her hands about a foot apart, gazing at Linda*]

Linda: That's pretty big.

Daphne: A big. And— [*interrupted by mother*]

Mother: Now tell her, about Diane. What'd Diane do? [*Diane is Daphne's eight-year-old sister*]

Daphne: [*reaches for her toy stethoscope*] It were a big— [*ignoring mother's question*]

Mother: What'd Diane do?

Daphne: Like this. [*still ignoring mother's question, demonstrates the size of the fish by stretching out her stethoscope*] It went over there, like this.

Mother: [*apparently giving up on her questions about Diane*] And what was the fishes doing? Show her how it was wiggling.

Daphne: [*flaps her hand up and down, gazing at Linda*]

Mother: Trying to get off the hook.

Daphne: Trying to get off the hook. [*still wiggling her hand*]

Mother: And show her, tell her how you was running.

Daphne: [*sits up abruptly, gazing at mother*]

Mother: [*suppresses a laugh*] You was. You was scared.

Daphne: [*firmly shakes her head, "No"*]

Like the mothers in the previous two examples, Daphne's mother encourages the completion of a story that allows her child to present a skillful, cute performance of a rehearsed family story. However, she also attempts to cast her as a member of a close-knit family, and, failing that, as the subject of an incident that the family (but not Daphne) thought humorous. This positioning of the child in both positive and negative lights was frequent across all types of narrative in this community, providing an interesting counterpoint to the self-affirming nature of other ways of telling.

In sum, when poor and working-class children are studied in settings where interlocutors find their talk to be intelligible and meaningful, it becomes possible to "hear" their narrative voices and discern the storytelling pathways on which they embark. In South Baltimore and Daly Park these pathways were marked by dramatic self-narration, engagement with and comic relief from life's harsh realities, and early immersion in hard individualism (Kusserow 2004), and yet they were subtly different from one another. In the Black Belt of Alabama, pathways were characterized by diverse ways of telling, each situating the child prominently as a performer in both real and imagined worlds. In all three communities, telling and listening to stories of personal experience was second nature to children by the age of three. Although middle-class children also learn to tell stories of personal experience in family contexts, working-class children have a distinct advantage and may well be more developmentally advanced in this area. Unfortunately, there may be little scope in the classroom for further cultivation of narrative skill. When Miller and Robert Mehler (1994) observed three kindergartens in Daly Park, they found that opportunities to engage in oral narrative were extremely limited. Although show-and-tell occurred daily in one classroom, it was not defined as a narrative event. When personal stories did occur, whether told by teachers or children, they were not as complex as those told in homes in Daly Park.

The lines of research recapped in this section illustrate but one type of routine communicative practice. In addition to personal storytelling, young children from South Baltimore engaged in pretend play, interactions in which adults taught valued knowledge (for example, names of people and things, skills of self-assertion), and a form of teasing involving play with the pragmatics of language (Miller 1982; Miller and Garvey 1984; Miller and Sperry 1987). Some low-income communities practice speech genres linked to their ethnic or cultural heritage, such as Navajo skinwalker stories (Brady 1984) and Western Apache place-name and historical tales (Basso 1996), or to their history of oppression (Basso 1979; Morgan 1980). Immigrant children whose bilingual expertise outstrips their parents' may hone their metalinguistic skills by translating for family members. For example, Lisa Dorner, Marjorie Orellana, and Christine Li-Grining (2007) found that Mexican American immigrant children who frequently served as translators developed sophisticated metalinguistic awareness, which conferred an advantage in school. Specifically, a higher rate of "language brokering" was associated with higher scores on fifth- and sixth-grade reading tests. In short, when approached on their own terms, diverse lower-income communities emerge as places that offer a range of resources and opportunities for children to cultivate specific verbal strengths, strengths that could be extended in classrooms with curricula more sensitive to these culturally mediated abilities (Genishi and Dyson 2009; Michaels 2005).

MISRECOGNITION AND LANGUAGE INEQUALITY AT SCHOOL

Despite the evidence that children master the languages and genres practiced in their homes and communities, when the focus shifts to school a different picture emerges: children from low-income families are less successful academically than their middle-class peers. According to the Nation's Report Card (National Center for Education Statistics 2009), the average reading score for all fourth-graders in its 2009 assessment was 221. However, while children qualifying for free-lunch programs scored 204 points, the average score for children who did not qualify was 232. How can these divergent images be resolved?

One explanation, compatible with perspectives from the language socialization tradition and sociolinguistics, appeals to cultural mismatches between the communicative practices that children bring with them from home and the communicative practices that they encounter in school (Cazden, John, and Hymes 1972). From this standpoint, the issue is not that there is something wrong with the verbal experiences of low-income children but that the skills they acquire and the genres they come to value differ from those of the classroom. Middle-class children, in contrast, experience a seamless continuity between the verbal styles and discourses of home and classroom, placing them at an academic advantage relative to their less economically privileged peers.

Shirley Brice Heath's (1983) *Ways with Words* provides a well-known example. Adopting methods from the language socialization tradition, Heath documents the literacy and narrative practices that flourished in two geographically contiguous working-class communities, one African American (Trackton) and the other European American (Roadville). Although these communities differed dramatically from each other, enacting opposing values toward fictionalization and literal truth, for example, linguistic practices in both communities differed from those used by middle-class families (both African American and European American). Moreover, middle-class ways of using language permeated the classrooms that all the children attended. Building on these sociolinguistic profiles, Heath records the successful efforts of one second-grade teacher to involve speakers from Roadville in her classroom. This innovative teacher created curricula that encouraged the children to become "language detectives," introducing them to a sociolinguistic vocabulary for thinking about language difference.

In effect, what Heath attempted to do was to cultivate metalinguistic awareness in all parties—children and teachers alike. Drawing on Pierre Bourdieu (1991), we might say that her educational innovation was designed to disrupt the process by which ways of speaking that departed from the middle-class norm were misrecognized as linguistically deficient. Bourdieu (1991) defines misrecognition as the process through which both middle-class and working-class speakers come to view the ways of speaking commanded by dominant groups as inherently more desirable. From Bourdieu's standpoint, the Roadville and Trackton children, by virtue of being human, were endowed with the capacity to learn language, but the social conditions under which they realized this capacity limited their access to ways of speaking considered legitimate in the educational marketplace. In other words, the problem was not that they lacked linguistic competence but that their competence did not count as legitimate. Systematic misrecognition essentializes the authority of dominant modes of speaking and the lesser legitimacy of other ways of speaking, becoming a key mechanism through which symbolic domination of minority speakers is achieved. Misrecognition and symbolic domination help to explain how macro-level "dominant" political and economic orders—in this case, class-based inequalities in educational achievement—are reproduced at the micro-level in schools and other institutions.

Research on dominant and nondominant ways of narrating experience in classrooms reveals how misrecognition happens in face-to-face interaction and illustrates the disproportionate social, psychological, and educational costs of misrecognition in classrooms for poor, working-class, and minority children. In show-and-tell or "sharing time" in a first-grade classroom, for example, a subtle but powerful mismatch between the teacher's middle-class narrative style and African American children's narrative style effectively denies these children equal access to oral preparation for literacy (Michaels 1981; Michaels and Cazden 1986). By following one child, Deena, over time, Michaels (1991, 303) was able to document the "dismantling" of her narrative development through the well-meaning but undermining responses of her competent, highly experienced teacher. Although the teacher effectively collaborated with the middle-class children, whose narrative style more closely resembled her own, she was not able to do so with Deena and her working-class African American peers, who used a topic-associating style. The teacher's repeated interventions demonstrated her misrecognition of the child's narratives as incoherent and pointless rather than discursively different. As this pattern continued, Deena became increasingly frustrated and annoyed with the teacher, and the teacher began to see Deena as less capable of producing organized texts.

A similar pattern emerged in William Corsaro, Luisa Molinari, and Katherine Rosier's (2002) study of the educational transitions of Zena, a low-income African American child. Zena flourished in Head Start, where most of her peers and teachers followed African American norms of speaking. Her teachers judged her academic performance favorably, and Zena's skill with adversarial and narrative speech allowed her to interact effectively with peers and take a leadership role in dramatic play. Zena continued to excel in kindergarten, but in first grade the same verbal strengths stigmatized her in the eyes of her white middle-class teacher and peers. Her verbal style was judged to be offensive and she was perceived as bossy and moody; conflict with peers impacted her academic achievement.

The misrecognition that Deena and Zena experienced in the everyday oral language of the classroom, a social context that is not directly assessed through standardized testing, is gradually transformed into a context that will be assessed as these young children travel the pathway to written literacy in the early primary years. Young speakers of nonmainstream English often experience a bewildering hodgepodge of spoken and unspoken rules and instruction concerning the relation-ships between oral and written language in the classroom. Genishi and Dyson (2009) relate a story about Tionna, a first-grade speaker of African American Vernacular English (AAVE). Tionna's teacher recognizes her as a fluent writer of prose, yet she is perplexed by the grammatical inconsistencies in Tionna's writing relative to main-stream English, inconsistencies that stem from normal discrepancies between sound and written symbol. For example, Tionna writes *is* for *i's*, a reasonable written substi-tution for the sound of the contraction for *it is* in AAVE. Throughout Tionna's school year, her teacher goes to great effort to help her learn mainstream English, yet with mixed results. When Dyson visits with Tionna a year later, Tionna reads Lucille Clif-ton's *Three Wishes* for her, a children's book written in AAVE. Although Tionna re-sponded to the same book with great enthusiasm a year earlier, she is now confused and even a bit frustrated by what she perceives to be portions of the book that contain "some words [that] need to be fixed" (Genishi and Dyson 2009, 31). Although Tionna has undoubtedly made considerable progress in her acquisition of an alternative dia-lect (mainstream English), her progress has come through the rote learning of new rules, rules that have distanced her from her home dialect.

Bourdieu's notion of misrecognition implies that the systematic underestimation of the verbal competence of children like Deena, Zena, and Tionna goes hand in hand with the misattribution of exceptional ability to children who use the middle-class discursive styles valorized in the educational market. Studies of the latter type of misrecognition are strikingly rare. Sarah Michaels and Richard Sohmer's (2000) anal-ysis of fourth-grade science lessons is an important exception. Although none of the children correctly understood the phenomenon in question (seasonal change), the middle-class children sounded "smarter" and more "scientific" in their explanations compared with their working-class counterparts, who used narrative accounts to in-terpret seasonal change. Reflecting on these results, Michaels notes, "Nathaniel was considered a brilliant student but he never understood how the inscriptions he spouted related to his phenomenal experience; Christopher, in contrast, struggled to do just that by recruiting his embodied experience via narrative accounts but he was rarely thought of by his teacher as a thoughtful, capable learner" (Michaels 2005, 142).

The research mentioned here provides a compelling answer to the question raised at the beginning of this chapter: how are misperceptions of language deficiency cre-ated and sustained? Classrooms, like the wider society in which they are embedded, are not neutral spaces in which language differences are arrayed on a grid of equiva-lent values. Instead, they are places in which some children experience a smooth ex-tension of the home socializing trajectory and others experience a discontinuity, re-sulting in progressive curtailment and alienation in the classroom. By exposing the discursive clashes or dovetailings that occur routinely in face-to-face interaction, these studies not only help to explain how macro-level patterns of unequal school achievement are established; they also point to an important process by which the discourse of deficiency is reproduced. In interaction after interaction participants ex-perience the language of the less economically privileged through the lens of mis-recognition: that is, as less coherent, less "nice," less correct, or less intelligent than the language of middle-class speakers.

The systematic misrecognition of poor and working-class children's oral narratives is especially poignant because, as discussed in the previous section, this genre is a routine source of enjoyment and an arena for precocious mastery and display for these youngsters before they enter school. Yet it is precisely this verbal advantage that is misrecognized as a verbal limitation. Furthermore, because these micro-level interpretive processes occur largely outside participants' awareness, they promote misrecognition of self and other in terms of social stereotypes (Bourdieu 1990; Gumperz 1982). In other words, as Labov (1972a) notes, these tacit, habitual interpretations align with the discourse that stereotypes low-income children as linguistically deficient, shadowing face-to-face interaction and keeping this discourse alive. Such misrecognition may become reinforced over time as children move through the educational system and eventually into adult-oriented institutions. This may be one route by which less economically privileged individuals learn to assume a posture of constraint when interacting in mainstream institutions (Lareau 2003).

MISRECOGNITION AGAIN

We return at this point to Genishi and Dyson's (2009) image of the contemporary classroom as increasingly regimented and standardized at a time when the school population is increasingly poor and diverse. These changes leave less room for the kinds of home-based language practices described earlier or for educational innovations that would recruit such practices as strengths (see Dudley-Marling and Lucas 2009; Michaels 2005, 2011), and they likely exacerbate the misrecognition of lower-income children's verbal skills. Thus it is easy to feel disheartened by these educational trends.

This situation also raises questions about how research on the language of poor and working-class children gets translated into educational policy. When we searched the U.S. Department of Education website, we found eighty-eight citations for Hart and Risley (1995) and only one reference each to work by Dyson and Heath. By contrast, we could find no mention of the skills that poor, working-class, or culturally diverse children bring to the classroom, even though the relevant knowledge base is now greater than ever (see Duranti, Ochs, and Schieffelin 2011; Shweder et al. 2009). A similar pattern emerged from a search of the U.S. Department of Health and Human Services website. Even if we set aside all methodological and conceptual challenges and take Hart and Risley's finding at face value—namely, that parents from the poorest families addressed far fewer words to their preschoolers than parents from the wealthiest families—what could be the rationale for devoting so much attention to a disadvantage in vocabulary and so little attention to other aspects of children's language experience, including their advantage in oral narrative? Wouldn't teachers be better equipped to cultivate low-income children's language and literacy development if they knew the full spectrum of their verbal resources, both strengths and weaknesses?

Margaret Mead and Frances Macgregor (1951) offered a perspective that is relevant here. In their book on Balinese childhood, they anticipated that their findings would be filtered through a culturally shaped climate of opinion such that some findings would be embraced and others, equally well substantiated, would not. They understood this filtering to be part and parcel of how social science works in relation to the wider society: "A new discovery in the field of human behavior has no efficacy at all until it is diffused, absorbed, and made part of a way of life by human beings, by physician and patient, by teacher and pupil, by writer and reader" (Mead and Macgregor 1951, 7). They argued that research on child development should include an analysis of the cultural currents likely to affect how findings are received and which findings are taken up and translated into practice.

Following Mead and Macgregor (1951), we ask, Which findings about the language of poor and working-class children are likely to be heard in policy discussions or embraced by public opinion? We contend that a largely implicit discourse of deficiency is at work in these arenas, just as it is in classrooms, prompting experts, teachers, and citizens alike to selectively accept evidence of the verbal limitations of less privileged children and to selectively disregard evidence of their strengths. Richard Valencia (1997, 196) notes that although deficit thinking may be sanitized in public discourse by a notion of being "at risk," the very concept of risk "tends to overlook any strengths and promise of the student so-labeled, while drawing attention to the presumed shortcomings of the individual." Susan Gal (1998) has called this selective view of others "erasure," a semiotic process common to ideologies of linguistic differentiation. Gal describes this process as follows: "Erasure occurs when an ideology simplifies a sociolinguistic field, forcing attention on only one part or dimension of it, thereby rendering some linguistic forms or groups invisible or recasting the image of their presence or practices to better fit the ideology" (Gal 1998, 328). The erasure of low-income children's verbal competencies in the marketplace of ideas may provide another answer to the question of how misperceptions of their language continue to be sustained. We suspect that an implicit hierarchy of methods (privileging quantitative studies with large sample sizes over in-depth, ecologically and culturally valid ethnographic research) may play a role in this process. An important goal for future research will be to examine the language ideology of deficiency from a multidisciplinary perspective, involving cultural, historical, political, and institutional analysis. Such work may help to increase awareness about the permutations of this discourse and support efforts to improve teacher education (Dudley-Marling and Lucas 2009).

Among the cultural currents that likely sustain the discourse of deficiency is the deeply held American belief that those who do not rise into the middle class have only themselves to blame. Consistent with this belief are current anxieties about American competitiveness relative to China and other emerging economies. Not surprisingly, the mediocre school performance of American children compared with Chinese children is frequently cited as a reason we fall behind. How, then, are we supposed to "catch up"? The educational reform program No Child Left Behind would suggest that we hold children to higher academic standards at earlier ages and assess their academic performance more rigorously. Genishi and Dyson (2009) imagine another approach. While refusing to sacrifice high standards for children or accountability for educators, they argue that regimentation does not equal success, especially for young children entering school. They advocate developmentally appropriate practice, reminding us that not only does development take time, but it does not necessarily occur on schedule.

Genishi and Dyson's (2009) view may gain support from a different cultural current, namely the belief that young children's psychological well-being and individuality should be respected. This belief aligns with the traditional understanding of kindergarten as a low-key transitional space designed to ease children's socialization into school, foster peer relations, and allow self-paced learning. Interestingly enough, this belief does not reference social class. Yet if classrooms were redesigned according to Genishi and Dyson's vision, all children would be likely to benefit, especially those from low-income and culturally diverse backgrounds.

In conclusion, we bring up one more factor that might be involved in sustaining an implicit discourse of deficiency in the realm of educational policymaking, namely reliance on outcome variables, such as vocabulary, that are thought to be easily measurable. Although Hart and Risley studied many aspects of children's verbal environment (for example, styles of taking turns in conversation), these are seldom noted. The finding that has been most widely disseminated is the disparity in vocabulary. Although no scholar of child development would assert that vocabulary is the only aspect of language that matters in school, the fact remains that it is this finding that has found fertile ground in the policy and public arenas.

While putting the final touches on this chapter, we heard a broadcast on National Public Radio (2011) describing an intervention program based on Hart and Risley's vocabulary findings. The purpose of the intervention? To teach low-income parents how to talk to their babies. We have no doubt that this program was motivated by the best intentions. However, the message that "fixing" low-income parents' communicative style will close the achievement gap cannot but reinforce the discourse of deficiency. Low-income children, their parents, and their teachers would be better served by a more balanced picture of children's verbal skills, one that recognizes their strengths as well as their limitations. The discourse of language deficiency leaves vital information out of the frame, compromising everyone's chances of success.

NOTES

1. For an overview of this large literature, see Duranti, Ochs, and Schieffelin (2011); for reviews see Garrett and Baquedano-Lopez (2002) and Kulick and Schieffelin (2004).
2. The Black Belt is a crescent-shaped swath of land stretching across the middle of Alabama from Georgia in the east to Mississippi in the west. The term itself is a double entendre, denoting on the one hand the dark, fertile soil of this productive agricultural region and on the other hand high proportion of African Americans living in the region. The term has been used by many authors and historians, notably Booker T. Washington in his 1901 autobiography *Up from Slavery* (New York: Doubleday, Page).

REFERENCES

Bakhtin, Mikhail M. 1986. *Speech Genres and Other Late Essays*. Edited by Carl Emerson and Michael Holquist. Austin: University of Texas Press.

Baldwin, Alfred, and Clara P. Baldwin. 1973. "The Study of Mother-Child Interaction." *American Scientist* 61(6): 714–21.

Bamberg, Michael, ed. 1997. "Oral Versions of Personal Experience: Three Decades of Narrative Analysis." Special issue, *Journal of Narrative and Life History* 7(4).

Baratz, Joan C. 1973. "Language Abilities of Black Americans." In *Comparative Studies of Blacks and Whites in the United States,* edited by Kent S. Miller and Ralph M. Dreger. New York: Seminar Press.

Basso, Keith H. 1979. *Portraits of "The Whiteman": Linguistic Play and Cultural Symbols Among the Western Apache.* New York: Cambridge University Press.

————. 1996. *Wisdom Sits in Places: Landscape and Language Among the Western Apache.* Albuquerque: University of New Mexico Press.

Bauman, Richard. 1986. *Story, Performance, and Event: Contextual Studies of Oral Narrative.* New York: Cambridge University Press.

————. 2004. *A World of Others' Words: Cross-Cultural Perspectives on Intertextuality.* Malden, Mass.: Blackwell.

Bereiter, Carl, and Seigfried Engelmann. 1966. *Teaching Disadvantaged Children in the Pre-School.* Englewood Cliffs, N.J.: Prentice Hall.

Bernstein, Basil B. 1972. "A Critique of the Concept of Compensatory Education." In *Functions of Language in the Classroom,* edited by Courtney B. Cazden, Vera P. John, and Dell Hymes. New York: Teachers College Press.

Bourdieu, Pierre. 1990. *The Logic of Practice.* Cambridge, Mass.: Polity.

————. 1991. *Language and Symbolic Power.* Cambridge, Mass.: Harvard University Press.

Brady, Margaret. 1984. *Some Kind of Power: Navajo Children's Skinwalker Narratives.* Salt Lake City: University of Utah Press.

Burger, Lisa K., and Peggy J. Miller. 1999. "Early Talk About the Past Revisited: A Comparison of Working-Class and Middle-Class Families." *Journal of Child Language* 26(2): 1–30.

Cazden, Courtney B., Vera John, and Dell Hymes. 1972. *Functions of Language in the Classroom.* New York: Teachers College Press.

Cho, Grace E., and Peggy J. Miller. 2004. "Personal Storytelling: Working-Class and Middle-Class Mothers in Comparative Perspective." In *Ethnolinguistic Chicago: Language and Literacy in the City's Neighborhoods,* edited by Marcia Farr. Mahwah, N.J.: Erlbaum.

Cole, Michael, and Jerome S. Bruner. 1971. "Cultural Differences and Inferences About Psychological Processes." *American Psychologist* 26(10): 867–76.

Corsaro, William, Luisa Molinari, and Katherine B. Rosier. 2002. "Zena and Carlotta: Transition Narratives and Early Education in the United States and Italy." *Human Development* 45(5): 323–48.

Deutsch, Martin P. 1963. "The Disadvantaged Child and the Learning Process." In *Education in Depressed Areas,* edited by Harry A. Passow. New York: Teachers College Press.

Dorner, Lisa M., Marjorie F. Orellana, and Christine Li-Grining. 2007. "'I Helped My Mom,' and It Helped Me: Translating the Skills of Language Brokers into Improved Standardized Test Scores." *American Journal of Education* 113(3): 451–78.

Dudley-Marling, Curt, and Krista Lucas. 2009. "Pathologizing the Language and Culture of Poor Children." *Language Arts* 86(5): 362–70.

Duranti, Alessandro, Elinor Ochs, and Bambi B. Schieffelin. 2011. *The Handbook of Language Socialization.* Malden, Mass.: Blackwell.

Gal, Susan. 1998. "Multiplicity and Contention Among Language Ideologies: A Commentary." In *Language Ideologies: Practice and Theory,* edited by Bambi B. Schieffelin, Katherine A. Woolard, and Paul V. Kroskrity. New York: Oxford University Press.

Garrett, Paul B., and Patricia Baquedano-Lopez. 2002. "Language Socialization: Reproduction and Continuity, Transformation and Change." *Annual Review of Anthropology* 31: 339–61.

Genishi, Celia, and Anne Haas Dyson. 2009. *Children, Language, and Literacy: Diverse Learners in Diverse Times*. New York: Teachers College Press.

Goodwin, Marjorie H. 1990. *He-Said-She-Said: Talk as Social Organization Among Black Children*. Bloomington: Indiana University Press.

Gumperz, John J. 1982. *Discourse Strategies*. New York: Cambridge University Press.

Haight, Wendy. 2002. *The Socialization of African-American Children at Church: A Sociocultural Perspective*. New York: Cambridge University Press.

Hart, Betty, and Todd R. Risley. 1995. *Meaningful Differences in the Everyday Experience of Young American Children*. Baltimore, Md.: Brookes.

———. 2003. "The Early Catastrophe." *Education Review* 17(1): 110–18.

Heath, Shirley B. 1983. *Ways with Words: Language, Life, and Work in Communities and Classrooms*. Cambridge: Cambridge University Press.

Hess, Robert D., and Virginia C. Shipman. 1965. "Early Experience and the Socialization of Cognitive Modes in Children." *Child Development* 36(4): 869–86.

Hudley, Edith V. P., Wendy Haight, and Peggy J. Miller. 2003. *"Raise Up a Child": Human Development in an African-American Family*. Chicago: Lyceum.

Kroskrity, Paul V., ed. 2000. *Regimes of Language: Ideologies, Politics, and Identities*. Santa Fe, N.M.: School of American Research Press.

Kulick, Don, and Bambi B. Schieffelin. 2004. "Language Socialization." In *A Companion to Linguistic Anthropology*, edited by Alessandro Duranti. Malden, Mass.: Blackwell.

Kusserow, Adrie. 2004. *American Individualisms: Child Rearing and Social Class in Three Neighborhoods*. New York: Palgrave.

Labov, William. 1972a. "The Logic of Nonstandard English." In *Language in the Inner City: Studies in the Black English Vernacular*. Philadelphia: University of Pennsylvania Press.

———. 1972b. *Language in the Inner City: Studies in the Black English Vernacular*. Philadelphia: University of Pennsylvania Press.

Labov, William, and Joshua Waletzky. 1967. "Narrative Analysis: Oral Versions of Personal Experience." *Journal of Narrative and Life History* 7(1–4): 3–38.

Lareau, Annette. 2003. *Unequal Childhoods: Class, Race, and Family Life*. Berkeley: University of California Press.

Leacock, Eleanor, ed. 1971. *The Culture of Poverty: A Critique*. New York: Simon and Schuster.

Mead, Margaret, and Frances C. Macgregor. 1951. *Growth and Culture: A Photographic Study of Balinese Childhood*. New York: Putnam's Sons.

Michaels, Sarah. 1981. "'Sharing Time': Children's Narrative Styles and Differential Access to Literacy." *Language and Society* 10(3): 423–42.

———. 1991. "The Dismantling of Narrative." In *Developing Narrative Structure*, edited by Allyssa McCabe and Carole Peterson. Hillsdale, N.J.: Erlbaum.

———. 2005. "Can the Intellectual Affordances of Working-Class Storytelling Be Leveraged in School?" *Human Development* 48(3): 136–45.

———. 2011. "Déjà Vu All Over Again: What's Wrong with Hart and Risley and a 'Linguistic Deficit' Framework?" Paper presented at the annual meeting of American Educational Research Association, New Orleans (April 8–12).

Michaels, Sarah, and Courtney Cazden. 1986. "Child Collaboration as Oral Preparation for Literacy." In *The Acquisition of Literacy*, edited by Bambi B. Schieffelin and Perry Gilmore. Norwood, N.J.: Ablex.

Michaels, Sarah, and Richard Sohmer. 2000. "Narratives and Inscriptions: Cultural Tools,

Power, and Powerful Sensemaking." In *Multiliteracies: Literacy, Learning, and the Design of Social Futures,* edited by Mary Kalantzis and Bill Cope. New York: Routledge.

Miller, Peggy J. 1982. *Amy, Wendy, and Beth: Learning Language in South Baltimore.* Austin: University of Texas Press.

———. 1994. "Narrative Practices: Their Role in Socialization and Self-Construction." In *The Remembering Self: Construction and Accuracy in the Self-Narrative,* edited by Ulric Neisser and Robyn Fivush. New York: Cambridge University Press.

Miller, Peggy J., Grace E. Cho, and Jeana R. Bracey. 2005. "Working-Class Children's Experience Through the Prism of Personal Storytelling." *Human Development* 48(3): 115–35.

Miller, Peggy J., and Catherine Garvey. 1984. "Mother-Baby Role Play: Its Origins in Social Support." In *Symbolic Play: The Representation of Social Understanding,* edited by Inge Bretherton. New York: Academic.

Miller, Peggy J., and Robert A. Mehler. 1994. "The Power of Personal Storytelling in Families and Kindergartens." In *The Need for Story: Cultural Diversity in Classroom and Community,* edited by Anne Haas Dyson and Celia Genishi. Urbana, Ill.: National Council of Teachers of English.

Miller, Peggy J., and Barbara B. Moore. 1989. "Narrative Conjunctions of Caregiver and Child: A Comparative Perspective on Socialization Through Stories." *Ethos* 17(4): 428–49.

Miller, Peggy J., and Linda L. Sperry. 1987. "The Socialization of Anger and Aggression." *Merrill-Palmer Quarterly* 33(1): 1–31.

———. 1988. "Early Talk About the Past: The Origins of Conversational Stories of Personal Experience. *Journal of Child Language* 15(2): 293–315.

Morgan, Kathryn L. 1980. *Children of Strangers: The Stories of a Black Family.* Philadelphia, Pa.: Temple University Press.

National Center for Education Statistics. 2009. *The Nation's Report Card: Reading 2009.* NCES 2010-458. Washington: U.S. Department of Education, Institute of Education Sciences.

National Public Radio. 2011. "Closing the Achievement Gap with Baby Talk." January 10. Available at: http://www.npr.org/2011/01/10/132740565/closing-the-achievement-gap -with-baby-talk (accessed November 11, 2011).

Ochs, Elinor, and Bambi B. Schieffelin. 1984. "Language Acquisition and Socialization: Three Developmental Stories and Their Implications." In *Culture Theory: Essays on Mind, Self, and Emotion,* edited by Richard A. Shweder and Robert A. LeVine. Cambridge: Cambridge University Press.

Philips, Susan U. 1983. *The Invisible Culture: Communication in Classroom and Community on the Warm Springs Indian Reservation.* New York: Longman.

Schieffelin, Bambi B., and Elinor Ochs. 1986a. "Language Socialization." In *Annual Review of Anthropology,* edited by Bernard Siegel. Palo Alto, Calif.: Annual Reviews.

———, eds. 1986b. *Language Socialization Across Cultures.* New York: Cambridge University Press.

Schieffelin, Bambi B., Katherine A. Woolard, and Paul V. Kroskrity, eds. 1998. *Language Ideologies: Practice and Theory.* New York: Oxford University Press.

Scollon, Ron, and Suzanne B. K. Scollon. 1981. *Narrative, Literacy, and Face in Interethnic Communication.* Norwood, N.J.: Ablex.

Shuman, Amy. 1986. *Storytelling Rights: The Uses of Oral and Written Texts by Urban Adolescents.* New York: Cambridge University Press.

Shweder, Richard A., Thomas R. Bidell, Anne C. Dailey, Suzanne D. Dixon, Peggy J. Miller, and

John Modell. 2009. *The Child: An Encyclopedic Companion.* Chicago: University of Chicago Press.

Sperry, Douglas E., and Linda L. Sperry. 2011. "Listening to All of the Words: Reassessing the Verbal Environments of Young, Low-Income Children." Paper presented at the biennial meeting of the Society for Research in Child Development, Montreal (March 31–April 2).

Sperry, Linda L., and Douglas E. Sperry. 1995. "Young Children's Presentations of Self in Conversational Narration." In *New Directions for Child and Adolescent Development*, edited by Linda L. Sperry and Patricia A. Smiley, vol. 69 of *Exploring Young Children's Concepts of Self and Other Through Conversation.* San Francisco, Calif.: Jossey-Bass.

———. 1996. "Early Development of Narrative Skills." *Cognitive Development* 11(3): 443–65.

———. 2000. "Verbal and Nonverbal Contributions to Early Representation: Evidence from African American Toddlers." In *Communication: An Arena of Development*, edited by Nancy Budwig, Ina C. Uzgiris, and James V. Wertsch. Norwood, N.J.: Ablex.

Valencia, Richard R. 1997. *The Evolution of Deficit Thinking: Educational Thought and Practice.* London: Falmer.

Wiley, Angela R., Amanda J. Rose, Lisa K. Burger, and Peggy J. Miller. 1998. "Constructing Autonomous Selves Through Narrative Practices: A Comparative Study of Working-Class and Middle-Class Families." *Child Development* 69(3): 833–47.

CHAPTER 7

CLASS RULES, STATUS DYNAMICS, AND "GATEWAY" INTERACTIONS

Cecilia L. Ridgeway and Susan R. Fisk

How do social-class differences affect the status dynamics of interpersonal encounters? That is, how do class differences affect who is listened to, taken seriously, and judged as competent, so that he or she becomes, or fails to become, respected and influential in group situations? Because status is an evaluative ranking among individuals or groups based on social esteem and respect, such interpersonal dynamics of evaluation and influence are best understood as status dynamics (Ridgeway and Walker 1995). It is typical for implicit status hierarchies of influence and esteem to emerge in interpersonal encounters, especially those that are goal oriented (Berger et al. 1977; Correll and Ridgeway 2003; Fiske 2010). It is important to understand how these hierarchies are shaped by class, as they mediate the valued social outcomes of the encounters. Interpersonal encounters between people from different sectors of society (for example, races, genders, social classes) play a powerful role in social stratification and inequality in society, as sociologists and social psychologists have increasingly recognized (Correll and Ridgeway 2003; Fiske 2010; Ridgeway and Walker 1995).

Consider, for instance, the following encounter. Frank and Christopher submit their identical resumes to an elite banking firm, and each is invited to meet at a French restaurant to interview for the available position. They have equivalent grades, majors, and extracurricular activities and even attended the same college. They are both Caucasian, tall, and handsome. However, Frank hails from an upper-middle-class family, as both of his parents are lawyers, while Christopher was raised by working-class parents who never attended college. Frank and his interviewer bond over their shared love of tennis, while Christopher's interviewer has a difficult time understanding his southern accent. Christopher also unknowingly commits a number of faux pas, such as wearing an inexpensive suit with an imperfect fit and mispronouncing his dinner order. Following the interviews, the firm decides that Frank is the superior candidate. The interviewers believe that he is more qualified, more competent, more likable. Christopher is upset by the rejection but concludes that he would not have wanted to work with "a bunch of stuffed shirts anyway."

As this example illustrates, the outcomes of interpersonal encounters are especially consequential for social inequality when they take place in what we refer to as gateway institutions. *Gateway institutions* are public organizations such as educational, workplace, and health institutions that mediate access to valued life outcomes by which we commonly judge inequality. These outcomes include good jobs, income, health, power, and social status. The hierarchies of influence and evaluation that develop in encounters within such institutions point individuals toward or away from greater access to such outcomes. Frank's and Christopher's interviews are one example of such critical gateway encounters. Others are student or parent interactions with educational institutions and patient interactions with medical personnel. In this chapter, we are interested in how social class affects the status dynamics (that is, the dynamics of evaluation and influence) in gateway social interactions. We are especially concerned with understanding how the effects of class in gateway encounters lead to lesser outcomes for those who are disadvantaged by their class standing.

Understanding the status dynamics of cross-class encounters is not a simple matter; it requires that we go well beyond standard accounts of interpersonal status processes such as those offered by status characteristics theory (Berger et al. 1977; Correll and Ridgeway 2003). To avoid confusion, we begin with a brief discussion of class as we use the concept. Next we turn to an examination of the social contexts in which cross-class interactions occur in the contemporary United States and the normative climate that surrounds them. Then we examine how this information about class and the contexts of cross-class encounters fits with current accounts of status processes in interaction. Status involves both group differences and shared status beliefs about an evaluative hierarchy between the groups, both of which affect status dynamics between individuals in encounters. To understand how this works in the case of class, we need to give special attention to the between-group aspect of class as it affects status between individuals. In particular, we argue, following Pierre Bourdieu (1984), that the distinctive nature of the contexts in which cross-class interactions do and do not occur gives rise to class-based rules for interaction. The status hierarchy between classes (as social groups with which individuals identify) shapes the content of these class rules in ways that have consequences for cross-class encounters. It also creates the foundation for in-group biases and class-based knowledge gaps that further shape the status dynamics of cross-class interactions. Finally, we present an analysis of how status beliefs and class rules jointly shape key gateway interactions in ways that systematically disadvantage individuals from lesser class backgrounds.

SOCIAL CLASS

To understand the status dynamics of cross-class interactions we first need some conceptual clarifications about social class itself and how we define it in this chapter. Like others, we broadly characterize social class as an individual's socioeconomic ranking in society. Defining social class more specifically, however, is a famously complex and controversial problem (Grusky 2008). In this chapter, we are interested in class as it impinges on interpersonal judgments and relations. Therefore, for these narrow purposes, we define *class* in terms of three simplified factors that we argue are important for interactional status dynamics. The first two are the standard sociological indicators of occupation and education. Occupations are taken as a powerful proxy indicator for social class in the United States and thus are a significant means by which class is signaled in social encounters (Centers 1949). This is especially true in regard to manual and nonmanual occupations (Goldthorpe et al. 1969; Vanneman and Pampel 1977; Gagliani 1981). Indeed, some sociologists argue that in an advanced industrial society, occupation effectively *is* social class because it brings with it education, income, status, and shared beliefs and work associations (Grusky and Sørensen 1998). In interaction, education also acts as a signal of social class. In terms of its perceived importance for class membership, education level has been rated nearly as high as occupation and higher than money, beliefs and feelings, style of life, and kind of family (Jackman and Jackman 1983). A college degree signals middle class rather than working class (Vanneman 1980).

As described by Bourdieu (1984), the third factor by which we define a person's social class at the interpersonal level is cultural-class identity. A cultural-class identity reflects the class-based cultural context in which a person was raised or to which a person has acculturated. We use the term *identity* here to capture an individual's sense of membership in a group based on shared cultural practices. Cultural-class identities are often implicit and taken for granted (Bourdieu 1984), but they can be explicit as well (Ostrove and Cole 2003). Either way, they mark for the individual the sense of difference between "us" and "them" on the basis of social class. Cultural-class identity is especially important for the status dynamics of cross-class encounters, as it was for Frank and Christopher. Typically, of course, occupational class, educational attainment, and cultural-class identity are tightly linked (Vanneman 1980), but since this is not always the case, it is useful to distinguish them. Each can independently affect status dynamics in cross-class interactions.

THE CONTEXTS OF CROSS-CLASS INTERACTIONS

To understand the status dynamics of cross-class interactions, we must also begin with an appreciation of the social contexts in which cross-class interactions do and do not occur and the normative climate that surrounds such encounters. When we do so, we confront a basic empirical fact: almost all encounters between Americans of different classes occur at work or in other such public, goal-oriented institutional contexts (schools, hospitals). In contrast, socially oriented interaction in the contemporary United States is astonishingly segregated by class. The root cause for this is the intense segregation of American residential neighborhoods by income (Iceland and Wilkes 2006). Although still not as strong as racial segregation, neighborhood segregation by income has increased substantially over recent decades (Massey, Rothwell, and Domina 2009). Since all residences in a given neighborhood cost about the same, they have similarly advantaged or disadvantaged occupants. Areas of residence shape shops, restaurants, bars, and other local gathering places, which encompass most contexts of nonwork interaction. It is not hard to see, then, why voluntary associations with others in America are highly homophilous with respect to social class (McPherson, Smith-Lovin, and Cook 2001). According to recent studies, Americans report their networks of acquaintances to be nearly as segregated by indicators of class as by those of race (DiPrete et al. 2011). The striking class segregation of social life in the United States means that people go from social contexts in which they are with those of their own class (their household, family, and neighborhood) to work or other such public places in which they may encounter those of other classes. Any account of the interpersonal aspects of class must be situated within these empirical realities.

The obvious implication is that most cross-class encounters, because they take place within public institutions, are embedded in interactions that are defined by the formal organizational roles of the interactants. For instance, the construction worker and architect interact at a building site, and the working-class patient interacts with the upper-middle-class physician at a clinic. As a result, the effects of class on behavior in these encounters, which include the gateway encounters we are most interested in, are complexly mixed with the requirements of organizational roles. Many cross-class interactions are simply organized as work-related cross-occupational interactions. In this case, class-as-occupation is an explicit part of the formal organization of the encounter.

It is important to recognize, however, that some critical cross-class interactions in public institutions, including some gateway interactions, involve organizational roles that are not occupationally defined. These are roles that can be occupied equally by people from multiple class backgrounds. Examples are student or parent interactions with school officials and patient interactions in health organizations. In these interactions, the occupational status and class background of the student or patient may act as latent, implicit factors that shape the interaction, but they are not explicitly part of the role requirements that organize the encounter. In other gateway interactions, such as the job interview discussed at the beginning of this chapter, class differences enter not through occupation but implicitly, through cultural-class identity. Understanding the explicit and implicit ways that class is embedded within role-defined interaction in public organizations is essential to understanding the status dynamics of cross-class interactions.

THE NORMATIVE CLIMATE OF CLASS-BASED INTERACTION IN THE UNITED STATES

The restriction of most cross-class encounters to public, goal-oriented organizational contexts may be driven by the material reality of residential segregation by income, but it is also supported and enforced by a distinctive normative climate. We claim that common cultural practice in the United States dictates that interactions explicitly based on social class are socially legitimate only in task- or work-oriented settings, in which class is recast as a task-relevant expertise based on occupation or education. An example would be interaction between a plumber and a physician over either a leaking faucet or an injured wrist. For Americans, social class is, or at least should be, the ultimate achieved form of social status. We believe in equal access to unequal outcomes (Lipset and Bendix 1967; Schwalbe 2008). Therefore, interactional assertiveness and deference based on occupational or educational differences seem legitimate when they are task relevant. In a sense, there is no dishonor in them in this situation.

The other side of this point is that Americans find the explicit acknowledgment of class differences and the organization of interaction based on them to be improper and illegitimate unless it is based on functionally relevant occupational or educational expertise (hooks 2000). The hidden risk in our faith in equal access to unequal outcomes is that we could be seen to "deserve" the place we hold in the class system. Thus when not functionally relevant, explicit stances of assertiveness or deference based on class difference imply that the actor assumes not just occupational expertise differences between self and other but some deeper, more basic "quality" or competence difference. Although little systematic work has been done on this topic, it is our observation that Americans find this assumption improper, unfair, or, at the very least, rude. For example, when in early 2010 it was leaked to the press that a Cornell sorority had an explicit, highly classed dress code by which they evaluated the female students who were rushing their sorority, the public reacted with disgust and outrage (Moss 2010). The code included directives such as "If you're wearing cheapo shoes, make sure they don't look like it," have a manicure and pedicure, wear Tory Burch shoes (which cost upward of $195), and avoid satin dresses unless you weigh less than 130 pounds and the dress is "from Betsey Johnson or Dolce and Gabbana" (both of which are expensive designer labels).

Some evidence, admittedly unsystematic, suggests that explicit acknowledgments of class and assertions of interactional status on the basis of class are culturally understood as especially improper when the interaction is not work oriented at all. In social contexts or even in socially focused interaction in work contexts, Americans find explicit interactions on the basis of class to be awkward and socially uncomfortable (hooks 1989). Indeed, it seems almost shameful to assert class differences at social gatherings. Ethnographic interviews suggest that such assertions of class differences, say, at the company party, are experienced as insulting by those from lower-status class backgrounds (Gorman 2000; Williams 2010).

The improperness of explicitly acting on class differences in settings in which it is not functionally relevant does not, of course, make concern over class go away. It merely drives it underground to an implicit level of maneuvering. Some of the most powerful and consequential ways that class shapes the outcomes of cross-class encounters are hidden from view, taking place at an implicit level that is outside the ostensible focus of the interaction.

In particular, the improperness of explicitly addressing class gives people who would be disadvantaged by their class in a given context an incentive to hide or obscure their class background, if possible, in middle- or upper-class-dominated contexts. For instance, contemporary ethnographic studies of how college students talk about class report that working-class students often elide their background in relations with middle-class students (Stuber 2006). As one working class student put it, "When you get closer in relationships you always feel uncomfortable, you know, telling them about your past. You wonder if they're going to think less of you" (Stuber 2006, 303). This adds to the sub rosa nature of cross-class dynamics in interpersonal encounters.

The normative awkwardness of introducing class distinctions in contexts where they are not recast as functionally relevant expertise further reinforces people's tendencies to avoid, as much as they can, non-work-related cross-class encounters (Bourdieu 1974). In this way, class differences create a barrier of social awkwardness that potentially discourages some class-disadvantaged individuals from seeking out gateway encounters with the class advantaged in order to improve their access to valued social outcomes (hooks 2000). Individuals, of course, sometimes reach past such barriers to make useful cross-class encounters (see chapter 4, this volume, on cross-class mentoring), but normative and structural impediments make these interactions rarer than they might be. This normative climate, then, supports and helps enforce the patterns of class-segregated interaction that are driven by residential segregation according to income.

Now that we have some conceptual distinctions for discussing class in interaction and a better appreciation of the social contexts in which cross-class interaction does and does not occur in the contemporary United States, the next task is to gain a better understanding of the status dynamics of encounters. The first step is to consider how class and the contexts of cross-class interaction fit together with what is already known about status processes in interaction. We begin with a brief discussion of status as a form of social inequality and then turn to the established accounts of how status shapes social interaction. While the standard account provides a useful beginning, it must be expanded to incorporate the ways in which the effects produced by the class segregation of social life also shape interpersonal status dynamics in cross-class encounters.

CLASS-BASED STATUS PROCESSES IN INTERACTION

In contrast to other bases of social inequality, such as material wealth or power, social status is distinctive in that it is inherently a multilevel phenomenon. It involves both evaluative rankings between social groups or categories of people in society (classes, races, sexes) as well as interpersonal hierarchies of esteem between individuals. Status between groups and status between individuals are linked by cultural-status beliefs. Status beliefs are widely shared cultural beliefs that people in one social group (for example, the middle class, whites, men) are more respected and diffusely more competent, especially at the things that matter most in society, than people in another group (the working class, people of color, women). In an achievement-oriented society such as ours, the presumption of differences in competence provides a foundation for the inequality in esteem. Status beliefs derive their power from the fact that they are implicitly consented to by all groups in a society, even by those who are disadvantaged by them (Cuddy, Fiske, and Glick 2007; Ridgeway and Correll 2006).

A well-developed program of research in sociology has shown that status beliefs link group and individual status by shaping the influence and esteem people develop in goal-oriented encounters (Berger et al. 1977; Correll and Ridgeway 2003). It argues that interpersonal hierarchies of influence and esteem are shaped by participants' status characteristics, which are salient social attributes of individuals that have corresponding status beliefs in the surrounding society. Class indicators like occupation and education are status characteristics in the United States because they are associated with widely shared beliefs that link certain categories of the attribute (professionals, the highly educated) with higher status and with presumptions of greater competence compared with other categories (blue-collar workers, the less well educated; Cuddy, Fiske, and Glick 2007; Fiske et al. 2002; Webster and Foschi 1988). Social class itself, however indicated, is also a powerful status characteristic because it carries with it widely accepted stereotypes that middle-class and rich people are more competent than working-class and, especially, poor people (Cuddy, Fiske, and Glick 2007).

When a status characteristic (such as occupation or class background) is salient in an encounter, either because the participants perceive that they differ on it or because they see it as relevant to the goals of the setting, status beliefs linked to the characteristic shape the participants' expectations for one another's competence and performance (Berger et al. 1977; Correll and Ridgeway 2003). These implicit performance expectations are consequential because they have self-fulfilling effects on people's behavior and judgments of one another, creating a corresponding influence hierarchy among them. For instance, when people who differ in occupation interact on a jury, status beliefs shape their behavior so that the occupationally advantaged, such as a professional, speak up more and act more assertive, both verbally and nonverbally, while the occupationally less advantaged, such as a delivery person, tend to hesitate. In the process, the advantaged, by speaking up more confidently, are perceived as having better ideas and more ability. As a result, they end up having more influence over decisions in comparison with the less advantaged, as research has shown (Strodtbeck, James, and Hawkins 1957; Webster and Foschi 1988). Status beliefs coordinate interpersonal assertion and deference in this way because the advantaged and the disadvantaged share the cultural assumption that some occupations and class backgrounds are more respected and imply greater competence than others (Jost and Burgess 2000; Ridgeway and Erickson 2000).

Research on status characteristics provides important insights into the processes by which class and its dominant indicators, occupation and education, shape the hierarchies of influence and esteem that develop in cross-class encounters. However, to make proper use of these insights, we must draw on the distinctions made earlier about how class enters into the public, institutional contexts in which most cross-class interaction occurs.

In the simplest case, cross-class interaction is organized in terms of the work-related occupations of the interactants. In these settings, the competence associated with each occupation is understood as having greater or lesser functional relevance to the situational task. Status characteristics research shows that the greater the task relevance, the greater the impact occupation will have on influence and deference. Even lower-status occupations command influence in situations in which their skills are directly relevant to the task at hand. For instance, a physician will defer to a plumber about fixing a toilet, even though the plumber has lower occupational status and is the "hired help" (see Correll and Ridgeway 2003). However, it is unlikely that the physician will defer to the plumber in any context other than this narrowly functional one, especially since hiring "help" legitimizes his or her broader status advantage over the plumber. Since class is recast as task-relevant expertise in such work-related settings, the interactional hierarchies of influence, deference, and esteem that emerge seem legitimate to all. The class status associated with occupations combines with the authority attached to the formal job role to smoothly structure the interaction in ways that can be precisely described by status characteristics research (Webster and Foschi 1988).

These well-understood cross-class interactions, however, are not the ones we are most interested in because they rarely function as gateway interactions. As noted earlier, most gateway interactions involve differential outcomes for people of different classes even when interactants act in similar roles (for example, patients) within institutions. Or they act in a similar occupational role, as job applicant or candidate for promotion, but have different cultural-class backgrounds.

What can status characteristics research tell us about the effects of class on these interactions? It suggests that for class-based status beliefs to shape interaction in these settings, class differences must first become implicitly salient for the participants. This is not unlikely, however, as people tacitly read one another's cultural-class identity from social cues of appearance, cultural knowledge, or life experiences (Stuber 2006; Gorman 2000; Argyle 1994; Bourdieu 1984). It is straightforward to extend the standard status characteristic argument to suggest that any cues of behavior or appearance that signal cultural-class differences will make salient status beliefs about class itself (Berger et al. 1986). In this context, however, class difference is unlikely to be explicitly acknowledged in the interaction. Instead, it operates as a kind of implicit background to the interactants' judgments of one another.

Once class difference is implicitly recognized in gateway interactions, status characteristics research suggests that it will bias expectations for the competence and performance of working-class participants compared with middle-class ones. Biased expectations, in turn, shape behavior in a self-fulfilling fashion. For instance, a physician, expecting less competence from the working-class diabetes patient, prescribes a simpler, though slightly less effective, treatment regime than is suggested for the middle-class patient (Luftey and Freese 2005).

Although class is not as immediately identifiable as race and gender, much evidence suggests that people are closely attuned to reading one another's class identities from social cues. Bourdieu (1984) provides an extensive discussion of how tastes vary systematically by class, especially in regard to food, music, and art. Other research has shown that dress and speech can be used to quickly classify social class. Clothing can signal occupation (for example, dirty clothing often indicates a blue-collar job) and can even carry status value (Kaiser 1990). Even if the style of clothing is the same, subtle differences often signal social class (Argyle 1994). These differences in dress correspond to differences in treatment, as studies have found that individuals sporting conventional and neat attire receive more help and cooperation from others (Suedfeld, Bochner, and Matas 1971). Speech style varies between classes and is therefore a primary and almost immediate cue to social class, often tied to powerful stereotypes (Bourdieu 1991; Giles and Coupland 1991; chapter 6, this volume). Studies in the United States, Canada, and Australia have found that individuals with higher-status accents are generally thought to be more competent, even by those with a lower-status accent (Argyle 1994). Ethnographic studies find that respondents often use an individual's style of grammar and sentence construction as a proxy indicator of social class (Stuber 2006; Gorman 2000). Peggy Miller and Douglas Sperry, in chapter 6 of this volume, detail the ways in which classed differences in speech further disadvantage working-class individuals within educational contexts.

CLASS RULES AND STATUS BELIEFS

Perhaps the most consequential way that people implicitly signal and read class differences in interaction, however, is through the use of what we term *class rules for interaction*. Americans do their socializing with others in highly segregated class contexts. This is particularly the case for socially oriented interaction that is not formally structured by the requirements of institutional roles and, therefore, more available for individuals to organize in their own ways. Segregated contexts for socializing, particularly in living contexts, foster the development of class-specific cultural rules or practices for interpersonal relations (Bourdieu 1984). These class rules embody ways of being in interpersonal relations (for example, modest or self-assertive) and relating to others (for example, warmly expressive or diffident) that are normatively expected, valued, and rewarded within that class (Hochschild 1979; Kraus, Côté, and Keltner 2010; chapter 5, this volume)

Because these cultural practices for relating to others develop and are used repeatedly among people in a socially homogeneous environment, they become taken-for-granted consensual rules for behavior by those within the class. Since, as Bourdieu 1977, 1984, 1988) notes, they are learned simply through growing up in or living in a segregated class context, people absorb their class rules as unspoken, socially valid practices that are largely invisible to them until challenged in a different class context. These class rules for interpersonal behavior are among the most powerful ways that people mutually, if unintentionally, reveal their cultural-class identity in cross-class encounters and trigger class-based status biases. For instance, it has been shown that the middle and upper classes have more elaborate rules for meals than the lower classes (DeVault 1991). As Joan Williams (2010, 173) observes, "TV during dinner is a dead giveaway that one is not in a professional-managerial household." Furthermore, the upper-middle-class dinner party is full of norms such as "Don't start until everyone is served, talk to the person on either side of you, don't clear until everyone is finished," in comparison with informal, working-class social events (DeVault 1991). Ignorance of such rules can signal membership in a different class.

It is useful to think about class rules for interaction in terms of class-based status beliefs. Embedded in status beliefs is a cultural presumption of a difference between groups, as well as a shared evaluative ranking of the groups on the basis of that difference. As noted earlier, class-based status beliefs coordinate behavior in cross-class encounters because they are implicitly accepted as a matter of social reality by both higher- and lower-class groups (Jost and Burgess 2000; Ridgeway and Erickson 2000). While the ranking may be culturally shared across classes, however, the social difference is not. By cultural definition, a working-class person is not a middle-class person. Yet although the difference is not shared, the nature or content of the difference is culturally presumed by shared beliefs to represent and express the status ranking between the groups.

Class rules for interaction constitute a fundamental aspect of the difference dimension that is embedded in class-based status beliefs. Therefore, we should expect the content of class rules to carry not only a connotation of cultural difference (for example, mere "style") but a public connotation of better and worse in worthiness and competence. To understand how this works, we need to look more closely at the between-group aspect of status and class rules for interaction. In addition to evoking status beliefs, class rules for interaction also create the basis for knowledge gaps between people of different classes and for in-group biases based on class, both of which are consequential for cross-class gateway interactions (Bourdieu 1984). Our arguments are admittedly speculative, but we follow them with empirical examples of the phenomena we describe.

The Hierarchical Content of Class Rules

The status hierarchy between class groups provides a lens through which to examine the content of the class rules for interaction produced by segregated living. Some years ago, sociologists and psychologists demonstrated that middle-status members of interpersonal groups show the greatest conformity to the norms and values that define membership in the group as a whole (Blau 1960; Harvey and Consalvi 1960; Dittes and Kelley 1956). More recently, Damon Phillips and Ezra Zuckerman (2001) have shown the generality of this effect even for firms within markets. Among Silicon Valley law firms, middle-status firms were more likely than both high- and low-status firms to conform to the market norm of serving high-tech corporations rather than branching out to include deviant legal specialties such as family law (Phillips and Zuckerman 2001). The logic behind these findings is that middle-status members of groups are sufficiently endowed to excel at group norms and values (in comparison with low-status members) but (in contrast to high-status members) are not so securely high status that they have nothing to prove to the group. Bourdieu (1984, 249) comments as well on the insecurity of the (middle-class) petit bourgeois and nouveau riche compared with the upper class, "who . . . have the privilege of not worrying about their distinction." Applied to the status hierarchy between class groups, this logic suggests how the content of middle-class rules might vary systematically in relation to the content of working-class rules for interaction.

Following this logic, we should expect middle- and upper-middle-class cultural rules for being and relating not only to embody consensual American values such as independence, individual agency, and achievement striving but also to represent an actual intensification of these values (chapter 5, this volume; Twenge 2006). This intensification is inherently comparative and hierarchical because it suggests that proper middle-class behavior should be understood as more independent, self-assertive, and achievement oriented than working-class behavior (Douvan 1956). Nicole Stephens, Stephanie Fryberg, and Hazel Markus (chapter 5, this volume) describe this middle-class stance as an "independent" rather than "interdependent" model of agency. For instance, one study found that middle-class participants, in comparison with working-class ones, valued a choice less if it appeared less "independent" because others had made a similar choice (Stephens, Markus, and Townsend

2007). Other research has found that middle-class parents give their children more independence to express their own views than do working-class parents, whose children have to defend and earn the right to express their own opinion (chapter 6, this volume).

In addition, this middle-class project of being the best at what is collectively esteemed fosters a rule for being an early adopter of whatever emerging cultural practices start to be seen as valued, high status, and "cool." For instance, if it starts to be cool to smoke, or to not smoke, or to jog, or to take your child to soccer practice, middle-class rules encourage their holders to quickly jump on the bandwagon. As Michael Argyle (1994, 85–86) has observed, "Middle-class parents are the first to read new books and to start the new fashions. They were the first to read Spock, the first to adopt feeding infants on demand and to be permissive about infant sexuality." A wide variety of contingent social processes, largely filtered through institutions dominated by middle-class values (media attention, expert praise, association with high-status actors or objects), can cause a cultural practice to gain status value with the public and be adopted by some initial members of the middle class. But once this happens, the imperative to be best at what is collectively valued acts in combination with social comparisons within a homogenous middle-class environment to cause the new practice to be quickly noticed by other middle-class people and to spread rapidly among them.

As a result of this early-adopter dynamic, the specific practices of middle-class culture change over time. For instance, middle-class expectations of what mothers should do for their children have significantly intensified in recent years, according to some research (Hays 1996). While the particular practices of the middle-class are moving targets, they are driven by a consistent, underlying cultural rule of being the relative best at embodying collectively valued American themes. And, of course, since middle-class people have more resources and occupy more powerful institutional positions in society than working-class people, they are better able to establish their perceptions of best cultural practices as culturally dominant in the society as a whole.

The class rules for social interaction within the working class similarly develop in a class-comparative context. Working-class people share consensual American values but, in an intergroup process, resist, to some extent, middle-class claims about the best ways to embody those values. As studies of the "hidden injuries of class" (Sennett and Cobb 1973) suggest, working-class people resent the implication inherent in middle-class rules that working-class practices are inferior realizations of collective values (Gorman 2000; Lamont 2000). They have their own counternarratives about the value of the greater emphasis they put on people and kin compared with material goods and the value of doing physically skilled work rather than deskwork (Gorman 2000; Lamont 2000; Vanneman and Cannon 1987). For instance, working-class individuals will often argue that college-educated, white-collar workers do not do real work (Gorman 2000), that professionals have the wrong priorities and do not put family first (Williams 2010), and that the economically advantaged are less morally pure (Lamont 2000; Stuber 2006; Bourdieu 1984). Thus while working-class people acknowledge the power of shared status beliefs that advantage the middle class, they do not fully abandon in-group favoritism for their own class or resentment of the other (Jackman and Jackman 1983; Vanneman 1980). We refer to this maintenance of a preference for their own class ways in the face of acknowledged social norms, rewards, and status beliefs that devalue those ways as a type of *working-class resistance*.

We argue that as a consequence of both their more constrained material circumstances and their intergroup resistance to middle-class claims, working-class people tend to delay adopting emerging new cultural practices that have already been embraced by middle-class people. Adopting new cultural practices often involves added expense, such as buying exercise equipment or paying for a child's special tutoring. Especially in a cultural context that questions whether these new practices are actually better embodiments of American values, these expenses can seem unreasonable. Furthermore, adopting such practices may come at a psychic cost to working-class members, as the adoption of a practice that is perceived as middle class may be seen as an affirmation of the superiority of the other group. Since these practices are less prevalent in the working class, members are also less exposed to local pressures from those in their own environment to adopt the new practices. Moreover, local pressure can actually urge against adopting such practices, as doing so may be viewed as a betrayal of the group. These processes combine to slow the rate at which working-class actors adopt new cultural practices that begin to gain status value in the society at large.

Although fostered by understandable cultural resistance, delayed adoption ends up disadvantaging working-class people at key sites of social achievement in society, like colleges, universities, and workplaces, since these sites are largely dominated by middle-class rules (Bourdieu 1984). It does so by creating implicit cultural knowledge gaps between working- and middle-class actors that put the working-class actors at a relative disadvantage in gaining the valued outcomes these middle-class-dominated gateway sites distribute. (For a more in-depth discussion of how the middle-class model of independence disadvantages the working class, see chapter 5, this volume.) These are some of the powerful ways in which the interactional aspects of class reproduce larger patterns of class-based inequality in resources and power.

Two Empirical Examples

To gain a feel for the subtle power of changing class rules for behavior to reproduce inequality, we describe two empirical examples of how this process plays out in contemporary universities. The first comes from Laura Hamilton and Elizabeth Armstrong's (2009) study of "hook-up" culture at a midwestern state university. "Hooking up" is an emerging new practice on college campuses that is supplanting the traditional date as the primary way that college men and women initiate sexual relationships with one another. In a hook-up, men and women go out together in casual groups (for example, for pizza), and individuals break off from the group for sexual contact based on interest (England, Shafer, and Fogarty 2008).

Hamilton and Armstrong (2009) occupied a room on an all-female floor of a campus dorm and engaged in extensive interviews and observations that revealed a strong class dynamic in student perspectives on hook-ups. Middle-class women in the dorm, the researchers found, viewed college as an essential site of self-development and career preparation, as they expected to take a few years after graduation to establish their lives before marrying and having children. This is a relatively recent view of the purpose of the college years for women. Contrast it with the saying from the early 1960s that women went to college not only to get their BA but also to get their MRS. The acceptance by middle-class college women of this new approach to their college years is a clear example of the early-adopter pattern. Hamilton and Armstrong observed that the middle-class women's view of college as an all-important time for self-development led them to also embrace the new cultural practice of hooking up, another example of early adoption. Hook-ups fit with their goals of delaying marriage and offered them a way to have a sex life without the time-consuming distraction of committed relationships.

About a third of the women in the dorm were from working-class backgrounds. Hamilton and Armstrong (2009) report that many of these students found the hook-up culture perplexing and uncomfortable. Unlike the middle-class students, they had not been raised to expect that their education and career preparation should greatly delay their formation of a family. Instead, they still assumed that their early twenties was a time to find a committed relationship. From this perspective, the dorm culture of going out drinking in casual mixed-sex groups every weekend and having uncommitted sex made no sense and alienated them from the other students.

Here we see working-class resistance to newly adopted middle-class rules that dominate in the university context. However, from a social inequality perspective, this resistance on the part of working-class women did them little good. Although the causality is surely complicated, working-class women who reported more alienation to hook-up culture were more likely to drop out of college over the years of the study. Most of the working-class women who did not drop out gradually took on the middle-class perspective about college and self-development and expressed increasing alienation from their old high school friends at home. In other words, the working-class students in this study were compelled to convert to middle-class rules for behavior to rise in the setting; if they resisted those rules, they tended to fail.

Jenny Stuber (2009) describes a similar class-rules dynamic in her study of the extracurricular activities pursued by midwestern college students. Middle-class students engaged in these activities in addition to their studies in order to meet middle-class injunctions to build their resumes for future job achievement. These middle-class rules for college behavior represent an intensification of the shared American value for achievement. Stuber found that in the process of engaging in extracurricular activities, the middle-class students also formed an expanded range of social ties that brought them added cultural capital that they could draw on when they began seeking jobs.

Working-class students, in contrast, found these extracurricular activities culturally less familiar, as well as expensive (Stuber 2009). They reported to Stuber that they did not really understand the point of putting time into these activities rather than simply concentrating on studying. As one student said, "I don't really see how being in all these clubs and stuff [will matter]" (Stuber 2009, 888). About travel and study abroad, another commented that "I like to be at a place where I know people. . . . I don't know how much [travel] would really help me" (Stuber 2009, 887). But after graduation, these working-class students' slimmer resumes and more limited social contacts disadvantaged them as they tried to find good jobs.

The Spread of Class Rules to Organizational Contexts

These studies illustrate how the early- or delayed-adoption process creates a changing terrain of class-based rules for being and relating that disadvantage working-class entrants into gateway institutions like universities. The studies show how both knowledge gaps between the classes and working-class skepticism about the presumed superiority of middle-class rules feed into that process. The studies, however, also implicitly illustrate a third factor emphasized by Bourdieu (1984) and many of the writers in this volume that plays a powerful role in disadvantaging working-class people in gateway institutions. In these universities, middle-class rules for being not only were the personal rules of individual middle-class students, they were also implicitly normative cultural practices that were part of the organizational culture of the universities themselves. For instance, in Stuber's (2009, 887) study of extracurricular activities, the working-class student who questioned the value of study abroad also said of her university's culture, "I feel like I'm hurting Benton's credentials, or whatever, by not going off campus because they do make such a big deal of it."

People bring the taken-for-granted class rules they acquire from segregated living contexts with them when they go to workplaces, schools, and other achievement-oriented sites that have major consequences for inequality. To the extent that people of their own class dominate a given work or educational context, their class rules become established as the cultural rules of interaction in that site. Consider, for example, the interpersonal culture of a construction site as compared with a hospital or a university. Class-differentiated interactional rules spread to work and education sites, constructing most of those sites as culturally "classed" as well. In these institutional sites, a given set of class rules has become part of the normative organizational culture by which people relate to one another in order to conduct the business of that institutional context. Note that this causes facility with the class-based rules of the setting to become an implicitly legitimate means to judge the performance and competence of participants (see chapter 6, this volume). Indeed, studies have found some evidence that employee competence in such cultural rituals can impact their success (Deal and Kennedy 1982; Kanter 1977; Packard 1962).

We suggest, then, that not only social settings but also most public, goal-oriented organizational contexts in the United States are culturally segregated, in that they are dominated by one set of class rules rather than another. As a consequence, when people enter into a class context other than their own, they enter as an implicit minority in a setting that operates according to a different set of class rules that are taken for granted and enforced by the largely homogeneous majority. They are put in the position of a nonadept who must interact with adepts.

Middle-class people are similarly disadvantaged by their nonadept position when they interact in organizational sites that operate according to working-class rules. The architect at the construction site, for instance, struggles to understand from the workers what is really going on with the project. But the architect retains his advantage in occupational status and organizational authority, so his lack of facility with the rules of the setting does not greatly impair the outcomes he or she receives from the encounter.

Most sites within gateway institutions (schools, workplace offices, medical contexts), however, operate according to middle-class rules of being and relating (see chapter 5, this volume). Positions of authority in these institutions, in particular, are dominated by people with middle-status occupations (teachers, professors, doctors, engineers), associated education, and primarily middle-class cultural identity (chapter 4, this volume). In these highly consequential contexts, it is working-class people who are in the position of being nonadepts. Their disadvantage with the rules of interaction is not often compensated for by any advantage in occupational status or organizational authority. As a result, working-class individuals' lack of facility with the rules of interaction in these institutions clearly signals their class background and only seems to confirm status biases about their lesser competence compared with that of others present. In cross-class encounters in gateway institutions, then, the knowledge gaps created by class-differentiated rules for interaction are not only a barrier to (working-class) nonadepts' own efforts to understand what is happening. They are also presumptive signals to the institutionally dominant (middle-class) participants that the nonadept is incompetent and does not "belong" in the setting.

We see an example of this in a study of admissions to highly selective colleges and universities. The researchers found that participating in extracurricular activities generally improved the likelihood of being admitted, but participating in certain activities that are less closely associated with contemporary middle class, especially urban middle-class, practices such as R.O.T.C., 4-H Club, and Future Farmers of America, decreased the odds of admittance (Espenshade and Radford 2010). Admissions officers seemed to believe that individuals who participated in these activities were less competent.

THE CLASS-BASED STATUS DYNAMICS OF GATEWAY INTERACTIONS

Gateway encounters, which take place in public institutions such as the workplace, educational institutions, or medical organizations, mediate people's access to the valued life outcomes on which equality is based. The analysis developed here suggests three primary factors that shape cross-class hierarchies of influence and evaluation in gateway encounters: class-related status characteristics (occupation, education, and cultural-class identity, however signaled), knowledge gaps between the participants about the rules of the setting, and in-group biases that encourage people to better appreciate those of their own class. Each of these factors affects the performance expectations that form for working-class actors in the encounter, others' willingness to grant them influence and esteem, and, consequently, the outcomes for the actors. Hidden behind all three factors are class-differentiated rules for interaction. These differences in social rules trigger status beliefs based on cultural-class identity, create knowledge gaps that particularly disadvantage working-class individuals, and provide the basis for in-group favoritism on the part of middle-class participants and defensiveness or resistance on the part of working-class individuals.

The best way to demonstrate how these factors work together to shape the status dynamics of cross-class gateway encounters is to consider some examples. Because of its intentional clarity, we start with our fictional example of Frank and Christopher, who are interviewed for a position in a banking firm. As in many gateway encounters, the two men are in the same organizational role, job applicant, and are in a low-authority position relative to the interviewers in the encounter. Frank and Christopher are also of the same occupational and educational status, but they differ in their class background and in their understanding of implicit class rules for interaction. Class differences in this encounter, then, are submerged and highly implicit and independent of job-related expertise.

What happens? The interactional rule differences between the interviewers and their interviewees quickly make class-based status beliefs implicitly salient in the setting. Frank's facility with middle-class rules allows him to connect with the interviewer over tennis. Christopher's lesser familiarity with these rules makes it harder for him to effectively present himself to his interviewer, and his knowledge gap causes him to make subtle social mistakes. Christopher's more awkward performance and low-status accent seem to confirm background status assumptions that he is less competent than Frank, despite similar training. And in-group biases make Frank seem more likable and more suitable for the position. Frank gets the job. Christopher is disappointed and confused, but he also experiences resistance owing to his own in-group biases. In all probability, none of these participants were consciously aware of these class dynamics, although Christopher likely knew something had happened without being able to say exactly what it was.

More convincing is real evidence from actual gateway encounters. Annette Lareau (2002) provides one such example in her description of the interactions she observed in pediatricians' offices with middle-class and working-class parents and children. Following middle-class rules for self-assertion, the middle-class mother prepped her ten-year-old son as they approached the doctor's office not only to answer the doctor's questions but to ask him questions as well. Once in the doctor's office, the son spoke right up and did this. The son soon established a friendly, surprisingly egalitarian banter with the middle-class doctor, who, despite his organizational position of authority, shared the boy's cultural-class identity. Sharing in the social ease with the doctor, the boy's mother felt free to volunteer problems with the child's eating habits and the fact that she had given up on giving the child a medication. From this richer trove of information, the doctor was able to give more detailed professional care for the child.

In contrast, Lareau (2002) describes a working-class mother and her son's interactions with their pediatrician as relatively more cautious, constrained, and uneasy. Impressed by the doctor's authority and feeling no counterbalancing kinship in class identity, the mother answered the doctor's questions minimally and seemed to resist revealing detailed information by which she might be judged negatively or that might confirm working-class stereotypes. Thus the information the doctor heard was less accurate and rich. The son, too, limited his interaction. He answered the doctor's direct questions but did not assert himself or initiate conversation with the doctor. In the end, the mother received less detailed feedback about her child's health.

Both of these encounters were organized as interactions between a patient and a doctor, but one is a cross-class interaction and the other is an in-group interaction. Following middle-class rules, the first mother and son actively and even strategically used their shared class background with the doctor to reduce the status distance between themselves and the doctor to equalize the conversation. Since he shared these cultural rules, the doctor responded in a positive, in-group-favoring manner, and information flowed freely between them, improving the health outcomes the patient received. In the second, cross-class, interaction, the mother and son seemed to feel from the beginning their class-status difference from the doctor. They were hesitant and deferential rather than assertive. The cultural knowledge gap between them and the doctor further strained the conversation. And, in a sign of working-class distrust of the middle-class setting, the mother resisted full disclosure to the doctor, further constraining the flow of health information and reducing the quality of outcomes mother and son received from the encounter. These differential outcomes were a joint effect of status beliefs triggered by class differences, knowledge gaps or similarities owing to class rules, and in-group biases that created bonding for the middle-class patients and implicit resistance for the working-class ones.

CONCLUSION

By our analysis, social class has a powerful impact on the status dynamics of cross-class encounters in gateway institutions. These complex effects, however, are almost entirely submerged beneath the surface of the encounter, obscuring their central importance for the unequal outcomes that people of different classes receive from their social encounters in gateway institutions.

At the heart of these effects of class on interpersonal status are implicit, class-based rules for interaction. These taken-for-granted rules are themselves embedded in widely accepted status beliefs that cast middle-class ways as better in general and indicative of greater competence than working-class ways. Tacit cultural rules for being and relating are produced and sustained by class-segregated living environments, but they spread to and become institutionalized as "the way things are done" in public organizations that are dominated by members of a given class. Since powerful public institutions that mediate individuals' access to valued life outcomes, like educational, health, and work organizations, operate largely according to middle-class rules, working-class people who enter them with different rules encounter a powerful but subtle cascade of disadvantages in their dealings with others. Their different ways of being trigger disadvantaging status beliefs that shape others' expectations, and even their own, for their competence in the setting. And their gap in knowledge about the invisible rules for relating makes it that much harder for them to figure out what is happening and successfully perform well according to the standards of the institution. Instead of the social ease of a shared cultural background, they face the awkwardness of relating as someone who is different and does not quite know the rules. Together, these interactional disadvantages, taking place in key gateway institutions, subtly point working-class people toward lower levels of valued life outcomes than otherwise similar middle-class people. In this way, cross-class encounters in these institutions routinely sustain social inequality in society.

We do not believe, however, that this situation is inevitable. Although gateway institutions are presently saturated with class-based rules for interaction, it may be possible to devise interventions that reduce the extent to which cross-class encounters within them perpetuate inequality. As a necessary first step, key gatekeepers in institutions must be educated about the nature and consequences of class-differential treatment for those who come through the institution. Doctors could be given sensitivity training to compensate for class-based differences; college admissions officers could be required to give the class disadvantaged the same consideration they give racial minorities; job interviewers can be taught to be aware of their own class biases. Second, institutions can devise specifically tailored support programs for members of lower-status class groups who enter the institution. For instance, Stanford University has created a First-Generation Low Income Partnership (FLIP) that works to "create a safe environment at Stanford in which students can talk openly about class issues, access consolidated resources, and empower prospective first-generation and/or low-income students through service initiatives" (Nguyen 2011). Many other colleges have similar initiatives. Bias toward those who are disadvantaged by their class status is not inescapable. However, it will not be overcome unless we increase our awareness of class-based discrimination in gateway interactions.

REFERENCES

Argyle, Michael. 1994. *The Psychology of Social Class*. London: Routledge.

Berger, Joseph, Hamit Fisek, Robert Norman, and Morris Zelditch. 1977. *Status Characteristics and Social Interaction*. New York: Elsevier.

Berger, Joseph, Murray Webster, Cecilia Ridgeway, and Susan Rosenholtz. 1986. "Status Cues, Expectations, and Behaviors." In *Advances in Group Processes: Theory and Research*, vol. 3, edited by Edward Lawler. Greenwich, Conn.: JAI Press.

Blau, Peter M. 1960. "Structural Effects." *The American Sociological Review* 25(2): 178–93.

Bourdieu, Pierre. 1974. "The School as a Conservative Force: Scholastic Achievement and Cultural Inequalities." In *Contemporary Research in the Sociology of Education*, edited by John Eggleston. London: Methuen.

———. 1977. *Outline of a Theory of Practice*. Cambridge: Cambridge University Press.

———. 1984. *Distinction: A Social Critique of the Judgment of Taste*. Translated by Richard Nice. Cambridge, Mass.: Harvard University Press.

———. 1988. "On Interest and the Relative Autonomy of Symbolic Power." *Working Papers and Proceedings of the Center for Psychosocial Studies*, no. 20. Chicago.

———. 1991. *Language and Symbolic Power*. Translated by Gino Raymond and Matthew Adamson. Cambridge, Mass.: Harvard University Press.

Centers, Richard. 1949. *The Psychology of Social Classes*. Princeton, N.J.: Princeton University Press.

Correll, Shelley J., and Cecilia L. Ridgeway. 2003. "Expectation States Theory." In *The Handbook of Social Psychology*, edited by John Delamater. New York: Kluwer Academic/Plenum.

Cuddy, Amy J., Susan T. Fiske, and Peter Glick. 2007. "The BIAS Map: Behaviors from Intergroup Affect and Stereotypes." *The Journal of Personality and Social Psychology* 92(4): 631–68.

Deal, Terrence E., and A. A. Kennedy. 1982. *Corporate Culture: The Rites and Rituals of Corporate Life.* Reading, Mass.: Addison-Wesley.

DeVault, Marjorie L. 1991. *Feeding the Family: The Social Organization of Caring as Gendered Work.* Chicago: University of Chicago Press.

DiPrete, Thomas A., Andrew Gelman, Tyler McCormick, Julien Teitler, and Tian Zheng. 2011. "Segregation in Social Networks Based on Acquaintanceship and Trust." *The American Journal of Sociology* 116(4): 1234–83.

Dittes, James E., and Harold H. Kelley. 1956. "Effects of Different Conditions of Acceptance Upon Conformity to Group Norms." *The Journal of Abnormal and Social Psychology* 53(1): 100–107.

Douvan, Elizabeth. 1956. "Social Status and Success Strivings." *The Journal of Abnormal and Social Psychology* 52(2): 219–23.

England, Paula, Emily Fitzgibbons Shafer, and Alison C. K. Fogarty. 2008. "Hooking-Up and Forming Romantic Relationships on Today's College Campuses." In *The Gendered Society Reader,* 3rd ed., edited by Michael S. Kimmel and Amy Aronson. New York: Oxford University Press.

Espenshade, Thomas J., and Alexandria Walton Radford. 2010. *No Longer Separate, Not Yet Equal: Race and Class in Elite College Admission and Campus Life.* Princeton, N.J.: Princeton University Press.

Fiske, Susan T. 2010. "Interpersonal Stratification: Status, Power, and Subordination." In *Handbook of Social Psychology,* 5th ed., edited by S. T. Fiske, D. T. Gilbert, and Gardner Lindzey, vol. 2. New York: Wiley.

Fiske, Susan T., Amy J. Cuddy, Peter Glick, and Jun Xu. 2002. "A Model of (Often Mixed) Stereotype Content: Competence and Warmth Respectively Follow from Perceived Status and Competition." *The Journal of Personality and Social Psychology* 82(6): 878–902.

Gagliani, Giorgio. 1981. "How Many Working Classes?" *The American Journal of Sociology* 87(2): 259–85.

Giles, Howard, and Nikolas Coupland. 1991. *Language Contexts and Consequences.* Pacific Grove, Calif.: Brooks/Cole.

Goldthorpe, John H., David Lockwood, Frank Bechhofer, and Jennifer Platt. 1969. *The Affluent Worker in the Class Structure.* Cambridge: Cambridge University Press.

Gorman, Thomas J. 2000. "Cross-Class Perceptions of Social Class." *The Sociological Spectrum* 20: 93–120.

Grusky, David B., ed. 2008. *Social Stratification: Class, Race, and Gender in Sociological Perspective.* 3rd ed. Boulder, Colo.: Westview.

Grusky, David B., and Jesper B. Sørensen. 1998. "Can Class Analysis Be Salvaged?" *The American Journal of Sociology* 103(5): 1187–1234.

Hamilton, Laura, and Elizabeth A. Armstrong. 2009. "Gendered Sexuality in Young Adulthood: Double Binds and Flawed Options." *Gender and Society* 23(5): 589–616.

Harvey, O. J., and Conrad Consalvi. 1960. "Status and Conformity to Pressures in Informal Groups." *The Journal of Abnormal Social Psychology* 60(2): 182–87.

Hays, Sharon. 1996. *The Cultural Contradictions of Motherhood.* New Haven, Conn.: Yale University Press.

Hochschild, Arlie Russell. 1979. "Emotion Work, Feeling Rules, and Social Structure." *The American Journal of Sociology* 85(3): 551–75.

hooks, bell. 1989. *Talking Back: Thinking Feminist, Thinking Black*. Boston, Mass.: South End Press.

———. 2000. *Where We Stand: Class Matters*. New York: Routledge.

Iceland, John, and Rima Wilkes. 2006. "Does Socioeconomic Status Matter? Race, Class, and Residential Segregation." *Social Problems* 53(2): 248–73.

Jackman, Mary R., and Robert W. Jackman. 1983. *Class Awareness in the United States*. Los Angeles: University of California Press.

Jost, John T., and Diana Burgess. 2000. "Attitudinal Ambivalence and the Conflict Between Group and System Justification Motives in Low Status Groups." *The Personality and Social Psychology Bulletin* 26(3): 293–305.

Kaiser, Susan B. 1990. *The Social Psychology of Clothing and Personal Adornment*. 2nd ed. New York: Macmillan.

Kanter, Rosabeth Moss. 1977. *Women and Men of the Corporation*. New York: Basic Books.

Kraus, Michael W., Stéphane Côté, and Dacher Keltner. 2010. "Social Class, Contextualism, and Empathic Accuracy." *Psychological Science* 21(11): 1716–23.

Lamont, Michèle. 2000. *The Dignity of Working Men: Morality and the Boundaries of Race, Class, and Immigration*. Cambridge, Mass.: Harvard University Press.

Lareau, Annette. 2002. "Invisible Inequality: Social Class and Childrearing in Black Families and White Families." *The American Sociological Review* 67(5): 747–76.

Lipset, Seymour Martin, and Reinhard Bendix. 1967. *Social Mobility in Industrial Society*. Berkeley: University of California Press.

Luftey, Karen, and Jeremy Freese. 2005. "Toward Some Fundamentals of Fundamental Causality: Socioeconomic Status and Health in the Routine Clinic Visit for Diabetes." *The American Journal of Sociology* 110(5): 1326–72.

Massey, Douglas, Jonathan Rothwell, and Thurston Domina. 2009. "The Changing Bases of Segregation in the United States." *The Annals of the American Academy of Political and Social Science* 626(1): 74–90.

McPherson, J. Miller, Lynn Smith-Lovin, and James M. Cook. 2001. "Birds of a Feather: Homophily in Social Networks." *The Annual Review of Sociology* 27:415–44.

Moss, Hilary. 2010. "Cornell Sorority Issues ABSURD Dress Code Guidelines." *The Huffington Post*, January 22. Available at: http://www.huffingtonpost.com/2010/01/22/sorority -sisters-fashion_n_433491.html (accessed October 19, 2010).

Nguyen, Ivy. 2011. "Woo to Lead New First-Gen, Diversity Effort." *The Stanford Daily*, January 19. Available at: http://www.stanforddaily.com/2011/01/19/woon-to-lead-new-first-gen -diversity-effort/ (accessed February 17, 2011).

Ostrove, Joan M., and Elizabeth R. Cole. 2003. "Privileging Class: Toward a Critical Psychology of Social Class in the Context of Education." *The Journal of Social Issues* 59(4): 677–92.

Packard, Vance. 1962. *The Pyramid Climbers*. New York: Crest.

Phillips, Damon J., and Ezra W. Zuckerman. 2001. "Middle-Status Conformity: Theoretical Restatement and Empirical Demonstration in Two Markets." *The American Journal of Sociology* 107(2): 379–429.

Ridgeway, Cecilia L., and Shelley Correll. 2006. "Consensus and the Creation of Status Beliefs." *Social Forces* 85(1): 431–53.

Ridgeway, Cecilia L., and Kristan G. Erickson. 2000. "Creating and Spreading Status Beliefs." *The American Journal of Sociology* 106(3): 579–615.

Ridgeway, Cecilia L. and Henry Walker. 1995. "Status Structures." In *Sociological Perspectives on Social Psychology*, edited by Karen Cook, Gary Alan Fine, and James S. House. New York: Allyn and Bacon.

Schwalbe, Michael. 2008. *Rigging the Game: How Inequality Is Reproduced in Everyday Life*. Oxford, U.K.: Oxford University Press.

Sennett, Richard, and Jonathan Cobb. 1973. *The Hidden Injuries of Class*. New York: Vintage.

Stephens, Nicole M., Hazel Rose Markus, and Sarah S. M. Townsend. 2007. "Choice as an Act of Meaning: The Case of Social Class." *The Journal of Personality and Social Psychology* 93(5): 814–30.

Strodtbeck, Fred L., Rita M. James, and Charles Hawkins. 1957. "Social Status in Jury Deliberations." *The American Sociological Review* 22(6): 713–19.

Stuber, Jenny M. 2006. "Talk of Class: Discursive Boundaries and Social Reproduction Among Working- and Upper-Middle-Class College Students." *The Journal of Contemporary Ethnography* 35(3): 285–318.

———. 2009. "Class, Culture, and Participation in the Collegiate Extra-Curriculum." *The Sociological Forum* 24(4): 877–900.

Suedfeld, Peter, Stephen Bochner, and Carol Matas. 1971. "Petitioners' Attire and Petition Signing by Peace Demonstrators: A Field Experiment." *The Journal of Applied Social Psychology* 1(3): 278–83.

Twenge, Jean M. 2006. *Generation Me: Why Today's Young Americans Are More Confident, Assertive, Entitled—and More Miserable than Ever Before*. New York: Free Press.

Vanneman, Reeve D. 1980. "U.S. and British Perceptions of Class." *The American Journal of Sociology* 84(4): 769–90.

Vanneman, Reeve, and Lynn Weber Cannon. 1987. *The American Perception of Class*. Philadelphia, Pa.: Temple University Press.

Vanneman, Reeve, and Fred Pampel. 1977. "The American Perception of Class and Status." *The American Sociological Review* 42(3): 432–37.

Webster, Murray, Jr., and Martha Foschi. 1988. "Overview of Status Generalization." In *Status Generalization: New Theory and Research*, edited by Murray Webster and Martha Foschi. Stanford, Calif.: Stanford University Press.

Williams, Joan C. 2010. *Reshaping the Work-Family Debate: Why Men and Class Matter*. Cambridge, Mass.: Harvard University Press.

CHAPTER 8

THE INTERSECTION OF RESOURCES AND RANK: SIGNALING SOCIAL CLASS IN FACE-TO-FACE ENCOUNTERS

Michael W. Kraus, Michelle L. Rheinschmidt, and Paul K. Piff

The psychological study of social class—or socioeconomic status—has traditionally focused on the disadvantaged social environments that surround individuals from lower social-class backgrounds. Inhabiting environments of reduced educational attainment, occupational prestige, and economic wealth, lower-class individuals are at increased risk, relative to their upper-class counterparts, for a number of health and psychological hardships (Adler et al. 1994). More recently, the psychological study of social class has turned to examining how the contrasting environments of lower- and upper-class status give rise to different cultural identities, a critical feature of social class that significantly influences interpersonal behavior (see, for example, Johnson, Richeson, and Finkel 2011; Kraus, Piff, and Keltner 2009, 2011; Snibbe and Markus 2005; Stephens, Markus, and Townsend 2007). In this chapter we build on this cultural identity framework by examining how higher and lower social-class environments shape different subjective perceptions of social class rank vis-à-vis others and, in turn, give rise to rank-relevant patterns of cognition, emotion, and behavior in everyday face-to-face social encounters.

We make three central theoretical claims: First, that social-class identity is rooted in subjective perceptions of one's social-class rank relative to others. Second, that social-class identity activates rank-relevant social cognitive tendencies, specifically greater independence and freedom of self-expression among individuals from higher social-class backgrounds and greater interdependence and perceived environmental constraint among individuals from lower social-class backgrounds. Third, that social-class identity is signaled in face-to-face social encounters through expressions of these rank-related independent versus interdependent behavioral profiles. We draw on evidence from recent laboratory research to bolster each of our theoretical claims and to demonstrate that face-to-face behaviors are a fundamental feature of how social-class identity is experienced and expressed by individuals. We conclude the chapter with a discussion of how the behavioral profiles of individuals from lower social-class backgrounds provide both challenges and opportunities for these individuals to excel in academic institutions and thereby improve their standing in the social hierarchy.

In this chapter, we use the term *upper class* to describe individuals from social environments of relatively elevated income, educational attainment, or occupational prestige. We use the term *lower class* to describe individuals from social environments of relatively lower income, educational attainment, or occupational prestige.

SOCIAL CLASS: RESOURCES AND RANK

Social class is traditionally defined by differences in material environments—such as those shaped by occupational position or material wealth—that fundamentally distinguish the lives of lower- and upper-class individuals. Karl Marx (Marx and Engels 1973) frames the class divide as a distinction between those who control the forces of production (for example, factories and businesses) and those working within those forces. Other theorists ground individual social-class position in one's role in the division of labor in society—a social position based on one's individual talents and skills (Durkheim 1997). More recently, theorists define social-class position in terms of type of employment, individuals in lucrative executive positions and more autonomous jobs occupying the top social-class positions and individuals engaged in unskilled, supervised labor occupying the bottom positions (Coleman and Rainwater 1978; Gilbert 2002; Thompson and Hickey 2005).

These varied definitions of social class underscore a critical point: material resources fundamentally shape people's social environments. Recent psychology research supports this perspective. Material resources impact happiness and well-being. For example, a recent meta-analysis reveals that people living at or near poverty—across cultures—report lower life satisfaction relative to people from higher-income environments (Howell and Howell 2008). Material resources also shape class-based disparities in academic achievement: individuals from lower social-class backgrounds show reduced scores on academic testing owing to a number of factors that reflect the lesser resources these individuals possess (for example, constrained educational opportunities, reduced school choice) relative to their upper-class counterparts (Nisbett 2008). Perhaps the most compelling demonstration of the influence of material resources on class-based outcomes arises from the field of health psychology, which finds increased mortality rates for people from lower-class occupations relative to their upper-class counterparts (Adler et al. 1994). Disparities in material resources significantly shape people's outcomes throughout the life course.

Material resources also shape individuals' perceptions of social-class rank in society. Individuals from higher social-class backgrounds with high levels of annual income, educational attainment, and occupational prestige have increased access to valued material possessions (for example, nutritious foods, home ownership) and elite social institutions (for example, prestigious colleges and universities, social clubs). By contrast, individuals from lower social-class backgrounds, who may be aware of these valued objects and elite institutions—through the media or daily observation of others' possessions—are often unable to obtain these valued symbols of elevated rank in society, owing to their reduced economic wealth and access. Even when individuals from lower-class contexts are able to attend elite social institutions, such as a prestigious university, these institutions seldom provide support for the unique challenges lower-class individuals experience, such as feelings of alienation in a context where students and professors from relatively upper-class families are the majority group (Johnson, Richeson, and Finkel 2011; Ostrove and Long 2007; Stephens, Markus, and Townsend 2007). Material indicators of elevated rank in society saturate social life, are visible when one is engaging in even the most mundane activities (for example, surveying the cars that others drive to work), and can influence daily perceptions of social-class rank—the sense of where one stands in the social-class hierarchy.

Symbols of social-class rank are ubiquitous and readily observable and give rise to subjective perceptions of social-class rank. Among individuals from higher social-class backgrounds, the possession of valued materials—fashionable clothing, expensive housing, prestigious academic degrees—shapes a social-class identity rooted in the sense that one has elevated social rank in society and has the freedom and wherewithal to obtain valued goods and services. For individuals from lower social-class backgrounds, the perception that one does not possess valued material resources but others do possess those resources shapes a social-class identity grounded in the sense that one occupies a lower social rank in society and that one's outcomes and desires are beyond personal control—constrained by external social forces and by other individuals (Kraus, Piff, and Keltner 2009).

Converging areas of research support the claim that subjective perceptions of social-class rank may shape the social lives of lower- and upper-class individuals. Among nonhuman species, social rank is a primary determinant of how individuals perceive and respond to their social environments. Social rank among nonhuman species shapes a number of important social outcomes, such as health (for example, cortisol reactivity; Sapolsky, Alberts, and Altmann 1997), exposure to aggression from others (Belzung and Anderson 1986; Southwick 1967), and the sharing of valued social resources (grooming, reproductive behavior, and so on; Abbott 1984; Watts 2000; Wickings and Dixson 1992). Although the highest-ranking animals in unstable or contentious social hierarchies—hierarchies characterized by intense competition for high-ranking positions—can experience poor health, in more stable social hierarchies, similar to those experienced by upper- and lower-class individuals, reduced rank negatively affects health, social life, and reproductive success in nonhuman species (for a review, see Sapolsky 2004).

Among humans, perceptions of social-class rank also shape how individuals from higher and lower social-class backgrounds think about the social world and relate to other individuals (for a similar line of reasoning, see Crosby 1976; Wilkinson 1999). Guided by the large body of research suggesting that objective indicators of elevated social class (for example, higher income and educational attainment) predict positive health outcomes (for a review, see Adler et al. 1994), researchers recently examined whether subjective perceptions of social-class rank independently impact health. In this research, social-class rank perceptions were assessed using a measure of subjective socioeconomic status developed by Nancy Adler and colleagues (2000). In this measure, participants ranked themselves in society or in their local community in terms of education, income, and occupation status by indicating their position on a ladder with ten rungs representing ascending levels of socioeconomic position. This subjective measure of socioeconomic status, relative to objective indicators of social class, more strongly and independently predicted self-rated health (Adler et al. 2000) and physiological health outcomes, such as body fat distribution (Adler et al. 2000), resting heart rate (Adler et al. 2000), diabetes (Singh-Manoux, Adler, and Marmot 2003), susceptibility to cold-causing viruses (Cohen et al. 2008), and respiratory illness (Singh-Manoux, Adler, and Marmot 2003).

This research suggests that perceptions of social-class rank vis-à-vis others are a crucial component of the social-class identities of upper- and lower-class individuals. In this fashion, social-class identity—shaped by subjective perceptions of social-class rank—is likely to shape patterns of thought and action among individuals in terms of both their current rank perceptions in a given context and their perpetual social-class rank within society as a whole. In the sections that follow, we describe how rank-related social cognitive tendencies shape class-based behavior during face-to-face encounters.

SOCIAL-CLASS IDENTITY: EXTERNAL CONSTRAINT VERSUS SOCIAL INDEPENDENCE

Our conceptual analysis of social-class identity—rooted in subjective perceptions of social-class rank—highlights the ways in which behavior among individuals from higher and lower social-class backgrounds is likely to vary in face-to-face social encounters. For individuals from higher social-class backgrounds, perceiving one's elevated rank in society fosters a sense that one has the freedom to act independently of the needs and wishes of other individuals (see, for example, Keltner et al. 2008; Snibbe and Markus 2005; Stephens, Markus, and Townsend 2007). By contrast, lower-class individuals' perceptions of their subordinate social-class rank relative to others fosters a sense that one's outcomes are largely determined by external social forces—that is, one's own personal motivations and goals are perceived to be controlled by external forces or by other individuals (Lachman and Weaver 1998; Johnson and Krueger 2005, 2006; Kraus, Piff, and Keltner 2009). These class-based differences in perceptions of independence and external constraint are likely to affect behavior across diverse social domains, including how individuals from higher or lower social-class backgrounds perceive and respond to others' emotions, behave in interactions with strangers, and help others in need.

Social Perception

Increased perceptions of external constraint may cause individuals from lower social-class backgrounds to view both social opportunities and obstacles as primarily determined by other individuals and external social forces. Research supports this assertion: for example, participants who reported lower subjective socioeconomic status were more likely than their upper-status counterparts to explain broad political events (for example, economic inequality in society) and social outcomes that individuals experience (for example, being laid off at work) as influenced by other individuals or external social forces (for example, the political influence of other individuals, educational opportunities; Kraus, Piff, and Keltner 2009). Moreover, class-based differences in explanation were accounted for, in part, by lower-class individuals' elevated perceptions that their lives were constrained by the external social environment.

Because lower-class individuals view social outcomes as primarily constrained by external influences and other individuals, the accurate perception of others' internal states, intentions, and emotions is particularly crucial for lower-class individuals. As a result, we would expect lower-class individuals to be more accurate in their perceptions of the intentions and emotions of others relative to their more independent upper-class counterparts.

Research on a rank-relevant construct related to social class—social power—provides indirect evidence in support of this prediction. Power is defined as a person's capacity to influence the rewards and punishments of other individuals (Fiske 1993; Keltner, Gruenfeld, and Anderson 2003). The control and freedom that high-power individuals experience relative to low-power individuals tend to focus these individuals on their own interests and goals rather than on the social context and the individuals within it (for example, Fiske 1993, 2010; Guinote 2007a, 2007b). One consequence of this inattention to others is that high-power individuals become less likely to accurately perceive the emotions that others experience. For example, individuals primed with power made more errors on a test of the ability to recognize emotions in pictures of others (Galinsky et al. 2006). As a second example, in a social interaction, high-power individuals perceived the emotions of low-power partners with less accuracy than did low-power individuals judging the emotions of their high-power partners (Gonzaga, Keltner, and Ward 2008).

Social class influences empathic accuracy in a similar fashion. Michael Kraus, Stéphane Côté, and Dacher Keltner (2010) brought two pairs of strangers into a job interview, where they were interviewed for a lab manager position by an experimenter. The researchers found that in this job interview, participants from higher social-class backgrounds were less able than lower-class participants to estimate the emotions of their partners. In a second study, the researchers examined how a manipulation of temporary perceptions of social-class rank might also influence emotion perception. This manipulation was used to disentangle social-class influences on emotion perception from confounding third variables (for example, ethnicity, neighborhood effects) that covary with social class and to determine whether rank perceptions, in part, account for class-based patterns of emotion perception.

Participants were instructed to imagine an interaction with a person at the very top or bottom of the social-class hierarchy. The researchers expected that participants who imagined interacting with a person at the very top of the social-class hierarchy would be primed to think about their subordinate rank relative to this upper-ranking interaction partner and, as a result, would be better able to perceive emotion. They expected participants imagining interacting with a person at the bottom of the social-class hierarchy to think about their elevated social-class rank and, in turn, to read emotions less accurately. Similar methods have been used in previous research to manipulate cultural patterns of independence and interdependence to assess the causal influences of these culture-specific cognitive patterns on behavior (Oyserman and Lee 2008). Consistent with predictions, upper-class participants who imagined interacting with a lower-class individual felt higher in social-class rank and also tended to perform worse on a standard test of emotion recognition, the Mind in the Eyes Task (Baron-Cohen et al. 2006), in which participants were asked to identify emotions displayed in subtle micro-expressions of the eyes. That these effects occurred using a measure of social class in society as a whole—educational attainment—and in terms of participants' current perceptions of their rank in an anticipated interaction is also noteworthy: the momentary activation of class-specific rank influences emotion perception in ways that are consistent with emotion perception patterns based on one's perpetual or chronic social-class rank in society more generally.

Experience of Emotion

In addition to influencing the ability to infer others' emotions, social-class differences in independence and constraint may impact how individuals from higher and lower social-class backgrounds experience emotions during interactions. Owing to their increased independence from other individuals, the emotions of upper-class individuals may be relatively unaffected by the emotion experiences of individuals around them. However, individuals from lower social-class backgrounds, owing to their elevated perceptions of external influences on their outcomes, are likely to be highly attuned to other individuals' emotions and, as a result, to shift their emotions in line with the emotion experiences of others.

Research on social power supports this prediction: In a longitudinal study of roommates' emotional experience over the course of several months, participants reporting a lower sense of power experienced a change in emotions over time, such that their emotions became more similar to the emotions experienced by their higher-power roommate—that is, low-power roommates' emotions converged with those of their high-power roommates over several months. By contrast, the high-power roommates' emotions remained unchanged over the same time period (Anderson, Keltner, and John 2003).

A similar pattern of emotion convergence may occur among interaction partners from higher or lower social-class backgrounds. In research by Kraus and colleagues (2011), female friendship pairs of university students—differing in family income and education—participated in a social interaction in which they were instructed to tease each other. Teasing is a potentially hostile form of interaction in which the teaser typically comments on a negative aspect of another person by using playful language and gestures (Keltner et al. 1998). In this research, differences in social class between friends predicted which partner would adapt her hostile emotions (for example, anger, contempt) to mirror those of her friend. Whereas the upper-class friend reported stable levels of hostile emotion throughout the interaction, the lower-class friend shifted her hostile emotions during the interaction to become more similar to the hostile emotions of the upper-class friend, indicating emotion convergence. Moreover, that these patterns occurred when researchers examined social-class rank within a friendship is noteworthy and is consistent with previous research showing associations between measures of chronic or perpetual lower social-class rank and increased self-reports of cynical mistrust and hostility (Gallo and Matthews 2003). Given that lower-class environments are perpetually more uncertain and hostile relative to middle-class environments, perhaps these patterns reflect, in part, the greater chronic emotion reactivity of lower-class individuals.

Physiological responses also reflect similar patterns of reactivity among individuals from lower social-class backgrounds. For instance, Elizabeth Page-Gould, Katrina Koslov, and Wendy Mendes (2011) recruited a sample of adults from the Boston area and had these strangers engage in a social interaction where they were asked to play a board game (for example, Taboo) while their physiological responses were measured with an electrocardiogram and impedance cardiography. During the interaction, participants from lower social-class backgrounds showed physiological responses that paralleled those experienced by their interaction partner. More specifically, lower social-class participants' pre-ejection period—a measure of cardiac contractility that indexes sympathetic nervous system activation—was significantly associated with the pre-ejection period of their partner from one minute earlier in the interaction. That is, lower social-class participants' physiological responses were changing to become more similar to the earlier physiological responses of their partner. No such physiological attunement was observed among upper social-class participants (Page-Gould, Koslov, and Mendes 2011).

Social Independence
Versus Interdependence

Social-class identity also predicts class-based differences in the extent to which individuals rely on others in their social environments, leading to face-to-face differences in behaviors reflecting relational independence versus interdependence. Disposed to feel elevated social-class rank, individuals from higher social-class backgrounds tend to perceive that they have both the resources and social influence to "go it alone"—in effect, feeling capable of achieving desired outcomes through their own control and influence (Kraus, Piff, and Keltner 2009; Keltner et al. 2008; Snibbe and Markus 2005; Stephens et al. 2007). By contrast, individuals from lower social-class backgrounds—prone to experience external constraints on their behavior—perceive that their social outcomes are disproportionately determined by external social forces (Kluegel and Smith 1986; Kraus, Piff, and Keltner 2009). To adapt to these external constraints on their life outcomes, lower-class individuals are motivated to behave in ways that enhance social connection and interdependence with others (for similar reasoning on how elevated social threat engenders relational interdependence, see Bowlby 1979; Pickett and Gardner 2005; Taylor 2006).

Empirical evidence suggests that upper- and lower-class individuals display divergent patterns of social independence during face-to-face interactions (for example, Rusbult et al. 1991; Stephens, Markus, and Townsend 2007; Stephens et al. 2009). For instance, upper-class individuals show elevated patterns of social independence and freedom of self-expression in their behavior. Evidencing this relative freedom of expression among upper-class individuals, a study of Icelandic children found that children of upper-class families described themselves by expressing more of their own unique thoughts and feelings compared with children from lower-class families (Hart and Edelstein 1992). In addition, parents in upper-class families tend to place a greater emphasis on children's individual wants and desires (Kusserow 2004; Lareau 2003) than do parents in lower-class families, reflecting differences in parents' encouragement of social independence.

In contrast to the relational independence exhibited by individuals from higher social-class backgrounds, lower-class individuals are more interdependent—that is, more socially engaged and attentive to others during face-to-face interactions (Kraus and Keltner 2009). Demonstrating these behavioral patterns of engagement, studies of grade-school children found that children from lower-class backgrounds were more likely than their upper-class counterparts to play in close proximity with other children (Scherer 1974) and to smile to elicit their classmates' and teachers' attention (Stipek and Ryan 1997).

Individuals from lower social-class backgrounds also exhibit behaviors that reflect increased engagement and interest in others, even when interacting with complete strangers. In a study of university students whose families were from upper- or lower-class backgrounds, participants came to the laboratory in pairs and were instructed to engage in a brief get-acquainted interaction with their experiment partner. In the first sixty seconds of the interaction, lower-class individuals showed more behaviors that reflect social engagement (for example, head nods, eyebrow raises, laughs) and fewer behaviors showing disinterest or disengagement (for example, checking a cell phone, self-grooming, drawing during the interaction) than did their upper-class counterparts (Kraus and Keltner 2009).

Prosocial Behavior

Differences in interdependence also shape prosocial motivations to be helpful and generous. For example, in a study examining cultural variation in generosity, Joseph Henrich and colleagues (2001) gave participants from fifteen different cultures a specific good (for example, money) and allowed them to share the good at their discretion. Individuals from more interdependent cultures—where resources are scarce and large-scale cooperation is common—were more likely to share the goods with an anonymous stranger (for similar claims about the association between helping and interdependence, see Oyserman and Lee 2008; Wong and Hong 2005). Research also suggests that the increased social interdependence of lower-class individuals engenders greater helping behavior among these individuals relative to their upper-class counterparts. For example, a large-scale survey of charitable donations found that people with lower incomes gave a higher percentage of their salaries to charity than did those with higher incomes (Toppe, Kirsch, and Michel 2001).

Differences in independence between individuals from higher and lower social-class backgrounds are also likely to engender divergent patterns of helping and generosity in face-to-face encounters. Research examining prosocial behavior in laboratory interactions (for example, helping behavior, generosity) has yielded results consistent with this prediction. In one study, Paul Piff and colleagues (2010) engaged participants in a dictator game in which they were asked to divide ten points (which would later be converted into actual money) between themselves and an unidentified other person. The researchers found that lower-class individuals—assessed in terms of subjective socioeconomic status rank perceptions—were more generous than their upper-class counterparts.

Another study assessed beliefs about how much people should give to charity each year. Here, participants were randomly assigned to imagine an interaction with a person at the top of or at the bottom of the social-class hierarchy. Participants imagining an interaction with a person at the top of the social-class hierarchy experienced subordinate social-class rank and reported that people should donate an average of 4.7 percent of their annual salary to charity. By contrast, participants imagining an interaction with a person at the bottom of the social-class hierarchy experienced elevated rank and reported that people should donate only an average of 3.0 percent of their salary to charity. This latter result experimentally demonstrates that temporarily manipulating social-class rank can lead to differences in interdependence and helping behavior among lower- and upper-class individuals in ways that are consistent with chronic or perpetual measures of social class. Moreover, this manipulation of temporary perceptions of rank allows researchers to pinpoint rank as a fundamental mechanism in influencing class-based psychological tendencies.

Thus far, we have detailed how social-class identity is shaped by subjective perceptions of social-class rank in society and how these perceptions of rank engender class-based differences in perceptions of external constraint and independence that shape behavior in face-to-face interactions. In the following section, we discuss how perceptions of external constraint and independence, which arise from social-class identity, underlie social behaviors and preferences that signal social class in face-to-face encounters.

SIGNS OF SOCIAL CLASS

Although perhaps not as easily discernable as other social categories (for example, gender, ethnicity), rank can be signaled in social hierarchies through a number of cultural practices and behaviors (Bourdieu 1985; Bernstein 1971; Tiedens and Fragale 2003; Veblen 1994; Zahavi and Zahavi 1998). For example, nonhuman species have been known to signal their enhanced reproductive or physical capabilities by engaging in costly metabolic actions (for example, growing a brightly colored peacock tail to attract a potential mate, jumping high in the air to discourage predators from giving chase; Zahavi and Zahavi 1998).

Recent empirical evidence suggests that human behavioral patterns reflecting class-based differences in independence may signal social-class identity during even the briefest face-to-face encounters. In the aforementioned get-acquainted interaction study, Kraus and Keltner (2009) had a separate sample of participants watch videotapes of these interactions between strangers and then attempt to estimate the social class of the participants based solely on what they observed in the videos. Interestingly, the judges were remarkably accurate in discerning the social class of participants, even after accounting for participant gender and ethnicity. What led to these accurate judgments of social class? Evidence suggests that the behaviors reflecting class-based differences in independence led judges to their inferences of social class. That is, judges perceived participants as higher in social class if they displayed more disengaged behaviors (for example, checking a cell phone) and lower in social class if they displayed more engaged behaviors (for example, head nods, laughs). Although other signals could have contributed to the accurate perception of social class during these interactions (for example, use of language, clothing), these initial results provide some of the first evidence suggesting that brief and nonverbal behaviors may also signal social class.

Converging with the findings from this study that social class is signaled in face-to-face encounters, several theoretical accounts suggest that other class-based behavioral patterns—arising from differences in rank-related perceptions of external constraint and independence—are likely to signal social class in interactions. The sociologist Thorstein Veblen (1994) argues that people signal their elevated social class by engaging in conspicuous leisure activities. That is, actively pursuing leisure activities signals to others that a person is free from the external constraints of a lower-class manual labor job and is able to use his or her time for leisure or intellectual pursuits. Applied to current social life, upper-class individuals might signal their elevated status by behaving in ways that give off an air of casualness or comfort with their environment, of being "at ease" with themselves (Kuriloff and Reichert 2003). These behaviors may demonstrate an uninhibited, self-reliant quality that is characteristic of upper-class standing and, in turn, may signal this status to others.

Individuals can also signal their upper-class rank through pursuits that reflect intellectual and artistic independence from others. Pierre Bourdieu (1985) suggests that people signal their upper-class status through displaying manners, tastes, and preferences that reflect social distinction and sophistication. According to Bourdieu, individuals from upper-class backgrounds display their elevated social-class rank by demonstrating their knowledge of, for example, social manners, sophisticated ways of speaking, and fine art and music that demonstrate to others one's privileged status in society.

More recently, Alana Snibbe and Hazel Markus (2005) extended this theorizing by showing that different preferences in music between upper- and lower-class individuals reflect differences in rank-related social independence. In their research, European Americans from working-class backgrounds (for example, high school educated) favored country music whose themes reflected external constraints and struggles with the external environment. Middle-class European Americans (for example, college educated), in contrast, favored rock music, ostensibly because its themes reflected concerns for independence, personal choice, and individual freedom.

We have provided some initial examples of the various ways in which social class is signaled in face-to-face encounters. Several other channels of communication may provide additional cues about social-class position that are based on rank-relevant perceptions of external constraint and independence. For instance, the voice may be a channel through which people signal their social-class position. Underscoring this possibility, the sociologist Basil Bernstein (1971) argues that people of differing class backgrounds have unique language codes they use to communicate. Perhaps these codes include patterns of speech that reflect the relational independence versus interdependence emphasized in different social-class contexts. Clearly, future research examining the various ways in which social class is signaled is warranted.

It is also important to consider how these signals of social-class rank can reinforce one's social-class identity. More specifically, to what extent do social-class signals lead others to make reliable inferences of one's social class, and how do these signals reinforce a person's own perceptions of his or her social-class rank? (For similar claims about how social characteristics reinforce social category identification, see Ridgeway 1991; Turner and Reynolds 2010.)

SOCIAL CLASS AND THE REINFORCEMENT OF SOCIAL INEQUALITY

An understanding of social-class signals is especially important because these cues may guide the expectations and behaviors of individuals within social interactions. More generally, expectations (for the self and imposed by others) of how individuals from different social classes should think and behave may constrain actual cognitive and behavioral responses. In this section, we argue that the behavioral and perceptual patterns that arise from the social-class identities of upper- and lower-class individuals have the capacity to reinforce face-to-face inequality and strengthen status differences between individuals. We first discuss how class-related behaviors and perceptions may serve to reinforce inequality through legitimizing beliefs about social-class hierarchy. We then turn to a discussion of behavioral patterns that develop among individuals from higher and lower social-class backgrounds that could hinder academic performance and, in turn, constrain the social mobility of lower-class individuals. Finally, we outline some ways in which class-based behavioral patterns may improve the social positions of individuals from lower-class backgrounds.

Our conceptual analysis and empirical review argues that social-class position is associated with specific cultural practices, behavioral patterns, and cognitive tendencies. These class-based differences inform inferences of others' social class based on brief interactions and accentuate class disparities between people in face-to-face encounters. Given the ease and regularity with which social class is perceived in interactions, social-class signals could serve to legitimize inequality in society between those from upper- and lower-class backgrounds.

Social-class inequality may come to be viewed as legitimate when signals of social class are thought to represent essentialist or innate qualities of upper- and lower-class individuals. Essentialist lay theories suggest that differences between social groups are inherent, stable, and unchangeable (Allport 1954; Haslam, Rothschild, and Ernst 2000; Keller 2005; Yzerbyt, Rocher, and Schadron 1997). An endorsement of essentialist theories means that one believes that individuals belong to the same social category because they share a specific feature in common, that category membership is unchangeable and provides accurate information about the individual (Keller 2005; Yzerbyt, Rocher, and Schadron 1997), and that members of the same category share similar biological characteristics (for example, physiological responses, genetically based traits; Keller 2005; Williams and Eberhardt 2008).

Several studies suggest that essentialist beliefs have hierarchy-justifying functions. For example, individuals who endorsed biological essentialism—the belief that social categories are determined primarily by genetic factors—were more likely to show prejudice and discrimination toward out-groups (Keller 2005) or low-status minority groups (for example, gays and lesbians; Haslam, Rothschild, and Ernst 2002). Similarly, people exposed to essentialist beliefs about racial categories tended to more readily excuse racial inequality in society (Williams and Eberhardt 2008). Research also suggests that essentialist beliefs are particularly instrumental in justifying elevated social rank in society. In one study, men who endorsed essentialist beliefs and learned as part of the experiment that gender inequality was decreasing reported more sexist attitudes, presumably as a means to maintain their elevated positions in an unstable gender hierarchy (Morton et al. 2009). Essentialist theories—by rendering group differences as stable, unchangeable, and even biological—can serve to justify status differences and inequality in society.

The ease with which social class is signaled and perceived through behavior accentuates group differences between individuals from upper- and lower-class contexts. These group differences are likely to promote essentialist lay theories of social class—views that differences between upper- and lower-class individuals reflect internal and biological characteristics rather than differences in external environmental circumstances. This may be especially true for upper-class individuals, whose elevated status in face-to-face encounters and emphasis on dispositional traits and characteristics can render essentialist theories of social-class particularly attractive.

Research in support of this assertion is limited but suggestive. For example, survey research in India found that upper-caste Indians endorsed statements suggesting that their caste membership was fixed at birth, reflecting an essentialist conception of social-class identity. By contrast, lower-caste Indians were more likely to endorse statements suggesting that their caste membership was a socially acquired identity (Mahalingam 1998). Similarly, research involving a hypothetical scenario in which participants imagined the brain of a lower-caste person placed in the head of an upper-caste person and vice versa found that lower-caste Indians felt that physical appearance was the sole determining factor of caste status (Mahalingam 2003). These findings argue that lower-caste Indians believed that social perceptions of external appearance—not internal biology—determine caste status (Mahalingam 2003). Evidence from the United States further suggests that individuals from higher social-class backgrounds are likely to endorse essentialist lay theories. For example, researchers have found that people with elevated income are more likely than lower-income participants to attribute disparities in wealth to internal, stable factors (for example, ability and talent; Kluegel and Smith 1986; Kraus, Piff, and Keltner 2009). Upper-class individuals' endorsement of stable and internal explanations of inequality is consistent with an essentialist outlook on social class.

Class differences in perception may also inadvertently promote legitimizing beliefs about the structure of society, which may decrease social mobility among lower-class individuals. People typically favor their own social group over other social groups (Allport 1954; Pettigrew and Tropp 2006; Tajfel and Turner 1986). However, given that individuals from lower social-class backgrounds perceive greater external constraints on their social outcomes relative to those from higher social-class backgrounds (Kraus, Piff, and Keltner 2009; Lachman and Weaver 1998), lower-class individuals may be less motivated to engage in social or political actions that favor their group over dominant groups in society. In essence, external constraints may create situations in which lower-class individuals see favoring other groups (for example, upper-class groups) as one means of obtaining desired social outcomes. This relative lack of favoritism for the lower-class in-group may be most likely among individuals from lower social-class backgrounds who perceive relations with upper-class individuals as harmonious or legitimate (for example, Saguy et al. 2009).

Evidence of system-justifying beliefs among lower-class individuals supports this assertion (Jost and Banaji 1994). For instance, in a sample of students from universities differing in prestige, students from the lower-prestige institution showed favoritism toward the students from the more prestigious university, whereas the higher-prestige students showed typical in-group favoritism (Jost, Pelham, and Carvallo 2002). In addition to explicit dominant-group favoritism, evidence suggests that lower-class individuals are also more likely to engage in political judgments and activities that favor the prevailing social hierarchy. For instance, in a national survey, lower-class individuals were more likely than their upper-class counterparts to support legislation limiting government criticism, more inclined to say that pay disparities foster motivation and effort, and more likely to view economic inequality as legitimate (Jost et al. 2003). These findings indicate that individuals from lower social-class backgrounds, despite their subordinate rank in society, may actually endorse beliefs that serve to legitimize inequality, constrain social mobility, and reinforce the status quo.

SOCIAL CLASS AND THE REINFORCEMENT OF EDUCATIONAL INEQUALITY

Beyond shaping beliefs about social mobility, the salience and perceived legitimacy of external constraints may also guide individuals' educational pursuits. Individuals from lower social-class backgrounds perceive greater external constraints on action and, as a result, may be less likely to attend to their own personal goals, wishes, and motivations (Guinote and Vescio 2010; Keltner, Gruenfeld, and Anderson 2003) and more likely to attend, instead, to their social connections and relations to others. This perceptual pattern may prove problematic in goal pursuit, particularly in academic contexts, where personal goals for academic success may be less salient for lower-class individuals than for individuals from higher social-class backgrounds.

Research on social power suggests that goal-setting behavior may underlie social-class differences in academic performance. This work indicates that low levels of power inhibit strategic problem solving and goal pursuit. For instance, individuals primed with relatively lower power showed delays in deciding on a plan of action and initiating goal-directed behavior (Guinote 2007b). During a role-playing exercise, individuals who felt relatively more powerful were more likely to use diversified approaches to solve a difficult problem, quicker to identify ineffective problem-solving approaches, and more likely to persist in finding a solution (Guinote 2007b). High-power individuals also seize opportunities to pursue their own goals more readily than lower-power individuals. In one study, individuals experimentally induced to feel less powerful showed deficits in their ability to selectively attend to information compared with those induced to feel more powerful (Guinote 2007a).

This body of research on the influence of social power on goal pursuit suggests that students from lower social-class backgrounds may be particularly susceptible to negative academic outcomes in university contexts when confronted with students from more privileged, upper-class backgrounds. That is, students from lower social-class backgrounds may perceive disparities in rank between themselves and other students whose families have long histories of university attendance. A low or devalued social position in relation to one's peers—perceived by individuals from lower social-class backgrounds—could chronically inhibit goal-directed academic behavior, academic persistence, willingness to seize educational opportunities, and attentional focus.

Lower-class students may also be particularly vulnerable to the cognitive and behavioral patterns characteristic of learned helplessness. Specifically, lower-class students may develop patterns of thought and behavior—arising from perceived external constraints on action—that hinder academic functioning (Shell and Husman 2008). Research on learned helplessness in academic settings suggests that children who perceive lower correspondence between their effort and outcomes, and who assume less personal responsibility for their performance, show significant achievement deficits (Dweck and Reppucci 1973). Recall that subjectively lower-class individuals were more likely than their upper-class counterparts to endorse contextual or external explanations for various outcomes, including educational opportunities (Kraus, Piff, and Keltner 2009). These findings suggest that lower-class students may perceive less personal control over their educational outcomes and less correspondence between their individual academic efforts and potential personal rewards (for example, upward mobility).

Barriers to academic achievement may also be more significant to individuals from lower social-class backgrounds. These students are likely to be more familiar with external obstacles to obtaining a college education (for example, tuition cost) relative to upper-class students, and the salience of these barriers could diminish educational attainment. Experimental research highlights the dangers of salient external obstacles to educational achievement for lower-class individuals. In one study, students who were encouraged to view their path to college as "open" and feasible (that is, possible with financial aid) planned to spend more time on their schoolwork and received better grades—because they perceived a direct connection between their current efforts and future outcomes—than students primed with a "closed" and less feasible (that is, expensive) view of college (Destin and Oyserman 2009). These results indicate that students who perceive fewer barriers to achievement may be more motivated to engage in goal-directed behaviors—such as studying or adhering to deadlines—that are critical to success in educational settings.

Elite university settings are contexts primarily shaped and inhabited by upper-class individuals (Johnson, Richeson, and Finkel 2011; Stephens, Markus, and Townsend 2007). The lower-ranking social identities of individuals from lower social-class backgrounds may be particularly salient in these contexts, and identity-based concerns may create an additional barrier to academic achievement. For instance, undergraduates who were more sensitive to rejection based on their ethnicity showed more difficulty in adjusting to college, fewer feelings of belonging at the institution, and greater grade decline over time (Mendoza-Denton et al. 2002). As with other types of status-based rejection concerns (for example, race, gender), worries about rejection based on social-class membership may significantly interfere with social and academic functioning. In support of this assertion, Sarah Johnson, Jennifer Richeson, and Eli Finkel (2011) found that undergraduates' concerns about academic competency at an elite university were associated with greater perceptions of having a low (that is, stigmatized) socioeconomic background relative to peers. Furthermore, they demonstrated that managing academic concerns requires greater effort for students from lower social-class backgrounds, as they experienced more self-regulatory depletion, measured in terms of candy consumption and poor performance on an attention task, than upper-class students while speaking about academic achievement but not nonacademic domains. As well, research shows that worries about confirming negative stereotypes of academic performance—concerns that are prevalent among individuals from lower-class backgrounds in elite university contexts—lead to poorer performance among these students relative to their upper-class counterparts (Croizet and Claire 1998).

COMBATING INEQUALITY BY BRIDGING THE SOCIAL-CLASS DIVIDE

Although individuals from lower social-class backgrounds face numerous barriers to social mobility, even once admitted to colleges and universities, there are several ways in which institutions can help them flourish in such settings. For instance, if higher education were made more financially accessible to students from lower-class backgrounds—as several national universities have recently aimed to do (Espenshade and Radford 2009)—the stigma of social class might be reduced. However, once a student has matriculated, issues of access still confront lower-class students (for example, affordability of class textbooks, social activities, foods). Such issues are likely to present unique financial challenges to lower-class students and contribute to feelings of alienation. Educational institutions that aim to break down these access barriers, as well as barriers to admission, will best serve their students from lower social-class backgrounds.

The ways in which students are tested in academic settings must also be scrutinized if institutions hope to improve the academic performance of students from lower social-class backgrounds. Though individuals from lower social-class backgrounds show worse performance on a number of different intelligence and academic tests (Nisbett 2008; Hackman and Farah 2009), these assessments were designed by individuals from higher social-class backgrounds and do not necessarily assess the unique skills that develop from lower-class contexts. The greater prosociality and empathic accuracy that lower-class individuals display in social interactions with others may have many potential social and academic benefits when harnessed appropriately. For instance, research on empathic accuracy in occupational settings suggests that the ability to read others' emotions accurately can improve job satisfaction and performance (Côté and Miners 2006) and leads to more mutually beneficial outcomes during negotiations (Elfenbein et al. 2007). Further research is necessary to better understand the ways in which these behavioral profiles can translate to elevated performance in classroom contexts. It is possible that group work—which typically benefits from empathic accuracy and mutual cooperation—may more accurately capture the academic performance of lower-class individuals.

CONCLUSION

Social class is intertwined with the very fabric of everyday life. In this chapter, we have argued that social-class identity is fundamentally shaped by subjective perceptions of rank vis-à-vis others. Specifically, we have outlined how rank perceptions guide the behaviors of upper- and lower-class individuals and provide the basis for the ways in which social class is signaled in face-to-face interactions. An understanding of these behavioral profiles provides insight into the unique challenges that individuals from lower social-class backgrounds experience in academic contexts and the ways in which educational institutions can be more sensitive to the cultural contexts and identities of all students.

REFERENCES

Abbott, David H. 1984. "Behavioral and Physiological Suppression of Fertility in Subordinate Marmoset Monkeys." *The American Journal of Primatology* 6(3): 169–86.

Adler, Nancy E., Thomas Boyce, Margaret A. Chesney, Sheldon Cohen, Susan Folkman, Robert L. Kahn, and S. Leonard Syme. 1994. "Socioeconomic Status and Health: The Challenge of the Gradient." *The American Psychologist* 49(1): 15–24.

Adler, Nancy E., Elissa S. Epel, Grace Castellazzo, and Jeannette R. Ickovics. 2000. "Relationship of Subjective and Objective Social Status with Psychological and Physiological Functioning: Preliminary Data in Healthy, White Women." *Health Psychology* 19(6): 586–92.

Allport, Gordon W. 1954. *The Nature of Prejudice*. Oxford, U.K.: Addison-Wesley.

Anderson, Cameron, Dacher Keltner, and Oliver P. John. 2003. "Emotional Convergence Between People over Time." *The Journal of Personality and Social Psychology* 84(5): 1054–68.

Baron-Cohen, Simon, Howard Ring, Xavier Chitnis, Sally Wheelwright, Lloyd Gregory, Steve Williams, Mick L. Brammer, and Ed Bullmore. 2006. "fMRI of Parents of Children with Asperger Syndrome: A Pilot Study." *The Brain and Cognition* 61(1): 122–30.

Belzung, Catherine, and James R. Anderson. 1986. "Social Rank and Responses to Feeding Competition in Rhesus Monkeys." *Behavioural Processes* 12(4): 307–16.

Bernstein, Basil. 1971. *Class, Codes, and Control*. Vol. 1. London: Routledge and Kegan Paul.

Bourdieu, Pierre. 1985. "The Forms of Capital." In *Handbook of Theory and Research for the Sociology of Education*, edited by John G. Richardson. New York: Greenwood.

Bowlby, John. 1979. *The Making and Breaking of Affectional Bonds*. London: Tavistock.

Cohen, Sheldon, Cuneyt M. Alper, William J. Doyle, Nancy Adler, John J. Treanor, and Ronald B. Turner. 2008. "Objective and Subjective Socioeconomic Status and Susceptibility to the Common Cold." *Health Psychology* 27(2): 268–74.

Coleman, Richard P., and Lee Rainwater. 1978. *Social Standing in America*. New York: Basic Books.

Côté, Stéphane, and Christopher T. H. Miners. 2006. "Emotional Intelligence and Job Performance." *The Administrative Science Quarterly* 51(1): 1–28.

Croizet, Jean-Claude, and Theresa Claire. 1998. "Extending the Concept of Stereotype Threat to Social Class: The Intellectual Underperformance of Students from Lower Socioeconomic Backgrounds." *The Personality and Social Psychology Bulletin* 24(6): 588–94.

Crosby, Faye J. 1976. "A Model of Egoistic Relative Deprivation." *The Psychological Review* 83(2): 85–113.

Destin, Mesmin, and Daphna Oyserman. 2009. "From Assets to School Outcomes: How Finances Shape Children's Perceived Possibilities and Intentions." *Psychological Science* 20(4): 414–18.

Durkheim, Emile. 1997. *The Division of Labour in Society*. New York: Free Press. First published in 1802.

Dweck, Carol S., and N. Dickon Reppucci. 1973. "Learned Helplessness and Reinforcement Responsibility in Children." *The Journal of Personality and Social Psychology* 25(1): 109–16.

Elfenbein, Hillary Anger, Maw Der Foo, Judith B. White, Hwee Hoon Tan, and Voon Chuan Aik. 2007. "Reading Your Counterpart: The Benefit of Emotion Recognition Accuracy for Effectiveness in Negotiation." *The Journal of Nonverbal Behavior* 31(4): 205–23.

Espenshade, Thomas J., and Alexandria Walton Radford. 2009. *No Longer Separate, Not Yet Equal: Race and Class in Elite College Admission and Campus Life*. Princeton, N.J.: Princeton University Press.

Fiske, Susan T. 1993. "Controlling Other People: The Impact of Power on Stereotyping." *The American Psychologist* 48(6): 621–28.

———. 2010. "Interpersonal Stratification: Status, Power, and Subordination." In *Handbook of Social Psychology*, 5th ed., edited by Susan T. Fiske, Daniel T. Gilbert, and Gardner Lindzey. New York: Wiley.

Galinsky, Adam D., Joe C. Magee, M. Ena Inesi, and Deborah H. Gruenfeld. 2006. "Power and Perspectives Not Taken." *Psychological Science* 17(12): 1068–74.

Gallo, Linda C., and Karen A. Matthews. 2003. "Understanding the Association Between Socioeconomic Status and Physical Health: Do Negative Emotions Play a Role?" *The Psychological Bulletin* 129(1): 10–51.

Gilbert, Dennis. 2002. *The American Class Structure in an Age of Growing Inequality*. 6th ed. Belmont, Calif.: Wadsworth.

Gonzaga, Gian C., Dacher Keltner, and Daniel Ward. 2008. "Power in Mixed-Sex Stranger Interactions." *Cognition and Emotion* 22(8): 1555–68.

Guinote, Ana. 2007a. "Power Affects Basic Cognition: Increased Attentional Inhibition and Flexibility." *The Journal of Experimental Social Psychology* 43(5): 685–97.

———. 2007b. "Power and Goal Pursuit." *The Personality and Social Psychology Bulletin* 33(8): 1076–87.

Guinote, Ana, and Teresa K. Vescio. 2010. *The Social Psychology of Power*. New York: Guilford.

Hackman, Daniel A., and Martha J. Farah. 2009. "Socioeconomic Status and Brain Development." *Trends in Cognitive Sciences* 13(2): 65–73.

Hart, Daniel, and Wolfgang Edelstein. 1992. "The Relationship of Self-Understanding in Childhood to Social Class, Community Type, and Teacher-Rated Intellectual and Social Competence." *The Journal of Cross-Cultural Psychology* 23(3): 353–65.

Haslam, Nick, Louis Rothschild, and Donald Ernst. 2000. "Essentialist Beliefs About Social Categories." *The British Journal of Social Psychology* 39(12): 127–39.

———. 2002. "Are Essentialist Beliefs Associated with Prejudice?" *The British Journal of Social Psychology* 41(1): 87–100.

Henrich, Joseph, Robert Boyd, Samuel Bowles, Colin Camerer, Ernst Fehr, Herbert Gintis, and Richard McElreath. 2001. "In Search of Homo Economicus: Behavioral Experiments in 15 Small-Scale Societies." *The American Economic Review* 91(2): 73–78.

Howell, Ryan T., and Colleen J. Howell. 2008. "The Relation of Economic Status to Subjective Well-Being in Developing Countries: A Meta-Analysis." *The Psychological Bulletin* 134(4): 536–60.

Johnson, Sarah E., Jennifer A. Richeson, and Eli J. Finkel. 2011. "Middle Class and Marginal? The Influence of Socioeconomic Status on the Self-Regulatory Resources of Students at an Elite University." *The Journal of Personality and Social Psychology* 100(5): 838–52.

Johnson, Wendy, and Robert F. Krueger. 2005. "Higher Perceived Life Control Decreases Genetic Variance in Physical Health: Evidence from a National Twin Study." *The Journal of Personality and Social Psychology* 88(1): 165–73.

———. 2006. "How Money Buys Happiness: Genetic and Environmental Processes Linking Finances and Life Satisfaction." *The Journal of Personality and Social Psychology* 90(4): 680–91.

Jost, John T., and Mazarin R. Banaji. 1994. "The Role of Stereotyping in System-Justification and the Production of False Consciousness." In "Stereotypes: Structure, Function, and Process." Special issue, *The British Journal of Social Psychology* 33: 1–27.

Jost, John T., Brett W. Pelham, and Mauricio R. Carvallo. 2002. "Non-Conscious Forms of System Justification: Implicit and Behavioral Preferences for Higher Status Groups." *The Journal of Experimental Social Psychology* 38(6): 586–602.

Jost, John T., Brett W. Pelham, Oliver Sheldon, and Bilian Ni Sullivan. 2003. "Social Inequality and the Reduction of Ideological Dissonance on Behalf of the System: Evidence of Enhanced System Justification Among the Disadvantaged." *The European Journal of Social Psychology* 33(1): 13–36.

Keller, Johannes. 2005. "In Genes We Trust: The Biological Component of Psychological Essentialism and Its Relationship to Mechanisms of Motivated Social Cognition." *The Journal of Personality and Social Psychology* 88(4): 686–702.

Keltner, Dacher, Deborah H. Gruenfeld, and Cameron Anderson. 2003. "Power, Approach, and Inhibition." *The Psychological Review* 110(2): 265–84.

Keltner, Dacher, Gerben A. Van Kleef, Serena Chen, and Michael W. Kraus. 2008. "A Reciprocal Influence Model of Social Power: Emerging Principles and Lines of Inquiry." In *Advances in Experimental Social Psychology,* vol. 40, edited by Mark P. Zanna. New York: Academic Press.

Keltner, Dacher, Randall C. Young, Erin A. Heerey, Carmen Oemig, and Natalie D. Monarch. 1998. "Teasing in Hierarchical and Intimate Relations." *The Journal of Personality and Social Psychology* 75(5): 1231–47.

Kluegel, James R., and Elliot R. Smith. 1986. *Beliefs About Inequality: Americans' Views of What Is and What Ought to Be.* Hawthorne, N.Y.: Aldine De Gruyter.

Kraus, Michael W., Stéphane Côté, and Dacher Keltner. 2010. "Social Class, Contextualism, and Empathic Accuracy." *Psychological Science* 21(11): 1716–23.

Kraus, Michael W., E. J. Horberg, Jennifer L. Goetz, and Dacher Keltner. 2011. "Social Class, Threat Vigilance, and Hostile Reactivity." *Personality and Social Psychology Bulletin* 37(10): 1376–88.

Kraus, Michael W., and Dacher Keltner. 2009. "Signs of Socioeconomic Status: A Thin-Slicing Approach." *Psychological Science* 20(1): 99–106.

Kraus, Michael W., Paul K. Piff, and Dacher Keltner. 2009. "Social Class, the Sense of Control, and Social Explanation." *The Journal of Personality and Social Psychology* 97(6): 992–1004.

———. 2011. "Social Class as Culture: The Convergence of Resources and Rank in the Social Realm." *Current Directions in Psychological Science* 20(4): 246–50.

Kuriloff, Peter, and Michael C. Reichert. 2003. "Boys of Class, Boys of Color: Negotiating the Academic and Social Geography of an Elite Independent School." *The Journal of Social Issues* 59(4): 751–69.

Kusserow, Adrie S. 2004. *American Individualism: Child Rearing and Social Class in Three Neighborhoods.* New York: Palgrave MacMillan.

Lachman, Margie E., and Suzanne L. Weaver. 1998. "The Sense of Control as a Moderator of Social Class Differences in Health and Well-Being." *The Journal of Personality and Social Psychology* 74(3): 763–73.

Lareau, Annette. 2003. *Unequal Childhoods: Class, Race, and Family Life.* Berkeley: University of California Press.

Mahalingam, Ram. 1998. "Essentialism, Power, and Theories of Caste: A Developmental Study." *Dissertation Abstracts International* 60(2-B).

———. 2003. "Essentialism, Culture, and Power: Representations of Social Class." *The Journal of Social Issues* 59(4): 733–49.

Marx, Karl, and Friedrich Engels. 1973. "Manifesto of the Communist Party." In *The Revolutions of 1848: Political Writings,* vol. 1., edited by David Fernbach. Harmondsworth, U.K.: Penguin. First published in 1848.

Mendoza-Denton, Rodolfo, Geraldine Downey, Valerie Purdie, Angelina Davis, and Janina Pietrzak. 2002. "Sensitivity to Status-Based Rejection: Implications for African-American Students' College Experience." *The Journal of Personality and Social Psychology* 83(4): 896–918.

Morton, Thomas A., Tom Postmes, S. Alexander Haslam, and Matthew J. Hornsey. 2009. "Theorizing Gender in the Face of Social Change: Is There Anything Essential About Essentialism?" *The Journal of Personality and Social Psychology* 96(3): 653–64.

Nisbett, Richard. 2008. *Intelligence and How to Get It: Why Schools and Cultures Count.* New York: Norton.

Ostrove, Joan M., and Susan M. Long. 2007. "Social Class and Belonging: Implications for College Adjustment." *The Review of Higher Education* 30(4): 363–89.

Oyserman, Daphna, and Spike W. S. Lee. 2008. "Does Culture Influence What and How We Think? Effects of Priming Individualism and Collectivism." *The Psychological Bulletin* 134(2): 311–42.

Page-Gould, Elizabeth, Katrina Koslov, and Wendy B. Mendes. 2011. "Powerful and Contagious: Social Power Drives Physiological Synchrony During Social Interactions." Unpublished paper, University of Toronto.

Pettigrew, Thomas F., and Linda R. Tropp. 2006. "A Meta-Analytic Test of Intergroup Contact Theory." *The Journal of Personality and Social Psychology* 90(5): 751–83.

Pickett, Cynthia L., and Wendi L. Gardner. 2005. "The Social Monitoring System: Enhanced Sensitivity to Social Cues as an Adaptive Response to Social Exclusion." In *The Social Outcast: Ostracism, Social Exclusion, Rejection, and Bullying,* edited by Kip Williams, Joe P. Forgas, and William von Hippel. New York: Psychology Press.

Piff, Paul K., Michael W. Kraus, Stéphane Côté, Bonnie H. Cheng, and Dacher Keltner. 2010. "Having Less, Giving More: The Influence of Social Class on Prosocial Behavior." *The Journal of Personality and Social Psychology* 99(5): 771–84.

Ridgeway, Cecilia L. 1991. "The Social Construction of Status Value: Gender and Other Nominal Characteristics." *Social Forces* 70(2): 367–86.

Rusbult, Caryl E., Julie Verette, Gregory A. Whitney, Linda F. Slovik, and Isaac Lipkus. 1991. "Accommodation Processes in Close Relationships: Theory and Preliminary Empirical Evidence." *The Journal of Personality and Social Psychology* 60(1): 53–78.

Saguy, Tamar, Nicole Tausch, John F. Dovidio, and Felicia Pratto. 2009. "The Irony of Harmony: Intergroup Contact Can Produce False Expectations for Equality." *Psychological Science* 20(1): 114–21.

Sapolsky, Robert M. 2004. "Social Status and Health in Humans and Other Animals." *The Annual Review of Anthropology* 33: 393–418.

Sapolsky, Robert M., Susan C. Alberts, and Jeanne Altmann. 1997. "Hypercortisolism Associated with Social Subordinance or Social Isolation Among Wild Baboons." *The Archives of General Psychiatry* 54(12): 1137–43.

Scherer, Shawn E. 1974. "Proxemic Behavior of Primary School Children as a Function of Their Socioeconomic Class and Subculture." *The Journal of Personality and Social Psychology* 29(6): 800–05.

Shell, Duane F., and Jenefer Husman. 2008. "Control, Motivation, Affect, and Strategic Self-Regulation in the College Classroom: A Multidimensional Phenomena." *Journal of Educational Psychology* 100(2): 443–59.

Singh-Manoux, Archana, Nancy E. Adler, and Michael G. Marmot. 2003. "Subjective Social Status: Its Determinants and Its Association with Measures of Ill-Health in the Whitehall II Study." *Social Science and Medicine* 56(6): 1321–33.

Snibbe, Alana C., and Hazel R. Markus. 2005. "You Can't Always Get What You Want: Educational Attainment, Agency, and Choice." *The Journal of Personality and Social Psychology* 88(4): 703–20.

Southwick, Charles H. 1967. "An Experimental Study of Intragroup Agonistic Behavior in Rhesus Monkeys (*Macaca mulatta*)." *Behaviour* 28(1): 182–209.

Stephens, Nicole, MarYam G. Hamedani, Hazel M. Markus, Hilary B. Bergsieker, and Liyam Eloul. 2009. "Why Did They 'Choose' to Stay? Perspectives of the Hurricane Katrina Observers and Survivors." *Psychological Science* 20(7): 878–86.

Stephens, Nicole, Hazel M. Markus, and Sarah S. M. Townsend. 2007. "Choice as an Act of Meaning: The Case of Social Class." *The Journal of Personality and Social Psychology* 93(5): 814–30.

Stipek, Deborah J., and Rosaleen H. Ryan. 1997. "Economically Disadvantaged Preschoolers: Ready to Learn but Further to Go." *Developmental Psychology* 33(4): 711–23.

Tajfel, Henri, and John C. Turner. 1986. "The Social Identity Theory of Intergroup Behavior." In *Psychology of Intergroup Relations*, 2nd ed., edited by William G. Austin and Stephen Worchel. Chicago: Nelson-Hall.

Taylor, Shelley E. 2006. "Tend and Befriend: Biobehavioral Bases of Affiliation Under Stress." *Current Directions in Psychological Science* 15(6): 273–77.

Thompson, William E., and Joseph V. Hickey. 2005. *Society in Focus: An Introduction to Sociology.* 5th ed. Boston, Mass.: Allyn and Bacon.

Tiedens, Larissa Z., and Alison R. Fragale. 2003. "Power Moves: Complementarity in Submissive and Dominant Nonverbal Behavior." *The Journal of Personality and Social Psychology* 84(3): 558–68.

Toppe, Christopher M., Arthur D. Kirsch, and Jocabel Michel. 2001. *Giving and Volunteering in the United States*. Washington, D.C.: Independent Sector. Available at: http://www.cpanda.org/pdfs/gv/GV01Report.pdf (accessed June 2008).

Turner, John C., and Katherine J. Reynolds. 2010. "Self-Categorization Theory." In *Handbook of Theories of Social Psychology*, 2nd ed., edited by Paul A. Van Lange, Arie W. Kruglanski, and E. Tory Higgins. New York: Sage Publications.

Veblen, Thorstein. 1994. *The Theory of the Leisure Class*, New York: Penguin. First published in 1899.

Watts, David P. 2000. "Grooming Between Male Chimpanzees at Ngogo, Kibale National Park," pt. 1, "Partner Number and Diversity and Grooming Reciprocity." *The International Journal of Primatology* 21(2): 189–210.

Wickings, Elizabeth J., and Alan F. Dixson. 1992. "Development from Birth to Sexual Maturity in a Semi-Free-Ranging Colony of Mandrills (*Mandrillus sphinx*) in Gabon." *The Journal of Reproduction and Fertility* 95: 129–38.

Wilkinson, Richard G. 1999. "Health, Hierarchy, and Social Anxiety." *The Annals of the New York Academy of Sciences* 896: 48–63.

Williams, Melissa J., and Jennifer L. Eberhardt. 2008. "Biological Conceptions of Race and the Motivation to Cross Racial Boundaries." *The Journal of Personality and Social Psychology* 94(6): 1033–47.

Wong, Rosanna Yin-mei, and Ying-yi Hong. 2005. "Dynamic Influences of Culture on Co-operation in the Prisoner's Dilemma." *Psychological Science* 16(6): 429–34.

Yzerbyt, Vincent Y., Steve J. Rocher, and Georges Schadron. 1997. "Stereotypes as Explanations: A Subjective Essentialistic View of Group Perception." In *The Social Psychology of Stereotyping and Group Life*, edited by Russell Spears, Penelope J. Oakes, Naomi Ellemers, and S. Alexander Haslam. Oxford, U.K.: Basil Blackwell.

Zahavi, Amotz, and Avishag Zahavi. 1998. "The Handicap Principle: A Missing Piece to Darwin's Puzzle." *Evolution and Human Behavior* 19: 343–46.

PART IV

INDIVIDUALS AND SOCIAL CLASS

CHAPTER 9

BEHAVIORAL DECISION RESEARCH, SOCIAL CLASS, AND IMPLICATIONS FOR PUBLIC POLICY

Crystal C. Hall

In 2009 the American Community Survey estimated that roughly 14 percent of Americans were living below the poverty line (U.S. Census Bureau 2010). Despite policies and programs to address achievement gaps and behavior differences between individuals from different ethnic and socioeconomic backgrounds, striking discrepancies persist between the experiences, performance, and outcomes of working-class and middle-class individuals. In this chapter, I explore the applications and implications that behavioral decision research has for policy design and implementation in the domain of services and benefits for low-income populations.

INTRODUCTION

Traditionally, two perspectives have been taken within the social sciences to explain poverty and the behavior of low-income individuals. One viewpoint describes individuals living in poverty as people who, like the rest of society, engage in actions that align with their goals, in a rational manner. The second describes these individuals' behavior as emanating from a "culture of poverty" that renders their behavioral patterns highly misguided. Neither of these perspectives has strong empirical support as a plausible explanation for the behaviors of individuals in this population. Marianne Bertrand, Sendhil Mullainathan, and Eldar Shafir (2006) argue that neither is an effective viewpoint for understanding and predicting behavior.

The first viewpoint—one that presupposes rationality—assumes that all choice results from consistent, informed preferences that exhibit internal coherence (Sen 1987). This viewpoint, which makes no exceptions for individuals from specific social groups, assumes that those in poverty, like all others, pursue their goals efficiently, with little need for outside intervention. From a policy perspective, this point of view suggests that broad antipoverty efforts are ill advised and wasteful.

The second viewpoint takes note of a controversial opinion discussed in the literatures of anthropology and sociology. Oscar Lewis (1959, 1966) argues that low-income individuals possess a unique system of values and a pathological inability to make well-informed choices. According to Lewis, this "culture of poverty" separates low-income groups from mainstream society and keeps them mired in poverty. He describes a subculture that perpetuates a cycle that socializes children into patterns of behavior, social norms, and social understanding that further impede their ability to break out from the underclass. Therefore, the culture of poverty view does not accept the explanation that the lives of low-income individuals, as a group, have been transformed by poverty. Instead, it argues, the cause of poverty is the pathology of low-income individuals. Although there has been no compelling empirical support for Lewis's model, his ideas persist in the public understanding of poverty (Goode and Eames 1996). In the context of public policy, this perspective implies that antipoverty programs may be effective only in the short term. If the culture of poverty notion were true, these efforts would serve to alleviate only the symptoms of a deeper problem.

A third framework, the behavioral perspective, provides a different lens through which to examine the behavior of individuals living in poverty. The use of a behavioral framework entails adapting the assumption that low-income individuals (like those from other demographics) suffer from biases and are susceptible to influences stemming from the specific situational factors they face. This perspective allows researchers, policymakers, and practitioners to more effectively explain some behavioral puzzles of the low-income group. Why do low-income individuals often fail to open bank accounts? Why is take-up of public assistance programs often strikingly low? Professionals addressing these types of questions can benefit from tools derived from the insights of psychology, a field that has been conspicuously silent regarding these issues.

The primary goal of my research agenda, through a nuanced analysis of the factors considered when engaging in judgment and choice, is to shed light on some aspects of the behavior of low-income individuals. The overarching theme throughout this work is the differences in the psychology of low-income earners compared with middle- and upper-class individuals. This perspective, drawn from the field of psychology, suggests that understanding the behavior of any human is quite complex. People often exhibit poor judgment, have preferences that change often, and sometimes behave impulsively and myopically, especially when they lack the cognitive resources necessary for self-control.

A closer examination of the behavior of low-income decisionmakers (using the tools of social psychology and behavioral decision research) suggests that the differences derive from the contextual features that matter most to the two groups and how each group weighs these features when making decisions. To specifically confirm this, I provide experimental evidence through examples based on existing knowledge within the psychological literature. Furthermore, I discuss instances where low-income decisionmakers behave in a manner that would be considered more "rational" than that of their high-income counterparts. There is insufficient appreciation for these cases, as they undermine popular opinion that low-income individuals are short sighted, misguided, and in need of outside intervention.

There are two secondary outcomes I hope to accomplish in this exploration of behavior in the context of poverty. The first is to more effectively consider the viewpoint of low-income individuals. Social psychology suggests that individuals' social environment and norms drive their behavior, and I consider specifically how this occurs for those in the context of poverty. To do this, I use the existing theoretical frameworks as an anchor, but I move beyond existing generalizations that have lumped low-income actors in the same group as the middle-class majority. The second goal is to connect these research findings to a real-world context and real policy issues. Application of this research outside of controlled lab settings will provide policymakers and low-income advocates with an additional set of tools to use when engaging with this population.

RECENT WORK EXPLORING DECISIONMAKING IN THE CONTEXT OF POVERTY

The research presented here provides illustrative examples of how the fields of behavioral decision research and psychology contribute to a more nuanced understanding of the decisionmaking of low-income and high-income individuals. As social psychology has long demonstrated, the power of the situation, when determining behavior, is often critically underestimated (Jones and Harris 1967). Behavioral decision research demonstrates how fine distinctions in context (in the form of differences such as framing or the existence of channel factors) can produce tangible and predictable shifts in behavior.

Claude Steele and David Sherman's (1999) notion of afforded psychology provides an excellent example of the use of this type of perspective on low-income behavior. The authors apply the theory to the case of low-income mothers as it relates to social mobility and economic security. The theory of afforded psychology is based on the notion that the circumstances of severely disadvantaged people are unreliable and unpredictable—both socially and financially. Steele and Sherman (1999) argue that low-income mothers suffer from a combination of economic disadvantage, restricted social and financial opportunities, and general social isolation. Without the ingredients that produce a secure life (for example, child care, health care, stable employment and housing), they face a series of complex dilemmas on a constant basis. This leads, the authors suggest, to a nuanced psychology with a series of components.

First of all, and somewhat ironically, these women cling strongly to a sense of independence and self-reliance. Although they might appear highly dependent from the perspective of outsiders, they must be highly self-reliant, as they have often lacked concrete and consistent support. In addition, the constant instability and uncertainty makes them distrusting of potential opportunities for upward mobility. Because of this lack of trust, they are unable to effectively implement their desire for self-reliance and independence. Consequently, severely disadvantaged mothers are driven by their immediate needs rather than long-term goals for themselves and their families.

There are numerous opportunities for experimental psychologists to contribute to both theoretical and practical debates about the behavior of individuals living in the context of poverty (Bertrand, Mullainathan, and Shafir 2006). The voices of the fields of both social psychology and judgment and decisionmaking have been considerably faint in the ongoing theoretical and practical debates in these areas. I provide examples of my own work and similar work from other researchers who demonstrate the usefulness of a behavioral perspective in understanding and predicting judgment and choice. This research spans the specific areas of decisions at tax time, the structure of mental accounting and decisions to save, and choices relevant to long-term physical and financial health.

Self-Affirmation and Identity as Behavioral Interventions

In this section, I draw on two distinct but related theories: stereotype threat and self-affirmation. Stereotype threat refers to the anxiety experienced by a person who is in a position to confirm a negative stereotype about a social group to which he or she belongs. Self-affirmation theory affirms the capacity of an individual to reduce the impact of a possible psychological threat by focusing on a separate area where he or she feels competent. Both of these concepts are useful tools for exploring social-class effects on behavior. Low-income individuals face opportunities to confirm negative stereotypes about their group on a daily basis. The psychological threat associated with the social identity tied to poverty can be especially prevalent when low-income individuals participate in programs or services geared toward them. A low-income worker who has been asked to participate in a financial planning seminar may have a fear of showing incompetence in this area in the presence of a higher-status outgroup member. This might cause the individual to make mistakes or disengage altogether.

Several studies have shown that stereotype threat can have an impact on the attitudes, behavior, and performance of stigmatized individuals. The research on stereotype threat shows that when people in a stigmatized group (owing to factors such as race, gender, social class) are forced to perform in the stereotype-relevant domain, they may inadvertently conform to and demonstrate that stereotype by performing at a lower level (Steele and Aronson 1995). A member of a marginalized group, worrying about being judged or treated in terms of a stereotype, might engage in a behavior that confirms that stereotype. This generates a psychological burden or distraction from the fear of being seen through the lens of a specific stereotype.

A recent meta-analysis shows that stereotype threat appears to impact the performance of both women and blacks on the Scholastic Aptitude Test (Walton and Spencer 2009). The concept of stereotype threat has also been demonstrated for low-income individuals (Croizet and Claire 1998). In this study, undergraduate students completed a task that involved a series of word problems. The participants were classified by socioeconomic status based on parental occupation and amount of financial aid. The verbal task was described as being one that would "assess intellectual ability" for solving the problems in the experimental condition or "test several hypotheses about the role attention plays" in the function of verbal and lexical performance, the control condition. The intent was to arouse feelings of stereotype threat in the experimental condition. In fact, the high-status students performed better than their low-status counterparts but only in the experimental condition, where the task was framed as an intelligence test. Very little follow-up work has been done specific to low-income individuals in the area of stereotype threat.

Related to this, self-affirmation theory is based on the general premise that individuals are motivated to protect their perceived sense of self-worth. Individuals often find themselves in situations that have the potential to threaten feelings of self-worth. As first discussed by Steele (1988), self-affirmation theory is based on the premise that people are motivated to protect and maintain their perceived integrity (see also Aronson, Cohen, and Nail 1999; Sherman and Cohen 2006). When this sense is threatened, individuals must find a way to restore their integrity. These threats may occur in reference to an individual or to a group identity (for example, race or gender).

In studies on affirmation, the threat response is most commonly induced through a short written exercise. Participants are shown a list of values—for example, religious affiliation, relationships with friends and family, a sense of humor—and asked to mark the ones they believe are important. They are then asked to choose one value and describe, in a short essay, why this value is personally important to them. Finally, participants are asked to describe several specific personal experiences where this value has been important and what positive feelings about themselves the experience might have produced. In the comparison condition, participants write about a value from the same list but are told to write about a value that they have not rated as personally important. In one study (run with Americans citizens) conducted after the 2001 attacks on the United States, self-affirmation eliminated partisan divergence between self-described U.S. patriots and nonpatriots in their interpretation of a report analyzing the terrorist attacks (Cohen et al. 2007). When participants were affirmed before reading the report, the correlation between patriot status and response to the report was no longer observed. In other words, a self-affirmation manipulation virtually eliminated any correlation between identity and openness to the report. Cohen and colleagues argue that individual attempts to protect the integrity of one's self-concept may threaten the integrity of interpersonal relationships. A self-affirmation appears to be effective at decreasing bias and increasing open-mindedness in a negotiation.

Other examples within the literature show the use of self-affirmation as a behavioral intervention. In a review of studies that used this method (McQueen and Klein 2006), the majority of manipulations "affirmed" participants by instructing them to focus on a highly valued personal characteristic or ideal. While specific exemplars are typically generated by participants (usually in the form of a short essay), there are cases in which the experimenter prompts participants to consider a specific domain. However, most of the dependent variables measured in these studies are cognitive. There are few examples of experiments that examine the influence of self-affirmation on more consequential behaviors, and the overwhelming majority of studies that use affirmation as a manipulation have been completed using undergraduate student participants.[1] Few studies have tested the potential effectiveness of self-affirmation manipulation outside of the laboratory, an application that has implications for real behavior.

However, recent work has shown that simple affirmation interventions have been effective in reducing the race achievement gap between high school students of different ethnicities (Cohen et al. 2006). In an experiment with real outcomes at stake, a brief in-class writing assignment improved the grades of African American students, reducing the racial achievement gap by 40 percent. Students spent fifteen minutes writing about a specific value that either was important to them (affirmation condition) or might be important to someone else (neutral condition). The decrease in the achievement gap was not a short-lived effect—the measured differences were seen over the course of an entire semester. Results like these suggest that the use of simple, cost-effective psychological interventions could go a long way toward alleviating identity- and stereotype-related stress and producing tangible, real-world benefits. The research by Cohen and colleagues is groundbreaking because it explores the beneficial effect of an affirmation manipulation on a tangible outcome in a natural setting, one that is subject to countless sources of interference over an extended period. In the context of social class, affirmation might be particularly useful as a means of decreasing stereotype threat for low-income individuals. When it comes to real-world service provision, stereotype threat might make this population less receptive to programs and services that might make them more aware of the negative stereotypes and stigma associated with their group.

In my own work, I have used a self-affirmation intervention among a group of low-income individuals (Hall, Zhao, and Shafir, forthcoming). In our first study, after random assignment to either a self-affirmation or neutral condition, participants' interest in a financial benefits program was measured. Individuals who had been affirmed showed a greater interest in receiving information about the Earned Income Tax Credit (EITC) program. The EITC is the largest and most-often claimed tax credit for low-income families. It is calculated as a supplement to earned income, money received from working for pay. It was originally approved in 1975 as a work incentive; households below a certain income level, whose tax burden is low or nonexistent, receive the EITC as a refund.

In this study, volunteers in a soup kitchen were randomly assigned to engage in one of two verbal tasks. In the affirmation task, participants described a specific personal episode during which they had experienced some type of personal success. Individuals in the control condition described what they ate on a daily basis, in detail. These interventions were unique, as they are distinct from the usual written affirmation prompts. We felt that an oral manipulation would be more appropriate for a population that might experience anxiety over writing.

After this task the participants were compensated and led to believe the task was complete. After leaving the room, they were subsequently greeted by a third individual (ostensibly unrelated to the study) and asked to stop and discuss the EITC and local free tax-preparation opportunities. While participants in each group were just as likely to stop and talk when approached, individuals in the affirmation condition were more than twice as likely to receive information about the EITC and tax preparation as those in the neutral control condition (79 and 36 percent, respectively).

We have replicated these findings using a set of simple cognitive tasks that show that low-income individuals who have been affirmed also are significantly less likely to show cognitive depletion (a decreased capacity for completing simple tasks that require working memory and undivided attention), as measured through two tasks. The participants completed one of two verbal manipulations, the same tasks as in the preceding study, reporting on personal success or daily diet. After this, they completed two additional tasks. The first, Raven's Progressive Matrices, is a set of multiple-choice nonverbal measures of reasoning and is often considered a measure of general intelligence (Raven 1936). In this task, the participant must choose the missing symbol or element that completes a pattern. The second test we used was based on simple studies on cognitive control, the ability to allow behavior to adapt from moment to moment based on shifting goals in a task. Participants completed both tests after completing the affirmation or neutral task. Those in the affirmation condition performed better on each task.

The theory of self-affirmation suggests that individuals seek the protection of their perceived integrity. There is no reason to suspect that this would not also be the case for low-income decisionmakers. In fact, low-income individuals might be more likely to engage in these processes, given that they are exposed to more stereotype threats in their everyday lives. When engaging in a situation that involves discussion of finances, for example, a low-income individual may be fearful of appearing to be unintelligent and incapable of achieving financial stability and independence. From the standpoint of service provision these results also suggest that lay intuitions' reasons for why low-income individuals do not often take up beneficial programs (lack of understanding the programs, lack of valuing the programs) may not apply. A decision not to engage with an individual or organization offering a service or program may stem from an immediate unwillingness to deal with a potential psychological threat.

In addition, I have conducted a small study using a different type of priming specifically focused on a specific social identity. Prior work has demonstrated that it is possible to render specific aspects of an individual identity salient during a given moment, and this may have an impact on judgment and choice (Turner 1985, 1987). This can come from salience in a cultural or social identity (such as race or ethnicity) or from a more specialized role (such as being a parent or teacher). This is possible because individuals possess a multifaceted, malleable self-concept (Turner 1985; Markus and Kunda 1986). For example, students primed with their scholarly identity are more likely than students primed with their social identity to choose scholarly magazines, such as *The Economist* or the *Wall Street Journal* (LeBoeuf, Shafir, and Bayuk 2010).

A recent pilot study I conducted explores identity salience among low-income consumers. Individual adults who reported living with dependent children were primed in either their parental identity or a neutral condition. They were subsequently asked to perform a task in which they allocated a hypothetical $1,000 tax refund to various categories (such as savings, paying off debt, buying gifts). Participants in the parental prime reported a greater interest in saving a portion of their refund (11 percent) than those in the control condition (2 percent). When stepping away from this finding, one can imagine how, for the resource- and time-strapped lower class, a chronic focus on the benefits of saving for a child's future is relatively difficult. However, a timely short-term prime with one's children could increase behavior toward that end. For the middle and upper class, a greater amount of resources makes this a less important issue. While they might also benefit from this prime, they also have the luxury of being able to concentrate more resources and attention on a particular financial goal. Lower-income families must struggle with so many immediate, short-term concerns that they find it harder to focus on long-term goals.

Overall, these studies suggest provocative insights for understanding effective marketing and program delivery to encourage take-up of savings products among low-income consumers. For example, decisions not to take up beneficial programs or services may stem not from a lack of interest or understanding on the part of an individual but from a fear of confirming a stereotype about the group. This may be especially prevalent when a low-income individual is interacting with someone perceived to be from a wealthier out-group. These factors might cause individuals to disengage where they might otherwise express interest in a program or service.

In addition, these studies provide useful extensions to the existing research on social identity and self-affirmation. Evidence gathered from these studies supports the notion of stereotype threat, self-affirmation, and identity salience outside the confines of race and gender, where they have been extensively studied.

Future research ought to further examine the usefulness of these techniques in simple, low-cost behavioral interventions to encourage positive behaviors such as saving and take-up of financial and social benefits. When a policymaker, service provider, or advocate for the poor has a better understanding of the impact of poverty on judgment and behavior, it will be possible to better work with the poor population. As more evidence demonstrates that low-income individuals are subject to the same types of irrationality as middle- and upper-class individuals, it is easier to see that the previous notion of the culture of poverty is insufficient to describe and predict behavior. In the next section, I explore this point further through an examination of a well-established finding regarding preference for saving on simple purchases by low- versus high-income consumers.

Mental Accounting and Savings Preferences

In the decisionmaking literature, another prominent area of exploration has been the study of mental accounting. Researchers study how individuals perceive, categorize, and evaluate their financial choices and outcomes (for a review, see Thaler 1999). Most research on mental accounting falls into one of three categories: how outcomes are perceived and experienced, how activities are assigned to specific "accounts," and the frequency with which accounts are reevaluated. The purpose of studying mental accounting is to broaden the general understanding of the psychology of choice. For the most part, the findings are that when making financial decisions, individuals do not incorporate all relevant factors (such as current wealth, future wealth, and the probability of outcomes). Instead, people often use simplified rules, which the study of mental accounting helps to describe.

While the mental accounting literature has contributed to the understanding of general consumer behavior, no work to date has examined these phenomena with respect to low-income consumers. In terms of simple, everyday decisions regarding buying and saving, low- and high-income decisionmakers make many of the same choices. Deciding whether or not to spend more time to save a certain amount of money is a common choice for both groups, but these choices might be more consequential for lower-income individuals. In addition, low-income individuals might be more used to focusing on smaller amounts, amounts that may carry less meaning for those with greater incomes. Saving a modest amount on a pair of shoes might appeal to both groups, but for low-income individuals, the lack of a financial buffer experienced might make them less sensitive to the proportion saved. If low-income consumers were to focus instead on the absolute amount saved, this would suggest that, in this context, low-income consumers are potentially more rational than their higher-income counterparts. Such a finding would go directly against the notion that low-income individuals are incapable of making beneficial financial choices, as a "culture of poverty" framework suggests.

To explore this, I conducted a series of studies that attempted to replicate a well-established finding in the area of mental accounting. Amos Tversky and Daniel Kahneman (1981, 457) investigated a decision to save with the following classic example:

> Frame 1: Imagine that you are about to purchase a jacket for $125 and a calculator for $15. The calculator salesman informs you that the calculator you wish to buy is on sale for $10 at the other branch of the store, located a 20 min. drive away. Would you make the trip to the other store?

> Frame 2: Imagine that you are about to purchase a jacket for $15 and a calculator for $125. The calculator salesman informs you that the calculator you wish to buy is on sale for $120 at the other branch of the store, located a 20 min. drive away. Would you make the trip to the other store?

In both of these questions, the individual is faced with the prospect of saving $5 on a purchase. However, participants are far more likely to make a trip to save $5 when it represents a larger proportion of the total price. The majority of participants, 68 percent, were willing to travel to save in the first frame, compared with only 29 percent in the second. Many researchers have replicated this finding (Mowen and Mowen 1986; Ranyard and Abdel-Nabi 1993; Moon, Keasey, and Duxbury 1999).

In two sets of studies comparing low- and high-income adults (Hall and Shafir, forthcoming), low-income individuals did not repeat the traditional pattern of mental accounting. This is initially shown through adapted versions of Tversky and Kahneman's (1981) original stimuli, examining willingness to travel to save money. In these studies, high-income participants replicated the expected pattern of results, while the low-income participants did not show the preference reversal that has been previously demonstrated.

When asked to decide between two saving options, higher-income participants preferred the savings option that reflected the greater proportion, replicating previous findings. When the amounts saved were not identical, high-income participants still chose the greater proportion, even when it was a lower absolute amount. Low-income participants did not replicate this; instead, they appeared to rely more on absolute values. Without the financial buffer enjoyed by higher-income individuals, these individuals may be more sensitive to absolute amounts, even under similar types of choice scenarios. A second set of studies more rigorously extends this using a novel design that forces participants to choose between various saving scenarios. These studies provide further support for the notion that low-income participants are more focused on absolute amounts. These patterns of results cause the low-income consumers to appear to be relatively more rational in this domain of choice. This finding provides a compelling example of how the relative rationality of low-income consumers is often underappreciated.

This effect does not appear to be a function of numeracy among low-income individuals, as more recent research shows. Previous work has demonstrated that low-numerate individuals are less likely to show the proportional savings effect (Peters et al. 2006). Recent data I have collected replicate this effect among high-income individuals, but both high- and low-numerate low-income participants fail to show this effect.

While preliminary, these results have the potential to be informative for policymakers and advocates of low-income populations, and they could be especially relevant for marketing programs directed at low-income individuals. While an individual with a higher income may be inclined to respond to highlighted cost ratios (save 30 percent on your heating bill!), this research suggests that, when targeting the low-income population, it may be more beneficial to highlight absolute amounts (save $30 on your heating bill!). The original proportional savings finding is a robust effect but one that seems to apply to the middle-class majority. This work suggests that low-income consumers do not have the same preference for proportions, a finding that could potentially be crucial for individuals designing efforts to encourage general saving and other positive financial choices. The same intuition that makes a prospect seem attractive to a middle- or upper- class policymaker or poverty advocate might not resonate with a low-income consumer.

If advocates for those living in poverty can have a better understanding of what features are most important to the low-income group, they can alter their message to be received more effectively. Although, in this case, low-income individuals appear to make choices that are more financially rational, they may still be susceptible to the framing of a choice that capitalizes on the preference for absolute savings. Future research will be needed to tease this apart further, as the current evidence most strongly supports the notion that low-income individuals do not replicate the commonly seen preference for proportional savings. There is not sufficient evidence to clearly describe what features seem to be driving their pattern of choices in this context. However, it is clear that this is a case where low-income individuals are engaging in financial preferences that are more coherent than those of their high-income counterparts. This striking pattern of behavior lends support to the notion that this population is not necessarily in need of interventions stemming from culture of poverty assumptions about their behavior and preferences.

Overall, findings of this nature provide further support for the broader argument that assumptions stemming from the middle-class majority may not adequately describe and predict the behavior of low-income individuals. In this case, the evidence demonstrates that this group does not replicate the findings of a robust, well-known psychological effect (preference for higher proportional savings) in the literature. As discussed in the next section, this approach is becoming more common in the scholarly literature, and these findings provide an additional set of tools for understanding low-income behavior, designing policy, and implementing specific programs.

Risk and Choice Among Low-Income Consumers

The work I have conducted with my collaborators builds on an increasingly common perspective from both within and outside of the behavioral sciences. It was at one time quite uncommon to use this approach, as the notion of a culture of poverty prevailed in theorizing about behavior of the poor. However, contemporary research exploring the behavior of low-income populations seems more willing to consider the implications of societal inequality on social environments (whether explicitly or not). This work capitalizes on the insights of social psychology and behavioral decision research and is particularly useful in the context of poverty, as it allows for a more realistic exploration and analysis of how individuals actually respond to policies and programs.

Under this behavioral approach, low-income consumers are shown to have the same biases and limitations as all humans, including such factors as low self-control, procrastination, and problems with commitment. If individuals living in poverty really suffered from a culture of poverty, these factors would not matter, because any observed financial and social choices would be driven by internal, learned factors as opposed to factors that were external and a function of the situation.

In one of the first articles that embraced this approach to understanding the behavior of low-income populations, Brian Zikmund-Fisher and Andrew Parker (1999) explored motivations behind the demand for rent-to-own contracts. Rent-to-own contracts provide an opportunity for individuals to purchase durable goods over an extended period of time. Individuals may return the item at any time but might end up paying two to four times the total standard retail price. Zikmund-Fisher and Parker study constraints on liquidity (the degree to which an asset can be purchased or sold without losing value), high intertemporal discounting (the tendency to give greater value to rewards as they move closer to the present), self-management of financial myopia, and risk aversion as possible explanations for the demand for these contracts. They find that this behavior is best explained as a response to risk aversion and expense shocks that low-income consumers face. In other words, the escapability of the contracts in the face of a financial crisis is an attractive feature. Families were more likely to choose rent-to-own contracts when their income streams were less stable.

This finding sheds light on the fact that assumptions about underlying causes of these types of choices (lack of knowledge, myopia) may not be entirely accurate. In fact, in the short run, a compelling argument can be made that low-income individuals are being at least somewhat rational with the decision to use this contract versus a more traditional use of a line of credit or payment plan. This is, of course, in conflict with the fact that behavior of this sort may make it difficult for a low-income family to build long-term wealth and assets. The dilemma is recognized by Steele and Sherman's (1999) afforded psychology theory and provides further evidence of the predicament that many low-income families may face when trying to balance short- and long-term financial goals.

Another set of findings, also in the domain of financial decisionmaking, explores the decision to play the lottery by low-income consumers. It has been well established that low-income households spend a significant portion of their income on lotteries (Clotfelter and Cook 1987, 1989). This is particularly alarming, because state lotteries have the lowest expected payout of any other form of legal gambling (Clotfelter and Cook 1989); typically, lottery players earn about fifty cents for each dollar spent. It has been estimated that, among families with earnings of less than $10,000, roughly 3 percent of income is spent on lottery tickets (Clotfelter et al. 1999). This propensity to gamble by low-income populations relative to the wealthy (Clotfelter et al. 1999) is clearly unfortunate, as these behaviors undermine efforts by public and nonprofit programs and services to help individuals deal with short-term financial crises and build longer-term financial stability.

However, a recent set of experiments suggests that highlighting income inequality and an individual's relative wealth can have an impact on the propensity to purchase lottery tickets (Haisley, Mostafa, and Loewenstein 2008). When primed with their income as relatively low (using the response scale in a survey), participants were more likely to "purchase" lottery tickets as their compensation for participation—nearly twice as much as those who were primed with their income as being more middle of the road. This finding supports the hypothesis that a perception of low income (relative to some implicit standard) is enough to increase consumption of lottery tickets. This result is particularly striking as the income response scale was embedded in a series of various demographic questions. Furthermore, the study also showed that low-income consumers were more likely to exhibit a demand for lottery tickets when they were presented with situations in which either rich or poor people received advantages. Participants answered questions about how likely a rich, middle-class, or low-income person would be to experience different life outcomes (for example, being awarded a scholarship, being elected mayor, finding money, or winning at a slot machine). These questions implicitly highlighted the fact that all individuals who play have an equal chance of winning a lottery. Without being explicitly asked whether a low- or higher-income person would have a better chance of winning the lottery, those in this experimental condition were more likely to "purchase" lottery tickets as their compensation.

These results suggest that the decision to participate in lotteries by low-income individuals may be (consciously or otherwise) motivated by factors that are more nuanced than simple cognitive errors or ignorance. In this case, a visible, relatively low income level has a stronger impact on choice than either a strictly rational influence or the influence of a culture of poverty. This is not entirely surprising, as theories such as social comparison (Festinger 1954) and relative deprivation theory (Crosby 1976) suggest that people do not evaluate the absolute value of their income, performance, and assets but instead are highly influenced by comparisons with others. Both of these sets of findings show how assumptions about two patterns of behavior among low-income groups (interest in rent-to-own contracts and purchase of lottery tickets) may not be simply explained by a lack of information or understanding of the situation. Instead, they are driven by situational factors specific to this population. In the next section, a similar logic applies to understanding choice in a completely different domain: food preferences.

Food Choice Among Low-Income Families

Health-related choices and behaviors are a major concern of policymakers and low-income advocates. One specific area in this domain explores food choice. The U.S. government spends millions of dollars annually on programs to supplement healthy eating. The federal Special Supplemental Nutrition Program for Women, Infants, and Children, commonly known as WIC, provides grants to states to supplement food, health care, and nutrition education for low-income pregnant women, nursing women, and children up to the age of five years who are at some nutritional risk. In addition, the federal SNAP program (Supplemental Nutrition Assistance Program, formerly known as the food stamps program) has provided cash benefits and nutrition education to low-income Americans since the late 1930s. In addition, thousands of food banks operating across the country provide food to low-income families. In all of these programs and services, an emphasis is put on encouraging low-income individuals to eat fresh, healthy food. It is well known that low-income individuals are less likely to consume healthy food (Lock et al. 2005), which contributes to the health gap between relatively low- and high-income individuals (Kant 2004).

More recently, specific efforts such as the Farmers Market Nutrition Program (affiliated with WIC) have attempted to increase the consumption of fresh produce by low-income individuals. These programs assist families with the purchase of fruits and vegetables, in particular. Farmers can enroll in the program as vendors and are reimbursed after accepting vouchers from customers at farm stands and markets. Previous strategies to increase the decision to consume targeted foods (such as fruits and vegetables) have not been widely tested. However, a recent study shows that WIC-eligible postpartum women in Los Angeles who received vouchers for fresh produce (redeemable at grocery stores or at farmers markets) increased their consumption of these foods (Herman et al. 2008). This increase was sustained during the intervention period and persisted six months after the intervention ended.

While this study was relatively small, and not representative by any means, it suggests that more focused efforts be made to change behavior in these domains. A shift in the availability of specific types of food and incentives to consume certain types of food could have a great impact. A lack of consumption of healthy food by low-income households may not simply reflect disinterest in this food but may instead be a function of availability. The concept of "food deserts" highlights the impact of disparities in food prices and of geographic constraints in access to traditional grocery stores (Walker, Keane, and Burke 2010). Recent research indicates that food deserts may contribute to difficulties regarding access to affordable, nutritious food (U.S. Department of Agriculture 2009). Besides providing access to healthy food, public programs attempt to provide opportunities and support for stable housing, a much more expensive endeavor. The logic of a behavioral approach to understanding housing choice also applies.

Housing Subsidies and Neighborhood Outcomes

The federal Moving to Opportunity program provides low-income families with the chance to move to less disadvantaged communities. At the time the program was put in place, it was suspected that providing low-income families with a voucher to move to a higher-income neighborhood (along with providing housing counseling) would lead to better schooling opportunities (Brooks-Gunn et al. 1993; Kaufman and Rosenbaum 1992). However, four to seven years later, there were no improvements in educational outcomes observed for the treatment group compared with those who did not receive housing subsidies (Orr 2003; Sanbonmatsu et al. 2006).

In a large mixed-methods study, the impact of the Moving to Opportunity program on educational outcomes was directly explored. Using surveys, interviews, and a comprehensive data set, the study found that parents, for the most part, did not move their children to neighborhoods with higher-performing schools (DeLuca and Rosenblatt 2010). Specifically, many parents expressed the belief that moving to a better school would not necessarily help their children. They believed that effort and motivation on the part of the student was more important than the educational environment or quality. Furthermore, many families lacked information about school quality and had exceptionally low expectations for all schools. These beliefs persisted, despite the fact that families, for the most part, emphasized the importance of education for their children. As with the prior examples, assumptions about the intentions of low-income individuals (in this case, the desire to move to neighborhoods with better schools) did not sufficiently describe their behavior.

Implications of Previous Research

A behavioral perspective gives both researchers and practitioners the opportunity to refine commonly held assumptions about the behavior of low-income populations. Many of the well-established findings in the fields of social psychology and behavioral decision research have been tested almost exclusively using members of the middle and upper class. Exploring some of these phenomena in the context of low-income settings can help researchers understand the boundary conditions on some of these effects. My previous research on mental accounting suggests that the social environment of poverty facilitates behavior that actually looks more rational than the behavior of middle- and upper-class individuals. The work on self-affirmation and identity salience describes specific cases where the social environment may have an impact on behavior and suggests potential methods for communicating with and designing interventions for this population.

The research on rent-to-own and lottery ticket purchases suggests that decisions to seek out seemingly costly financial contracts and engage in gambling with very low expected payouts may not be solely the result of myopia, lack of intelligence, or lack of information. Features of the decision environment may have direct impacts on many of these choices. A better understanding of both the assumptions and reality behind decision motivations and other features of the social context may allow researchers, policymakers, and advocates to work to generate more creative solutions to many of these issues. It is crucial, from a policy perspective, to understand how people actually respond to incentives, taking into account their social environments. Based on the nuanced understanding of the demand for lotteries provided by the work of Emily Haisley, Romel Mostafa, and George Loewenstein (2008), some researchers are working with practitioners to explore the efficacy of lottery-linked savings for low-income consumers. They are considering the notion that the cognition and emotions that low-income individuals have toward lotteries may be powerful motivators for increasing take-up of programs and services. This is a creative approach that could potentially facilitate powerful long-term benefits for these individuals. This type of approach will not only help researchers better understand the limitations of existing theory but will also facilitate a better comprehension of how these principles can be effectively applied as interventions in the real world.

Finally, many of these findings question some of the core, repeatedly replicated findings in behavioral research. They also provide evidence that low-income decisionmakers are not as irrational as often described. A reconsideration of these central assumptions about the behavior and preferences of this population could lead to vastly different approaches to policy design and implementation.

FUTURE DIRECTIONS

There is a growing desire among practitioners to apply behavioral science in a way that is powerful and meaningful. This desire has largely originated within the field of asset building and financial education but is expanding to domains such as housing and health care, as well. There are countless behavioral puzzles that can be explored using this approach, but efforts by policy-minded researchers ought to address questions and issues that carry implications for both theory and practice.

In this final section, I discuss future directions in my own research agenda. With this work, my first goal is to push the boundaries of the theory toward describing behavior for low-income Americans. In addition, I want to test the effectiveness of these tools as behavioral interventions. I suggest two research approaches, one using an underused form of field testing, the other studying cultural identity and its implications for choice.

Intervention Testing in the Field

Even the simplest research design requires thoughtful and careful implementation to be tested outside of lab settings. Even for simple survey research, testing in the field can often prove difficult when dealing with a population such as low-income individuals. Often this work must be conducted with the cooperation of nonprofit and government agencies. Effective collaboration is often difficult, given that these organizations are often overworked and understaffed.

However, I have worked with organizations to set up small "lab sites" to explore large-scale behavioral interventions. I have recently secured funding that will allow this work to be taken to a much larger scale. Presently, Volunteer Income Tax Assistance (VITA) sites provide the best opportunity to do this. More than twelve thousand VITA sites are open nationwide, helping close to a million low-income tax filers complete their tax returns each year. The Internal Revenue Service continues to expand its partnerships with nonprofit and community organizations. These sites represent an enormous opportunity to conduct quality field research in a controlled setting.

For example, if a low-cost, easy way to increase savings at tax time were tested and proved successful at one site, it would be relatively easy to implement it at similar VITA sites. The VITA sites are ideal settings in which to insert well-designed nudges that can help people make the best decisions possible. They also happen to be ideal places for behavioral scientists to run studies, well suited to observing people and collecting data. Sites are filled with a population that is often difficult to reach, demographics data are collected and stored as a matter of course, the sites are staffed with committed personnel able to manage large numbers of people, and people are guided through a series of important decisions that can be easily tweaked to create a potentially powerful intervention.

Staff and volunteers can be trained to work as research assistants who can implement the studies and monitor data collection. In this way, the research is an almost seamless part of the site's daily process. In addition, having program staff serve as research assistants allows researchers to dramatically increase the number of people who can be part of the study, moving sample sizes from hundreds to thousands. With my current collaborators, I will attempt to replicate findings of my previous research in the context of tax-time decisionmaking. This includes the use of self-affirmation as a behavioral intervention and identity priming (parental identity). This work will also explore the finding that low-income consumers tend to underestimate their tax refunds (Romich et al. forthcoming) and that informing them of this might be a useful tool for encouraging savings at tax time.

In this initial attempt to explore these research questions on a larger scale, there are two guiding practical questions. First, how can we increase take-up of savings products? Second, how can we increase enrollment in public benefit programs? These questions have an impact on scores of low-income consumers. Any lessons we learn in these studies have significant potential for scale and portability, as VITA sites across the country can possibly implement similar interventions.

Interactions of Class and Culture and the Implications for Choice

More recent work I am conducting explores how home and school experience interacts with features of the social context to influence the self-perceptions, judgments, and behaviors of youth from working-class backgrounds. In particular, we seek to examine risk perception among two dimensions of social identity: cultural background (European Americans, Asian Americans, and immigrants) and class background (working class and middle class). Building on the existing literature within cultural psychology (Markus and Kitayama 1991; Nisbett et al. 2001), I hope to expand the theoretical discussions regarding what aspects of social identity contribute to decisionmaking around risk. Specifically, the proposed research is significant because it has the potential to demonstrate that decisionmaking around risk varies across contexts (home, school) and to link variation in decisionmaking around risk with aspects of social identity (social class, culture).

Individuals who are born and raised in a working-class context but have transitioned into a middle-class context such as community college or university become essentially bicultural individuals, having knowledge and experience in two social classes. The same logic applies to individuals who have extensive experience in both individualist (American, Western European) and collectivist (East Asian) cultures. Using a recently developed and pilot-tested methodology, a colleague has found evidence that reasoning about risk differs in the contexts of home and school among immigrant Asian youth, especially those from working-class backgrounds. That is, immigrant youth make decisions about marriage, career, and breaking the law to help a family member when they are primed to think of home that are different from decisions about marriage, career, and breaking the law when they are primed to think of school. This frame-switching behavior is a function of culture and class and is not observed in nonimmigrant youth.

There is support for this pattern in the few other studies that examine decisionmaking around risk in diverse settings. East Asians have been found to take more financial risks and fewer social risks compared with European Americans (Weber and Hsee 1998; Hsee and Weber 1999), and individuals with lower socioeconomic status use a different set of heuristics for making financial decisions compared with middle-class individuals, as previously discussed.

CONCLUSION

As the U.S. population continues to diversify, behavior and achievement gaps between individuals from different social classes have persisted. Policymakers continually attempt to understand why many negative outcomes tend to afflict lower-income populations and to design programs and interventions to counteract them. A prominent issue is how cultural and ethnic background and social class might interact to produce differences in judgment and choice. Decisionmaking around risk allows individuals to negotiate an array of social and financial choices.

Understanding the sociocultural and contextual influences on decisionmaking in general can have far-reaching implications, both for the basic processes underlying judgment and decisionmaking and for public policy in an increasingly pluralistic society. A reconsideration of the often implicit assumptions that low-income consumers behave irrationally is a critical step in the right direction. Advancement in this field (at the scholarly and practical levels) has the potential to inform education and financial policies that affect the next generation, many of whom come from working-class communities.

NOTE

1. Participants in only two of the studies in the review paper by Amy McQueen and William Klein (2006) were not college students. One of these studies used Israeli soldiers, the other used elementary school students.

REFERENCES

Aronson, Joshua, Geoffrey L. Cohen, and Paul R. Nail. 1999. "Self-Affirmation Theory: An Update and Appraisal." In *Cognitive Dissonance: Progress on a Pivotal Theory in Social Psychology,* edited by E. Harmon-Jones and J. Mills. Washington, D.C.: American Psychological Association Books.

Bertrand, Marianne, Sendhil Mullainathan, and Eldar Shafir. 2006. "Behavioral Economics and Marketing in Aid of Decision Making Among the Poor." *The Journal of Public Policy and Marketing* 25(1): 8–23.

Brooks-Gunn, Jeanne, Greg J. Duncan, Pamela K. Klebanov, and Naomi Sealand. 1993. "Do Neighborhoods Influence Child and Adolescent Development?" *The American Journal of Sociology* 99(2): 353–95.

Clotfelter, Charles T., and Philip J. Cook. 1987. "Implicit Taxation in Lottery Finance." *The National Tax Journal* 40: 533–46.

———. 1989. *Selling Hope: State Lotteries in America.* Cambridge, Mass.: Harvard University Press.

Clotfelter, Charles T., Philip J. Cook, Julie A. Edell, and Marian Moore. 1999. *State Lotteries at the Turn of the Century.* Durham, N.C.: Duke University, National Gambling Impact Study Commission.

Cohen, Geoffrey L., Julio Garcia, Nancy Apfel, and Allison Master. 2006. "Reducing the Racial Achievement Gap: A Social-Psychological Intervention." *Science* 313(5791): 1307–10.

Cohen, Geoffrey L., David K. Sherman, Anthony Bastardi, Lillian Hsu, Michelle McGoey, and Lee Ross. 2007. "Bridging the Partisan Divide: Self-Affirmation Reduces Ideological Closed-Mindedness and Inflexibility in Negotiation." *The Journal of Personality and Social Psychology* 93(3): 415–30.

Croizet, Jean-Claude, and Theresa Claire. 1998. "Extending the Concept of Stereotype Threat to Social Class: The Intellectual Underperformance of Students from Low Socioeconomic Backgrounds." *The Personality and Social Psychology Bulletin* 24(6): 588–94.

Crosby, Faye. 1976. "A Model of Egotistical Relative Deprivation." *The Psychological Review* 83(2): 85–113.

DeLuca, Stefanie, and Peter Rosenblatt. 2010. "Does Moving to Better Neighborhoods Lead to Better Schooling Opportunities? Parental School Choice in an Experimental Housing Voucher Program." *The Teachers College Record* 112(5): 1443–91.

Festinger, Leon. 1954. "A Theory of Social Comparison Processes." *Human Relations* 7(May): 117–40.

Goode, Judith, and Edwin Eames. 1996. "An Anthropological Critique of the Culture of Poverty." In *Urban Life: Readings in the Anthropology of the City,* edited by George Gmelch and Walter Zenner. Prospect Heights, Ill.: Waveland.

Haisley, Emily, Romel Mostafa, and George Loewenstein. 2008. "Subjective Relative Income and Lottery Ticket Purchases." *The Journal of Behavioral Decision Making* 21(3): 283–95.

Hall, Crystal C., and Eldar Shafir. Forthcoming. "Mental Accounting in the Context of Poverty." Working paper, University of Washington.

Hall, Crystal C., Jiaying Zhao, and Eldar Shafir. Forthcoming. "Self-Affirmation as an Intervention Among the Poor." Working paper, University of Washington.

Herman, Dena R., Gail G. Harrison, Abdelmonem A. Afifi, and Eloise Jenks. 2008. "Effect of a Targeted Subsidy on Intake of Fruits and Vegetables Among Low-Income Women in the

Special Supplemental Nutrition Program for Women, Infants, and Children." *The American Journal of Public Health* 98(1): 98–105.

Hsee, Christopher K., and Elke U. Weber. 1999. "Cross-National Differences in Risk Preference and Lay Predictions." *The Journal of Behavioral Decision Making* 12(2): 165–79.

Jones, Edward E., and Victor A. Harris. 1967. "The Attribution of Attitudes." *The Journal of Experimental Social Psychology* 3(1): 1–24.

Kant, Ashima K. 2004. "Dietary Patterns and Health Outcomes." *The Journal of the American Dietary Association* 104(4): 615–35.

Kaufman, Julie E., and James E. Rosenbaum. 1992. "The Education and Employment of Low-Income Black Youth in White Suburbs." *Educational Evaluation and Policy Analysis* 14(3): 229–40.

LeBoeuf, Robyn A., Eldar Shafir, and Julia B. Bayuk. 2010. "The Conflicting Choices of Alternating Selves." *Organizational Behavior and Human Decision Processes* 111(1): 48–61.

Lewis, Oscar. 1959. *Five Families: Mexican Case Studies in the Culture of Poverty.* New York: Basic Books.

———. 1966. *La Vida: A Puerto Rican Family in the Culture of Poverty: San Juan and New York.* New York: John Wiley.

Lock, Karen, Joceline Pomerlau, Louise Causer, and Dan R. Altmann. 2005. "The Global Burden of Disease Attributable to Low Consumption of Fruit and Vegetables: Implications for the Global Strategy on Diet." *The Bulletin of the World Health Organization* 83(2): 100–08.

Markus, Hazel, and Shinobu Kitayama. 1991. "Culture and the Self: Implications for Cognition, Emotion, and Motivation." *The Psychological Review* 98(2): 224–53.

Markus, Hazel, and Ziva Kunda. 1986. "Stability and Malleability of the Self-Concept." *The Journal of Personality and Social Psychology* 51(4): 858–66.

McQueen, Amy, and William Klein. 2006. "Experimental Manipulations of Self-Affirmation: A Systematic Review." *Self and Identity* 5(4): 289–354.

Moon, Philip, Kevin Keasey, and Darren Duxbury. 1999. "Mental Accounting and Decision Making: The Relationship Between Relative and Absolute Savings." *The Journal of Economic Behavior and Organization* 38(2): 145–53.

Mowen, Maryanne M., and John C. Mowen. 1986. "An Empirical Examination of the Biasing Effects of Framing on Business Decisions." *Decision Sciences* 17(4): 596–602.

Nisbett, Richard E., Incheol Choi, Kaiping Peng, and Ara Norenzayan. 2001. "Culture and Systems of Thought: Holistic Versus Analytic Cognition." *The Psychological Review* 108(2): 291–310.

Orr, Amy J. 2003. "Black-White Differences in Achievement: The Importance of Wealth." *The Sociology of Education* 76(4): 281–304.

Peters, Ellen, Daniel Västfjäll, Paul Slovic, C. K. Mertz, Ketti Mazzocco, and Stephan Dickert. 2006. "Numeracy and Decision Making." *Psychological Science* 17(5): 407–13.

Ranyard, Rob, and Deborah Abdel-Nabi. 1993. "Mental Accounting and the Process of Multiattribute Choice." *Acta Psychologica* 84(2): 161–77.

Raven, John C. 1936. "A New Series of Perceptual Tests: Preliminary Communication." *The British Journal of Medical Psychology* 16: 97–104.

Romich, Jennifer R., Crystal C. Hall, D. Jody Miesel, and Nicole Keenan. Forthcoming. "How EITC Eligible Tax Filers Estimate Their Refunds." Working paper, University of Washington.

Sanbonmatsu, Lisa, Jeffrey R. Kling, Greg J. Duncan, and Jeanne Brooks-Gunn. 2006. "Neighborhoods and Academic Achievement: Results from the Moving to Opportunity Experiment." *The Journal of Human Resources* 41(4): 649–91.

Sen, Amartya K. 1987. *On Ethics and Economics.* Oxford, U.K.: Blackwell.

Sherman, David K., and Geoffrey L. Cohen. 2006. "The Psychology of Self-Defense: Self-Affirmation Theory." *Advances in Experimental Social Psychology* 38: 183–242.

Steele, Claude M. 1988. "The Psychology of Self-Affirmation: Sustaining the Integrity of the Self." *Advances in Experimental Social Psychology* 21: 261–99.

Steele, Claude M., and Joshua Aronson. 1995. "Stereotype Threat and the Intellectual Test Performance of African Americans." *The Journal of Personality and Social Psychology* 69(1): 797–811.

Steele, Claude M., and David A. Sherman. 1999. "The Psychological Predicament of Women on Welfare." In *Cultural Divides: Understanding and Overcoming Group Conflict,* edited by Deborah A. Prentice and Dale T. Miller. New York: Russell Sage Foundation.

Thaler, Richard H. 1999. "Mental Accounting Matters." *The Journal of Behavioral Decision Making* 12(3): 183–206.

Turner, John C. 1985. "Social Categorization and Self-Concept: A Social Cognitive Theory of Group Behavior." In *Advances in Group Processes: Theory and Research,* vol. 2, edited by E. J. Lawler. Greenwich, Conn.: JAI Press.

———. 1987. *Rediscovering the Social Group: A Self-Categorization Theory.* New York: Blackwell.

Tversky, Amos, and Daniel Kahneman. 1981. "The Framing of Decisions and the Psychology of Choice." *Science* 211(4481): 453–58.

U.S. Census Bureau. 2010. *American Community Survey Briefs.* Available at: http://www.census.gov/prod/2010pubs/acsbr09-1.pdf (accessed November 22, 2011).

U.S. Department of Agriculture. 2009. "Access to Affordable and Nutritious Food: Measuring and Understanding Food Deserts and Their Consequences." Available at: http://www.ers.usda.gov/Publications/AP/AP036/AP036fm.pdf (accessed November 22, 2011).

Walker, Renee E., Christopher R. Keane, and Jessica G. Burke. 2010. "Disparities and Access to Healthy Food in the United States: A Review of Food Deserts Literature." *Health and Place* 16(5): 876–84.

Walton, Gregory M., and Steven J. Spencer. 2009. "Latent Ability: Grades and Test Scores Systematically Underestimate the Intellectual Ability of Negatively Stereotyped Students." *Psychological Science* 20(9): 1132–39.

Weber, Elke U., and Christopher Hsee. 1998. "Cross-Cultural Differences in Risk Perception, but Cross-Cultural Similarities in Attitudes Towards Perceived Risk." *Management Science* 44(9): 1205–17.

Zikmund-Fisher, Brian J., and Andrew M. Parker. 1999. "Demand for Rent-to-Own Contracts: A Behavioral Economic Explanation." *The Journal of Economic Behavior and Organization* 38(2): 199–216.

CHAPTER 10

WHEN HARD AND SOFT CLASH: CLASS-BASED INDIVIDUALISMS IN MANHATTAN AND QUEENS

Adrie Kusserow

Like many graduate students in cultural anthropology, I sat for hours in seminars where learned professors introduced me to the subtleties and complexities of ethno-conceptions of the self in Africa, Southeast Asia, and Latin America only to come "home" in their comparisons to a generic, almost caricatured description of the American self as simply individualistic. And while the individualistic conceptions of self they described as a backdrop to these more "exotic" selves resonated with my own upper-middle-class background and upbringing (and that of many of the academics in Cambridge, Massachusetts), I could not imagine how the working-class parents from nearby Somerville, where I lived and worked part time, would react to this definition of themselves, given the kind of individualism they practiced and fervently believed was the best way to raise their children. Surely not all communities practice, perceive, or socialize the same strands of individualism. Working in a preschool with kids and parents from working-class Somerville was my first experience of the distance between what my professors were casually referring to and what I was seeing and hearing every day.

This was the very beginning of what I would later (after finishing my dissertation fieldwork on preschools in New York) refer to as two different types of individualism, namely, "hard" and "soft" individualism. There was the "soft" individualism of the middle and upper middle classes, which focused on the cultivation and expression of unique and personal feelings, thoughts, ideas, and preferences. The sociologist Steven Tipton (1982) calls this emotion-focused style of individualism "psychologized individualism." And there was the "hard," working-class individualism, which focused on the cultivation of self-reliance, perseverance, determination, protectiveness, street smarts, stoicism, and toughness. These two styles of individualism are by

Table 10.1   Soft and Hard Individualisms in Manhattan and Queens

	Soft (Manhattan)	Hard (Queens)
Individualism means	emotional expression; creativity, uniqueness	emotional control; self-reliance; toughness; perseverance
The self is	delicate, full of promise, like a flower	hard, protective; like a fortress, rocket, Superman
Caregivers should	give praise, encouragement; mirror emotions; foster creativity	tease, discipline, toughen; nurture without spoiling
The world is	safe and welcoming; competitive; open to uniqueness	potentially dangerous; forbidding; filled with ups and downs
Jobs demand	thinking outside the box; creativity	discipline; hard work; working with others
The future holds	success, personal achievement; a job that fits your personality and interests	uncertainty, struggle; fulfillment with hard work; compromise; structure

Source: Author's compilation.

no means rigid boxes; people of all social classes can and do fluidly use each style. However, the working-class Queens, New York, residents in my research leaned more toward a hard individualistic style, whereas the upper-middle-class Manhattan residents tended more toward soft individualism.

Hard and soft individualisms not only reflect class differences in material worlds and everyday realities but also shape the everyday attitudes and habits of parents, teachers, and children. They correspond to the class-based futures that parents and teachers envision for their children—trajectories that are seen as normal and natural, the obvious choices. Insofar as children internalize these different styles of individualism, social inequality is reproduced, generation after generation, despite the myth of American mobility. For example, the two individualisms have different conceptions of self, the world the child will encounter, and the type of future the child will inhabit; and they used different metaphors to envision, describe, and guide the child's self. Each type arises from the demands, concerns, and perceptions of its local wealthy or working-class environment. Years later, after I finished my fieldwork in New York, I jotted down some thoughts on these different kinds of individualism (table 10.1). Clearly, laying a cookie-cutter version of individualism on America, I could see, ignored the very fiber of the social classes and subcultures in which these individualisms flourished.

During my research in New York, I encountered two preschools in which classrooms were privileging this kind of upper-middle-class version of individualism despite the working-class individualism children and parents brought to these schools and experienced at home. There was a dissonance between the two kinds of individualism, one promoted by the middle-class-informed Board of Education, the other a hard individualism lived in the homes and streets of the working class. My research led to many more questions that I have yet to fully explore: What different kinds of individualism are fostered in the local terrains (demands, concerns, hopes, expectations) of different social classes? What kind of selves do these individualisms promote and assume to be natural and normal? How are these individualisms expressed in the ways parents and teachers from different social classes talk about socializing their young children? What is the effect on a working-class child of being asked to do projects that are steeped in middle-class psychologized and individualistic pedagogy? In what ways is a working-class child put at a disadvantage when asked to learn and perform a different kind of individualism? When such dissonance exists, is the switch from home to school awkward, painful?

In this chapter I further describe the different conceptions of self and kinds of individualism that I observed in Manhattan and Queens, in particular the individualisms practiced and cultivated by parents in the socialization of their children, and the ways in which these individualisms can sometimes clash, like two different cultures, in certain preschool settings.

FIELDWORK

Despite my professors' caution not to do anthropological research in the United States, I began my fieldwork in Manhattan and Queens, hoping to contribute to the dehomogenization of the American concept of self by exploring the complexities and subtleties of parental conceptions of the child's self, particularly among white American parents and teachers of preschool-age children from different social classes and communities. Working in three communities, I discovered that parental conceptions of the child's self did not reflect stereotypical bipolar class constructs (a solely conforming working class and a self-directed upper middle class), nor was one generic brand of individualism sufficient to characterize them all. Individualisms arise in local worlds. Hence to explore how Americans from different social classes think about, internalize, and express their individualism, I spent one year interviewing parents and teachers, observing classrooms, attending parent-child workshops and community school–related events for parents, and conducting home visits in two New York communities, which I refer to as Parkside, a predominantly white, upper- to upper-middle-class community on the Upper East Side of Manhattan; and Queenston, a racially mixed, lower-working-class community in Queens. In the interest of controlling the race variable for both communities, I interviewed white parents and teachers in Queenston.

Studying the verbal and nonverbal socialization of the self-concepts among white four-year-olds in these preschools made up half of my research. This involved a microanalysis of the ways cultural and class construction of the self were embedded in everyday discourse and social interactions between teacher and child, daily preschool activities, ideology, spatial set-up, and discipline. The other half of my fieldwork comprised extensive semi-structured interviews with the parents of these children. In talking to parents, great effort was made not to question them directly about the concepts of individualism but rather to see what images, stories, phrases, and metaphors arose when they spoke about the children in response to more indirect questions about child-rearing beliefs and methods. Hence rather than bluntly asking people, "What does individualism mean?" I studied the way parents and teachers talked about (including the metaphors they used in describing their children), disciplined, and interacted with their preschool-aged children. I also asked them what they felt their children would need to be successful and happy in life. By studying the teachers and parents of preschoolers, I not only learned more about social-class differences in understandings of individualism but also examined how those different ideas are transmitted to new generations.

PARKSIDE AND QUEENSTON CONCEPTIONS OF SELF

The Upper East Side of Manhattan is bounded on the west by Central Park and to the east by the East River and runs from 59th to 96th Streets. Parkside is a wealthy, mainly white, neighborhood that consists of neo-Georgian townhouses, Beaux Arts mansions, art galleries, boutiques, and museums. The streets are wide and clean and well manicured. The neighborhood has long been known for its intense concentration of wealth. The 1990 census shows that the blocks between 59th and 110th Streets from Fifth Avenue to the East River have the highest per capita income of any urban quarter in the nation. Arriving in Manhattan, I decided to try my luck living on the Upper East Side as an au pair. I was offered a position by one family who would give me free room and board in exchange for babysitting their nine-year-old daughter after school for a few hours a day. From their apartment on Park Avenue it was an easy walk to many Parkside preschools as well as a weekly adult workshop on parenting hosted by a local therapist who specialized in early childhood development.

All of the Parkside parents I interviewed had enrolled their children in private preschools. Competition to get into these preschools was fierce, consisting of a long application process, multiple interviews with the parents and the child, with the parents alone, and then with the child alone. Intelligence tests and recommendations were also required. Many parents expressed a good deal of anxiety anticipating their child's performance during the interview process. Many Parkside parents saw the admissions process as only the start of competition for their children. When I asked one father, an investment banker whom I interviewed in his office, whether his three-year-old needed privacy, he answered, "It's important . . . for them. They're out there competing, developing, and learning and so they need this down time, where they aren't under a microscope, they aren't being pushed."

In Parkside's relative safety, comfort, and affluence, soft individualism thrived. The child's emotions and personal opinions, which were thought to be the markers of the idiosyncratic, "true" self, were valued highly. Parkside parents also linked the careful cultivation of psychologized individualism to their children's eventual achievement: in their interior well of emotions and thoughts, children can find both the uniqueness that will set them apart from their peers and the motivational fuel to propel them ahead of their peers. Hence, the values of psychologized individualism were often linked with success, achievement, and leadership in a competitive society. As one father said, "It gives them more of an ability to be a leader, self starter, a stand out." Being true to the self's genuine idiosyncrasies was thus tied to taking risks, being unique, standing out, and being creative. One father said, "It all comes down to this creativity thing. The more individual she is, the more creative she's going to be. We want them to freewheel and do what they want to do." Psychologized individualism was tied to ensuring that the child opened out into the world and found the right societal outlet, into a successful career that capitalized on his or her best qualities.

In Parkside, individualism was largely directed to the emotional health of the child. It was a philosophy used to protect and legitimate the unfolding of the child's psychologized self. The parents and teachers that I observed emphasized the delicacy and uniqueness of the child's self and the extreme care, resources, wide range of opportunities, and gentle touch needed to help this fragile self unfold and realize its full potential. One of the most common metaphors used to describe the unfolding of the child was that of a flower growing, blossoming, and blooming to reveal its unique contents—the child's feelings, desires, talents, tastes, imagination, and creativity. One teacher spoke of the importance of teaching the child to explore and release the emotions and how this was tied to leadership and a sense of liberation. "You really have to look for the times when you release and explore those emotions and let them feel confidence that they can lead, even if it's just leading a line of classmates, everything is within the realm of possibility."

Because the unfolding of the psychologized self is a delicate process, Parkside parents were alert to any large, clumsy, or harsh interference that might stunt it. One father, John, described to me what it meant to "mirror" a feeling, a technique he had learned in a parent guidance workshop. "I absolutely believe in all the nurturing stuff. One time my daughter left the group and told me what had happened and I mirrored her feeling rather than discounted it, saying, 'Oh, you must be really sad about that.' . . . It was validation, so important." Many of the Parkside parents and teachers I met refrained from giving stern direct commands to their children and instead disciplined them through gentle, almost tentatively voiced questions. ("Do you really think you should be bouncing that ball now, Timmy?") Parkside parents and teachers also tried to save face, voicing their concerns more often than working-class Queenston parents, masking their anger, annoyance, and frustration with children so as not to hurt their feelings or keep them from opening up.

Like many of the Manhattan preschools I observed, Parkside encouraged a number of child-oriented bodily practices and behaviors designed to protect the child's self-esteem and to encourage the opening up of the child's unique self.

Saving face: Teachers made an effort not to look bored, angry, or frustrated.

Saving voice: Teachers used a soft, gentle tone, avoiding whining, frustration, or anger directed at the child. They called children by their first name and avoided calling them by group names. For example, one teacher said she never referred to working with the children as "herding cows." The one group name used was the more egalitarian "friends"; otherwise, personal names were used.

Verbal stimulation: Teachers maintained a steady stream of talking, avoiding silence. They sought to stimulate the child by voicing observations; making lessons out of any given moment; encouraging questions, stories, and opinions.

Child-appropriate dress: Teachers were expected to dress in clothing that would appeal to and stimulate the imaginations of the children—flowers, patterns evoking children's drawing, and cartoon-type patterns.

Child-appropriate styles of communication: Teachers bent down to sit near the child so that the teacher's eyes were at the level of the child's eyes.

Physical affection: Teachers were encouraged to cuddle the children, to rub the childrens's backs, and to allow them to sit on their lap.

Across the East River from Parkside is Queenston, where harder realities give rise to harder individualisms. Queenston is a lower-working-class community that includes housing projects, a school for juvenile delinquents, and miles of chipped cement, graffiti-covered signs, garbage, broken crack vials, and the occasional prostitute. For Queenston parents, the tough environment (gangs, drugs, racism, violence), their often-difficult pasts (child abuse, alcoholism, drug addiction, divorce), and their belief that the future holds struggle and hardship give rise to a hard individualism. Queenston was by far the most difficult place to establish connections with parents. Queenston teachers had told me that the "parents won't talk, we can't even get them to leave their soap opera to talk about their child's behavior" and that many of them would "feel suspicious of me" or intimidated and just avoid me. I often called parents five or six times without reaching them; some of the apartments had no working phone. Quite often I scheduled an interview for which the parent did not show up. Sometimes this happened two or three times with the same parent. Many parents were divorced, and frequently both the men and the women were visibly exhausted, overworked, overwhelmed.

Trying to contact some of the families that did not have a telephone, I visited without notice, knocking on doors, feeling invasive, even like a stalker at times, arriving in the midst of dinner or discipline. Many parents were self-conscious about where they lived, so I interviewed more than half of the Queenston parents at school. I felt I was sometimes seen as an authority from the educational system or a case worker from the department of child welfare who was there to pass judgment on how they were raising their child. Some of these parents lived in housing projects, others in dilapidated apartments with shades drawn and doors locked, crushed crack vials littered on the street outside. Many of these mothers seemed harried, overtired, and at the end of their ropes. They had none of the luxuries most of the Parkside parents enjoyed (babysitters, air-conditioning, on-site washer and dryer, free time, housecleaners). They greeted me at the door, hesitant and sometimes defensive, in the sweltering heat, one child on a hip, others in the background jumping on the couch, a dog barking, a TV blaring in the background.

For those who had struggled in the past with the social welfare system, marriage, or drugs and come away defeated, individualism served as a legitimate philosophy that espoused a certain degree of isolation and a right to be left alone. It was a time when some parents licked their wounds in solitude or in the company of the few family members they trusted, often peering out into the world they had removed themselves from with a great deal of bitterness and mistrust. These were parents who had often been in positions of dependency on or trust in a person, community, or system, had been disappointed, and had built a philosophy of self-reliance—"You can't depend on anyone or anything except yourself." Other elements of their tough pasts might include beatings from parents who were drunk or high on drugs, repeated verbal abuse, and a total lack of communication with their own parents. The accepted tenets of individualism allowed these parents to be respected as individuals and left alone to "live their own lives the way they wanted." Individualism served a protective, healing role. These parents often spoke of independence as something they adopted later in life, after being stupid enough to think that they could be dependent on the system or a person. They spoke proudly of the process of "wising up."

When I asked one mother (who had been beaten a lot as a child while her mother was trying to stay off drugs) what things she'd like her child to have, she answered, "Independence, self reliance, 'cause other people are gonna let you down and it's a burden to other people if you can't do it yourself. . . . You really need to be able to rely on yourself or else you're in big trouble in the real world." When I asked her what happens to those who do not learn independence, she replied, "I think people take advantage of them, I do. I think people can pick up, like when people are not confident. People can sense that. It's not good. They'll take you for a ride." Mothers in Queenston, living in beat-up "bungalows" off the small side streets near the boardwalk, seemed generally fed up, tired, and bitter about their lives. They described the hardships of being left alone at the age of six, raised by drug-addicted mothers whose own fathers and husbands had left them, getting pregnant at fourteen, subway and street violence, dropping out of high school, trying to raise four kids on welfare. The themes of independence, self-reliance, and perseverance were all mentioned as a kind of embittered retreat for the adults, a way of barricading children from the inevitable disappointments in life and helping them resist the pull of the street life of gangs, the wrong crowd, peer pressure, alcohol, or drugs. The self should be resilient enough to get the child through the times "when things don't go right for them," including the hurdles and mistakes that are an inevitable part of life (hard work, low wages, little vacation, divorce and separation, loss, loneliness).

Phrases like "staying put," "standing your ground," "minding your own business," "keeping up your pride," and "not letting others get under your skin" were common. Parents implied that these tough boundaries of a dense, resilient self are the best tools to help children resist the negative influences of the street (gangs, peer pressure, violence, alcohol, drugs). Hence individualism in the form of "not relying on or trusting anyone else," self-determination, privacy, and self-reliance were often seen as ways of surviving the rigors of a bad system, a world that could not be trusted.

Techniques for raising a hard individual are different from those for raising a soft individual. Teasing, yelling, spanking, issuing direct commands without a "please" or "thank you," openly expressing one's annoyance or boredom with a child, directly contradicting a child's story, and delaying response to a child's questions or crying were all practices that Queenston adults used regularly without the guilt and trepidation that inhibited Parkside adults. Through these acts, the Queenston parents revealed not only that they wanted their children to become tougher and more resilient but also that they believed their children were tougher and more resilient to begin with. Parents often used phrases like "tough guy," "sturdy kid," "solid, "rough it through"—in fact, statements about physical punishment were never paired with any kind of worry or rumination over whether this might bring about a more fragile, more impaired, less confident child with lower self-esteem. Unlike Parkside parents, Queenston parents did not wait around after they lost their temper, nonverbally scanning the child's face for signs of weakened confidence or a deep wound to the child's self-esteem, as many Parkside parents did.

While Parkside parents were more often apt to ask children how a scolding had made them feel or cuddle them if they seemed hurt by a direct command, saying something like, "You know you aren't bad, it's what you did that was bad," working-class parents continued on with adult conversations or making dinner, without turning to their child to scan for a possible wounded reaction. In their parents' eyes, working-class kids, by their very nature, were sturdy. Physical punishment, not saving face or voice to spare the child, made perfect sense, given that the child was tough to begin with, hence there was often no need to check in with the child and see if she or he had been hurt by direct commands, slaps, or annoyance. Given the notion that such behaviors bounced off the child without impairing the delicate interior of self-esteem highly guarded by the Parkside parents, these parents spanked or yelled and moved on, assured that the child's self was resilient and, in fact, in need of such parental discipline.

DISSONANCE BETWEEN HOME AND SCHOOL IN RELATION TO PSYCHOLOGIZED INDIVIDUALISM

Education is allegedly America's great social leveler, the institution through which people, regardless of their class backgrounds, are sorted according to their intelligence, talent, perseverance, and fortitude. Social reproduction theorists have long emphasized the ways in which the class structure is reproduced from one generation to the next. In looking for institutions that reproduce the social relations of a capitalist society, they are often led to one institution in particular: the school. Despite popular belief that the school is the ultimate neutral ground, where classless, unbiased texts and classless, culture-neutral pedagogies are doled out to every child in equal parts, the school has proved to be one of the greatest sites of the reproduction of social inequality. (See, for example, Bowles and Gintis 1976; Bourdieu 1977; Bernstein 1975; Heath 1983; Willis 1977; MacLeod 1995; Giroux 1983.) As Pierre Bourdieu (1977) has emphasized, school culture is most often predicated on the values and practices of the middle class, and the preschools that I describe in this chapter, with the exception of two, followed the same pattern. In one preschool where working-class children were taught upper-middle-class, soft, psychologized individualism (Kusserow 2004), this was largely because the New York Board of Education insisted that teachers socialize the child's self in this softer way, and it was also the dominant pedagogy for those working-class teachers who were able to get advanced degrees in early childhood education.

For example, in a few of the Head Start programs I observed, the distance between the hard and soft individualisms was often manifest in the silence of the lower-working-class children, seemingly mystified by the gentle ways of the teacher, who moved around the classroom with a constant glow and smile, showering praise on them. Many of these children came from families where conformity to group life was taught through practices such as teasing, public shaming, blaming, direct commands, and threats. The processes of handling and crafting the self of the child had distinctly different styles, Parkside's being a loosening, and Queenston's a blunting, of the self. Another striking difference lay in what was considered damaging to the child's self. Freely expressing boredom or annoyance, speaking to a child in an angry or demanding way, or failing to communicate with a child at eye level was not seen by many Queenston parents as in any way damaging to the child's self-esteem. Nor was simply being silent with them in the car (instead of engaging the child in conversation) seen as understimulation.

Queenston parents seemed to have more confidence in a certain plucky inevitability to the child's intellectual development and natural curiosity. They did not feel they were mowing over delicate flowers; rather, they viewed these "harsher" practices in the context of building a healthy, spunky, resilient self of the child. It was from this sense of the child's sturdy ego base that they teased or yelled. They did not assume this would shatter the child's self-esteem or confidence; rather, they thought they were merely thickening the child's self in preparation for life's tumbles. Parents were helping their children adapt and grow, starting from what they felt their children could handle.

One mother, Sara, talked about how silly and "soft" her sister's discipline of her children was. She also spoke disparagingly of the "mushiness" of her oldest son. Of her sister, she says, "She's into all that time-out stuff. She says to her kid, 'You're not bad, what you've done is bad.' I mean give me a break. Of course the kid is bad sometimes." Sara said that when she was growing up her mother would sit in the corner with her coffee, and if Sara did something wrong, her mother would throw a spoon at her from across the room. She also said she was afraid her husband was getting "too soft" with the kids. Despite her shy personality, during the interview Sara would switch suddenly into loud, harsh yells and scream at the kids to leave her alone while she was talking. Neither the child nor the parent flinched from these outbursts. Both resumed normal play or conversation, as if it were part of the natural ebb and flow of life in the house. She then talked about her eldest son, who was the "mushiest" because he got the most attention. Asked if too much attention leads to that, she replied, "You shouldn't pay too much attention to any emotion and you shouldn't baby them too much, give them too much praise. You don't want them to be too soft."

Discipline

The Queenston children were confused when a middle-class teacher, interrupting a scuffle, would take them aside and ask them to explain why they wanted to hit one another and how it made them feel to be hit. Accustomed to being spanked, shamed, or simply ignored for fighting, they seemed bewildered by the new, therapeutic way of dealing with conflict. Some children did not seem even to know they were being disciplined and hence had to be frequently reminded. Used to direct commands, harsh voices, and assertions of their lower place in the hierarchy, they sometimes could not distinguish between comments or questions and "real" discipline, at least the type they were used to at home. Sometimes in conjunction with a soft, slightly hesitant tone of voice and a number of qualifiers, teachers made statements like "Josie, I can think of lots of other things you could do besides hitting Tommy that would make you feel a lot better. Can you name one of these for me?" or "Sam, do you think you could think about doing something more gentle with your body?" or "You know what I am noticing? Has anyone noticed that people are talking without raising hands?"

In a soft individualistic attempt to give the child some power and to avoid the appearance of hierarchy, often considerable time was spent with a child in this question-and-answer mode in which the teacher tried gently to orient the child toward the right answer without issuing a stern command. This involved using several questions over and over again. If a child used a hammer to pound in a tack when he could push it in with his finger, one teacher asked, "Do you think that's the best thing to use? *[Silence, long pause]* It's up to you, but do you think you should use that? Can you think of anything better to use?" Furthermore, the child's behavior, not the child, was named as problematic, making direct discipline less direct than the working-class children were used to: "Tommy, you're not using your listening ears today, are you? . . . Why not?" Hence those children coming from homes where discipline consisted of physical punishment and strong, direct commands sometimes responded poorly to the discipline at the Head Start program—lengthy mediation of fights, a balanced hearing of children involved in a disagreement, no preconceived notions of who was right and who was wrong when an issue was being aired out—perhaps because they could not recognize it as discipline at all.

Privacy

One of the other interesting areas of dissonance between the soft, psychologized individualism favored in the Parkside schools and the hard individualism of working-class homes was the domain of privacy. Privacy was one of the concepts that also revealed a less psychologized conception of the child's self on the part of Queenston parents. I learned a great deal about conceptions of the self by asking parents and teachers whether, and why, they felt their children needed privacy. Interestingly enough, the Queenston parents gave quite a mix of replies. Many of them felt that children needed privacy but not necessarily a psychological privacy aimed at protecting or nourishing the unique emotional terrain and feelings of the child. They did not feel that the child's psychologized self needed shelter or space to the extent that the Parkside parents did. Whereas Parkside parents almost universally spoke of the privacy needed for the psychological aspects of the self of each child, at least half of the Queenston parents referred to the privacy needed for the general sexual aspects of the child or said that children did not need privacy at such a young age.

Some of these parents felt the child did not need privacy at all until puberty, at which point it was this sexual aspect of development that deserved space and shelter, not necessarily the emotions, moods, feelings, or personality of the child. Often what was meant by privacy for the Queenston parents was a privacy and shelter for the budding sexuality of the body, a privacy defined by gender, especially privacy from the opposite sex, most often expressed as girls' need for privacy from their fathers. One Queenston mother, Ellen, in response to my question as to whether children needed privacy at the preschool age, spoke of her four-year-old daughter: "I don't know. Yeah, I think so. Dawn is very private. The other kids would run around with no clothes on, but not her. She can't even change her shirt in front of her grandfather. . . . So yeah, I think they have to learn that. . . . I have three girls, and we're all the same sex. They have to learn what's theirs is theirs. No one's allowed to touch." Another Queenston mother, Diane, spoke of the need for privacy in terms of the daughter's need to respect her own body. "Privacy shows them to respect . . . themselves and to respect everybody else—don't want them growin' up fourteen, fifteen years old usin' the bathroom with your mom, walkin' in the room like it's no big deal."

In the Queenston preschool where soft individualism was promoted, one of the bathrooms for the children was in the classroom itself, surrounded by a dense piece of cloth the size of a shower curtain. Children could use this bathroom if they chose, or they could go down the hall to the real bathrooms. Interestingly enough, two working-class parents complained that this did not guarantee full privacy for their children, that no one should be hearing them go pee in the middle of class. This same arrangement in one of the Parkside preschools was not addressed as mentioned as a problem by any of the parents. Rather, the parents' more common complaint about privacy was that the children did not have enough emotional down time, time-out corners, individual spaces to just do a craft or play however they wanted to do.

In speaking of privacy from siblings, parents also referred to the rights of ownership of various objects that belonged to the child. Dawn's mother remarked, "You don't go into Dawn's room and start playing with her little games. That's hers. What I also did with each of them, since they share a room, and they have bunk beds. So I build shelves in each of their beds for their own private things. If they go to a birthday party, and they bring home like those little things in goodie bags, they put it on their shelf. No one else can touch what's on their shelf."

When I finally purposely asked one Queenston mother about privacy that might not be related to being in the bathroom (that is, a more psychologized privacy), she said she wouldn't push it, because then they're going to expect it and it's hard to get that in a big family. Privacy was seen as more a luxury they could do without than a basic need.

I also discovered that at times, when parents talked about a child's privacy, they were referring to psychological privacy appropriate for an older child, because the presumption was that a child of preschool age did not need privacy. Sometimes these parents would automatically switch to talking about their oldest child, assuming that was whom my privacy question referred to.

One father, James, said, "At four, no. I mean privacy when he goes to the bathroom, yes. But in his own room, I don't, no, not important right now, doesn't need it 'cause he wouldn't want it anyway. He's just three. I mean, if you say, 'Here's your private time. Go in your room and think.' I mean [laughs], what privacy do they need? I mean these questions are for a little bit older children." This same father, when I asked him about the quiet spot in the Queenston preschool classroom where only one child could go in at a time, said it seemed like a total waste of space.

Another Queenston mother who adopted some of the upper-middle-class methods of child rearing similar to those practiced at Parkside emphasized the same thing: "My son has his own room. The oldest one, Matthew, has bunk beds. When it's time out, you go upstairs, you play by yourself, you relax." When I asked, "What's good about privacy?" she replied, "To see themselves, you know, to, [it's] a question of independence. They won't need another person to play [with]. They can play by themselves and relax, and Matthew reads his books and stuff."

For these parents, privacy was tied to learning self-reliance. As one of the strands of individualism felt to be important among these parents, privacy taught the boy independence, to entertain himself, to rely on himself. Queenston parents responded to questions about privacy in a variety of ways: some felt that young children had no need for privacy; others stressed the importance of physical, especially sexual, privacy and for protection of personal property and information; still others saw privacy as a way of learning how to be alone or to be self-reliant in a world where there will not always be people around to help you. It comes as no surprise, then, that in the Queenston preschool, where soft individualism was promoted, certain working-class parents were confused by the "need" for a quiet space in the preschool. During an orientation session at the preschool, one parent said, "Why go to preschool, then, if you're just going to need time alone? It seems a little silly if you ask me." They were also bothered by the lack of physical privacy in the classroom's shower-curtained bathroom in a way that Parkside parents would not have been.

Creativity

Working-class children may also be flummoxed by some of the more softly individualistic academic requirements and pedagogical practices. One teacher said, "I tell these kids to use their imagination, and they say, 'What do you mean? I don't have imagination.'" Parkside children were used to daily rituals involving verbal self-expression in front of an audience, elaboration of personal stories about experiences outside of school, art projects based on imagination, the use of emotion words to describe inner states, as well as asking questions, being curious, inquisitive, precocious. This identification of soft individualism as natural, innate behavior masks the process that middle-class children had gone through to learn it, making soft individualism seem even more mysterious to working-class children. Bourdieu (1977, 495) writes of this Catch-22 in "Cultural Reproduction and Social Reproduction": "An educational system which puts into practice an implicit pedagogic action requiring initial familiarity with the dominant culture, and which proceeds by imperceptible familiarization, offers information and training which can be received and acquired only by subjects endowed with the system of predispositions that is the condition for the success of the transmission and of the inculcation of the culture. By doing away with giving explicitly to everyone what it implicitly demands of everyone, the educational system demands of everyone alike that they have what it DOES NOT GIVE" (emphasis in original).

The invisible and never explicitly taught cultural capital of school can seal children into the mindset that education is not for them. In a New York upper-middle-class preschool, a child of Puerto Rican immigrants who is told at home not to talk back to adults, to be quiet, to speak only when spoken to, and to remember his or her place may be written up in an evaluation as anything ranging from naturally shy to sullen, rebellious, recalcitrant, stubborn, lacking communication skills, or dull. Because the angelic, fairylike behavior that is expected of them is so different from what they have been used to, some children, rather than try it out like a role in a play, may perhaps get stage fright and became caricatures of their own cultural capital or view it as ludicrous, effeminate, spineless.

One of the most striking juxtapositions between the two individualisms was manifested in one child, Amanda. In a classroom adorned with posters advocating soft individualism, Amanda told me that her brother had "smacked her on the back," so she "punched him back." Her mother then smacked him for smacking her, and then smacked them both, she reported. Amanda was four years old, very plucky and perhaps my favorite of the children because of her colorful nonverbal behavior and theatrics. I was impressed with the sophistication of her negative facial expressions. She had already learned how to posture a somewhat jaded, cynical, snide look and seemed to take pride in her facial antics. During free play, with a rumpled apron tied around her waist, she would clean house and laugh at how pathetic the other children's play was, as if they were naïve and clueless and had not wised up. She would look over at me, as if acknowledging our status as fellow outsiders, and make an exaggerated snide face, as if all of this playing house stuff was too quaint. She stood with one hand on her hip, dustpan in the other, and mimicked a tough, bitchy expression on her face.

Other times, I noticed she was snide to the other children, laughing at them, making faces at them, as if to imply they were losers. Another child would say something to her and she would roll her eyes with a look of disgust, making a fist, as if she would like to hit the child. She did all of this quite skillfully outside the gaze of the teachers, knowing she had to work under the radar to avoid getting into trouble. She had accepted their authority and knew not to get caught threatening it or disturbing the peace of the classroom. She had perfected the art of tough individualism within the established hierarchy of the classroom. Self-determined, she moved quietly out of view of the teachers, showing her cocky and defensive stance only to the other children and to me, not letting any child push her down or get in her way.

POETRY AND PORTFOLIOS: PARENTAL RESISTANCE TO THE PSYCHOLOGIZATION OF THE CHILD'S SELF

Portfolios were a perfect example of the Board of Education's attempt to promote upper-middle-class psychologized teaching methods in Queenston preschools, in which most of the teachers were working class and had not been trained in these methods. When I was doing my fieldwork in Queenston, portfolios had just been introduced into one of the classrooms I observed. Portfolios were books put together by the teachers for each child, with samples of the child's work. Portfolios included selected pieces of artwork, the activities the child chose in class, or things said by the child. All of these together were said to represent the uniqueness of the child's self more fully than a grade or a generic teacher report.

While I was observing at this preschool, one of the educational administrators from the New York City Board of Education, Miss Thompson, came in for a weekly meeting with the preschool teachers to make sure the portfolio process was being "correctly implemented." About half of the preschool teachers, those who had been teaching in the school for some time and were not presently pursuing a degree in education, saw Miss Thompson as a nuisance. The teachers felt they did very well on their own, without what they described as a rather nosy, controlling, and uptight woman telling them what they should do with their class. Most often her words were taken with a grain of salt. The teachers nodded as if in agreement and then secretly rolled their eyes when she turned away. Miss Thompson represented the new upper-middle-class "sensitive" and child-centered teaching methods and techniques that the Board of Education was hoping would filter down into every New York classroom. These methods often focused on protecting the child's self-esteem and showing appropriate appreciation for his or her uniqueness and individuality.

Some of the requirements of elementary school may even directly conflict with a working-class family's values or notions of masculinity. Teacher Mrs. O'Neil recalled one such instance: "One of the last projects in my class was putting together a poetry book. So this working-class kid wrote these very sweet poems about how weird it is to feel yourself growing into a man. I asked him, 'Don't you want to take your poetry book home?' And the kid said: 'Oh no. If my dad saw these he would beat me.' O'Neil says that although the student was joking about the beating, he was serious about how deep his embarrassment would run should his sensitivity and imagination be discovered and his masculinity be questioned.

Nowhere was this disparity in class cultures more evident than in circle time, one of the classic preschool rituals, where children are given a chance to speak by themselves, telling a story about anything they want. Ironically, it is democratically called sharing, yet the differences between the stories of the Queenston kids and the Parkside kids could be dramatic. I could not help but think of Peggy Miller's (1994) research among middle- and working-class parents in Baltimore. One of the ways that working- and middle-class parents socialize hard versus soft individualism lies in how they help their children tell stories. Middle-class parents of preschoolers allow their children to include incorrect or fantastical elements in their versions of stories, rather than correcting them. When they do correct their children's narratives, they do so gently and discreetly, so as not to impinge on the child's right to express his or her own view of the experience—a softly individualistic impulse. In contrast, working-class parents regularly challenge their preschool children's stories and neither soften their oppositions nor give in quickly. In this way, children get used to defending their versions of reality. Thus storytelling becomes a training ground on which preschoolers learn to defend themselves against affronts—a component of hard individualism.

In my own fieldwork, during circle time, Parkside kids seemed confident and physically almost jumped out of their assigned places on the rug, ready to take flight into fantasy realms (purple dragons and castles made of chocolate) and expected a rapt and awestruck audience. Their confidence was stunning, as if they were used to having an audience that oohed and aahed at whatever they said. Metaphors and similes would later come to them easily, as might the exercise of poetry. In contrast the Queenston preschoolers had more realistic, flattened (in the sense of less fantastical) stories about what they did the day before, such as, "I went to the grocery store with my mother."

Other kinds of creative projects involving self-introspection can be viewed by working-class parents as selfish or a waste of time. One Queenston parent said of her preschooler's older brother, "Yeah, all this journal stuff, they're trying to turn him into a little Woody Allen—I'm like get over yourself, you've got bigger fish to fry. I told him the project was stupid."

Around the preschool classroom were a sprinkling of small poster-like pieces of paper illustrating different ways a teacher or parent could phrase something so as not to hurt the child's self-esteem. For example, one phrase might be, "It's not that you're bad, Megan, it's that what you've done is bad." These sheets also included advice on how to ask children what they would like to do, instead of commanding them, as well as various clever ways to give praise to children, thereby raising their confidence and belief in themselves. These stayed on the walls and did not seem to receive a great deal of attention. Whereas in the Parkside preschools these approaches were practiced on a daily basis without reminders hanging on the walls, most of the Queenston teachers (with the exception of the youngest, who had a higher degree in teaching than the others and seemed to mimic the posters word for word) did not seem to feel their teaching needed more sensitivity, attentiveness, praise, or warmth.

What was most interesting were some of the parents' responses to these portfolios. For example, I asked Mr. James, a prison guard and construction worker living in Queenston, whether his child needed privacy. He said no, without hesitation, and talked disparagingly and bitterly about the children's portfolios at preschool. Mr. James resisted the psychologization of a four-year-old. He felt kids should not be treated so cautiously and thought about so seriously all the time.

> I went over there—they have a class, a school meeting, and Miss Tarlin is telling me, "Well, we drew these pictures with finger paints. What do you see in them?" I said, "I see a mess. What do you see?" I mean, don't try to read into a four-year-old finger painting. It's not too—I mean, can you pick out a psychological murderer at four years old? I don't think, I mean, don't try to read into it. I mean, don't even give me all this hogwash. I really don't want to hear it. This is a four-year-old kid. Don't tell, I mean, they have stacks of paper on a four-year-old kid!

I then asked him if he could tell me about his child's portfolio. "Portfolio. It's how they get along. They put [in] their pictures and try to analyze them. What do you see after this child paints a picture? What is it? How do you see your father here, or where do you see the flower in this? And then they'll try and explain it to you." "Psychoanalysis?" I said jokingly, sensing his frustration.

> Psychoanalysis, yeah. I mean, you're psychoanalyzing a four-year-old kid that is standing there with their hand in paint. If you ask them draw a picture of a flower and they drew a weed, maybe you could figure something out there, but I don't think you're gonna figure out hand paintin', so I told her it was just a little too much, and I said you're gettin' a little too serious with four-year-olds. She said,

"Well, this is the Board of Education's rules, now, so we have to do it, we have to explain it." And I said, "Well, I don't want to hear it. This is bullshit." You know what I mean. I'm not—there are people I know in Manhattan who I know people who have a two-year-old and the two-year-old says instead of da da, says ta ta, and they fuckin' analyze it, and I mean, shit! It's unbelievable. You're better lettin' 'em go into a pile of mud and put it on the wall. It's the same shit.

Similar small instructional posters hung on the walls of the parent room in Queenston. The parent room was meant as a meeting place for parents to talk about their children and take mini-courses on crafts, cooking, and holiday gift ideas. Rarely did I see parents in this room. Mothers and especially fathers had to be pushed and prodded to come in. I interviewed a group of about four Queenston parents who had been urged by the parent room coordinator, Ms. Costado, to come in one day so I could talk with them. Most often when I asked the group a question, the parents would reply one way and Ms. Costado would tell them the way they should have responded. The dynamic of the group interview was my asking "serious" questions and the parents responding with jokes. I was torn between just giving up on the interview and laughing along with them or continuing with my job. I expect I seemed to them a prudish anthropologist asking serious questions.

At no time did the child-centered psychologized philosophy seem more foreign than at that moment. In fact, throughout the interview, Ms. Costado, trying to get a more serious response from the parents, emphasized the child-centered philosophy espoused by the New York Board of Education: that parents should be more sensitive to children's needs, more empathetic, they should try to understand how the children are feeling, build their confidence, sometimes let children tell you what they want to do instead of dictating to them, praise them more, and remember to tell them that though their behavior may be bad, they are not bad people.

Most of the parents did not seem to take her advice seriously and, in fact, the interview turned out to be more of a laughing session where the parents joked around about their children, gossiped with one another, and snickered at the craziness of some of Ms. Costado's suggestions. Ms. Costado seemed embarrassed by how the parents were responding to my questions and would often say things like, "Oh, come on, you know better than that. How should you really do it?" Ms. Costado had grown up in the area and was well liked by the parents. Unlike Miss Thompson, she was down-to-earth and unpretentious, more like one of them, despite her attempts to change the way they raised their children. Ms. Costado was able to get close to the parents because of her similar background, sense of humor, and understanding of where the parents were coming from. As much as she could, amid the mutual teasing and laughter, she tried to introduce suggestions on how to treat children with respect, but most of the parents did not pay much attention. When I asked a question, parents would often reply with a joke. Asked, "When are you most proud of your child?" one mother, a large, gruff woman whose husband was a police officer and whose son was the class rabble rouser, replied, "When he shuts his mouth!" and laughed. The whole group laughed with her. Ms. Costado looked disappointed. She tried to get the interview back on track. "Be serious, now. Come on. You know that's not what you mean. Go ahead, Adrie [to me]. Now listen to her; listen up [to the group]."

Occasionally the parents were having such a good time laughing and joking that I could not be heard. They took seriously neither the interview itself nor new information on child rearing and the children's feelings. One last time I meekly asked, feeling totally out of place, "What are some qualities you are most proud of in yourself that you hope the child will have?" One young father, John, full of machismo, said, "I'm a great sex lover; that's what I hope he's like." The whole group laughed again. I laughed along with them, trying not to be too serious but also trying to get them to engage with me. "How do you discipline your kids?" I asked. The large woman, Mary, answered, "Smack 'em upside the head." To this John said, "No, spank 'em on the butt; that's better." Most of the interview continued like this, Ms. Costado piping in afterward with, "You know you're not supposed to hit them first. Come on, John, be serious. Help this lady out. She's trying to do her school thesis."

In response to this, John tried to contain his laughter, finding it hard to resist the chance to entertain the group, but this only made them laugh harder. Most of the time the laughter seemed to be over the difference between the way they disciplined their children or sometimes felt about their children and the ways Ms. Costado suggested they should act and feel. Spanking and hitting and being irritated or frustrated with the child were offered up as answers, and laughter soon followed over how far from correct their answers were.

REPRODUCTION OF INEQUALITY: THE IMPULSE TO NATURALIZE

I hope this chapter has led to some insights into the different kinds of individualisms different social classes and their local landscapes foster, practice, and embody and what happens when hard and soft individualisms clash. I also hope this chapter can begin to open further conversations about how the socialization of these individualisms, insofar as they are such a deep part of a child's basic worldview, can contribute to a kind of reproduction and continuation of social inequalities. Class-based individualisms are not easily tried on and shed, like so many hats. They often form the visceral core of a child's being and of a child's worldview—of what is possible in life, what is real, dangerous, silly, or normal, what constitutes success, the goals one should aspire to achieve. Insofar as parents and teachers used distinctly different metaphors, such as a flower as at Parkside or the fortresslike images of protection at Queenston, in talking about and disciplining their children, they begin to establish children's naturalized conception of their own nature, their "natural" environment, their future place in the world.

In "Cultural Reproduction and Social Reproduction," Bourdieu (1977) writes that the pedagogic culture that schools transmit mirrors the dominant culture. Pedagogies of the upper middle class are privileged in schools in a way that disadvantages children who have not been socialized in these forms of cultural capital. Why? The reason is that in large part, the transmission of school knowledge and culture "depends on the previous possession of the instruments of appropriation . . . requiring initial familiarity with the dominant culture" (Bourdieu 1977, 493–94).

Focusing on individual agency shifts a teacher's attention from the unequal social environment to the children's individual talents and natural traits. Who ever thinks of questioning the value of generosity, creativity, artistic talent, and hard work? On the Upper East Side of Manhattan, it is a given, not a luxury, that children should be allowed to discover themselves, what they are good at, through lessons in art, ballet, and tennis. In lower-income parts of Queens, it is a given that no child should be spoiled too much because the world is not like that. We all need to look out for ourselves, that is just part of what it means to live. Yet time and time again, working-class parents and teachers praise the toughness and stubborn spirit of their children, while upper-middle-class parents praise the precociousness of theirs, as if these were individual traits given at birth.

Upper-middle-class parents consciously and unconsciously teach their children how to communicate with teachers and other adults in power. These children are curious, are inquisitive, and know how to ask questions. As a result, when they show up for their first day of school, they have already mastered a large, albeit implicit, portion of the curriculum. These behaviors then get called "talent," "sensitivity," "intelligence," "imagination," and other traits that are supposedly inborn and supposedly necessary for scholastic success—rather than class-based knowledge learned in Parkside homes and local environments like story hour at Barnes and Noble or a visit to the Museum of Natural History. As children and parents disengage, instead of being labeled as culturally out of sync, they are labeled as uncooperative, dumb, hard to reach, or lazy. The children start to feel that education is not for them, and they often get tracked into lower-level and remedial classes.

HEGEMONY OF THE "SOFT"

Much more research needs to be done on how working-class parents and children feel about the dissonance between class culture in the home and at school. Do they feel slighted, baffled, bemused, intimidated? To what extent is the convergence of these hard and soft realities jarring, uncomfortable, or even traumatic? Wendy Luttrell (1997), in her book *Schoolsmart and Motherwise: Working-Class Women's Identity and Schooling*, describes the degradation and disdain that schools steeped in upper-middle-class pedagogy inflict on students from working-class backgrounds. The anthropologist Philippe Bourgois (1996) describes the agony of having to choose between the culture of home and family and that of school in his book *In Search of Respect: Selling Crack in El Barrio*. He describes the trauma of first contact with the public school system from the perspective of a recent Puerto Rican immigrant and Primo, her second-generation son. Bourgois (1996, 177) writes, "It is in school that the full force of middle-class society's definitions of appropriate capital and symbolic violence comes crashing down on a working-class Puerto Rican child."

Primo's mother, a former rural plantation worker, worked in an inner-city sweatshop. Her functional illiteracy and her inability to communicate with the educational bureaucracy were passed on to Primo, who consequently appeared uncooperative and slow-witted to his kindergarten teachers. Perhaps feeling he had to protect himself, he resisted his teachers lest they unconsciously insult or hurt him should he make the mistake of trying to please them—and inevitably failing. Despite his anxious mother's admonishments that he respect his teacher and do well in school, Primo felt that success in the classroom would have betrayed his love for her (Bourgois 1996, 176).

The kind of hegemony of the soft, psychologized individualism and its clash with hard individualism, explored in this chapter at the site of the preschool, has wider implications. It can also be felt between predominantly middle- and upper-middle-class social service providers and the lower- and working-class clients they serve.

In addition, the rift between individualisms can undermine well-intentioned social sector attempts at building cross-class coalitions. Betsy Leondar-Wright (2005, 85), a social justice activist and the author of *Class Matters: Cross-Class Alliance Building for Middle-Class Activists*, recounts one such class clash:

> I was facilitating a mid-Atlantic regional antinuclear meeting in 1979. There were about 50 people there—mostly white, mostly middle class. We were planning a massive No Nukes march on Washington D.C. We were doing our first go-round of introductions, and to make it more playful, I had asked people to answer the question, "If you were an animal, what animal would you be?" Then in walked about six union guys, all with short hair, suits and ties, from the United Mine Workers of America. These guys don't do animal names. They didn't do small groups. Their muckety-muck gave his speech, and then the union guys just walked out, most of them without saying a word.

The United Mine Workers of America did not send delegates to the Washington march. "I knew I had done something wrong, but I didn't know what."

As Bourgois (1996) notes, even when former crack dealers tried their hardest to keep low-level jobs in middle-class workplaces, they could not change the ways they spoke, moved, and dressed enough to satisfy managers. After donning white button-down shirts, removing their gold chains, and cutting down on their swearing—all acts that called into question their sense of their own masculinity—these men still found that the better jobs of receptionist or plant caretaker were reserved for those who looked, spoke, and acted in keeping with middle-class soft individualism.

A number of difficult ethical questions arise that pertain to both the school and the workplace: If the white-collar world is more softly individualistic, should lower- and working-class kids get taught this method in school to help them engage in the white-collar world? If not, how do schools handle multiple models and address this dissonance between home and school? Should schools and workplaces attempt to transcend class differences? If so, how would this be done? Furthermore, can social scientists, educators, and policymakers assume that middle- and upper-middle-class individualism is indeed the best and natural endpoint of development? The understated American discourse on what to do about class divides usually recommends that the lower classes assimilate to the middle- and upper-middle-class norm.

I would argue that building pedagogies and curricula that "transcend" class differences is perhaps not as easy as one would think. When Americans think about social class, we usually think about the material evidence: different forms of transit; different kinds of and sizes of houses; different neighborhoods; different jobs; different access to health care; different exposures to pollution and violence; different styles of music, clothes, food, and pastimes. But class is not just about the material world, and class cultures are not just skin deep. Class cannot be wiped off like the frosting on a cake. Class penetrates the very core of our being, down to the way we hold our forks, tell our stories, console and discipline our children, talk to our neigh-

bors, remember our pasts, hold and sculpt our bodies, and imagine our futures. Social class is lived in the flesh, viscerally, held in one's self-image and one's vision of
life's possibilities. Basic assumptions about the nature of the self, the future and reality (Is the world safe or dangerous? Do people need to express their feelings to be
happy? Should a child be teased? Spanked?) are at the root of these differing styles
and are not easily switched on or off in either the school or the workplace.

Assimilating to the middle class is not only difficult, it can also be painful. "Everyone talks about how wonderful upward mobility and the American dream are, but no
one mentions the loss and the cost," notes Felice Yeskel, codirector of Class Action, a
nonprofit organization that works to raise awareness about the impact of class on
individuals, relationships, and institutions. "People who change classes—what we
call straddlers—don't feel at home in either their class of origin or in their new class."
Some acknowledge the difficulty of straddling and yet still place the onus of assimilation on the lower classes. Ruby Payne is the founder and president of Aha! Process, a
company that teaches organizations about social-class cultures. "When you are required by law to participate in middle-class institutions, like education or legal institutions, and you don't know the hidden rules of the middle class, you can get cruci-
fied," she told me.

A number of questions arise: Whose job is it to assimilate to predominantly
middle-class schools and social sectors? Should Queenston kids eventually be forced
to assimilate into soft, psychologized individualism? Should schools challenge the
board of education's assumption that this is the ultimate educational and developmental goal? Should managers of working-class employees force them to learn how
to act like white-collar professionals? Should employers insist that managers learn
about their own working-class cultures and adapt the workplace to an ethos and feel
of hard individualism? Christina Hoff Sommers is not sold on the idea of one-way
assimilation. In *One Nation Under Therapy: How the Helping Culture Is Eroding Self-
Reliance*, written with Sally Satel (2005, 94), Sommers says, "We have a word for
middle-class people's preoccupation with their inner world. It's depression." She
asks, "Who would you rather have as a co-worker—someone from a precious
middle-class environment who expects lavish praise and falls apart at the first criticism, or someone with self-discipline and a strong work ethic?" Sommers suggests
that the working-class's harder selves may be what will restore the United States's
competitive edge in the global economy. "These working class kids might be able to
move ahead while the middle-class kids are sitting in circles sharing feelings and
wondering what happened."

In light of my own research I do not believe soft, psychologized individualism
should be the educational and developmental goal. Adopting either worldview to
the exclusion of the other seems unrealistic. Pedagogies that include both hard and
soft classroom approaches and assignments might be the ideal, but before this happens, students, managers, employees, and teachers need to begin looking at social
class in general. In a sense, social class needs to come out of the closet. Perhaps the
first step is becoming aware of one's own culture-based style of individualism and
the ways in which it unconsciously seems natural, right, true, and inevitable. Close
on the heels of this first step is to acknowledge that one's own class culture is not
necessarily the best or only way to live. The third step should involve learning about

the local worlds of other classes, those that are unfamiliar. Deeper knowledge of lower- and working-class contexts would give practitioners, managers, and teachers a sense of how tough, unfair, or helpful proposed assignments or changes would be for their students or clients, as well as how realistic certain changes really are.

Given that mainstream American culture is often dominated by middle-class practices, values, and institutions, isn't it the responsibility of the teacher, the parent, and the manager to teach these class-based ways to working-class students, children, and clients? There are no easy answers to this question. Perhaps the money and stability gained from a better job, more education, or different habits would be worth the discomfort of the shift in cultures. Or perhaps the soft, psychologized, middle-class culture would be so strange for the working class that it would not stick—even if liberally applied—or so jarring that it would cause shame or withdrawal. Since each case is different, the implications for social class should be carefully and explicitly addressed. At the most general level, the assumptions of social class should be admitted into the broader American discourse on social change. Doing so might ultimately guide us to more effective techniques for short-circuiting the perpetuation of social inequality.

REFERENCES

Bernstein, Basil. 1975. *Class, Codes, and Control*. London: Routledge and Kegan Paul.

Bourdieu, Pierre. 1977. "Cultural Reproduction and Social Reproduction." In *Power and Ideology in Education*, edited by Jerome Karabel and A. H. Halsey. New York: Oxford University Press.

Bourgois, Philippe. 1996. *In Search of Respect: Selling Crack in El Barrio*. New York: Cambridge University Press.

Bowles, Samuel, and Herbert Gintis. 1976. *Schooling in Capitalist America*. New York: Basic Books.

Giroux, Henry. 1983. *Theory and Resistance in Education*. London: Heinemann Educational.

Heath, Shirley Brice. 1983. *Ways with Words*. Cambridge: Cambridge University Press.

Kusserow, Adrie. 2004. *American Individualisms: Child Rearing and Social Class in Three Neighborhoods*. New York: Palgrave Macmillan.

Leondar-Wright, Betsy. 2005. *Class Matters: Cross-Class Alliance Building for Middle-Class Activists*. Gabriola Island, British Columbia, Canada: New Society Publishers.

Luttrell, Wendy. 1977. *Schoolsmart and Motherwise: Working-Class Women's Identity and Schooling*. New York: Routledge.

MacLeod, Jay. 1995. *Ain't No Makin' It: Aspirations and Attainment in a Low-Income Neighborhood*. Boulder, Colo.: Westview.

Miller, Peggy. 1994. "Narrative Practices and the Social Construction of Self in Childhood." *The American Ethnologist* 17(6): 292–311.

Sommers, Christina Hoff, and Sally Satel. 2005. *One Nation Under Therapy: How the Helping Culture Is Eroding Self-Reliance*. New York: St. Martin's.

Tipton, Steven. 1982. *Getting Saved from the Sixties: Moral Meaning in Conversion and Cultural Change*. Berkeley: University of California Press.

Willis, Paul. 1977. *Learning to Labor: How Working Class Kids Get Working Class Jobs*. Aldershot, U.K.: Gower.

CHAPTER 11

PUTTING RACE IN CONTEXT: SOCIOECONOMIC STATUS PREDICTS RACIAL FLUIDITY

Diana T. Sanchez and Julie A. Garcia

In the fall of 2007, the United States elected Barack Obama as its forty-fourth president and its first African American president. Not surprisingly, his election fueled conversations about the state of ethnic relations in the United States. Many considered his election to be a victory over racism. However, both his election and the media frenzy over his racial background suggest that we are far from achieving a color-blind society. Obama was born to a white mother and a black father; many people questioned his racial status. Headlines such as "Is Obama Black Enough?" (Coates 2007) shed light on the difficulty that many have in categorizing people with multiracial backgrounds. If Obama has white ancestry, does that make him any less black? Questions about Obama's racial categorization and the salience of his multiracial background revived discussions on definitions of race in American society. For example, who is considered black in American society, and why? In this chapter, we consider the oft-ignored role of socioeconomic status (SES) in racial categorization. Specifically, we discuss the growing literature on socioeconomic status and racial categorization to understand how class complicates the meaning of race.

Broadly speaking, examining how SES contributes to the experiences of racial minorities has played an important role in understanding the persistence of racial disparities between whites and minorities (especially African Americans) in the United States. These studies range from classic debates about the relative salience of race and class as markers of stratification (for example, Wilson 1978) to more recent attention to the intersection of race and class in accounting for racial disparities in health (for example, Williams and Collins 1995; Williams et al. 1997). It is well established that low SES both restricts access to and increases the need for quality health care. People of lower-SES backgrounds report greater stress and reactivity to stressful events and are exposed to greater environmental toxins, such as air pollution (Boer et al. 1997; Fiscella et al. 2000; Fiscella and Williams 2004; Lynch et al. 1998; Weinick, Zuvekas, and Cohen 2000). Low socioeconomic status presents health risk as early as fetal development (Hilmert et al. 2007), which disproportionately affects minorities, who are overrepresented in working-class and lower-SES groups. The intersections of race and class may suggest an important venue for understanding health risk among different communities.

While intersectional research on class and race has become more popular, little research examines how class itself may inform race or vice versa. The dearth of research on this topic is partly a result of the general tendency to view a person's race as both obvious—easily determined by appearance—and fixed. Historically, racial categorization has been dominated by the "one-drop rule" (see Davis 2001). The *one-drop rule* is a colloquial term coined in the nineteenth century to denote the standard that any person with "one drop" of African ancestry should be categorized as black. Rather than viewing multiracial ancestry in complex and malleable terms, the one-drop rule put racial distinctions in simplified and intractable categories. Most laypersons continue to see racial categories as static and easily identified despite the growing number of multiracial populations who challenge these notions (Williams and Eberhardt 2008).

In contrast, current race scholars tend to view race as socially constructed and malleable (see Smedley and Smedley 2005). This shift toward more constructionist thinking has corresponded with growing attention to the multiracial community. For example, a recent *New York Times* article finds that more and more young people define themselves as multiracial—full members of two or more racial categories (Saulny 2011). Some multiracial people have challenged the racial classification system entirely by choosing not to identify with any race at all (Rockquemore and Brunsma 2002). These examples highlight how multiracial people test racial boundaries and race "rules," with growing public recognition.

Over the centuries, we also see historical evidence for the malleability of racial categories. For example, the white racial category shifted and expanded in the early twentieth century to include Irish and Italian immigrants who were formerly considered and treated as minorities (Ignatiev 1995; Lee and Bean 2010; Roediger 2005). After they were perceived as white by the mainstream culture, Irish and Italian immigrants experienced less prejudice and discrimination. Thus merely perceiving these new immigrant groups as white, and therefore as integrated into the dominant culture, shielded them against discrimination. Not surprisingly, today these formerly immigrant groups tend to hold higher-status positions in the United States compared with immigrant groups that are not perceived as white or a part of the dominant culture.

Empirical research demonstrates the changing categorization of multiracial populations that further underscores the social construction of race and ethnicity (for example, Shih et al. 2007; Spickard 1992). Features of the environment, motivations of the perceiver, and the method of measurement affect both self-categorization (Doyle and Kao 2007; Harris and Sim 2002; Hitlin, Brown, and Elder 2006; Sanchez, Shih, and

Garcia 2009) and categorization by others (Pauker et al. 2009; Peery and Bodenhausen 2008; Willadsen-Jensen and Ito 2006, 2008) for people of multiracial ancestry. This flexibility in categorization is not limited to multiracial populations; recent research reveals significant levels of racial fluidity for monoracial populations, as well (Brown, Hitlin, and Elder 2006; Penner and Saperstein 2008). That is, even those who are not children of interracial marriages tend to experience shifts in their own self-proclaimed racial identification and the labels others use to define their racial identity. In this chapter, we review research on the fluidity of race, particularly as it pertains to socioeconomic status and other markers of status.

This chapter explores how socioeconomic factors affect racial fluidity (changes in racial identification and categorization). Specifically, we discuss data that reveal that individuals are less likely to be identified as white and more likely to be identified as black if they have ever experienced markers of low status: incarceration, living below the poverty line, or unemployment. We also examine how the personal value placed on one's minority background varies by indicators and correlates of socioeconomic status—unemployment rates and the racial composition of multiracial people's childhood neighborhoods.

FLUIDITY AND CONSTRAINT IN RACIAL IDENTIFICATION AND CATEGORIZATION

Individuals with multiracial ancestry can racially self-categorize in a multitude of different ways. For example, persons with Asian and white ancestry may view themselves as white, Asian, multiracial, or all three. Moreover, categorization with one group is not necessarily mutually exclusive of categorization with another group; some multiracial people highly identify with multiple racial categories (for example, Asian, white, and multiracial). Identification with any particular racial category often varies as a function of social context. Research that has explored the malleability of Asian American identity has found that being around racially similar others (Yip 2005), reading an Asian newspaper (Morris and Peng 1994), or speaking an Asian language (Yip 2005) increases the salience of one's ethnic identity. For multiracial people, people from multiple racial backgrounds could be construed as racially similar others.

Thus the racial composition of those in their immediate environment could account for fluctuations in racial identification. A person with mixed racial background may identify as multiracial when with family members who share multiple racial categories and later identify as a singular racial identity with friends who share only one racial category. Racial identification may also vary at different times in a person's life course (for example, adolescence and adulthood). During childhood, multiracial people may identify as their parents identify them, but as they move into young adulthood they may use their own personal experiences as guides for self-definition. Recent research on multiracial identification finds great variation in racial identification across the life course (for example, Hitlin, Brown, and Elder 2006).

Though the topic of identity fluidity and flexibility has dominated the discourse around multiracial identity for the past decade (Harris and Sim 2002; Hitlin, Brown, and Elder 2006; Rockquemore and Brunsma 2002; Rockquemore, Brunsma, and Delgado 2009; Sanchez, Shih, and Garcia 2009), recent studies have discovered racial identity fluidity among non-multiracial populations, as well (Harris and Sim 2002; Penner and Saperstein 2008). Despite evidence of racial fluidity, few studies have identified the contexts that may alter racial categorization and identification among multiracial and non-multiracial populations. Of those studies, only a small number have explored how socioeconomic status shapes identity for those with the most flexible racial identities. Most work on the identification patterns of multiracial individuals finds that the racial composition of those environments shapes racial identification for multiracial populations (Sanchez and Garcia 2009) and that the presence of minorities promotes affiliation with one's minority identity. However, neither the work on self-identified multiracial populations nor that on monoracial populations considers how SES and the racial composition of the context may be intertwined. Given that lower-SES neighborhoods tend to be more racially diverse than higher-SES neighborhoods, it could be the case that SES, not race, is driving variations in racial identification. Thus it is important to disentangle the effects of SES and racial composition in determining racial identification.

Growing research supports the notion that racial identification is a social construction, despite the prevailing belief that race has a genetic or biological component (Spickard 1992; Williams and Eberhardt 2008). The volitional nature of racial identification among multiracial people adds credence to the notion that racial identification is a social construction. But again, experiencing one's racial identity as a choice may not be unique to multiracial populations (Brown, Hitlin, and Elder 2006; Harris and Sim 2002; Penner and Saperstein 2008). For example, a third- or fourth-generation Latino person who has fully acculturated in American society (that is, no longer speaks Spanish or participates in Latino customs) may choose to identify as white despite having Latino ancestry. If racial identification is a choice, these identity choices are certainly constrained by face-to-face interactions with others and societal and institutional forces, all of which are nested within a socioeconomic context.

For those deciding how to racially identify, their choice will be influenced by several factors such as physical appearance (Ahnallen, Carter, and Suyemoto 2006; Good, Chavez, and Sanchez 2010), socioeconomic background, and the racial diversity of their social context (Sanchez and Garcia 2009; Yip 2005). These factors determine, in part, how perceivers will view and treat individuals and therefore how people will eventually racially identify. For example, whether an African American woman has more African physical features, such as darker skin or textured hair, influences how others categorize her, which may in turn affect how she identifies herself (Harris and Sim 2002; Khanna 2004, 2010; Nagel 1994). Having a physical appearance that resembles a low-status minority group (for example, Latinos, blacks) generally increases the likelihood that individuals will encounter racial discrimination and will be viewed in terms of negative racial stereotypes. As a result, people may self-identify with the racial group that treats them more positively as a coping strategy, which is usually a minority group for those who physically resemble the minority group. Psychological research suggests that minorities who highly identify with their minority identity tend to buffer themselves from the ill effects of discrimination on psychological functioning and physical health (for example, Sellers et al. 2003). Thus choices to racially identify in accordance with one's physical appearance can be beneficial but may simultaneously reinforce inequality based on physical appearance.

Notably, SES and physical appearance may be conflated because perceivers often categorize those with prototypical physical appearances into lower-status minority groups. For example, African Americans with darker skin are more likely to be in positions of economic disadvantage (occupying lower-status jobs, living in poverty, attaining lower levels of education) relative to their light-skinned peers (Maddox 2004). Researchers have argued that dark skin cues negative African American stereotypes (Maddox and Gray 2002), many of which are class based. A plethora of negative stereotypes, such as those that African Americans are dangerous, unintelligent, or primitive, are specifically geared toward lower-class minority groups.

Socioeconomic status and physical appearance together seem to reinforce racial categories and racial identification by determining, at least in part, what stereotypes and prejudices people face. In fact, some research suggests that we visually perceive people differently depending on their self-categorization and SES. Thus we may literally "see" race through a social-status lens. For example, faces of varying phenotypes (light to dark) that are accompanied by black identity labels tend to be viewed as being darker than they actually are (MacLin and Malpass 2003; Levin and Banaji 2006). Socioeconomic status itself "colors" physical appearance perception such that interviewers rate interviewees who indicate higher educational achievement as having lighter skin tones than the interviewees themselves report (Telles 2002; Telles and Lim 1998). Taken together, this research demonstrates that if a person of African descent identifies as black or has a low-SES background, he or she will likely be viewed as having dark skin. Socioeconomic status and self-categorization change how people are perceived physically and thus racially categorized.

IN THE EYES OF THE BEHOLDER: SOCIAL CLASS AND RACIAL CATEGORIZATION

With minimal information, people can accurately gauge socioeconomic status. Indeed, research shows that perceivers accurately "read" social class from observing individuals for only sixty seconds and then use those impressions to guide behavior and expectations in face-to-face interactions (Kraus and Keltner 2009). Perceiving that someone is from a low socioeconomic background has been associated with greater discrimination, such as giving longer sentences and guilty verdicts (Willis Esqueda, Espinoza, and Culhane 2008) and creating greater physical distance (Westie and Westie 1957). It is interesting that perceivers who are from low-SES backgrounds themselves are not immune to making these types of negative judgments (Willis Esqueda, Espinoza, and Culhane 2008). Increased discrimination against low-SES compared with high-SES minorities may result from the tendency for race to become more salient in the processing of low-SES groups (Weeks and Lupfer 2004) and the negative valence of stereotypes of lower-class groups (Bayton, McAllister, and Hamer

1956; Smedley and Bayton 1978). Taken together, these studies support the notion that SES guides reactions to minorities.

IMPACTS OF SOCIOECONOMIC STATUS ON BLACK AND WHITE CATEGORIZATION

To help shed light on how race and SES are intertwined, we examine one of the largest-scale explorations of racial classification by SES. Using a representative sample of American respondents to the National Longitudinal Survey of Youth from 1979 to 1998, Andrew Penner and Aliya Saperstein (2008) explored how social status affects perceptions of race by studying changes in racial classification as a function of SES. They examined the year-to-year changes in interviewers' black and white categorization of more than twelve thousand respondents to determine whether racial categorization had changed over time with changes in respondents' SES, defined in terms of living below the poverty line, incarceration, and unemployment. Penner and Saperstein found that the racial categorization of 20 percent of the respondents had changed across the nineteen years of the study. More important, the changes corresponded to changes in status.

Respondents who had been classified as white in the previous year were less likely to be classified as white if they were living below the poverty line, incarcerated, or unemployed. Because interviewers could categorize respondents as only black, white, or other, this finding also meant that previously identified white respondents were more likely to be identified as either black or other if they were of low status. In other words, having been imprisoned, unemployed, or living below the poverty line increased the likelihood that a respondent would be categorized as black. Notably, these results persisted when a number of other factors were accounted for, including whether the respondents were of Hispanic origin or of multiple races. Thus above and beyond self-identification and the fixed effects of phenotype, SES predicted racial categorization by perceivers for respondents of both multiracial and non-multiracial ancestry.

These findings highlight the fluidity of racial categorization. But perhaps more important, they demonstrate that social status corresponds with changes in how perceivers racially categorize others: respondents moving downward in status were more likely to be categorized as black than those moving upward in social status. These results mean that a black lawyer is less likely to be viewed as black because of his or her higher status, whereas a prison inmate is more likely to be categorized as black. In fact, a more recent study shows that homicide victims are more likely to be classified as black (Noymer, Penner, and Saperstein 2011), suggesting that status-related stereotypes inform racial classification. The social-status effects on racial categorization have the unfortunate consequence of reinforcing black stereotypes. If high-SES black Americans are no longer categorized as black, then the category black remains inextricably linked to low SES. We can therefore expect that Barack Obama, who holds the highest position in the United States, will soon be recategorized as multiracial or other, to maintain black stereotypes. Similarly, categorizing most people who have been incarcerated as black (regardless of how they self-identify) pre-serves the black stereotype of criminality whereby black group members are more likely to be seen as criminals and therefore dangerous and aggressive. The tendency to categorize higher-SES people as white (even if they self-identify as black) and lower-SES people as black (even if they self-identify as white) perpetuates harmful stereotypes about black Americans.

It is important to note that researchers have not yet examined whether social status shapes the racial categorization of other racial groups (for example, Asians and Lati-nos). However, other studies (for example, Willis Esqueda, Espinoza, and Culhane 2008) have found that SES shapes perceivers' judgments of Latinos, with harsher judgments and stereotyping of lower-SES Latinos. Therefore, we might expect similar processes to be at play for other low-status groups. Black Americans have also been shown to have the most constrained racial or ethnic options for self-identification (Doyle and Kao 2007; Waters 1990). Thus Penner and Saperstein's results for black and white categorization may be a conservative test of the relationship between ra-cial fluidity and SES.

Many unanswered questions remain about class and racial categorization: Do ob-servers intentionally use socioeconomic status as an indicator of race? Are these pro-cesses automatic? If categorization is, in part, deliberate, researchers should identify the psychological processes that may account for or moderate these links. For exam-ple, classification of others may operate similarly to reflected appraisals such that perceivers categorize others as they expect the targets would categorize themselves (Sanchez, Good, and Chavez 2011). Perceivers may hold stereotypes about low-SES-group members, overestimating the sheer number of minorities who live below the poverty line and underestimating the number of whites who live below the poverty line. They may also assume that low-SES-group members are highly racially identi-fied with their minority identity, an assumption that may reinforce categorization with a racial group. However, perceivers may believe that higher-SES-group mem-bers are less likely to be minority identified because minorities of higher SES are less likely to be viewed in terms of their race (Weeks and Lupfer 2004).

Racial categorization processes often occur without discussion. Perceivers are of-ten uncomfortable asking others about their race in intergroup contexts. Research on white perceivers suggests that whites avoid the topic of race and racial categorization when describing individuals of a different race, trying to appear colorblind so as not to appear racist (Apfelbaum, Sommers, and Norton 2008; Norton et al. 2006). At the same time, everyone engages in (often automatic) racial categorization of others. Fail-ing to discuss race openly (a common strategy to appear less racist repeatedly shown to backfire; see Apfelbaum, Sommers, and Norton 2008; Norton et al. 2006) may actu-ally encourage the use of stereotypes such as class judgments during racial process-ing and impression formation.

Some perceivers may have group interests in mind when using SES to racially categorize others. For example, perceivers may want to keep socially desirable peo-ple in their group and socially undesirable people out of their group. Numerous studies have shown that people want to keep "good" people in their group and "bad" people out of their group to make sure that the in-group maintains a positive group image and that its members feel positive about group membership (Marques, Yzerbyt, and Leyens 1988; Tajfel and Turner 1979). Given the tendency to view lower-SES groups as undesirable, unfavorable, and even subhuman (Cikara et al. 2010; Harris and Fiske 2006), people may be more likely to categorize lower-SES individuals into out-groups to maintain favorable group images. Thus perceiver characteristics such as race and interest in a positive group image may moderate racial categorization. For example, white people who hold strong and favorable views about their racial identity may be most likely to view a homeless person as black.

ASSIMILATION OR EXCLUSION: SOCIAL CLASS AND RACIAL IDENTIFICATION

Socioeconomic status plays an important role in guiding decisions and social cognition (see chapters 5 and 9, this volume). For example, people of lower socioeconomic status sometimes try to conceal their identity (Garcia, Hallahan, and Rosenthal 2007) and worry about confirming negative stereotypes about their group (Spencer and Castano 2007. Socioeconomic class can influence how much power people feel in interactions and what choices they feel that they have in the world (chapter 8, this volume). Thus we contend that SES also shapes how people think about themselves racially (that is, which racial categories they feel entitled to claim). Socioeconomic status may affect identification with either the white, higher-status group or with the minority, lower-status groups. Socioeconomic status may also shape membership in other social categories imbued with status (gender, culture, and ethnicity). For the purposes of this chapter, we focus on racial categories.

Racial fluidity may be predominantly a middle- or upper-class phenomenon because members of low-status minority communities are expected to identify strongly with their minority background and disidentify from white culture. For example, black Americans typically live in lower-SES communities and show racial solidarity by not marrying outside their race. When they do break these "race rules," they are often met with disapproval from their black peers (Childs 2005; Yancey 2009). Disapproval from black peers is likely heightened in racially segregated, low-income communities. Once again, it is unclear whether these are elective choices or forced choices. In other words, social class and intermarriage are so strongly linked, especially for black Americans, that lower-class black Americans may be shut out of interracial marriage with whites rather than themselves shunning interracial marriage (Gullickson 2006). For example, low-SES black Americans are the least likely to marry outside their race and the least likely to identify with their white or multiracial identity when they have mixed racial ancestry (Lee and Bean 2010). As a result of their lower levels of SES in the United States, fewer black Americans intermarry with white Americans, and thus fewer children of interracial marriages have black ancestry. Consequently, black Americans, as a result of their lower SES, may have less flexibility in racial identity because fewer of them have multiracial ancestry (which allows for greater racial fluidity). The combination of fewer multiracial black Americans and concerns about disloyalty to the black community may make racial categorization particularly more rigid in black communities (Doyle and Kao 2007; Lee and Bean 2010).

THE IMPACT OF SOCIOECONOMIC STATUS ON SELF-IDENTIFICATION AS BLACK OR WHITE

As with racial categorization, SES guides racial self-identification. To demonstrate this phenomenon, we turn again to Penner and Saperstein's study examining the self-identification patterns of Americans, which utilized that data from the 1979 and 2002 respondents in the National Longitudinal Survey of Youth. Penner and Saperstein (2008) explored the racial fluidity patterns of respondents as a function of SES. Specifically, they examined whether SES moderated the extent to which respondents who self-identified as black or European (for example, British, Irish, German) in 1979 used those same self-identifications again in 2002. As in their work on racial categorization discussed earlier, Penner and Saperstein used the following markers of low SES: living below the poverty line, unemployment, and incarceration. Again, all three SES indicators predicted racial identification. People who had ever been living below the poverty line, unemployed, or incarcerated during an interview between 1979 and 2002 were more likely to identify as black and less likely to identify as white in 2002 compared with those living above the poverty line, employed, and not incarcerated. These findings persisted even when the researchers controlled for reporting multiracial ancestry. In other words, both multiracial and non-multiracial respondents showed racial fluidity patterns wedded to socioeconomic status. For example, a participant who self-identified as white in 1979 and later experienced poverty was more likely to switch his or her racial identification to a nonwhite identity in 2002.

Similarly, a respondent who self-identified in the 1979 survey as black was more likely to switch to a nonblack identity in 2002 if he or she had maintained consistent employment. These findings demonstrate the powerful effect of SES on self-identification: racial fluidity is constrained by SES such that people who are of lower SES tend to be more likely to identify as minority and less likely to identify as white. However, it is unclear what drives this process. Is self-identification driven by the perceived value of identifying as white or black? To address this question, we turn to our data on the minority identification of multiracial respondents, who demonstrate the most racial fluidity.

THE IMPACT OF NEIGHBORHOOD SOCIOECONOMIC STATUS AND RACIAL COMPOSITION ON RACIAL IDENTIFICATION

While there is a clear connection between socioeconomic status and racial identification, the psychological processes that guide racial identification for different SES groups have yet to be established. Racial socialization practices that vary by SES, different rules about the acceptability of identifying as white or black, and differential experiences of discrimination and prejudice may affect minority identification.

To illustrate the interplay between SES and racial identification, we examine the hypothetical experiences of Sondra and Rosa. Sondra, a multiracial Latino-white girl growing up in an all-white, upper-class neighborhood, may be particularly aware of the privilege associated with her white identity and the drawbacks of holding onto her Latino identity because she often hears negative racial slurs and stereotyping that either are expressed by or go unchallenged by her white peers. As a result, Sondra may come to negatively view her Latino identity as she assimilates into the white culture, especially when she has the economic resources to be accepted into the white community. Moreover, Sondra is likely to have expertise in white culture by having lived a privileged lifestyle and learned the norms of white culture. Thus she may be able to "pass" as white regardless of her physical appearance as a result of her higher SES and greater access to white culture and customs. For example, Sondra might be comfortable living in a predominantly white neighborhood, shopping and eating at restaurants in an all-white neighborhood, and working in an all-white company. Simply put, she knows which fork is the salad fork, and knowing these rules allows her to identify more as white and less as Latino.

Rosa, in contrast, a Latino-white girl growing up in a racially diverse and lower-SES community, is less likely to feel comfortable in a predominantly white neighborhood because when she and her friends drive to all-white, upper-class communities, the police typically pull them over to make sure they are "not lost." And white store managers follow Rosa around the store when she goes shopping because, she suspects, they think she will steal from them. She is more comfortable in largely Latino communities because she has always felt accepted by other Latinos. From her experiences in white communities and conversations with other Latinos, she has learned that whites do not typically accept people like her and instead tend to look at Latinos with suspicion. She has learned that she cannot "pass" in white communities because she dresses differently, she moves differently, and she speaks differently from other white people. In her largely Latino neighborhood, she has seen that the Latino families on her block looked out for one another—watching one another's kids and bringing over food when in need. Thus she identifies less as white and more as Latino because she takes pride in her Latino culture and resents the way the white community has treated her.

As the experiences of Sondra and Rosa illustrate, self-identification depends on a level of acceptance by racial groups that is achieved by understanding culture. Sondra has had only white friends and lived in a white, upper-class culture. If Sondra had other Latino friends, she may not have fully assimilated into the white culture and devalued her minority identity. Thus to understand self-identification it is necessary to look at both SES and cultural context. Individuals exposed to different SES contexts such as neighborhoods, schools, or religious environments may have very different views about the value and meaning of identifying with a minority background: minority groups and minority culture may be more valued in lower-SES communities than in higher-SES communities as a result of the strong presence of minorities in lower-SES communities. Typically, communities of higher SES also have fewer minorities, which may reduce the emphasis on race, undervalue the benefits of diversity, and provide few minority role models for minority and multiracial youth.

Thus the effects of neighborhood SES on racial identification and the perceived value of their ethnic minority background may depend on the racial composition of the neighborhood. To test the possibility that SES and diversity of the context predict attitudes and identification with one's minority background, we examine whether multiracial respondents who had higher SES and grew up in predominantly white neighborhoods tended to show the lowest levels of racial identification with their minority background. Of course, neighborhood is only one environment in which class and race intersect to predict self-identification. School and work contexts, for example, represent other environments where the racial composition of one's peers may combine with SES background to predict self-identification. However, for the purposes of the chapter, we focus on the SES of the neighborhood, as the place where people live during their adolescence may play a primary role in racial socialization and identity development.

EVIDENCE OF MINORITY DISIDENTIFICATION BY MULTIRACIAL RESPONDENTS OF HIGH STATUS

To assess whether neighborhood SES is related to racial identification, we performed secondary data analysis on a survey sample of white-minority multiracial respondents living in New Jersey (New Brunswick area) and California (San Francisco area). Participants consisted of twenty-three black-white, twenty-nine Asian-white, and twenty-six Latino-white multiracial respondents who participated in a week-long diary data collection, including multiple daily reports assessing their momentary feelings about their minority identities. Using the 2000 census, we coded the zip codes of the respondents' neighborhoods for the percentage of the population residing in that neighborhood who were unemployed, the percentage who were white, and the median household income of the neighborhood. Participants came primarily from middle-class neighborhoods. Median household incomes for their childhood neighborhoods ranged from $22,304 to $129,375. Neighborhood unemployment ranged from 1 to 9 percent unemployed, with an average unemployment rate of 4 percent. Participants grew up in neighborhoods where, on average, 70 percent of the population was identified as white, ranging from 9 percent white to 95 percent white.

We analyzed the average scores across days for the participants on measures of minority identification (that is, how central their minority identity is to their definition of themselves), private regard (that is, how proud they are of their minority identity), and public regard (that is, how much they believe others value their minority identity). We examined whether neighborhood SES, diversity of the neighborhood, and the interaction between SES and diversity of the neighborhood predicted attitudes about one's racial identity, above and beyond the effects of age and self-perceived physical appearance. We found significant interactions between SES and the diversity of the neighborhood on attitudes toward one's minority background. Specifically, we found that multiracial people from higher-SES backgrounds and largely white contexts reported lower public regard of minorities, while SES did not predict public regard for multiracial people in more racially diverse settings. These findings suggest that multiracial people coming from higher-SES neighborhoods felt that others devalued their minority background when their neighborhoods were largely white.

Within an elite context of upper-class whites, multiracial people may be uniquely aware of the racial prejudice of whites. Moreover, these prejudices may occur with little repercussion, because whites may be comfortable expressing prejudices among other whites but are less likely to reinforce egalitarian values when few minorities are around. Therefore, racial stereotypes and jokes may be common and unchallenged in white contexts. As a result, multiracial people of higher SES may eventually come to identify with and assimilate into white racial categories and culture as a strategy for contending with the low acceptance of their minority background in largely white communities and in the absence of minority role models (Harris and Khanna 2010).

The pattern of results was similar for minority self-regard and self-identification such that coming from a diverse neighborhood mattered when SES was high. Multiracial participants from largely white neighborhoods reported less pride in their minority background and lower minority identification when they came from high-SES contexts. In other words, multiracial people from affluent backgrounds personally adopted negative views of their minority background and disidentified from their minority background when in contexts that had few minority role models. However, when SES was low, the diversity of the neighborhood did not predict minority pride or identification. Multiracial individuals showed the weakest minority identification and pride when they came from nondiverse neighborhoods of high SES. Similarly, multiracial respondents from contexts that were largely white and high SES also indicated that others had low regard for their racial identities. Together, these findings suggest that multiracial individuals are likely to lose their minority identity and have negative views of their minority background when they are surrounded by whites from upper-class backgrounds.

Not surprisingly, minority identification was strongly positively related to both private (that is, personal value) and public (that is, perception of others' value) regard. In other words, multiracial black-white respondents who personally value their black identity (private regard) and believe that society values their black identity (public regard) are more likely to identify with their black identity. Therefore, diversity and SES of the neighborhood may influence public and private regard, which in turn influences identification. We examined whether regard explained the observed effect of SES and diversity of neighborhood on minority identification. This was, in fact, the case. Specifically, our results suggest that the low levels of minority identification among multiracial individuals from high-SES and largely white neighborhoods may result from a lack of pride in one's minority background. Multiracial respondents in upper-class, white neighborhoods may have few minority role models. Moreover, they were raised within a culture that may deemphasize race and devalue minorities. Thus it is not surprising that multiracial people who grew up in these contexts may feel less pride in their minority identity and therefore be less likely to identify as minority.

While these results do not address white identification, it is plausible that less identification as minority corresponds with higher identification as white. Penner and Saperstein's (2008) findings suggest that high SES may increase white identification and decrease minority identification. This may be particularly true if high SES is combined with a largely white context (which it often is). Thus multiracial people in affluent, white communities are likely to assimilate into white culture by feeling ashamed of their minority background and emphasizing their whiteness. The process whereby high-SES multiracial people tend to identify as white and disidentify from their ethnic background may reproduce social inequalities by encouraging higher-SES-group members to exit minority categories and enter white racial categories. One root cause of this reproduction may be the fostering of white pride and negative views of minority identity in higher-SES neighborhoods. This may cause non-multiracial group members to move away from their minority backgrounds as well. Given that racial fluidity occurs among non-multiracial groups, these findings suggest that other minorities in higher-SES communities may also feel ashamed about their minority backgrounds if they are in largely white communities. The movement of higher-SES-group members away from their minority identity and toward a white identity also has implications for the resources within low-SES communities because higher-SES-group members may be less likely to distribute their wealth (through charities) to their minority communities if they do not identify with minority culture and identity.

SUMMARY AND CONCLUSIONS

Many psychologists who study race, racial identity, and racial disparities fail to fully consider the role of socioeconomic class. Instead, they "control" for socioeconomic status without discussing the inextricable ties between race and class. In particular, the study of racial prejudice in psychology has yet to fully integrate how targets' social class may change the nature of prejudice and discrimination. Sociologists, too, have long debated about how best to consider race and class, calling attention to the problem of examining race and class separately. Recent research on racial fluidity has revived this old debate by demonstrating again that these two dimensions of inequality, race and class, are conflated such that race is, in part, defined by socioeconomic status. Evidence from the literature on racial fluidity suggests that socioeconomic status determines how people racially categorize others and what racial categories people choose for themselves. Moreover, the work we present on multiracial individuals suggests that SES influences how people value the categories themselves. In other words, multiracial people in higher-SES (and white) communities may come to personally value white identity more than minority identity.

The differential meaning of white identity and minority identity in different communities may reinforce inequalities by encouraging higher-SES-group members with ethnic minority backgrounds to claim white identities. This is particularly problematic when large numbers of multiracial people come from middle- and upper-class backgrounds as a result of higher interracial marriage rates among higher-SES groups (Lee and Bean 2010). Thus multiracial individuals of higher SES and increasingly minorities of higher-SES backgrounds may disidentify as minority and identify as white, reinforcing the links between low SES and categorization as black or Latino.

Given that the reproduction of social inequality is maintained, in part, through the links between racial categorization, identification, and socioeconomic status, future research should examine the mechanisms (and moderators) that explain why and when race is tied to SES. For example, our findings suggest that people from lower-SES backgrounds and more diverse environments experience feelings of pride that increase minority identification. But how? Perhaps, having minorities in one's neighborhood fosters pride because it means that families, schools, religious organizations, and leaders in the community recognize and celebrate diversity. If one comes from a predominantly minority community, perhaps community leaders also share one's ethnic background, thereby increasing positive role models. Seeing more positive in-group role models may, in turn, increase ethnic pride. The presence of positive minority role models also challenges negative racial and ethnic stereotypes. Another possible explanation is that lower-SES minorities develop better strategies to cope with discrimination because they discuss race openly in their households, schools, and religious environments. As we discussed earlier, in mixed-race interactions people are less likely to mention race (Apfelbaum, Sommers, and Norton 2008; Norton et al. 2006).

This chapter also highlights how changes in SES may correspond with changes in categorization and identification. Earlier in this chapter we introduced Rosa, who grew up in a largely racially diverse and lower-income community where she learned to highly value her Latino identity and devalue her white identity. Rosa's father got a new job, which allowed him to move Rosa's family to a middle-class, mostly white neighborhood in the suburbs. Rosa goes to college, where she has mostly white friends from middle-class backgrounds. She rarely visits the urban neighborhood she used to live in. As a result of losing some of her minority role models and, perhaps, greater exposure to her white neighborhood and white culture, Rosa may come to identify more with her white identity than she did in the past. Also, others may come to categorize Rosa more as white and less as Latino because her mannerisms have changed to cue her white identity. As this example illustrates, the increases and decreases in status that multiracial and non-multiracial people experience through various life experiences will change how they view their racial identity and how others view them. For Rosa, her father's new job changed her status; for others, becoming unemployed or marrying into higher-status families may change socioeconomic status. Social status plays an important role in race and race relations in the United States. We hope that this chapter fosters a deeper understanding of how socioeconomic status constructs and reproduces racial meanings so that researchers can better understand the persistence of inequalities through the processes of categorization and identification.

REFERENCES

Ahnallen, Julie, Alice Carter, and Karen L. Suyemoto. 2006. "Relationship Between Physical Appearance, Sense of Belonging, Feelings of Exclusion, and Racial/Ethnic Self-Identification Among Multiracial Japanese-European Americans." *Cultural Diversity and Ethnic Minority Psychology* 12(4): 373–86.

Apfelbaum, Evan P., Samuel R. Sommers, and Michael I. Norton. 2008. "Seeing Race and Seeming Racist? Evaluating Strategic Colorblindness in Social Interaction." *The Journal of Personality and Social Psychology* 95(4): 918–32.

Bayton, James A., Lois B. McAllister, and Jeston Hamer. 1956. "Race-Class Stereotypes." *Journal of Negro Education* 25: 75–78.

Boer, J. Tom, Manuel Pastor Jr., James L. Sadd, and Lori D. Snyder. 1997. "Is There Environmental Racism? The Demographics of Hazardous Waste in Los Angeles County." *The Social Science Quarterly* 78(4): 793–810.

Brown, J. Scott, Steven Hitlin, and Glen H. Elder Jr. 2006. "The Greater Complexity of Lived Race: An Extension of Harris and Sim." *The Social Science Quarterly* 87(2): 411–31.

Childs, E. C. 2005. "Looking Behind the Stereotypes of the 'Angry Black Woman': An Exploration of Black Women's Responses to Interracial Relationships." *Gender and Society* 19(4): 544–61.

Cikara, Mina, Rachel A. Farnsworth, Lasana T. Harris, and Susan T. Fiske. 2010. "On the Wrong Side of the Trolley Track: Neural Correlates of Relative Social Valuation." *SCAN* 5: 404–13.

Coates, Ta-Nehisi P. 2007. "Is Obama Black Enough?" *Time Magazine*, February 1. Available at: http://www.time.com/time/nation/article/0,8599,1584736,00.html (accessed November 14, 2011).

Davis, F. James. 2001. *Who Is Black? One Nation's Definition*. University Park: Pennsylvania State University Press.

Doyle, J. Mihoko, and Grace Kao. 2007. "Are Racial Identities of Multiracials Changing? Self-Identification Among Single and Multiple Race Individuals." *The Social Psychology Quarterly* 70(4): 405–23.

Fiscella, Kevin, Peter Franks, Marthe R. Gold, and Carolyn M. Clancy. 2000. "Inequality in Quality: Addressing Socioeconomic, Racial, and Ethnic Disparities in Health Care." *The Journal of the American Medical Association* 283(19): 2579–84.

Fiscella, Kevin, and David R. Williams. 2004. "Health Disparities Based on Socioeconomic Inequities: Implications for Urban Health Care." *Academic Medicine* 79(12): 1139–47.

Garcia, Stephen M., Mark Hallahan, and Robert Rosenthal. 2007. "Poor Expression: Concealing Social Class Stigma." *Basic and Applied Social Psychology* 29(2): 99–107.

Good, Jessica J., George F. Chavez, and Diana T. Sanchez. 2010. "Sources of Self-Categorization as Minority for Mixed Race Individuals: Implications for Affirmative Action Entitlement." *Cultural Diversity and Ethnic Minority Psychology* 16(4): 453–60.

Gullickson, Aaron. 2006. "Education and Black/White Interracial Marriage." *Demography* 43(4): 673–89.

Harris, Cherise A., and Nikki Khanna. 2010. "Black Is, Black Ain't: Biracials, Black Middle-Classers, and the Social Construction of Blackness." *Sociological Spectrum* 30(6): 639–70.

Harris, David R., and J. J. Sim. 2002. "Who Is Multiracial? Assessing the Complexity of Lived Race." *The American Sociological Review* 67(4): 614–27.

Harris, Lasana T., and Susan T. Fiske. 2006. "Dehumanizing the Lowest of the Low: Neuroimaging Response to Extreme Out-Groups." *Psychological Science* 17(10): 847–53.

Hilmert, Clayton J., Christine D. Schetter, Tyan P. Dominguez, Cleopatra Abdou, Calvin J. Hobel, Laura Glynn, and Curt Sandman. 2007. "Stress and Blood Pressure During Pregnancy: Racial Differences and Associations with Birthweight." *Psychosomatic Medicine* 70(1): 57–64.

Hitlin, Steven, J. Scott Brown, and Glen H. Elder Jr. 2006. "Racial Self-Categorization in Adolescence: Multiracial Development and Social Pathways." *Child Development* 77(5): 1298–1308.

Ignatiev, Noel. 1995. *How the Irish Became White*. New York: Routledge.

Khanna, Nikki. 2004. "The Role of Reflected Appraisals in Racial Identity: The Case of Multiracial Asians." *The Social Psychology Quarterly* 67(2): 115–31.

———. 2010. "If You're Half Black, You're Just Black: Reflected Appraisals and the Persistence of the One Drop Rule." *The Sociological Quarterly* 51(1): 96–121.

Kraus, Michael W., and Dacher Keltner. 2009. "Signs of Socioeconomic Status: A Thin Slicing Approach." *Psychological Science* 20(1): 99–106.

Lee, Jennifer, and Frank D. Bean. 2010. *The Diversity Paradox: Immigration and the Color Line in 21st Century America.* New York: Russell Sage Foundation.

Levin, Daniel T., and Mahzarin R. Banaji. 2006. "Distortions in the Perceived Lightness of Faces: The Role of Race Categories." *Journal of Experimental Psychology* 135(4): 501–12.

Lynch, John W., Susan A. Everson, George A. Kaplan, Riitta Salonen, and Jukka T. Salonen. 1998. "Does Low Socioeconomic Status Potentiate the Effects of Heightened Cardiovascular Responses to Stress on the Progression of Carotid Atherosclerosis?" *The American Journal of Public Health* 88(3): 389–94.

MacLin, O. H., and R. Malpass. 2003. "The Ambiguous-Race Face Illusion." *Perception* 32: 249–52.

Maddox, Keith B. 2004. "Perspectives on the Racial Phenotypicality Bias." *The Personality and Social Psychology Review* 8(4): 383–401.

Maddox, Keith B, and Stephanie A. Gray. 2002. "Cognitive Representations of Black Americans: Reexploring the Role of Skin Tone." *Personality and Social Psychology Bulletin* 28(2): 250–9.

Marques, J. M., V. Y. Yzerbyt, and J. P. Leyens. 1988. "The Black Sheep Effect: Judgmental Extremity Towards Ingroup Members as a Function of Ingroup Identification." *The European Journal of Social Psychology* 18(3): 1–16.

Morris, Michael W., and Kaiping Peng. 1994. "Culture and Cause: American and Chinese Attributions for Social and Physical Events." *The Journal of Personality and Social Psychology* 67(6): 949–71.

Nagel, Joane. 1994. "Constructing Ethnicity: Creating and Recreating Ethnic Identity and Culture." *Social Problems* 41(1): 152–76.

Norton, Michael I., Samuel R. Sommers, Evan P. Apfelbaum, Natassia Pura, and Dan Ariely. 2006. "Colorblindness and Interaction: Playing the Political Correctness Game." *Psychological Science* 17: 949–53.

Noymer, Andrew, Andrew Penner, and Aliya Saperstein. 2011. "Cause of Death Affects Racial Classification on Death Certificates." *PLoS One* 6(1): e15812.

Pauker, Kristin, Max Weisbuch, Nalini Ambady, Samuel R. Sommers, Reginald B. Adams, and Zorana Ivcevic. 2009. "Not So Black and White: Memory for Ambiguous Group Members." *The Journal of Personality and Social Psychology* 96(4): 795–810.

Peery, Destiny, and Galen V. Bodenhausen. 2008. "Black + White = Black: Hypodescent in Reflexive Categorization of Racially Ambiguous Faces." *Psychological Science* 19(10): 973–77.

Penner, Andrew M., and Aliya Saperstein. 2008. "How Social Status Shapes Race." *The Proceedings of the National Academy of Sciences* 105(50): 19628–30.

Rockquemore, Kerry Ann, and David L. Brunsma. 2002. "Socially Embedded Identities: Theories, Typologies, and Processes of Racial Identity Among Black/White Biracial." *The Sociological Quarterly* 43(10): 335–56.

Rockquemore, Kerry Ann, David L. Brunsma, and Daniel J. Delgado. 2009. "Racing to Theory or Re-theorizing Race? Understanding the Struggle to Build a Multiracial Identity Theory." *The Journal of Social Issues* 65(1): 13–34 .

Roediger, David R. 2005. *Working Towards Whiteness: How America's Immigrants Became White.* Cambridge, Mass.: Basic Books.

Sanchez, Diana T., and Julie A. Garcia. 2009. "When Race Matters: Racially Stigmatized Others and Perceiving Race as a Biological Construction Affect Biracial People's Daily Well-Being." *The Personality and Social Psychology Bulletin* 35(9): 1154–64.

Sanchez, Diana T., Jessica J. Good, and George F. Chavez. 2011. "Blood Quantum and Perceptions of Black/White Biracial Targets: The Black Ancestry Prototype Model of Affirmative Action." *The Personality and Social Psychology Bulletin* 37(1): 3–14.

Sanchez, Diana T., Margaret Shih, and Julie A. Garcia. 2009. "Juggling Multiple Racial Identities: Malleable Racial Identification and Well-Being." *Cultural Diversity and Ethnic Minority Psychology* 15(3): 245–54.

Saulny, Susan. 2011. "Black? White? Asian? More Young Americans Choose All of the Above." *The New York Times,* January 29. Available at: http://www.nytimes.com/2011/01/30/us/30mixed.html (accessed November 16, 2011).

Sellers, Robert M., Cleopatra H. Caldwell, Karen Schmeelk-Cone, and Marc A. Zimmerman. 2003. "The Role of Racial Identity and Racial Discrimination in the Mental Health of African American Young Adults." *Journal of Health and Social Behavior* 44(3): 302–17.

Shih, Margaret J., Courtney Bonam, Diana T. Sanchez, and Courtney Peck. 2007. "Beliefs in the Social Construction of Race: Adaptive Strategies for Multiracials." *Cultural Diversity and Ethnic Minority Psychology* 13: 125–33.

Smedley, Audrey, and Brian Smedley. 2005. "Race as Biology Is Fiction, Racism as a Social Problem Is Real: Anthropological and Historical Perspectives on the Social Construction of Race." *The American Psychologist* 60(1): 16–26.

Smedley, Joseph W., and James A. Bayton. 1978. "Evaluative Race-Class Stereotypes by Race and Perceived Class of Subjects." *Journal of Personality and Social Psychology* 36(5): 530–35.

Spencer, Bettina, and Emanuele Castano. 2007. "Social Class Is Dead, Long Live Social Class! Stereotype Threat Among Low-Socioeconomic Individuals." *Social Justice Research* 20(4): 418–32.

Spickard, P. R. 1992. "The Illogic of American Racial Categories." In *Racially Mixed People in America,* edited by Maria P. P. Root. Newbury Park, Calif.: Sage.

Tajfel, Henri, and John C. Turner. 1979. "An Integrative Theory of Intergroup Conflict." In *The Psychology of Intergroup Relations,* edited by Stephen Worchel and William G. Austin. Monterey, Calif.: Brooks/Cole.

Telles, Edward E. 2002. "Racial Ambiguity Among the Brazilian Population." *Ethnic and Racial Studies* 25(3): 415–41.

Telles, Edward E., and Nelson Lim. 1998. "Does It Matter Who Answers the Race Question? Racial Classification and Income Inequality in Brazil." *Demography* 35(4): 465–74.

Waters, Mary C. 1990. *Ethnic Options: Choosing Identities in America.* Berkeley: University of California Press.

Weeks, Matthew, and Michael B. Lupfer. 2004. "Complicating Race: The Relationship Between Prejudice, Race, and Social Class Categorizations." *The Personality and Social Psychology Bulletin* 30(8): 972–84.

Weinick, Robin M., Samuel H. Zuvekas, and Joel W. Cohen. 2000. "Racial and Ethnic Differences in Access to and Use of Health Care Services, 1977 to 1996." *Medical Care Research and Review* 57(1): 36–54.

Westie, Frank R., and Margaret L. Westie. 1957. "The Social-Distance Pyramid: Relationships Between Caste and Class." *American Journal of Sociology* 63(2): 190–96.

Willadsen-Jensen, Eve C., and Tiffany A. Ito. 2006. "Ambiguity and the Timecourse of Racial Perception." *Social Cognition* 24(5): 580–606.

———. 2008. "A Foot in Both Worlds: Asian Americans' Perceptions of Asian, White, and Racially Ambiguous Faces." *Group Processes and Interpersonal Relations* 11(2): 182–200.

Williams, David R., and Chiquita Collins. 1995. "U.S. Socioeconomic and Racial Differences in Health: Patterns and Explanations." *The Annual Review of Sociology* 21: 349–86.

Williams, David R., Yan Yu, James Jackson, and Norman Anderson. 1997. "Racial Differences in Physical and Mental Health: Socioeconomic Status, Stress, and Discrimination." *The Journal of Health Psychology* 2(3): 335–51.

Williams, Melissa, and Jennifer Eberhardt. 2008. "Biological Conceptions of Race and the Motivation to Cross Racial Boundaries." *Journal of Personality and Social Psychology* 94(6): 1033–47.

Willis Esqueda, Cynthia, Russ K. E. Espinoza, and Scott E. Culhane. 2008. "The Effects of Ethnicity, SES, and Crime Status on Juror Decision Making: A Cross-Cultural Examination of European-American and Mexican American Mock Jurors." *The Hispanic Journal of Behavioral Sciences* 30(2): 181–99.

Wilson, William Julius. 1978. *The Declining Significance of Race: Blacks and Changing American Institutions.* Chicago: University of Chicago Press.

Yancey, George A. 2009. "Crossracial Differences in the Racial Preferences of Potential Dating Partners: A Test of the Alienation of African Americans and Social Dominance Orientation." *The Sociological Quarterly* 50(1): 121–43.

Yip, Tiffany. 2005. "Sources of Situational Variation in Ethnic Identity and Psychological Wellbeing: A Palm Pilot Study of Chinese American Students." *The Personality and Social Psychology Bulletin* 31(12): 1603–16.

CHAPTER 12

THE SECRET HANDSHAKE: TRUST IN CROSS-CLASS ENCOUNTERS

Susan T. Fiske, Miguel Moya, Ann Marie Russell, and Courtney Bearns

In *Lost in the Meritocracy*, Walter Kirn (2009) vividly describes the alienating experience of coming from rural Minnesota to college at Princeton, where he constantly felt like a misfit among the privileged. He grew to mistrust his roommates, who simply assumed he would chip in for their expensive furniture and alcohol purchases. At the same time, they evidently mistrusted him, excluding and ignoring him. Even now, some colleagues at Princeton describe the "secret handshake" that they are certain everyone else knows, as a subtle signal of belonging to the trusted upper-class club. More broadly, ethnographic accounts detail such class-membership codes (Fussell 1983), as do some other chapters in this volume. Here, we explore social psychological evidence for the role of trust in cross-class encounters, particularly when people from lower-class backgrounds enter higher-status settings, but we also touch on encounters between middle- and upper-class individuals in working-class contexts. We aim to describe how one social psychological mechanism, mutual mistrust, can widen social-class divides in interpersonal encounters. We describe social-class effects on perceivers' disparate orientations toward trust and social-class stereotypes of people as more or less trustworthy. Finally, we speculate about how to bring them together.

Our preliminary data on perceivers show that blue-collar and low-income people trust some members of their own in-group but have lower generalized trust of people from various social classes, which is likely to have consequences for cross-class interactions. On the other side, the higher-status groups looking down on lower-status groups, well-established findings indicate that the higher-income people have high generalized trust. We interpret this to mean trust in people in general, but poor people are excluded, largely ignored. Thus Kirn's privileged roommates gratuitously trusted him by assuming that he would want, as they did, to chip in for expensive furnishings. When he turned out not to be just like them, they were annoyed, and they gave up trying to understand him, deciding that he was not worth their time.

Conversely, Kirn felt that they had not accepted him, not sought to make connections, and not established trust, so he kept his distance, as a precaution against being exploited and further rejected.

One framework for understanding mutual social-class images is the well-established stereotype content model, which arrays images of social groups (including class) on fundamental dimensions of trusting or mistrusting the other's intentions (as warm or cold) and judging the other's ability or inability to enact those intentions (as competent or not). These images and reactions demonstrably play out during interpersonal encounters. The societal and interpersonal nature of the model demonstrates that social structure (not only status hierarchy but also interdependence) creates trust and mistrust in actual interactions.

Of course, class relations are not simple. Along the way, we also describe some preliminary work suggesting nuances in trust directed downward, toward poorer people, as likely a function of the latter's apparent work ethic and higher-income people's feeling entitled to judge others. Asserting one's own entitlement to judge (as Kirn's roommates did) is not likely to make other people trustful. Maybe higher classes' feeling of entitled judgment is part of what lower- and working-class people experience as the secret handshake.

Finally, we use the notion of interdependence across the status hierarchy to explore ways of facilitating mutual trust. Interdependence is the primary form of trust (the belief that each shares or at least appreciates the other's intentions). Status, in conveying presumed competence, has a second-order impact on trusting others to carry out their benign intentions. We close by suggesting future directions for bridging class divides and showing that the handshake could be universal.

CLASS ORIENTATIONS TOWARD TRUST

The social class of the perceiver may contribute to habitual forms of cross-class trust (or mistrust) through class culture (described variously in chapters 5, 6, 7, and 10, this volume). Several social psychological processes contribute to social class framing perceivers' perspectives on trust. For instance, social-class background can contribute to some class-specific patterns of values, cognition, and behavior (Kraus, Piff, and Keltner 2009; Snibbe and Markus 2005). Social class contributes to people's self-views (Stephens, Markus, and Townsend 2007) and social identity. Social class potentially contributes to a negative social identity or social stigma among lower-class individuals (Croizet and Claire 1998; Spencer and Castano 2007) and presumably a positive social identity among higher-class individuals. Moreover, upper-class individuals usually have economic independence and higher personal control over their life choices. In contrast, lower-class individuals experience a reduced sense of control over their own life outcomes, and as one coping strategy they work more with trusted others to help achieve their desired outcomes (Johnson and Krueger 2005a, 2005b; Lachman and Weaver 1998; Piff, Martinez, and Keltner, forthcoming). Any of these factors might contribute to habitual patterns of trust.

Blue-collar and middle- and upper-class styles of social thought and interaction apparently do differ, middle-class institutions being less receptive to the working-class cultural patterns. Here we begin to explore how styles of trust may vary across class, with implications for interactions in cross-class encounters. We start with working-class perceivers, who may specialize in relational trust, and then turn to middle- and upper-class perceivers, who may specialize in generalized trust.

A Note on How We Measure Social Class

One challenge to the psychological study of social class is the difficulty of defining and measuring social class itself. Social class is often defined by material wealth, income, occupation, and participation in educational and social institutions (Oakes and Rossi 2003). Although these types of ratings can tell us how participants compare with the population at large, they provide no information on where participants feel they stand in comparison with others in their reference groups.

Other research has addressed this issue by assessing subjective social status (Adler et al. 2000) in addition to more traditional, objective measures of social standing. This approach can help disentangle the material advantages and disadvantages of differences in socioeconomic status from the more subjective psychological consequences of feeling comparatively better or worse off than others. Our illustrative preliminary research considers objective status markers as well as subjective social class, measured by where people place themselves on a ten-rung ladder to reflect their relative rank in society (Adler et al. 2000). Respondents are instructed to

> think of this ladder as representing where people stand in the United States. At the top of the ladder are the people who are the best-off—those who have the most money, the most education, and the most respected jobs. At the bottom are the people who are the worst off—who have the least money, least education, and the least respected jobs or no job. The higher up you are on this ladder, the closer you are to the people at the very top; the lower you are, the closer you are to the people at the very bottom. Where would you place yourself on this ladder? Please place a large "X" on the rung where you think you stand at this time in your life, relative to other people in the United States. (587)

In the study conducted by Nancy Adler and colleagues (2000), subjective social class measured in this way predicted mental well-being and physical health, even when the researchers controlled for objective social class and habitual negative affect.

To study social class in the laboratory, the ideal scenario would be to manipulate social class to test its effects. Although real class manipulations are impossible, for obvious reasons, some recent success has been had by manipulating participants' social reference groups to alter their feelings of relative social status (Piff et al. 2010). This is a promising paradigm for future class-related laboratory studies, one that we endorse, but we are starting with descriptive surveys.

Hypotheses About Kinds of Trust

Our approach relies on some conceptions of trust that have generated the most research and are theoretically most relevant to cross-class encounters. We hypothesize that higher-class people score higher in generalized trust, while lower-class people score higher in relational trust. Briefly, higher-class people have more autonomy because they have more resources, so they can afford to maintain an optimistic view of people in general; positivity promotes approach, and being wrong has fewer consequences for them than for those with lesser resources. (Remember Walter Kirn's privileged roommates.) Lower-class people are more dependent on others to share resources (Kirn was not allowed to enjoy his roommates' wealth without reciprocating), and they cannot afford to take as many risks because of relative scarcity (Kirn was on scholarship), so they may specialize in a more circumscribed trust (fewer, but closer, friends). Generalized trust is well represented in the literature, but relational trust is less studied, and the two kinds have not often been compared.

Specifically, *generalized trust* is an overall belief in human benevolence, that most people can be trusted. Generalized trust encourages approaching others to form social relationships, moving out of one's comfort zone—particular, committed interpersonal relationships—and getting to know unfamiliar others, creating social opportunities (Yamagishi, Cook, and Watabe 1998). Generalized trust encourages cooperation with strangers (Yamagishi 1986), and it accepts social uncertainty. Measures (Yamagishi and Yamagishi 1994) include items such as "Most people are basically honest" and "Most people are trustworthy."

Survey data (Pew Social Trends Staff 2007) show that higher-income respondents report higher generalized trust (that is, they believe that most people can be trusted). Social class correlates with describing others as trustworthy, fair, and helpful (Weaver 2006). Subjective social class predicts general trust across thirty-three rich and middle-income countries (Elgar 2010).

In contrast, *relationism* (also called assurance, particularistic trust, or interpersonal trust) prioritizes the maintenance of secure relationships with specific people, generally friends or relatives. Relationism includes emotional, supportive connectedness of self with others (Uleman et al. 2000; Yamagishi 1998; Yamagishi and Yamagishi 1994). Because these others are known, their behavior is predictable, and one can feel secure that they will not be harmful (Hayashi et al. 1999). Thus relationism involves a sense of security coming from knowledge about, and therefore predictability of, specific people, so it overcomes social uncertainty. Measures (Kashima et al. 2004; see also Kashima et al. 1995) include items such as "It doesn't matter whether a person is useful to me; my relationship with the person is important."

Because people from the working class are more relationally interdependent (Stephens, Markus, and Townsend 2007), perhaps they will tend to trust those who share relationship connections. People with more interdependent self-concepts as group members (Maddux and Brewer 2005; Yuki et al. 2005) tend to trust those who share relationship connections or who share direct or indirect interpersonal links.

We aim to build on this prior work, especially focusing on the relational trust that lower- and working-class contexts encourage. Previous work has not sufficiently delineated how relational forms of trust might operate according to social class.

Lower-Class and Working-Class Perspectives

To anticipate, our exploratory data show higher relational trust and lower generalized trust among blue-collar and low-income people, which is likely to have consequences for their cross-class interactions. Over the 2010 to 2011 academic year, more than twelve hundred Americans, average age early thirties, both genders, mostly white, completed a series of scales online for Amazon marketplace credits (Mechanical Turk); subsamples of about two hundred each completed a variety of subscales. In the overall sample, although relationism and generalized trust correlated moderately, relationism correlated negatively and generalized trust positively with social class.

For lower- and working-class respondents, endorsing relationism emphasized a trusted inner circle, correlated with endorsing compassionate goals (supporting others, having compassion for mistakes, avoiding harm; Crocker and Canevello 2008) and prosocial orientation (Piff et al. 2010), as well as behavior choices in simulated interactions. They invested more points in a peer during a trust scenario, offered to cut their own salary to save colleagues in a lay-off scenario, and volunteered to go to a colleague's train station to start a shared journey. The specific scenarios were as follows:

> Imagine that you are working for a company and that you would go to a conference with a colleague. . . . You and your colleague have agreed to go there by train. . . . There were two train stations: (a) the station near your house, (b) the station near the house of the colleague.

> Suppose you had 30 points to play a game with a randomly selected partner who was also completing the survey. You could choose to give a portion of the points to your partner. As many points [as] you give to your partner would then be tripled, and your partner would have the opportunity to give back to you from this larger pool as many points as he/she would like. Please, write how many points you would decide to give to your partner (from 0 to 30).

> Imagine you are working in a small business. Due to the economic crisis, the owner of the company asks you if you are willing to accept a cut in the hours per week you work (with the corresponding cut in your salary) in order to keep other people with the same rank [as] yours. The owner tells you that it is up to you to make the decision. Do you accept this cut in your work time and in your salary?

Lower- and working class-respondents' relational trust predicted prosocial responses. Overall, these patterns fit the interdependence (chapter 5, this volume) and interpersonal attunement (chapter 8, this volume) indicated by other research programs.

Lower- and working-class relationism also decreased independent action control (Kuhl 1981), competitive zero-sum beliefs (feeling that one person's success depends on another's failure; beliefs that to succeed, it is sometimes necessary to step on others; Crocker and Canevello 2008), entitlement (feeling more deserving than others, that great things should come to one; Campbell et al. 2004), and self-image goals (focusing on how one wants to appear to others; Crocker and Canevello 2008). In short, a relational form of trust was not self-serving, not independent, and not autonomous. It also showed less tolerance for cognitive uncertainty (preferring structure) and emotional uncertainty (being upset by sudden changes).

All these responses could be interpreted as a functional response to limited financial resources: trusting and sharing within a known circle, pooling resources, demonstrating good faith, and avoiding risk. Such responses might constitute working-class solidarity as a functional solution to scarcity, given a history of mutual trust (Lamont 2000).

Middle-Class and Upper-Class Perspectives

On the other side of the class divide, the high-status perspective emphasized abstract, generalized trust in humanity as trustworthy; that people are basically honest, good, and kind; and that people are likely to reciprocate when trusted by others. Generalized trust predicted greater action control, that is, approaching current challenges, getting over negative events, and acting to solve them (Kuhl 1981). Generalized trust predicted a higher tolerance for emotional uncertainty than did relational trust. Generalized trust also predicted lower zero-sum beliefs but half as strongly as the working-class relationism did.

These responses could be interpreted as being open to opportunities because one's primary settings allow risk taking and one's past experiences have been mostly rewarding. Indeed, some of our other preliminary evidence indicates a sense of willingness to take interpersonal risks as an autonomous agent. Higher-income people feel entitled to judge others when social class is evident but not salient, despite the potential interpersonal consequences of doing so. However, when social class is made more salient by the simple expedient of asking participants to report their own social class at the start (versus end) of the study, higher-income people can adjust to act less entitled (Bearns and Fiske 2011). Conveying entitlement to judge is not likely to make other people trusting, but this too is an empirical question to be investigated. As suggested earlier, this feeling of entitlement may be part of what lower-class people experience as the secret handshake.

Class and Forms of Trust: Summary and Comment

For self-identified lower-class members in our study, trust more often took a relational form, focused on specific known familiars and correlated with an interdependent interpersonal orientation. When lower-class members look outside their secure, predictable, reliable inner circle, presumably their trust will be more limited. It is an empirical question, but presumably lower-class people would mistrust middle- and upper-class people as outsiders, consistent with the next section's description of stereotypes of rich people as cold and untrustworthy and as all the more threatening because they are stereotypically competent and effective.

For self-identified higher-class members, trust more often took a generalized abstract form: a belief in the goodness of humanity, correlated with a more self-serving, autonomous orientation. Looking down on the lower status, their high generalized trust might encompass trusting their own group and also the middle class, and maybe blue-collar people. This trust might not necessarily extend to poor people, who are likely ignored, given the stereotype (described next) of poor people as untrustworthy and incompetent, even dehumanized, according to some of our previous work (Harris and Fiske 2009). Admittedly, more data are needed to resolve these specific class-on-class perceptions, but they fit the data so far.

As a perceiver variable illustrated here, socioeconomic status determines people's lives to a great extent. From material aspects (what people eat, how they dress, or where they live) to cultural ones (the schools people attend or the social activities they engage in), to physical and psychological characteristics (health- and mood-related vulnerabilities, the values people defend, the identities they assume), almost all aspects of people's lives are affected by their social class (Kraus and Keltner 2009). To this list, as a potential mediating process, we may be able to add contrasting patterns of trust characteristic of social-class cultures.

IS TRUST MODERATED BY SOCIAL-CLASS STEREOTYPES?

People experience face-to-face cross-class encounters through respective expectations, which can undermine the mutual trust that eases social interaction. If people suspect the other's intentions as being self-serving, competitive, or exploitative, trust is undermined. Independently, if one person looks down on the other, neglecting or scorning that other person's perspective, the potential for mutual respect in the relationship is compromised (Fiske 2011). If one person sees the other as possessing out-of-reach tangible or intangible resources, the result can be envy, which also poisons the potential for constructive interactions. After framing social-class stereotypes in general, we summarize data on their interpersonal enactment and examine some nuances.

Stereotype Content Model for Social Class

Social class categorizes individuals by their behavior during social interactions (see, for example, Blascovich et al. 2001). Though the importance of social class in the United States is often minimized by lay people, social-class categorizations do influence how people are viewed and treated in consequential ways. According to the stereotype content model, people ask two fundamental questions about other people and other groups: are they friend or foe (that is, are they warm and trustworthy) and can they enact their intentions (that is, are they competent; Fiske et al. 2002; Fiske, Cuddy, and Glick 2007). Note that the warmth dimension focuses directly on trustworthy intentions. The competence dimension, in contrast, emphasizes the ability to enact those trustworthy intentions, so competence (as previewed earlier) is a second-order form of trust. That is, good intentions do not matter unless the person can be trusted to complete them. Directly or indirectly related to trust, these two dimensions, warmth and competence, account for more than of 80 percent of people's impressions of others (Wojciszke, Bazinska, and Jaworski 1998). To illustrate, consider each quadrant of this two-dimensional map of stereotypes, from the perspective of social class (see figure 12.1).

Middle-class people are the societal reference group in the model, so they are seen

Figure 12.1   Stereotype Content Model

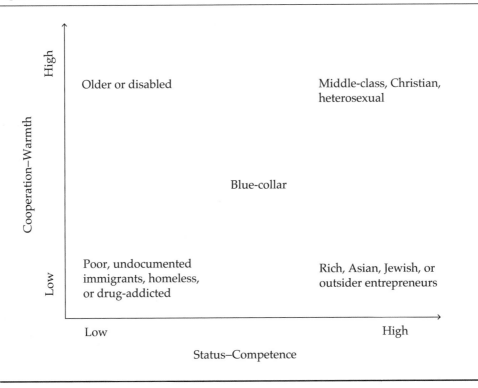

Source: Authors' figure.

as both warm (trustworthy) and competent. Rich people, in contrast, are viewed with ambivalence: they are granted competence, but they are seen as cold and untrustworthy. (In a contrasting form of ambivalence, people with disabilities are seen as warm and trustworthy but incompetent.) Poor people are seen as lacking both warmth and competence; apparently blamed for their poverty, they allegedly have untrustworthy intentions and are stereotypically incapable of doing better. Blue-collar workers fall somewhere between high and low competence, higher than poor people and lower than rich or middle-class people (Fiske et al. 2002). The four quadrants of the stereotype content model thus show how different social classes carry distinct stereotypes.

What are the origins of these stereotype dimensions, warmth and competence? Social status strongly predicts perceived competence, all over the world (Cuddy et al. 2009; Durante et al. 2011). Thus social class elicits an instant judgment that one deserves one's class, the poor being allegedly incompetent, the middle class and the rich being allegedly competent, the working class being ranked in between.

On the warmth dimension, the social structural factor of perceived cooperation or competition predicts perceived intentions for good or ill; competition can involve either tangible resources or symbolic values, and both predict perceived warmth and trustworthiness, again at high correlations (Cuddy et al. 2009; Durante et al. 2011;

Kervyn, Fiske, and Yzerbyt 2011). So on the warm-trustworthy dimension, both poor and rich people are seen to have values and resource priorities that compete with those of the middle class. Neither are entirely trusted by the rest of society. The poor may be seen as freeloading on society, whereas the rich may be seen as being out of sync with middle-class values, perhaps even exploiting the economic system.

Although the warmth dimension directly involves trustworthiness, the competence dimension bears indirectly on trust: as noted, low competence implies an inability to enact one's intentions, whether warm or cold. Thus either low-warmth or low-competence perceptions would tend to undermine mutual trust, as our research suggests in examining their affective and behavioral consequences (Cuddy, Fiske, and Glick 2007). For example, only the high-warmth–high-competence quadrant predicts strong, unambiguous positive feelings, such as pride. This middle-class quadrant predicts pride and admiration of social reference groups that land there (for example, in the United States, the middle class, Christians, and heterosexuals). Such trusted groups receive both active and passive aid from others.

In direct contrast, the allegedly incompetent, untrustworthy poor-people quadrant predicts contempt and disgust, as well as active and passive harm, for groups that land there (for example, poor people, homeless people, undocumented immigrants, and drug addicts). They are not at all trusted, either to have good intentions or to be able to enact any they do have. The net effect, however, is that their allegedly exploitative (uncooperative, untrustworthy, freeloading) intents can be mostly ignored because they allegedly are not good at achieving these ends. Our data indicate that, in general, poor people are fundamentally neglected and ignored (Harris and Fiske 2009).

For the ambivalently perceived quadrants, the feelings and behaviors are mixed. Allegedly competent but cold, rich people (for example, outsider entrepreneurs) elicit envy and jealousy as well as behaviors that imply association and going along to get along but also (under social breakdown) active attack. Consider the common targets of mob violence, rich businesses. Envy is a volatile emotion that involves feelings of injustice and resentment, with damaging results (Cikara and Fiske 2011, 2012; Cuddy, Fiske, and Glick 2007; Fiske 2011). The rich may be respected, but they are not entirely trusted.

The fourth quadrant (incompetent but warm) relates less directly to issues of social class, as older and disabled people land there, pitied, helped, and protected but also socially neglected. They may be trusted, but they are not respected. Although people who are disabled or older are disproportionately low income, they are not our focus here.

Interpersonal Evidence for the Stereotype Content Model and Social Class

Social class thus predicts evaluative, affective, and behavioral reactions on the intergroup level but also, most pertinent here, on the interpersonal level. Not only do people have abstract theories about how social class operates in society, but also social class leads to assumptions, for example, about individual people's intelligence and general competence. In one study, students were told they would interact with a target of either high or low social-class background (the target's parents were either a lawyer and a surgeon or a single-mother filing clerk); in fact, we had manipulated the targets' status to suggest one or the other social class. Even before meeting, participants indicated that they anticipated the poor target to be less competent than the rich target (Russell and Fiske 2008), and meeting the person made no difference. Simply arbitrarily designating one participant as the boss in another study also resulted in experiencing the boss to be more competent, even after the interaction, so the expectations reinforced confirmation during the encounter. Thus the interpersonal status effects mimic those at the societal level of the stereotype content model. This means that higher-class people do not expect lower-class people to be capable of enacting their intentions, whether good or ill, so they are not trusted but not consequential, either.

Getting Beyond Social-Class Stereotypes

In the studies just described, when cooperation-competition was also explicitly manipulated, it overrode default expectations about class-based untrustworthiness and independently predicted perceived warmth and trustworthiness. One route to overcoming second-order issues of trust (that is, status implies competence) is to intervene in the first-order forms of trust, namely, interdependence predicting perceived intent for good or ill. Cooperativeness equals trustworthiness, even in poor people.

Another intervention targets intentions by providing direct information about the other's motivations. If poor people by default are viewed as uncooperative and exploitative, then undoing these perceptions should alter perceived trust. Indeed, trust directed downward toward poor people is likely a function in part of their apparent work ethic, which expresses their willingness to abide by and cooperate with society's shared goals, contrary to the generic stereotype of indolent poverty. Although the interpersonal and societal research based on the stereotype content model do suggest a general antipathy toward poor or working-class individuals, reactions to lower-status social classes are far more complex than inevitable negativity. In judging the poor, perceived motivation (trustworthy intent) determines whether poverty seems deserved (meritocracy) and or undeserved (leading to pity and sympathy for the less fortunate; for example, Zucker and Weiner 1993). This kind of information about their apparent motivation polarizes reactions to the poor, exaggerating either positive (hardworking) or negative (lazy) interpersonal judgments, affect, and behavioral responses.

In a series of interpersonal-level studies (Russell and Fiske 2011), social class was found to polarize extreme reactions to job applicants, colleagues, and student peers. In one study, Princeton undergraduates reported their reactions to a peer whose background was manipulated as either rich or poor and who was further described as possessing a strong or weak work ethic. Not only did respondents give strongly negative ratings to the poor and allegedly lazy student, but they also gave strongly positive ratings to the poor but allegedly hardworking student; work ethic did not polarize ratings of the affluent student. We tested this effect in other domains and found that nonstudent adults did the same thing with their colleagues. Finally, to look at the real-world consequences of this social-class polarization, we asked nonstudent adults to evaluate a job applicant whose background and qualifications were held constant across condition except for social class and work ethic. Once again we found polarized appraisals of the applicant depicted as poor but not of the applicant presented as rich. Thus trust directed downward toward poor people is likely a function of their apparent work ethic, which reveals their intent for good or ill, overriding the stereotypic default that they are not well intended. It also overrides the stereotypic default that they are incompetent, because motivation is one requirement for competence.

The Stereotype Content Model: Summary and Comment

The social-class stereotypes addressed by the stereotype content model, well established at the societal level, demonstrably affect interactions between specific individuals identified primarily by social class. Together, the societal and interpersonal research aims to show that social structure (not only status hierarchy but also expected interdependence) undermines trust in actual interactions. The default stereotypes viewing both the rich and the poor as "on the other side" (competitors) against middle-class people, the societal reference group, shape trust in both directions. That is, as the societal data show, poor, blue-collar, and middle-class people, looking upward, mistrust the rich, and at the same time, blue-collar, middle-class, and rich people, looking downward, mistrust the poor because both the very poor and very rich are seen as potentially exploiting the rest of society.

Although cross-class trust is likely low, the perceivers' relative positions toward the lower and upper ends of the status hierarchy convey different forms of second-order trust, that is, a belief in the others' competence to enact their alleged exploitative intent. According to the model, lower classes should see the upper classes as especially untrustworthy because of their alleged ability (competence) to enact their self-serving, uncooperative intents. Conversely, the upper classes should see the lower classes as untrustworthy but inconsequential because of their alleged incompetence. This supports the distinct approaches to trust for people from different social classes, the topic of the first section's preliminary data on class differences in generalized and relational trust. That is, the lower and working classes trust their own relational circle because outsiders, especially richer ones, seem self-serving and ill intentioned. The middle and upper classes can afford generalized trust in abstract humanity but do not need to interact with anyone they view as incompetent and therefore irrelevant.

BRINGING THE TWO SIDES TOGETHER

So far, we have examined how social class affects people as trusting (or mistrusting) perceivers and then separately as stereotyped trustworthy (or untrustworthy) targets. It takes two to interact, so now we explore how these dynamics might operate together. Specifically, we explore whether viewing both the rich and the poor as "on the other side" (competitors, exploiters), arrayed against societal reference groups such as middle-class people, undermines trust at both ends: lower- and working-class people looking upward at middle- and upper-class people as well as middle- and upper-class people looking downward at lower- and working-class people.

How Trust Might Operate in Cross-Class Interactions

As we have suggested, trust may act as a mechanism in social-class encounters. Consider a cross-class encounter in a setting traditionally inhabited by privilege (for example, higher education). This is an unfamiliar environment for a person used to lower- and working-class contexts, who is more likely to be uncomfortable with that uncertainty. Without a history, trust depends on relationships, and being new would entail caution until relationships are established or network connections are discovered. For the person's middle- and upper-class counterparts in the same setting, trust is assumed, and the risk is tolerated. Untested optimism is the default. Moreover, the environment has familiar norms. One person will come across as brash, sociable, and entitled, the other as cautious, inhibited, and isolated. They are likely to puzzle each other at best and frustrate each other at worst.

Now consider the same two people encountering each other in a lower- or working-class environment (for example, as customers waiting in an auto repair shop). For a customer used to lower- and working-class contexts, this would be an environment to enter most comfortably if one had prior connections, such as knowing a friend or relative of the repair crew. If those connections exist, confidence, trust, and comfort are possible, perhaps even with someone of a higher status. Without those connections, a working-class person might avoid interaction, even in this context. But assuming they do encounter each other, the middle- or upper-class customer would have to provide evidence of connections, just like anyone else, or else be seen as an outsider. The middle- or upper-class person does not understand the point of this, assuming that people who are treated well, even strangers, will respond well in turn, and the other person's caution might be read as suspicion. The middle- or upper-class person expects everyone to be open and accepting without having to prove anything. The middle-class assumption of individualism shows generalized trust and belief in abstract humanity (for example, chapters 5, 8, and 10, this volume), yet this may appear remote and impersonal to a working-class perceiver because it fails to demonstrate a personal, relational stance. Abstract ideals may trip up higher-class people's cross-class encounters on the ground.

In society at large, differences between social classes could persist if lower classes tend toward relationism and higher classes toward generalized trust. For the middle and upper classes, generalized trust encourages people to approach others to form social relationships regardless of previous interpersonal relationships (Igarashi et al. 2008). Because most people are believed to be trustworthy, there should be no problem in starting relationships with an other, beyond the family or close friendship circles, encouraging social and economic opportunities (Yamagishi, Cook, and Watabe 1998). Thus, for instance, Toshio Yamagishi (1986) has found that people with high generalized trust are more likely to cooperate with strangers than are those with low levels of generalized trust. But as noted, they may not specifically bother to cross the social-class divide.

In contrast, lower- and working-class people's particularistic trust (relationism) may help them keep social relationships once these are formed because the emotional connection typical of particularistic trust can help maintain secure and committed social relationships. Therefore, although relationism may not stimulate people to seek new social opportunities and to establish new social relationships, it may strengthen the commitment to existing social relationships. Not surprisingly, then, poor people have the best chance of thriving in middle-class settings with a critical mass of similar others (Frable, Platt, and Hoey 1998). The mere presence of similar others buffers self-esteem from stressors inherent in mixed-class environments and boosts positive self-concept. Poor people may thus carry resources within them that promote their ability to rebound from the ongoing challenges of cross-class environments. What is more, resilience research suggests that, ironically, people with a history of confronting adversity have an advantage over people without such history when they cope with later adverse events (Seery, Holman, and Silver 2010).

Mobility and Inequality, from the Ground Up

To increase upward mobility and decrease inequality, higher and lower classes must interact, despite the social reality of their differing life conditions that influence feelings and behaviors. Regardless of popular conceptions of the United States as a classless society, economic distinctions here are increasingly pronounced, as social scientists know (Piketty and Saez 2003). Recent media have disparaged our "banana republic," noting that inequality in the United States surpasses that in many countries traditionally criticized for their social inequity (Kristof 2010). Differences between social classes, far from disappearing, are clearly significant and tend to perpetuate. For instance, in the short term, families' earnings correlate across generations (Bowles and Gintis 2002; Mazumder 2005).

Once established, these social-class divides can be tremendously difficult for individuals to overcome. American pride in meritocracy notwithstanding, social mobility in the United States is remarkably limited (Economic Mobility Project 2010). Even in our educational system, long heralded as the great equalizer, class differences are not only evident but reinforced (Carnevale and Rose 2003). In education, social-class background has a powerful effect on college completion (Rumberger 2010). A meta-analytic review of the literature on socioeconomic status and academic achievement in articles published between 1990 and 2000 found a medium to strong relation between socioeconomic status and achievement (Sirin 2005).

These entrenched levels of inequality have consequences on the ground. Social class not only differentiates people and groups but is one of the primary sources of inequality and discrimination among them. People from lower social classes suffer everyday hassles, harassment, and aggression (Fiske 2010), and difficulties for people from lower social classes occur in almost every domain. For instance, lower social class is associated with an elevated risk of mortality from diverse causes (Matthews and MacDorman 2008), and class can in some measure explain differences in mental health and physical functioning before the age of sixty (Jokela et al. 2010). Not only does this create a direct hit for the lower- and working-classes themselves, it also creates an indirect hit for the middle and upper classes to have distrustful, ill, and immobile lower and working classes.

In everyday encounters, rich and poor people everywhere are divided by status stereotypes (Cuddy et al. 2009; Durante et al. 2011), laying the groundwork for mutual mistrust. What is more, countries with the highest Gini indices of income inequality also show the most well-developed, complex social-class stereotypes (Durante et al. 2011). Just as the United States falls in the lowest third of income equality (Central Intelligence Agency 2010), it is one of the leaders in differentiated social-class prejudices. These complex social-class (and interethnic) stereotypes more easily resist change, so they help maintain the deeper social-class divides. Although we like to think of ourselves as free of social-class prejudices, Americans have robust social-class issues.

CONCLUSION

With further research into the psychological consequences of social class, we may be able to mitigate the challenges faced by those moving up the ranks. As social mobility becomes economically more difficult, attenuating some of the associated psychological challenges becomes even more crucial to making class barriers easier to overcome, thereby promoting a more equitable and meritocratic society.

Despite the obvious need to study the effects of social class, psychology has paid little attention to the issue, tending to treat social class as a confounding variable rather than a research focus (Fiske 2010). As a result, though social class has been studied elsewhere, most notably in economics and sociology, only minimal research has investigated the psychological processes relating to class differences. To help explain the perpetuation and consequences of social-class divides, social psychologists can investigate underlying mechanisms that may be making these economic obstacles even more difficult to overcome.

A social psychological analysis reveals the depth and breadth of the social-class divide in daily experience, as well as its prevalence. The consequences are thoroughgoing and urgently need to be addressed at individual, interpersonal, intergroup, and institutional levels if we are ever to reduce inequality, increase mobility, and narrow the divide.

The authors wish to thank the Russell Sage Foundation for supporting the exploratory conference on this topic, as well as the early stages of their research, and Susan Fiske's sabbatical year as a Visiting Scholar. In addition, Miguel Moya was supported by the Spanish Education Department (Program for Professors' and Researchers' Visits to Foreign Centers) during his sabbatical year at Princeton; Ann Marie Russell was supported by a Graduate Research Fellowship from the National Science Foundation; and Courtney Bearns was supported by a Princeton University First-Year Fellowship in Science and Engineering and a University Center for Human Values Prize.

REFERENCES

Adler, Nancy, Elissa Epel, Grace Castellazzo, and Jeannette Ickovics. 2000. "Relationship of Subjective and Objective Social Status with Psychological and Physiological Functioning: Preliminary Data in Healthy White Women." *Health Psychology* 19(6): 586–92.

Bearns, Courtney, and Susan T. Fiske. 2011. "Social Class Salience and Entitlement to Judge." Poster presented at the Society for Personality and Social Psychology Conference, San Diego, Calif. (January 27–29).

Blascovich, Jim, Wendy B. Mendes, Sarah B. Hunter, Brian Lickel, and Neneh Kowai-Bell. 2001. "Perceiver Threat in Social Interactions with Stigmatized Others." *The Journal of Personality and Social Psychology* 80(2): 253–67.

Bowles, Samuel, and Herbert Gintis. 2002. "The Inheritance of Inequality." *The Journal of Economic Perspectives* 16(3): 3–30.

Campbell, W. Keith, Angelica M. Bonacci, Jeremy Shelton, Julie J. Exline, and Brad J. Bushman. 2004. "Psychological Entitlement: Interpersonal Consequences and Validation of a New Self-Report Measure." *Journal of Personality Assessment* 83(4): 29–45.

Carnevale, Anthony, and Stephen Rose. 2003. "Socioeconomic Status, Race/Ethnicity, and Selective College Admissions." In *America's Untapped Resource: Low-Income Students in Higher Education*, edited by R. D. Kahlenberg. New York: Century Foundation Press.

Central Intelligence Agency. 2010. *The World Factbook*. Available at: https://www.cia.gov/library/publications/the-world-Factbook/fields/2172.html (accessed October 28, 2010).

Cikara, M., and Susan T. Fiske. 2011. "Bounded Empathy: Neural Responses to Outgroup Targets' (Mis)fortunes." *Journal of Cognitive Neuroscience* 23(12): 3791–803.

———. 2012. "Stereotypes and Schadenfreude: Behavioral and Physiological Markers of Pleasure at Others' Misfortunes." *Social Psychological and Personality Science* 3(1): 63–71.

Crocker, Jennifer, and Amy Canevello. 2008. "Creating and Undermining Social Support in Communal Relationships: The Role of Compassionate and Self-Image Goals." *Journal of Personality and Social Psychology* 95(3): 555–75.

Croizet, Jean-Claude, and Theresa Claire. 1998. "Extending the Concept of Stereotype and Threat to Social Class: The Intellectual Underperformance of Students from Low Socioeconomic Backgrounds." *Personality and Social Psychology Bulletin* 24(6): 588–94.

Cuddy, Amy J. C., Susan T. Fiske, and Peter Glick. 2007. "The BIAS Map: Behaviors from Intergroup Affect and Stereotypes." *The Journal of Personality and Social Psychology* 92(4): 631–48.

Cuddy, Amy J. C., Susan T. Fiske, Virginia S. Y. Kwan, Peter Glick, Stéphanie Demoulin, Jacques-Philippe Leyens, Michael H. Bond, Jean-Claude Croizet, Naomi Ellemers, Ed Sleebos, Tin Tin Htun, Hyun-Jeong Kim, Greg Maio, Judi Perry, Kristina Petkova, Valery Todorov, Rosa Rodríguez-Bailón, Elena Morales, Miguel Moya, Marisol Palacios, Vanessa Smith, Rolando Perez, Jorge Vala, and Rene Ziegler. 2009. "Is the Stereotype Content Model Culture-Bound? A Cross-Cultural Comparison Reveals Systematic Similarities and Differences." *The British Journal of Social Psychology* 48: 1–33.

Durante, Federica, Susan T. Fiske, Nicolas Kervyn, Amy J. C. Cuddy, Adebowale (Debo) Akande, Bolanle E. Adetoun, Modupe F. Adewuyi, Magdeline M. Tserere, Ananthi Al Ramiah, Khairul Anwar Mastor, Fiona Kate Barlow, Gregory Bonn, Romin W. Tafarodi, Janine Bosak, Ed Cairns, Claire Doherty, Dora Capozza, Anjana Chandran, Xenia Chryssochoou, Tilemachos Iatridis, Juan Manuel Contreras, Rui Costa-Lopes, Roberto González, Janet I. Lewis, Gerald Tushabe, Jacques-Philippe Leyens, Renée Mayorga, Nadim N. Rouhana,

Vanessa Smith Castro, Rolando Perez, Rosa Rodríguez-Bailón, Miguel Moya, Elena Morales Marente, Marisol Palacios Gálvez, Chris G. Sibley, Frank Asbrock, and Chiara C. Storari. 2011. "Inequality Predicts Ambivalence in Stereotype Content." Paper presented at meetings of the European Association of Social Psychology, Stockholm (July 13–16).

Economic Mobility Project. 2010. "Economic Mobility of Black and White Families." Executive summary. Available at: http://www.economicmobility.org/assets/pdfs/EMP_ES_Black _White_Families.pdf (accessed December 2, 2010).

Elgar, Frank J. 2010. "Income Inequality, Trust, and Population Health in 33 Countries." *The American Journal of Public Health* 100(11): 2311–15.

Fiske, Susan T. 2010. "Interpersonal Stratification." In *Handbook of Social Psychology*, 5th ed., edited by Susan T. Fiske, Daniel T. Gilbert, and Gardner Lindzey. New York: Wiley.

———. 2011. *Envy Up, Scorn Down: How Status Divides Us*. New York: Russell Sage Foundation.

Fiske, Susan T., Amy J. C. Cuddy, and Peter Glick. 2007. "Universal Dimensions of Social Perception: Warmth and Competence." *Trends in Cognitive Science* 11(2): 77–83.

Fiske, Susan T., Amy J. Cuddy, Peter Glick, and Jun Xu. 2002. "A Model of (Often Mixed) Stereotype Content: Competence and Warmth Respectively Follow from Perceived Status and Competition." *Journal of Personality and Social Psychology* 82(6): 878–902.

Frable, Deborrah E. S., Linda Platt, and Steve Hoey. 1998. "Concealable Stigmas and Positive Self-Perceptions: Feeling Better Around Similar Others." *Journal of Personality and Social Psychology* 74(4): 909–22. doi:10.1037/0022-3514.74.4.909.

Fussell, Paul. 1983. *Class: A Guide Through the American Status System*. New York: Touchstone.

Harris, Lasana T., and Susan T. Fiske. 2009. "Dehumanized Perception: The Social Neuroscience of Thinking (or Not Thinking) About Disgusting People." In *European Review of Social Psychology*, edited by Miles Hewstone and Wolfgang Stroebe, vol. 20. London: Wiley.

Hayashi, Nahoko, Elinor Ostrom, James Walker, and Toshio Yamagishi. 1999. "Reciprocity, Trust, and the Sense of Control: A Cross-Societal Study." *Rationality and Society* 11(1): 27–46.

Igarashi, Tasuku, Yoshihisa Kashima, Emiko S. Kashima, Tomas Farsides, Uichol Kim, Fritz Strack, Lioba Werth, and Masaki Yuki. 2008. "Culture, Trust, and Social Networks." *Asian Journal of Social Psychology* 11(2): 88–101.

Johnson, Wendy, and Robert F. Krueger. 2005a. "Genetic Effects on Physical Health: Lower at Higher Income Levels." *Behavior Genetics* 35(5): 579–90.

———. 2005b. "Higher Perceived Life Control Decreases Genetic Variance in Physical Health: Evidence from a National Twin Study." *Journal of Personality and Social Psychology* 88(1): 165–73.

Jokela, Markus, Archana Singh-Manoux, Jane E. Ferrie, David Gimeno, Tasmine N. Akbaraly, Martin J. Shipley, Jenny Head, Marko Elovainio, Michael G. Marmot, Mika Kivimäki. 2010. "The Association of Cognitive Performance with Mental Health and Physical Functioning Strengthens with Age: The Whitehall II Cohort Study." *Psychological Medicine* 40(5): 837–45.

Kashima, Yoshihisa, Teruyoshi Kokubo, Emiko S. Kashima, Dianne Boxall, Susumu Yamaguchi, and Kristina Macrae. 2004. "Culture and Self: Are There Within-Culture Differences in Self Between Metropolitan Areas and Regional Cities?" *Personality and Social Psychology Bulletin* 30(7): 816–23. doi:10.1177/0146167203261997.

Kashima, Yoshihisa, Susumu Yamaguchi, Uichol Kim, Sang-Chin Choi, Michele J. Gelfand, and Masaki Yuki. 1995. "Culture, Gender, and Self: A Perspective from Individualism-Collectivism Research." *Journal of Personality and Social Psychology* 69(5): 925–37.

Kervyn, Nicolas, Susan T. Fiske, and Vincent Yzerbyt. 2011. "Why Is the Primary Dimension of

Social Cognition So Hard to Predict? Symbolic and Realistic Threats Together Predict Warmth in the Stereotype Content Model." Manuscript under review, Princeton University.

Kirn, Walter. 2009. *Lost in the Meritocracy: The Undereducation of an Overachiever.* New York: Doubleday.

Kraus, Michael W., and Dacher Keltner. 2009. "Signs of Socioeconomic Status: A Thin-Slicing Approach." *Psychological Science* 20(1): 99–106. doi:10.1111/j.1467-9280.2008.02251.x.

Kraus, Michael W., Paul K. Piff, and Dacher Keltner. 2009. "Social Class, Sense of Control, and Social Explanation." *Journal of Personality and Social Psychology* 97(6): 992–1004. doi:10.1037/a0016357.

Kristof, Nicholas. 2010. "Our Banana Republic." *The New York Times,* November 6. Available at: http://www.nytimes.com/2010/11/07/opinion/07kristof.html?scp=1andsq=banana%20republicandst=cse (accessed November 6, 2010).

Kuhl, Julius. 1981. "Motivational and Functional Helplessness: The Moderating Effect of State Versus Action Orientation." *Journal of Personality and Social Psychology* 40(1): 155–71.

Lachman, Margie E., and Suzanne L. Weaver. 1998. "The Sense of Control as a Moderator of Social Class Differences in Health and Well-Being." *Journal of Personality and Social Psychology* 74(3): 763–73.

Lamont, Michèle. 2000. *The Dignity of Working Men: Money and the Boundaries of Race, Class, and Immigration.* New York: Russell Sage Foundation/Cambridge, Mass.: Harvard University Press.

Maddux, William W., and Marilynn B. Brewer. 2005. "Gender Differences in the Relational and Collective Bases for Trust." *Group Processes and Intergroup Relations* 8(2): 159–71.

Matthews, T. J., and Marian MacDorman. 2008. "Infant Mortality Statistics from the 2005 Period Linked Birth/Infant Death Data Sheet." *The National Vital Statistics Report* 57(2): 1–32.

Mazumder, Bashkar. 2005. "Fortunate Sons: New Estimates of Intergenerational Mobility in the United States Using Social Security Earnings Data." *The Review of Economics and Statistics* 87(2): 235–55.

Oakes, J. Michael, and Peter H. Rossi. 2003. "The Measurement of SES in Health Research: Current Practice and Steps Toward a New Approach." *Social Science and Medicine* 56(4): 769–84.

Pew Social Trends Staff. 2007. "Americans and Social Trust: Who, Where, and Why." Pew Research Center. Available at: http://pewsocialtrends.org/2007/02/22/americans-and-social-trust-who-where-and-why/ (accessed October 28, 2010).

Piff, Paul K., Michael Kraus, Stéphane Côte, Bonnie H. Cheng, and Dacher Keltner. 2010. "Having Less, Giving More: The Influence of Social Class on Prosocial Behavior." *Journal of Personality and Social Psychology* 99(5): 771–84.

Piff, Paul K., Audres G. Martinez, and Dacher Keltner. Forthcoming. "Me Against We: Ingroup Transgression, Collective Shame, and Ingroup-Directed Hostility." *Cognition and Emotion.* doi: 10.1080/02699931.2011.595394.

Piketty, Thomas, and Emmanuel Saez. 2003. "Income Inequality in the United States, 1913–1998." *The Quarterly Journal of Economics* 118(1): 1–39. Updated data available at: http://elsa.berkeley.edu/~saez/saez-UStopincomes-2008.pdf (accessed October 28, 2010).

Rumberger, Russell. 2010. "High School Dropout, Graduation, and Completion Rates: Better Data, Better Measures, Better Decisions." In *Expert Guidance on Next Steps for Research and Policy Workshop,* edited by Robert Hauser and Judith Koenig. Washington, D.C.: National Academies Press.

Russell, Ann Marie, and Susan T. Fiske. 2008. "It's All Relative: Social Position and Interpersonal Perception." *The European Journal of Social Psychology* 38(7): 1193–1201.

———. 2011. "A Tale of Two Paupers: Polarized Perceptions of the Poor." Unpublished manuscript, Princeton University.

Seery, Mark D., E. Alison Holman, and Roxane C. Silver. 2010. "Whatever Does Not Kill Us: Cumulative Lifetime Adversity, Vulnerability, and Resilience." *Journal of Personality and Social Psychology* 99(6): 1025–41.

Sirin, Selcuk R. 2005. "Socioeconomic Status and Academic Achievement: A Meta-Analytic Review of Research." *Review of Educational Research* 75(3): 417–53.

Snibbe, Alana C., and Hazel R. Markus. 2005. "You Can't Always Get What You Want: Educational Attainment, Agency, and Choice." *Journal of Personality and Social Psychology* 88(4): 703–20.

Spencer, Bettina, and Emanuele Castano. 2007. "Social Class Is Dead. Long Live Social Class! Stereotype Threat Among Low Socioeconomic Status Individuals." *Social Justice Research* 20(4): 418–32.

Stephens, Nicole M., Hazel R. Markus, and Sarah S. M. Townsend. 2007. "Choice as an Act of Meaning: The Case of Social Class." *Journal of Personality and Social Psychology* 93(5): 814–30.

Uleman, James S., Eun Rhee, Nenshad Bardoliwalla, Gün Semin, and Midori Toyama. 2000. "The Relational Self: Closeness to Ingroups Depends on Who They Are, Culture, and the Type of Closeness." *Asian Journal of Social Psychology* 3(1): 1–17.

Weaver, Charles N. 2006. "Trust in People Among Hispanic Americans." *Journal of Applied Social Psychology* 36(5): 1160–72.

Wojciszke, Bogdan, Roza Bazinska, and Marcin Jaworski. 1998. "On the Dominance of Moral Categories in Impression Formation." *Personality and Social Psychology Bulletin* 24(12): 1251–63.

Yamagishi, Toshio. 1986. "The Provision of a Sanctioning System as a Public Good." *Journal of Personality and Social Psychology* 51(1): 110–16.

———. 1998. *Shinrai no kouzou: Kokoro to syakai no shinka gemu* [The Structure of Trust: The Evolutionary Games of Mind and Society]. Tokyo: Tokyo University Press.

Yamagishi, Toshio, Karen S. Cook, and Motoki Watabe. 1998. "Uncertainty, Trust, and Commitment Formation in the United States and Japan." *American Journal of Sociology* 104(1): 165–94.

Yamagishi, Toshio, and Midori Yamagishi. 1994. "Trust and Commitment in the United States and Japan." *Motivation and Emotion* 18(2): 129–66.

Yuki, Masaki, William W. Maddux, Marilynn B. Brewer, and Kosuke Takemura. 2005. "Cross-Cultural Differences in Relationship- and Group-Based Trust." *Personality and Social Psychology Bulletin* 31(1): 48–62.

Zucker, Gail S., and Bernard Weiner. 1993. "Conservatism and Perceptions of Poverty: An Attributional Analysis." *Journal of Applied Social Psychology* 23(12): 925–43.

INDEX

Boldface numbers refer to figures and tables.